'The book offers a significan   in the
field. Working through phen   gnitive
psychology, neuroscience and   ıl, and
the authors respond to these fi

...........y of Leeds

What is the relationship between 'body' and 'mind', 'inner' and 'outer' in any approach to acting? How have different modes of actor training shaped actors' experiences of acting and how they understand their work? Phillip Zarrilli, Jerri Daboo and Rebecca Loukes offer insight into such questions, analysing acting as a psychophysical phenomenon and process across cultures and disciplines, and providing in-depth accounts of culturally and historically specific approaches to acting. Individual chapters explore:

- psychophysical acting and the legacy of Stanislavsky;
- European psychophysical practices of dance and theatre;
- traditional and contemporary psychophysical approaches to performance in India and Japan;
- insights from the new sciences on the 'situated bodymind' of the actor;
- intercultural perspectives on acting.

This lively study is ideal for students and practitioners alike.

Phillip B. Zarrilli is Professor of Performance Practice at Exeter University, UK, and the founding Artistic Director of The Llanarth Group, Wales, UK.

Jerri Daboo is Senior Lecturer in Drama at the University of Exeter, UK, and has worked as a performer and director for many years.

Rebecca Loukes is Senior Lecturer in Drama at the University of Exeter, UK, and Co-Artistic Director of RedCape Theatre, UK.

Theatre and Performance Practices explores key performance practices encountered in the study of modern and contemporary theatre. Each book in the series charts the critical and historical development of a mode of performance practice and assesses its contemporary significance. Designed to inspire students, scholars and practitioners, the series asks, what are the choices and responsibilities facing performance-makers today?

Theatre and Performance Practices

General Editors: Graham Ley and Jane Milling

Published

Christopher Baugh	*Theatre, Performance and Technology (2nd edition)*
Deirdre Heddon	*Autobiography in Performance*
Greg Giesekam	*Staging the Screen*
Deirdre Heddon and Jane Milling	*Devising Performance*
Helen Nicholson	*Applied Drama*
Cathy Turner and Synne K. Behrndt	*Dramaturgy and Performance*
Michael Wilson	*Storytelling and Theatre*
Philip B. Zarrilli, Jerri Daboo and Rebecca Loukes	*Acting: Psychophysical Phenomenon and Process*

Forthcoming

Mark Evans	*Performance, Movement and the Body*
Jason Price	*Popular Theatre*
Kerrie Schaefer	*Communities, Performance and Practice*

Theatre and Performance Practices Series

Series Standing Order ISBN 978–1–403–98735–8 (hardcover)
Series Standing Order ISBN 978–1–403–98736–5 (paperback)
(*outside North America only*)

You can receive future titles in this series as they are published by placing a standing order. Please contact your bookseller or, in the case of difficulty, write to us at the address below with your name and address, the title of the series and the ISBN quoted above.

Customer Services Department, Macmillan Distribution Ltd, Houndmills, Basingstoke, Hampshire, RG21 6XS, UK

Acting: Psychophysical Phenomenon and Process

Intercultural and Interdisciplinary Perspectives

PHILLIP B. ZARRILLI
JERRI DABOO
REBECCA LOUKES

palgrave
macmillan

First published 2013 by
PALGRAVE MACMILLAN

Palgrave Macmillan in the UK is an imprint of Macmillan Publishers Limited, registered in England, company number 785998, of Houndmills, Basingstoke, Hampshire RG21 6XS.

Palgrave Macmillan in the US is a division of St Martin's Press LLC, 175 Fifth Avenue, New York, NY 10010.

Palgrave Macmillan is the global academic imprint of the above companies and has companies and representatives throughout the world.

Palgrave® and Macmillan® are registered trademarks in the United States, the United Kingdom, Europe and other countries

ISBN: 978–1–403–99054–9 (hardback)
ISBN: 978–1–403–99055–6 (paperback)

This book is printed on paper suitable for recycling and made from fully managed and sustained forest sources. Logging, pulping and manufacturing processes are expected to conform to the environmental regulations of the country of origin.

A catalogue record for this book is available from the British Library.

A catalog record for this book is available from the Library of Congress.

Printed in China

Contents

List of Figures

Preface

Our interest in acting as a psychophysical phenomenon and process grows out of the fact that the three co-authors are practitioners – actor/ performers, makers, directors, and teachers. But this book is *not* about *how* to act; rather, as suggested in our title, we examine acting as an embodied, psychophysical phenomenon, and process. Although we do not address how to act, this book is nevertheless directed at contemporary actors throughout the world, as well as teachers, directors, and scholars of acting and performance. We would very much like actors and students of acting in Seoul, Singapore, Bangkok, Trissur, Amman, Malta, Nairobi, Berlin, Cardiff, and Chicago to read this book and find it informative and useful for how we think and talk about acting across cultures, and also for how one performs. Four primary assumptions have guided us in writing this book:

- Given our focus on acting as a phenomenon and process, we examine acting from the perspective of *the actor-as-practitioner 'inside' the embodied process, phenomenon, and experience of acting.*
- As an embodied phenomenon and process, we also assume that *acting is a psychophysical process equally engaging the 'inner' (psycho-) and 'outer' ('physical') dimensions of experience and embodiment* shaped in each historical context by specific cultural, aesthetic, and scientific models, and paradigms.
- Theories and practices of acting from the late-nineteenth century have been constantly (re)shaped by an ever-evolving set of global, intercultural techniques, practices, and aesthetics principles; therefore, *we assume that acting, actor training, and paradigms of acting today should be examined as an inter-cultural phenomenon.*
- Finally, to interrogate acting as an embodied, psychophysical phenomenon, process, and practice we will utilize *an interdisciplinary set of interpretive tools* from phenomenology, cognitive, and neuro-sciences, anthropology, area studies, and other relevant disciplines/perspectives.[1]

At the broadest level our approach to the subject of acting is guided by the field known as performance studies. Performance studies assumes that taking an intercultural and interdisciplinary approach to its subject is essential. It also assumes an integral 'relationship between studying performance and doing performance' (Schechner 2002:1).[2] An interdisciplinary/intercultural approach to research is also reflected in the stance taken by the International Federation for Theatre Research towards publication from 2003 to 2004:

> [I]t has become increasingly urgent for performance scholars to expand their disciplinary horizons to include the comparative study of performance across national, cultural, social, and political borders. This is necessary not only in order to avoid the homogenizing tendency to limit performance paradigms to those familiar in our home countries, but also in order to be engaged in increasing new performance scholarship that takes account of and embraces the complexities of transnational cultural production. (Reinelt and Singleton 2010:xi)

Given our focus on acting as a psychophysical phenomenon and process, we use the compound term 'psychophysical' to mark the dialectical engagement of the actor's bodymind in the 'inner' and 'outer' processes that constitute specific approaches to acting. We view the phenomenon of acting as an embodied, inter-subjective/inter-corporeal, experiential process of attending to and enacting tasks/actions, and of sensing, perceiving, feeling, remembering, and imagining – all shaped by historically and culturally specific assumptions and/or paradigms. Therefore, one of our purposes is to investigate and interrogate these specific modes of experience and engagement of the actor as they have been shaped by historically and culturally specific assumptions and/or paradigms. We also step back from these specific discussions to strategically consider more general questions about acting, including

- What constitutes the 'work' of the actor and how is that 'work' structured?
- What analytical tools (from philosophy, the new sciences, social sciences, etc.) are most useful in attempting to understand and articulate a 'general' (or meta-theory) of acting as a phenomenon and process?
- What is the relationship between 'body' and 'mind', 'inner' and 'outer' in any approach to acting?
- How have culturally/historically specific modes of actor training shaped how actors understand their work, and shaped their experience of acting?
- How might we begin to articulate and understand the complex process and phenomenon of the actor's consciousness?

One or more of the above concerns and/or questions are addressed by each of the authors from our own unique perspectives in the individual chapters we have authored. The choices for the subjects of the individual chapters have been made in accordance with the areas of expertise and interest of each author. Inevitably these choices can offer only a limited view of a vast subject, but they have been made to establish a dialogue across forms, paradigms, and cultures to allow for a complex interaction. The chapters within the book reflect both individual interests and perspectives, as well as shared concerns in relation to psychophysical acting.

To contextualize *Acting: Psychophysical Phenomenon and Process*, let us briefly consider how our approach to thinking and talking about acting compares with that of the many books published in English on acting. While not comprehensive, books on acting could be described as falling into one or more of the following major categories:

1. accounts of an approach to actor training and acting authored by the specific master teacher/director who has developed a particular approach (Stanislavsky 2008; Chekhov 1991, 1985; Grotowski 2002; Staniewski 2004; Suzuki 1986; Zarrilli 2009);
2. 'how to' trade books which describe and advocate a particular approach to acting (Adler 2000; Cohen 1978; Hagen 2008; McGaw 2012; Moore 1979, 1965, 1960);
3. a reinterpretation/updating of a particular approach to acting written by a professional actor/teacher (Merlin 2001, 2007);
4. collections of essays which offer historical, contextual, and practical overviews of a variety of approaches to actor training and acting (Hodge 2010 [2000]; Krasner 2000; Zarrilli 2002 [1995]);
5. in-depth socio-cultural/historical studies of a specific paradigm or approach to acting or training focused on a specific practitioner or period: on Stanislavsky (Pitches 2009; Whyman 2011; Carnicke 1998; on Brecht: Braun 1995, 1969; Pitches 2003; on Suzuki: Carruthers and Yasunari 2007; Allain 2009; about performing Beckett: Kalb 1989);
6. in-depth accounts of a particular traditional model and paradigm of actor training and acting within a specific non-Western cultural/historical context, such as Beijing Opera (Riley 1997) or *kathakali* dance-drama (Zarrilli 1984, 2000); and
7. accounts that reflect historically, culturally, inter-culturally, and/or meta-theoretically on acting (Cole 1992; Gordon 2006; Harrop 1992; Hornby 1992; Huston 1992; Lutterbie 2011; Rayner 1994; Schmitt 1990; Roach 1993 [1985]; Zarrilli 2009, 2002).

This book falls within the final three categories above in that we reflect historically, culturally, inter-culturally, and meta-theoretically on acting, and provide in-depth accounts of several specific socio-cultural/historical studies of specific approaches to actor training in several specific cultural contexts in order to reflect upon acting as a phenomenon and process across cultures.

More specifically this co-authored book extends key discussions in two previous publications by Phillip B. Zarrilli – his edited collection of essays, *Acting Reconsidered* (2002 [1995]) and his sole-authored book, *Psychophysical Acting* (2009). Similar to these earlier publications, *Acting: Psychophysical Phenomenon and Process* invites the reader to 'reconsider' acting by putting 'aside parochial preconceptions and points of view that propose acting as *a* truth (that is, one system, discourse, or practice)' in order to cultivate 'a critical awareness of acting as multiple and always changing' (2002:3). In order to prompt the reader to 'reconsider' acting as *a* truth, *Acting Reconsidered* provided accounts across a range of alternative paradigms, approaches to, and theories of acting and training, as well as a set of meta-theoretical essays 'reflecting more generally on the nature, practice, and phenomenon of acting' (2002:3). Zarrilli's more recent, sole-authored book, *Psychophysical Acting*, systematically addressed in more detail and depth than *Acting Reconsidered* the relationship between the actor-as-doer and what the actor does, and provided a sustained reflection on the nature of acting as a phenomenon and process.[3] Methodologically, *Psychophysical Acting* rejects representational and mimetic meta-theories of acting as inadequate and articulates an alternative conceptualization and model of the actor's work as an enactive phenomenon and process – a subject introduced in Chapter 1 and expanded upon by Rebecca Loukes in Chapter 6 in light of new sciences.

Finally, like *Acting Reconsidered* and *Psychophysical Acting*, this book is somewhat unusual in that it provides analysis and reflection on acting as a phenomenon and process in several specific cultural contexts, and also reflects on contemporary globalization of principles and techniques of acting and actor training in today's intercultural context.

In the general Introduction (Chapter 1), Phillip B. Zarrilli provides an overview of key issues and considerations in attempting to expand and reflect specifically upon acting as an embodied, psychophysical phenomenon and practice. He considers the actor as doer, the actor's performance score, an 'enactive approach' to acting and embodiment, intercultural perspectives on acting, and a concluding discussion that articulates one model for understanding the actor's 'consciousness' in performance.

In Chapters 2 and 3, Zarrilli then provides two specific case-studies examining the psychophysical paradigms and practices within two non-Western cultural contexts – India (Chapter 2) and Japan (Chapter 3). His choice to focus on India and Japan is idiosyncratic in that he writes about the two specific cultural contexts he knows best from previous research and from practical engagement with the performance traditions of India and Japan. Both chapters begin with an analysis of how specific embodied modes of acting practice are thought about and reflected upon in each cultural context. Chapter 2 provides an account of the work of the actor/dancer in India where modes and models of psychophysical training and embodiment such as yoga inform extant dance-drama traditions such as *kutiyattam* and *kathakali*, as well as the work of a number of important contemporary Indian performers such as Navtej Johar and Maya Krishna Rao. Chapter 3 examines psychophysical principles, processes, and practices of acting within selected Japanese traditions. The primary focus is on the Shinto/Buddhist-influenced tradition of *nō* performance, and the radical approaches to the inner and outer (bodymind) dimensions of psychophysical performance in post-war Japanese *butoh* (the 'dance of darkness'). The chapter concludes with brief discussions of the psychophysical work of the internationally known director Suzuki Tadashi, and the aesthetic of quietude as developed by Ōta Shōgo.

In Chapter 4, Jerri Daboo provides an account of the Russian actor and theatre director Konstantin Stanislavsky's (1863–1938) seminal work on redefining the actor's work in Russia in the late nineteenth and early twentieth centuries, and follows the legacy of Stanislavsky and into the twentieth and twenty-first centuries. This focus on Stanislavsky allows for an in-depth view of his development of a psychophysical approach, and the way that he drew on influences from yoga and the scientific paradigms from his day to create his system, as well as the many changes he made throughout his life. This is followed by an examination of ways in which aspects of his work were taken on and re-interpreted by others following him, particularly the Method School in America in relation to the Emotion Memory exercise. The chapter concludes by questioning the notion of 'inner' and 'outer' as a continuum in relation to psychophysical acting.

In Chapter 5, Rebecca Loukes focuses on the actor/performer within the process of making or generating movement – looking across historical examples drawn from the field of European 'embodied' psychophysical practices from both dance and theatre. Work examined here includes that of Mary Wigman, François Delsarte, Pina Bausch, Jerzy Grotowski, and Jacques Lecoq. And in Chapter 6, 'Beyond the Psychophysical? The

"Situated", "Enactive" Bodymind in Performance' Loukes brings us very much into the present moment of the early twenty-first century. This chapter picks up from the preliminary discussion in Chapter 1 on an 'enactive approach' to acting to explore how complementary perspectives on current scientific scholarship can reflect, inform, and challenge how we understand the bodymind of the twenty-first-century psychophysical performer including issues of the actor's consciousness in performance. Loukes grounds her discussion of insights from the new sciences on psychophysical performance practices by citing first-hand, phenomeno-logical descriptions of performing written from 'inside' the performer's perspective.

We have organized Chapters 2 through 6 chronologically. Since the Indian and Japanese paradigms of acting date from very early periods yet continue to inform acting and training practices today East and West, we introduce the reader to these modes of work first so that we may under-stand these psychophysical paradigms and practices in depth in their own right. In later chapters we trace the contemporary legacy and use of these traditions – for example, principles/practices of yoga have influenced Stanislavsky and Grotowski, and elements/principles *of nō* are embedded in the psychophysical processes of butoh practice, as well as informing the training of Tadashi Suzuki and Shōgo Ōta. As we shall see, non-Western elements and principles have been central to many of the alternative ways of thinking about acting, performance, the body, and body–mind relationship in the work considered in Chapter 5, and in re-situating the bodymind relationship in contemporary new sciences (Chapter 6).

A brief Afterword by Jerri Daboo revisits issues raised throughout the book in relation to dialogue and the paradox(es) of acting.

Phillip B. Zarrilli, Jerri Daboo, and Rebecca Loukes

Notes

1. This list is not intended to be exclusive. Interpretive tools drawn from literary or historiographical studies also play an extremely important part in an actor's preparation for certain types of roles by gaining an essential under-standing of an historical context or person.
2. Our approach is also informed by some elements of practice-based research in which we occasionally analyse specific examples of acting based on our own immersion in the practice of acting. See also Richard Schechner's useful discussion of the relationship between theory and practice in 'Towards Tomorrow Restoring Disciplinary Limits and Rehearsals in Time?' (2006:230–2).

3. *Psychophysical Acting* examines in practice and theory a psychophysical under-standing and approach to acting by elaborating and expanding upon the assumptions behind Constantin Stanislavsky's use of the compound 'psycho-physical' in the nineteenth century, and provides a specific description and account of one in-depth process of psychophysical training – that developed by Phillip B. Zarrilli through Asian martial arts and yoga as a pre-performa-tive training for actors – can be applied to specific problems of acting across a range of dramaturgies.

Acknowledgements

The authors would like to thank Jane Milling and Graham Ley for their thoughtful comments and support during the writing and editing of this book; all at Palgrave Macmillan for their patience; and Hannah Cummings for proofreading the text.

Phillip B. Zarrilli also wishes to thank the International Research Centre, 'Interweaving Performance Cultures' at Freie Universitat (Berlin) for its support while writing his contributions to this book. Thanks are also due to Carol Sorgenfrei, Richard Emmert, Maya Krishna Rao, Kunju Vasudevan Namboodiripad for their generous assistance and cooperation. Special thanks to Kaite O'Reilly.

Jerri Daboo would like to thank the Dartington Hall Trust, the Devon Heritage Centre, and practitioners and colleagues who have helped along the way through shared practice and discussions, including Dorinda Hulton, Peter Hulton, Bella Merlin, Joanna Merlin, the late Mala Powers, and Sandra Reeve. Special thanks to the memory of John Garrie Roshi for his training and understanding of the bodymind.

Rebecca Loukes would like to thank Claire Coaché, Giovanna Colombetti, Andrew Dawson, Cassie Friend, Sarah Loukes, Eva Schmale, Jo Tasker, Lisle Turner, Turtle Key Arts, Rachel White, and my colleagues and students at the University of Exeter. Special thanks, as always, go to Richard, Flinn, and Arran Brazier.

Notes on Authors

Phillip B. Zarrilli is an actor, director, actor-trainer, and scholar. He is the founding Artistic Director of The Llanarth Group (Wales, 2000). Over the past thirty-plus years he has developed a psychophysical process of training actors using Asian martial arts and yoga which is taught at his permanent studio in Wales and internationally in short and long-term residencies. He is Professor of Performance Practice in the Drama Department at Exeter University and has published numerous books and essays including *Psychophysical Acting: An Intercultural Approach After Stanislavski* (2009) which received the 2010 ATHE Outstanding Book of the Year Award at the ATHE annual meeting in Los Angeles, USA.

Jerri Daboo is Senior Lecturer in Drama at the University of Exeter. She has worked as a performer and director for many years. Her work focuses on a psychophysical approach to performer training, with a particular emphasis on the work of Michael Chekhov, along with aspects of Buddhism, yoga, and martial arts. She has published a book on the Southern Italian ritual of tarantism, and researches on the cultural history of the South Asian diaspora in Britain.

Rebecca Loukes is an actor-deviser and practitioner working with psychophysical approaches to training and performance. She has trained in the awareness practices of Elsa Gindler with Eva Schmale (Germany) and Charlotte Selver (USA) and Asian martial/meditation arts with Phillip B. Zarrilli and these approaches underpin her performance work, writing, and teaching. She is Co-Artistic Director of RedCape Theatre, Associate Editor of *Theatre, Dance and Performance Training* journal and is a part-time Senior Lecturer in Drama at University of Exeter.

1 Introduction: Acting as Psychophysical Phenomenon and Process

Phillip B. Zarrilli

... [A]cting, like riding a bicycle, is easier to do than to explain.

Sharon Carnicke (2010:6)

There are many historically variable and context-specific paradigms, practices, and approaches to acting and actor training. One need only think of the diversity of theatrical performances throughout the world – the subtle, nuanced expressivity and restraint of the actor/dancers in Japanese *nō* theatre (Figure 1.1); the expressive and exuberant physicality displayed in genres such as Kerala, India's, *kathakali* dance-drama (Figure 1.2) or nineteenth-century European and American melodrama, or British pantomime, where heightened performances bring larger than life demons, gods, villains, and/or heroes to the stage; the finely drawn, individualized characters of textually based realist performances of plays by Ibsen or Chekhov; or the overt and often literally exhausting physicality brought centre stage in performances by companies such as DV8 (Govan et al. 2007:166–168) or Goat Island (Goulish 2000; Bottoms and Goulish 2007). Historically as well as today, many actors who have been trained within specific genres or styles of performance such as *nō*, *kathakali*, commedia dell'arte or opera master the techniques, conventions, and style of playing a type of role within a specific genre and remain specialist/virtuosic performers within that tradition or role-type. An increasing number of performers trained in traditional genres of performance such as Indian performers Navtej Johar (originally trained in *bharatanatyam*, South Indian dance) and Maya Rao

Figure 1.1 Kita-nō school actor, Akira Matsui playing the *Mae-shite* (primary role of the first part), Woman in *Hashitomi* ascribed to Naitō Saemon. As explained in Chapter 3, this is one of the 'phantasmal' *nō* plays in which the actor playing Woman in the first part is revealed in the second part of the play as the ghost of Lady Yūgao. By permission of Akira Matsui.

(originally trained in *kathakali*) (Figure 1.3) continue to perform *within* these traditions, but have also chosen to bring the disciplined type of psychophysical embodiment, awareness, energetic engagement, and consciousness imbibed from their in-depth psychophysical trainings into alternative and more experimental ways of creating performances outside these traditions and their conventional modes of expression.[1]

Still others are like the Japanese performer/director Yoshi Oida. Oida originally trained with Okura-san [one of the great master-teachers] in the traditional comic theatre form known as *kyōgen*, but no longer performs *kyōgen*. Rather, Oida brings the subtle embodied modes of expressivity he learned from *kyōgen* and *nō* into his work as a contemporary performer/director on the global stage. Yoshi Oida began to reevaluate his work outside the Japanese traditions when he encountered Peter Brook at a Theatre of Nations experiment in Paris in 1968. After

Figure 1.2   *Kathakali* master-actor, Kalamandalam Gopi as King Rumamgada in a performance of *King Rugmamgada's Law*. Here Rugmamgada has loosened his hair and entered into a transformative state of 'fury' so that, as required, he will be able to cut off his son's head. (See Chapter 2, pp. 79–83 for a discussion of this scene.) (Photo by Phillip B. Zarrilli).

joining Brook's company, Yoshi explains in his 1992 book, *The Actor Adrift*, how he had to modify what he had learned from his in-depth training in Japan and to discover ways to apply, adjust, and translate what he had learned from these rich, embodied modes of learning. After a performance on tour of work-in-progress directed by Peter Brook in rural Iran, '...Peter said to me, "Your acting is too concentrated and strong for this style of work"...And I realized that just as there are many levels of performance, there is no one "right" way to act' (1992:72). As is clear from his professional career as well as his publications, Yoshi Oida has developed a new, self-consciously intercultural approach to performance in which non-Western concepts of and approaches to embodiment, acting process, and aesthetics inform how he performs in contemporary cosmopolitan settings throughout the globe today.[2]

Similar to the three performers briefly discussed thus far – Yoshi Oida, Navtej Johar, and Maya Rao – many contemporary actors trained in the West today do not wish to restrict their acting and performance work to one specific genre, style, or role-type. Many actors choose to

Figure 1.3 Maya Krishna Rao's *kathakali*-based, solo performance of *Khol Do*—an adaptation of the short story by Sadat Hasan Manto, created in 1993. Rao's hour-long performance is an unrelenting, forcefully embodied physicalization that communicates through her bodymind the complete and unrelenting pathos and terror of the experience of dislocation associated with the riots that ended in the division of India and the creation of Pakistan. (Photo by permission of Maya Krishna Rao.).

perform across a broad spectrum of dramaturgies, styles, and types of roles from fully rounded individual characters in a realist play to the many new, alternative, 'post-dramatic' (Lehmann 2006) dramaturgies inhabiting today's stages – the later plays of Samuel Beckett (1984);[3] open scripts such as Heiner Müller's body of work (*Medeaplay* or *Hamletmachine* 1984) or that of Martin Crimp (*Attempts on Her Life* [1997] or *Fewer Emergencies* [2005]; the alternative dramaturgies of contemporary non-Western playwrights such as Japan's Ōta Shōgo (*The Tale of Komachi Told by the Wind* 2004), Betsuyaku Minoru (*Sick* 2004), and Noda Hideki with Colin Teevan (*The Bee* 2006; *The Diver* 2008); or the wide range of aesthetics and dramaturgies that inform devised 'physical theatre'. As one example among many, UK RADA-trained actress Kathryn Hunter is particularly well known for the physicality of her performances and has therefore played across a vast range of roles, theatrical genres, and styles from *Fragments* (a collection of short Beckett plays directed by Peter Brook), to the inventive Lecoq-based work of Theatre de Complicite, to playing King Lear, to performing in the London performances and on international tour of Japanese playwrights Noda Hideki and Colin Teevan's *The Bee* (2006, 2012) and *The Diver* (2008).

Given the global flows of culture as well as the sheer diversity of theatrical styles, genres, modes of physicalization, and dramaturgies available on today's stages, it should be no surprise that theories of and approaches to acting[4] today

- are highly diverse,
- have often been influenced by intercultural concepts and/or techniques,
- may be contradictory, and
- are often idiosyncratic.

The idiosyncrasy of contemporary acting

If one consults *Actors on Acting* – Toby Cole and Helen Krich Chinoy's historically broad-ranging edited collection of reflections, interviews, accounts, manifestos, and essays on Western acting by or with actors, directors, and theorists first published in 1949 (Cole and Chinoy 1970) – it is immediately evident just how diverse, contradictory, and idiosyncratic theories and approaches to acting have historically been in the West from the early Greek theatre to the late twentieth century.

This diversity of opinions about and approaches to acting is also reflected in Mary Luckhurst and Chloe Veltman's *On Acting* (2001) – a series of interviews with an eclectic range of twenty 'successful' professional British and American stage and film actors ranging from Simon Callow to Willem Dafoe, Anna Deavere Smith, and Indira Varma. Not surprisingly, the editors' short introduction concludes that '*There are as many definitions of acting as there are actors*' (emphasis added, 2001:xii; see also Renaud 2010:79–80).

A careful reading of the interviews with the twenty Western actors in *On Acting* or a review of the many publications on acting and acting training available today[5] makes it clear that among highly visible and successful actors there is no *single* shared method or approach to acting or actor training. Among the actors interviewed by Luckhurst and Veltman, Simon Callow, Michael Sheen, and Aysan Celik received sustained training at drama schools or in formal acting programmes, while others such as Willem Dafoe and Barb Jungr, *had no formal acting training whatsoever.* Dafoe received his 'training by doing', that is, he 'simply performed a lot' – first with Theatre X in Milwaukee, then with the Performance Group in New York, and then the Wooster Group (DaFoe 2001:23). He eventually expanded his acting work to include films. For Barb Jungr 'it was music which brought me to theatre' (2001:49). With a childhood filled with music, singing, learning classical violin, and attending performances, Jungr describes herself as having been '"schooled," not trained' (2001:50). Her first schooling was in gospel music and then onstage for thirteen years in the alternative cabaret circuit where 'physically, vocally and politically, you went on stage and had to get your point across to an audience who had not necessarily come to see your act' (2001:50).

Many if not most professional actors today could be said to work in highly idiosyncratic ways, that is, each individual draws on the diverse modes of performance/acting and/or types of training or 'schooling' they have experienced to address the specific acting, devising, or dramaturgical problems faced in each new production context. The internationally known Welsh theatre, film, and television actor Michael Sheen, whose notable roles have included playing the former UK Prime Minister Tony Blair, Mozart in *Amadeus*, David Frost in *Frost/Nixon*, and The Teacher in National Theatre Wales' 2011 huge 48-hour Port Talbot community production of *The Passion*, explained how he does not 'specialize in a certain type of acting' and prefers to be as adaptable as possible (2001:115). And, Willem Dafoe, when asked, '*Do you have a definition of acting?*' responded:

> It is very flexible, because acting a role depends on what is required [...] It is all performing in one way or another. I like to think of it in terms of different acting for different kinds of performances, and some actors are clever enough to know what mode they have to be in, depending on the material. (2001:25)

The kind of adaptability and/or context-specific flexibility that Sheen and Dafoe describe has often been neglected in discussions of contemporary acting and actor training after the rise and misrepresentation of Stanislavsky's work as 'a' or 'The System'. There is no doubt that the work of Russian actor and theatre director Konstantin Stanislavsky (1863–1938) revolutionized Western approaches to acting and actor training in the late-nineteenth and early-twentieth centuries. Stanislavsky was engaged in a life-long process of practical research into the nature and processes of acting. Following common usage at the time, he attempted to articulate a 'psychophysical' (*psikhofizicheskii*) approach to Western acting focused both on the actor's inner work (guided by Ribot's 'psychology' among others), and an embodied physicality applied at first to textually based character acting. He later adjusted his approach to the unique inner and outer problems of a variety of then 'alternative dramaturgies'[6] including opera and the symbolist dramas of the Belgian playwright Maurice Maeterlinck (1862–1949). As explained in more detail in Chapter 4, for a variety of complex reasons, a historically balanced view of Stanislavsky's approach to acting and training actors should be viewed as an ever-evolving process where there was never 'a' system per se – a fact too often hidden behind representations and descriptions of Stanislavskian-based approaches to acting as 'a' system.

The dominance of Stanislavskian-based approaches to acting and actor training in the West throughout the twentieth century has often meant that acting and actor training are approached in terms of how to play a character in a textually based drama with an emphasis on the actor as an 'interpreter' of a role. As we well know from Stanislavsky, the process of interpreting a role engages the actor in a highly creative, psychophysical process that culminates in actualizing and 'living' or 'experiencing' that role as fully as possible on stage.

As discussed at length in Chapter 5, alongside this notion of the actor as 'interpreter', as processes of devising, co-creation, and performance-making developed in the work of such key figures as Jacques Lecoq (1921–1999), an additional model of the actor-as-creator began to develop. The subtitle to Lecoq's *The Moving Body* is '*teaching creative theatre*' (2000; see also Chamberlain and Yarrow 2002). The actor-as-creator or maker is another primary model utilized by many actors today working in ensemble acting companies such as Theatre de Complicite, Odin Teatret, the theatre of Suzuki Tadashi (see Chapter 3), and in Maya Krishna Rao's work (see Chapter 2), where a wide variety of improvisatory techniques are utilized to generate performance material that eventually is shaped into a performance score (Hulton 1998; Govan, Nicholson, and Normington 2007; Harvie and Lavender 2010). While examining the scope and full history of devised theatre-making is beyond the scope of this book and Chapter 5, our concern here will be with acting as a process and phenomenon which encompasses both the actor-as-interpreter and the actor-as-maker.

If contemporary acting is often highly idiosyncratic; if, as Yoshi Oida observes, 'there is no one "right" way to act' (1992:72); if, as Sharon

Carnicke has suggested, '... acting, like riding a bicycle, is easier to do than to explain' (Carnicke 2010:6); and if the actor can be both an 'interpreter' and a creative 'maker', what, if anything, can be said about acting without being reductive? What constitutes 'the work' of the actor? From what perspective(s) might it be productive to think, talk about, and (re)consider acting and actor training today?[7]

In the remainder of this introductory chapter I consider the question or problem of what can be said about acting from five perspectives:

1. *The actor as doer.* I begin by considering acting at the most general level by asking, 'What constitutes the "work" of the actor?' In the most general sense the actor can be considered a 'doer'.
2. *The actor as present to the sensorial field offered by performance.* I briefly consider here the actor as existing within the sensorial field offered by a particular training or performance and the stimuli offered by that field of experience.
3. *The actor's performance score.* Whatever the genre, approach to, or style of acting, one part of the actor's work (in training and/or rehearsals) is to structure or create a 'score' to guide the actor when performing. I consider how actors construct a specific 'score' for enactment, the dramaturgy that informs the score, the sub-score that may exist as part of the actor's score, and the relationship between each actor's score and the performance score as a whole.
4. *An enactive approach to acting and embodiment.* Stepping back from the specific nature of the actor's score and building on the notion of the actor as a 'doer', I draw on a set of interdisciplinary insights from phenomenology, cognitive science, and anthropological ecology to construct a 'meta-theory' of acting as an enactive process of psychophysical embodiment – a subject addressed in more detail in Chapter 6 by Loukes.
5. *Acting: an intercultural perspective.* Given that theories and practices of acting since the late nineteenth century have been shaped by a constantly evolving set of global, intercultural techniques, practices, and aesthetic principles, I address acting from an intercultural perspective.
6. *Acting as an embodied phenomenon and process.* Using the compound term 'psychophysical' to mark the dialectical engagement of the actor's 'inner' and 'outer' processes, I provide a brief description of acting as a phenomenon – as a constant process of sensing, perceiving, attending to, attuning, feeling, remembering, and imagining – and focus specifically on the actor's embodied consciousness.

All five of these perspectives either inform, or are addressed more specifically in Chapters 2–6.

What constitutes the 'work' of the actor? The actor as 'doer'

Let us begin this initial reflection by looking at the etymology of the English word 'acting'. The noun 'act' is derived from the Latin *actus, doing*' which in turn is derived from the past participle of the verb *agere*, meaning 'to do' (*Webster's Third New International Dictionary, Vol. I*, 1976:20). An 'act' is a thing done or being done' (ibid.). Although an archaic meaning, the verbal form, to 'act', means 'to carry out into action' (ibid.). The actor is 'one who does things' (Partridge 1983:5). The word 'actor' derives from the middle English, '*actour*, doer' (ibid.:23), i.e., the actor is a doer.[8]

Trevor Marchand reminds us that yet another facet of doing as-a-process was identified long ago by Aristotle in his *Nichomachean Ethics* (2010:1). Aristotle explained how both the arts as well as virtues 'are not endowed, but realized and reinforced [by doing] in practice' (2010:1):

> For the things we have to learn before we can do them, we learn by doing them, e.g. men become builders by building and lyreplayers by playing the lyre; so too we become just by doing just acts, temperate by doing temperate acts, brave by doing brave acts. (Aristotle, *Niochomachean Ethics*, book 2, Chapter 1:31–32; quoted in Marchand 2010:1)

Aristotle articulated a commonplace about skilled/virtuosic craftsmanship as a form of deep 'knowing' through embodied doing. Like master carpenters or musicians, actors learn by doing.

At virtuosic levels of skilled practice, in-depth embodied knowledge is manifest in the doer as an integrated psychophysical whole. 'Body' and 'mind' are one. An integrated, accomplished body-mind manifests 'physical skills' necessarily informed by requisite 'inner' modes of disposition/engagement – the type of focus/concentration of attention, sensory engagement, awareness/feeling-tone, et cetera essential to a specific form of artistry/skill.

The notion of an 'act' as a thing 'being done' also suggests the processual nature of the acting-as-doing, that is, acting is *enactment*. One meaning of the noun 'action', is 'the process of change or alteration' (ibid.: 21). This sense that there is 'change or alteration' at the centre of action points in two directions: (1) towards the actor's 'inner' process and experience in which psychophysiologically there is a sense/awareness of 'inner' movement taking place within the actor's body-mind *as the actions/tasks that constitute the actor's score shift and change*, and (2) the audience's perception and experience that something is happening given the shifts or changes taking place in the actor's score. Three important caveats are necessary here: (a) how a specific cultural paradigm of acting and embodiment interprets these shifts or changes varies from one culture or aesthetic to another, or between different approaches to and theories of acting; (b) an actor's 'inner' process and experience of these shifts and changes may be totally different from what the audience perceives/experiences from 'outside'; and (c) as discussed in more detail later, for the virtuosic actor this 'inner' experience/feel/awareness of movement, change, or alteration is most often understood as a non-intentional process. The virtuosic actor is not moving but 'being moved' in the moment of performance.

In his interview in *On Acting* cited above, Michael Sheen points to several key inter-related dimensions of the actor-as-doer's process when he describes the one constant throughout his work as attempting to bring 'a physical presence to what I do' (2001:116). What Sheen-the-actor 'does' is to perform an acting score. The shape, form, and aesthetic conventions guiding the actions/tasks that constitute a performance score are historically, culturally, and aesthetically variable. Sheen points to the obvious fact that actors, even when immobile, are nevertheless always 'psycho-physically' present and engaged in performing/doing the set of tasks or actions that constitute a specific performance score – even if/when that is nothing more than breathing in a position of immobility. But Sheen's statement that he 'attempts to bring a physical presence' to what he does points *beyond the merely physical* engagement of the actor-as-doer in what he does. Sheen's use of 'presence' calls *our* attention as readers to this *something more than the simply physical* – the inner processes at work. I interpret Sheen's use of 'physical presence' to mean that Sheen-as-actor (and equally as a human being) is fully 'present' to each embodied action in the moment of its doing. Ideally, he can be understood to bring every dimension of him-'self' into what he does, that is, his body-mind, attention, focus/concentration, sensory awareness/perception, imagination, memory, and feelings, are all fully available and 'present' for engagement in the moment as necessary. Optimally each task/action of his performance score is enlivened by being 'physically present' with one, more, or all of the repertory of embodied possibilities listed above.

What constitutes the sensorial field of the actor?

The notion of the actor being 'enlivened' points to the central importance of the actor being phenomenally and sensorially 'open' to her
performance environment when performing. A series of questions
arises:

- What constitutes the sensorial field of the actor from 'inside' his experience of training and/or performance?
- How do specific trainings 'attune' and open the actor to specific
  modes of sensory awareness, that is, to 'listening', to 'seeing', to 'touching', to 'balancing' and so on?
- What felt stimuli are offered by each element of performance whether
  produced by the actor himself, music/musicians, the other actors, or
  the stage environment?
- In what ways is the actor's experience shaped by these 'felt stimuli'?
  How does the actor absorb, respond to, reflect upon what is felt?

For the actor to be open to the sensorial field offered by a performance
means that the actor is not always 'active' as a 'doer', but is equally
'passive' in the sense of remaining open to what is felt, sensed, absorbed,
and received.

Western approaches to acting tend to (over) emphasize 'action' without
due consideration of how the actor can enter a state of open sensory/
perceptual receptivity in the moment. In addition, the Western textual
tradition of analysis has focused much on the actor's 'head-work', that is,
on analytically identifying 'actions' within a text. The sensorial dimensions
of training and performance too often remain under explored. Whether
'traditional' or contemporary, trainings that start from psychophysical,
embodied practice optimally lead to both an 'awakening' or 'enlivening' of
the actor's energy, and to an opening of the sensorium and perception. The
degree to which such an opening occurs, which senses are opened, and
how the awakened sensorium is animated in a performance score depends
on the specific cultural, training, and performative contexts. The list of
questions posed above is open-ended and can only be answered with
reference to particular approaches to actor training and performance.

Part of our explorations throughout this book focus on how specific
approaches to training and performance take account of and nourish or
develop a complete range of the actor's sensorium. As we will see in
Chapters 2, 3, 4, and 5 these concerns have been addressed in both

'traditional' and contemporary trainings from *nō* to Stanislavsky, and in Chapter 6 Loukes considers the actor's body-mind within the field of contemporary cognitive studies from a 'situated' perspective.

It is within the actor's specific performance score that the question of whether and how the actor's sensorium is to be stimulated and opened is immediately relevant. It is to the actor's score that we now turn our attention.

The actor's performance score

We may define the *actor's performance score* as follows: *that structure or sequence of actions determined in part or in full by conventional performance techniques, and/or through rehearsal processes (often responding to and embodying a dramatic text), and/or through devising/making processes. The acting score provides the actor with a repeatable template or map that guides her embodiment, senses, and experience of that score within each live performance.*

[Note: Where improvisation plays a role in live performance, the horizon of possibilities is not limitless; rather, improvisation always takes place within the context of a specific structure or set of rules within which one 'improvises'. And those who regularly improvise – such as stand-up comedians – must gain an understanding through rehearsals, training, or on-the-job experience of how to improvise in a certain way.]

It is almost ubiquitous today for the actor to understand her process during the rehearsal/devising period as culminating in the production of a performance score.[9] Three major types of processes can shape an actor's performance score:

1. As discussed in more detail in Chapters 2 and 3, most evident in genres of performance such as India's *kathakali* or *kutiyattam* and Japanese *nō* are the established or assumed set of conventions which, along with traditional aesthetic principles, guide and shape a performance's structure and dramaturgy. The score for a specific role within the repertory is often learned in painstaking detail under the careful guidance of a master teacher in a lengthy period of training and/or apprenticeship. Actors learn either complete performance scores for specific role categories or types, or performance units, sequences, or choreographed patterns that are assembled to shape,

structure and perform dramatic texts within a repertory of plays-in-performance. Actors in the *kutiyattam* tradition maintain manuals with extensive notes on the staging and acting techniques to be used for particular acts of each drama in their repertoire. From the outsider's perspective, conventionalized systems of training and acting mistakenly appear rigid, *but they are not.* There is a tremendous amount of individual variation among actors performing specific roles, and there is a great deal of freedom within certain aspects or sections of a performance where the virtuosic performer interprets and makes his mark on how a specific role is interpreted and performed.

The acting/performance scores for contemporary dramatic texts are usually developed during rehearsals rather than during periods of training. Rather than being determined by convention, the director guides and shapes the specific aesthetic logic of the production as a whole, works with designers on developing the *mise-en-scène*, and guides how the actors define, structure, and shape the actions/tasks that constitute their score. For texts in which there are clearly defined, individualized roles and characters, contemporary actors most often make use of a wide variety of tools drawn from approaches to acting developed by Stanislavsky which will be discussed in Chapter 4 (and/or those who followed him such as Strasberg, Adler, Meisner, Michael Chekhov, and so on). Within the notion of Total Theatre, scores are used to take into account the totality of the action and the *mise-en-scène*, such as Max Reinhardt's performance score for *The Miracle* (1911). A discussion of Total Theatre and its relation to other movements in Germany is found in Chapter 5. In many non-Western theatre traditions and in some post-dramatic texts, such as the plays of Samuel Beckett, there is no individualized 'character' per se but rather what might best be described as a 'figure' or 'persona' such as the primary 'doer' or *shite* in Japanese *nō*, or Mouth in Beckett's *Not I.* For Mouth, the actor's score and the governing aesthetic logic are guided by Beckett's specific vision and the constraints he places on the actor-in-performance. In the performance of other post-dramatic texts, the director and actors must search out the appropriate aesthetic logic that will guide the production as a whole as well as the shaping of an actor's score.

2. A third set of processes are those which take place when an actor's score is created as part of a production which is being devised, co-created, or made within the development/rehearsal period. The

point(s) of departure for the creative processes vary widely. As discussed in more detail in some of the examples at the end of Chapters 2 and 3, in Chapter 5, a solo artist working alone, a group of collaborators/co-creators, and/or a director develop a process or way of working, conceptualizing and then guiding an often evolving creative process and its aesthetic logic. Potential units or structures of performance are generated, assembled, discarded, and/or revised. The artist(s) weave together or montage structures or units of performance consisting of a set of tasks, actions, or images to constitute the performance score for the production as a whole and for each individual actor.[10]

In all these processes individual actors *may* have their own specific aesthetic logic, or their own interpretation of a role, figure, or set of actions/images guiding the development of their own individual scores, *even if this logic is not explicitly articulated or reflected upon.* Crucially, before going onstage most actors will have developed a repeatable performance score to guide them in/through each live performance. There may of course be places in this score that are open to 'play' or 'improvisation' within certain constraints in the moment of playing.

Let us consider two other accounts of the contemporary actor's score. When creating productions with Odin Teatret, Eugenio Barba uses the term performance score to mark

- the general design of the form in a sequence of actions, and the evolution of each single action (beginning, climax, conclusion);
- the precision of the fixed details of each action as well as the transitions connecting them (*sats*, changes of direction, different qualities of energy, variations of speed);
- the dynamism and the rhythm: the speed and intensity which regulate the *tempo* (in the musical sense) of a series of actions. This is the meter of the actions with their micro-pauses and decisions, the alternation of long or short ones, accented or unaccented segments, characterized by vigorous or soft energy;
- the orchestration of the relationships between the different parts of the body (hands, arms, legs, feet, eyes, voice, facial expressions). (2010:27–28)

John Lutterbie provides a description of the performance score that emphasizes its dynamic enactment in actual performance. For Lutterbie the actor's score is a series of intentional acts that interweaves creative associations discovered through analysis and improvisation with the dynamics of technique. These acts are performed through movement, language, and gesture. They combine memories – those retrieved from the past as well as those derived from working on the current production – with data from external perceptions and internal proprioceptions. The complex is generated by the desire to perform with (or without) other actors and for an audience. When all works, the result is a thoughtful, precise, intelligent, and effective series of actions that sustains the performer throughout the performance. (Lutterbie 2011:194)

All three descriptions of the performance score provided above emphasize the fact that the actor's score is a template and guide to enactment that is highly detailed, yet dynamic and in no way rigid or inflexible. However their performance scores are shaped, all virtuosic actors respond *in the moment* sensorially to what is happening within the performance environment; therefore, it is helpful to think of the actor's score as a 'dynamic system' developed and brought to actualization alongside and in relation to the scores of the other actors/performers. Each actor's score is dynamically actualized within the 'dynamic system' of the production score as a whole (Lutterbie 2011:210). When repeated sufficiently during training/rehearsals and when brought to performance, the score constitutes a dynamic horizon of moment-by-moment possibilities for the actor's embodied/sensory actualization in the moment of performance.

In the process of creating an actor's performance score, Eugenio Barba calls attention to the 'actor's dramaturgy' as part of this process. The 'actor's dramaturgy' is the aesthetic 'logic' that informs the construction of the actor's individual score, and which may 'not correspond to my intentions as a director, nor to those of the author' (Barba 2010:24). Although speaking of his work with Odin, Barba helpfully points out how an actor develops her own

logic from her biography, from her personal needs, from her experience and the existential and professional situation, from the text, the character or the tasks received, and from the relationships with the director and with the other colleagues. (2010:24)

The actor's aesthetic logic and dramaturgy in creating a specific performance score exists, but often remains hidden and is not publicly revealed.

articulates what happens within the actor's creative process of ₃ping a score and the dramaturgical/aesthetic logic that informs ₄t score. When devising or rehearsing, actors are often asked to improvise, i.e., to explore and see what happens or what is generated within the parameters of an exercise or structure. When performances are developed through devising/improvisatory processes, one of the difficulties for the performers is to be able to both remember what they have done, and then to recreate precisely the kind of embodied engagement produced in the moment of improvisation. Barba provides the following description of how actors find their way to repetition of a score generated through devising/improvisation in his work with Odin Teatret actors:

> A thread guided the actor in finding again the direction of the paths which divided and merged together in his body-mind while improvising. It was a thread made of stimuli, of mental energy and somatic memory, absolute subjectivity and imaginative freedom, permeated by timelessness and biographic episodes. This thread was the *subscore*. It was what the actor heard, saw and reacted to. In other words, the way he recounted the improvisation to himself through actions. This tale involved rhythms, sounds and tunes, silences and suspensions, fragrances and colours, people and clusters of contrasting images: a stream of stimuli or inner actions which turned into precise dynamic forms [....] The subscore is an inner support, a hidden scaffold which actors sketch for themselves. (2010:29)

A parallel account to Barba's is provided by Julia Varley – an actor with Odin Teatret since 1976. In *Notes from an Odin Actress*, Varley recounts her own process and perspective on creating both the performance score and subscore, and the logic that informs her work. She describes the subscore as

> an invisible physical/mental process, which accompanies, both in a fixed and fluctuating way, the actions that the spectator sees [...] It is not restricted to a conscious mental process based on images. The course that a subscore follows can be linked to physical sensations, abstractions, information processed in different ways by the brain and remembered/ forgotten by a memory, which I place in my cells rather than in my thoughts. (2011:79)

To summarize, the actor's performance score what might be best thought of as a tapestry of four interwoven layers, including

1. the performance score for the production as a whole, that is, the dramaturgy and 'general design' for what 'the spectator sees', tempo-rhythm and orchestration;
2. each individual actor's score consisting of the specific set of actions/tasks orchestrated rhythmically within the design of the whole;
3. the specific aesthetic logic or dramaturgy that informs an individual actor's often idiosyncratic creation of that score; and
4. the extremely subtle elements and threads of associations, memories, feelings, sensations, et cetera that constitute the subscore.

These four layers constituting the actor's score are suffused with the inherent *dynamic and energetic possibilities* that are available to the actor for embodiment and enactment of that score in the moment of performance.

But what is it that creates performance as an occasion that is out of the everyday and ordinary? What allows a 'text' or a 'score' to come 'off the page'? For an actor's score to be of interest Ingemar Lindh (1945–1997)[11] explains that the actor must

> transpose his actions to *another dimension*. If his work does not provoke resonance, it does not stimulate associations. For example, 'action' does not simply mean tearing a newspaper to shreds. The act has to stir a new world in the actor and in others; otherwise his score remains a corpse instead of enabling him to act and react [....] to facilitate the channeling of his energy. (2010:31, emphasis added)

This *other dimension* to which Lindh points is the territory Martin Sheen referred to in his statement about being present. To bring a performance to life – the actor has to engage fully her inner animating energy in the moment of performance. Only then will a performance 'resonate, 'vibrate', and thereby 'stir' or 'move' both the actor herself and the audience in a manner appropriate to a specific dramaturgy, its aesthetic logic, and its performance conventions. Specific maps of this process of inner resonation and vibration are offered in Chapters 2 and 3 with reference to India and Japan.

To attain an optimal, virtuosic ability to actualize this 'other dimension' in live performance, most actors either go through one or more of the following: (1) a long-term professional apprenticeship, such as traditionally occurred in Italian *commedia dell'arte* companies and in *kathakali* or *nō*; (2) like Willem Dafoe some actors may gain sufficient experience and the ability to 'vibrate' or 'resonate' simply through practice; and/or

(3) actors undergo some form of long-term psychophysical training(s) which includes repetition and experience. Although acting today can be said to be idiosyncratic in that there is no single 'right' way to train and thereby approach the wide variety of dramaturgies and styles of acting experience experienced on stages throughout the world today, reaching towards virtuosity requires of all actors the skilled ability to deploy kineaesthetic/bodymind 'knowledge' in the 'flow' of the moment – a kind of practical/professional knowledge. All actors are ideally able to make tactical adjustments to their acting scores in the moment of performance – adjusting as necessary their bodyminds and energy to the acting problem/environment at hand. Such tacit, sensory-motor knowledge is only acquired through long-term training and experience. Like any embodied practice, first and foremost is the kind of knowledge gained in and for an ever-deepening relationship to the embodied act of practice – a sense of assiduous attentiveness in the moment of doing. Second is knowledge *about* one's engagement *of* this experience of being/ doing. Thomas P. Kasulis describes the type of experience which evolves for actors through training/experience as 'sensory dependent knowledge' (1993:304). This is not 'knowledge' that is 'about', but rather a form of tacit 'knowledge' which one comes to actualize through a specific mode of embodied practice and which one is able to deploy in practice (see Zarrilli 2001).

Before elaborating further on the specifics of the actor's embodied process of being present to what she does, and to better understand this view of acting as a process of doing, I introduce an alternative paradigm for understanding acting as an enactive phenomenon and process.

An enactive approach to acting and embodiment[12]

Drawing on recent developments in phenomenology, cognitive science, and anthropological ecology, I introduce an enactive approach to under-standing of acting as a phenomenon and process. In Chapter 6 Rebecca Loukes expands on the question of how the new sciences shed light on psychophysical processes of acting.

In contrast to representational or mimetic theories of acting that are constructed from the position of the outside observer to the process/ phenomenon of acting, my concern is with articulating a way of under-standing acting from the perspective of the actor as enactor/doer from 'inside' the act of performing. I begin with an example: A brief description and discussion of acting Reader and Listener in Samuel Beckett's short post-dramatic text, *Ohio Impromptu* (Figure 1.4).

Figure 1.4 Reader (Phillip B. Zarrilli) and Listener (Andy Crook) in Samuel Beckett's *Ohio Impromptu*. As Reader reads the story from the pages of the well-worn book, the two figures sit motionless throughout most of the performance 'as though turned to stone' (Beckett 1984:287). (Photograph: Brent Nicastro. Photo by permission of Phillip B. Zarrilli and The Llanarth Group.).

The mise-en-scène and theatrical context of Beckett's *Ohio Impromptu*

Two figures – Reader and Listener – are identically dressed in long black coats with long white hair. They are seated as mirror images at a 4′×8′ white table with 'head[s] bowed proper on right hand[s]' (Beckett 1984:285). Open before Reader on the table is a 'worn volume' and a single wide-brimmed black hat. As Reader reads the story, the two figures sit 'motionless' throughout most of the performance 'as though turned to stone' (Beckett 1984:287). Reader reads the text 'without colour', i.e., without the typical vocal contours that characterize everyday conversation. Listener listens. Physical actions are minimal. Listener knocks on the resonant wooden table when he wishes Reader to stop and repeat a phrase, or when he wishes the reading to continue. When the story is complete, the last page turned, and the book closed, after a final knock Reader and Listener gradually raise their heads to look into one another's eyes.

The account I provide below of performing *Ohio Impromptu* is constructed from my perspective as an actor inside the performance score developed while on tour in the US with *The Beckett Project*. From this position inside the performance, I summarize how I deploy my psychophysical attention and awareness at the beginning of the performance. I then elaborate how an 'enactive approach' to acting views the actor as a skilled practitioner – a sentient being able to be, to do, to respond, and to imagine in specific (theatrical) environments. The implications of this view of acting as phenomenon and process are briefly explored.

Performing Reader in Beckett's *Ohio Impromptu*

September 15, 2006, the Gilbert Hemsley Theatre, Madison, Wisconsin. Tonight is the first of eight performances of *The Beckett Project*. We have just received our five minute call for *Ohio Impromptu*. Andy Crook (Listener) and I (Reader) leave our dressing room, mirror images of one another in our long black coats, black trousers, and long white wigs. Since we have not yet taken our places within the specific on stage environment Beckett envisaged for *Ohio Impromptu*, anyone encountering us backstage as we walk down the short corridor into the theatre would find us laughable – are we a pair of daft Goths who have wandered in off the street, or perhaps we have arrived over a month early for Madison's infamous Hallowe'en street party?

Entering the theatre we double check the placement of our straight-backed white chairs, check with the house manager about how much time we have until they want to open the doors and let the audience enter. 'Three minutes.' We take our seats at the '4 x 8' white table. Andy and I settle into our chairs. As Reader I am situated to Andy's right, and as Listener he is to my left. I begin my final personal preparations. I check my placement on the chair, sensing the feel of the chair against my thighs and buttocks. I arrange and rearrange my long black coat so that it is not caught up beneath me. I let my awareness open from my 'centre' (lower abdominal area, or *dantian*) down through my lower body and out through the soles of my feet. I sense the relationship of the soles of my feet to/through the floor.

'Two minutes.' I double-check the precise placement of the book on the table before me. Following up on our earlier vocal warm-up, I place the palm of my right hand on my sternum and repeat a set of strong, resonant vocal pulses – 'ha, ha, ha, ha' – in a pitch that vibrates my sternum. With my external focus directed outward through the theatre, my voice 'sounds' both my body and the space. Andy and I settle into our identical physical positions under the watchful eye of our acting colleague, Patricia

Boyette. As each of our right hands frames our foreheads, she ensures that from the audience's perspective we do indeed look identical. Patricia makes any final adjustments to this nearly still-life image we will inhabit for fifteen to seventeen minutes, lowering a knuckle of a finger for one of us and ensuring a wisp of hair is not loose. In the final few moments before the house is open and the audience enters, I 'sound' the text by seeing if I hit the chest resonator so that I 'vibrate' at the correct pitch on the opening line, 'Little is left to tell…' I sense the act of articulation of the 't' and 'tt's in the line as my tongue hits the back of my teeth, waking up my mouth, filling my body.

My attention shifts to my breath. I follow my in-breath as it slowly drops in and down to my lower abdomen. Keeping my primary attention on my in-breath and out-breath, I open my auditory awareness to Andy about three feet to my left…Listening for his breath. I open my awareness further beyond Andy to the periphery, out through the top of my head toward the back of the theatre, and behind me. We are 'ready.' Patricia gives the house manager the all clear. The doors are opened, and the audience, chatting as they enter, are like a wall of energy and sound moving into the space. Their sound passes through me. I am aware of it, but not distracted by it. My sensory awareness and attention are not singular, but multiple – taking in my breathing as it begins to synchronize with Andy's. Now, we are breathing together…in…and out…as one. Our perceptual awareness is open to each other. My awareness simultaneously takes in the audience…reaching toward the back row of the space and the rustling presences there. They begin to sit, and settle. I sense the heat of the lengthy lighting cue as its warmth begins to touch my hands and as the brightness of the light hits the table and illuminates the text before me. The audience further settles.

I am perched on the edge of speech, sensing the potential words in my mouth, sensing the touch of the page of the book on the table with my left hand, and the touch of the weight of my forehead against my thumb and first two fingers. Following my breath, when I sense the lighting cue is at its full warmth and intensity, and that the audience has indeed fully settled and the last cough has been coughed, the first line of the text 'unexpectedly' is shaped in and emerges from my mouth riding a breath on a pitch with little color but that nevertheless resonates in my sternum: 'Little is left to tell…In a last attempt…' The sharp, resonant sound of knuckles hitting the surface of the table stops my reading. I follow my breath, sensing its synchronization with Andy's, inhabiting with that breath this space-time between us.

Just as my sensory and perceptual awareness are open, my imagination and memory are also open. As I read the opening line, associations may momentarily present themselves to me at the periphery of my consciousness/awareness. Usually there is a sense of an impending end…the end of *this* particular reading of the story – there is only one page left to turn in this book…the end of a life – my father's…my mother's…my own…?

What I have just described, as best I can, is how as a stage actor I simultaneously inhabit, act within, and respond as a sentient, perceptual being to the very specific (theatrical) environment that constitutes the *mise-en-scène* of Beckett's *Ohio Impromptu*. As Reader, the actions I initiate – reading the text, turning a page, closing the book – and my responses to stimuli – my reading of the first line or being interrupted in my reading by Andy's knock – are specific to the play's dramaturgy and my overt performance score as actualized in this theatre on this day. Precisely when does Andy's knock with the knuckles of his left hand stop my reading of the text? Ideally, I never know. By being perceptually responsive to Andy's actual presence in this environment my reading is stopped by his knock as/when it happens in each performance. The word or part of a word that is interrupted differs every night. Precisely what my imagination will conjure in response to that first line, 'Little is left to tell', I do not know with absolute precision. What is conjured imaginatively or from my memory has not been reduced to a single possibility, but rather falls within *a range of appropriate possibilities* triggered by my engagement with reading/hearing/speaking the sentence at the moment of its saying/hearing.

Andy Crook and I are not abstract constructs, but rather specific sentient beings acting. We are sensing, perceiving, imagining, remembering as living human organisms in the moment to all the stimuli in the environment. These stimuli include the book open before me as both material object and the words it contains, Beckett's text that I read from the book, the other actor, and the environment. In this view, *acting may be defined as that dynamic embodied/enactive psychophysiological process by means of which a (theatrical) world is made available at the moment of its appearance/experience for both the actors and audience.*[13]

However pedestrian, the above description of acting in *Ohio Impromptu* is intended to provide some idea of just how complex the embodied phenomenon and experience of acting is at the moment it takes place. Although any such account can never completely describe the phenomenon of acting in all its complexities, following the philosopher Alva Noë I have tried to 'catch experience in the act of making the world available' (2004:176).

The problem of the body and body-mind dualism

Contemporary theories and accounts of acting and of Western psychological realism in particular, are susceptible to body-mind dualism because they often assume a static, essentialist model when representing acting. If body-mind dualism remains a problem, how are we to think and talk about the body, mind, and their relationship in acting? In Chapters 2 and 3 we explore Indian and Japanese ways of understanding the relationship between body and mind where historically within certain specific schools of thought, it has long been assumed that body and mind are fundamentally related. Within our Western traditions, several complementary tools can be used to address the body-mind relationship in acting and acting as an embodied process: a post-Merleau-Ponty phenomenology;[14] philosophical linguistics which reconsider the foundational role of embodiment and experience in linguistic/cognitive formations;[15] the branch of cognitive science which views the human organism (mind, body, consciousness, experience) as 'an embodied dynamic system' (Thompson 2007:4–13); and an ecological approach to perception developed by the social anthropologist Tim Ingold (2000, 2011).

My focus here and our focus throughout this book is on the livedness of the actor's modes of psychophysical embodiment, perception, sensory awareness, and experience from the actor's perspective inside training and performance. This perspective is intended to overcome the inherent body-mind dualism often assumed in how we think and talk about acting.

Beginning in the seventeenth century, Western philosophers came to identify the body as a physical object much like other material objects – as having certain anatomical and functional properties that could be characterized as following certain scientific principles. Thomas Kasulis explains how

> since the modern West considered the body a mechanism existing in an external relation to the spirit or mind, it naturally assumed we could discover the processes of the body through autopsies. Although the mind was no longer functional in a corpse, the body continued to be itself even after the relationship was severed by death. Western physiology owes its birth to that way of thinking. (1993:305)

As we shall see in more detail in Chapter 2 in India, and in Chapter 3 in Japan as well as China; dissection and autopsies were not central to the development of their indigenous medical systems. Rather, these cultures developed specific paradigms and practices which focused on 'the whole mind-body complex' (Kasulis 1993:305).

Among those Western philosophers who systematically challenged a mechanistic understanding of the body as an object during the 1960s was Maurice Merleau-Ponty. His three books – *Phenomenology of Perception* (1962, 2012), *The Primacy of Perception* (1964, 2012), and *The Visible and the Invisible* (1968) – marked a paradigmatic shift in Western thinking about the role of the body in the constitution of experience when he raised the fundamental philosophical problem of the body's role (or lack thereof) in constituting experience. Merleau-Ponty critiqued the hitherto static, objective nature of most representations of the body and experience:

> [T]hinking which looks on from above, and thinks of the object-in-general must return to the 'there is' which underlies it; to the site, the soil of the sensible and opened world such as it is in our life and for our body – not that possible body which we may legitimately think of as an information machine but that actual body I call mine, this sentinel standing quietly at the command of my words and acts. (Merleau-Ponty 1964:160–161)

Rejecting the exclusive assumption of the natural sciences and modern psychology that treated the physical body (*Körper*) as a thing, object, instrument, or machine under the command and control of an all-knowing mind, and thereby challenging the Cartesian *cogito*, Merleau-Ponty (re)claimed the centrality of the lived body (*Leib*) and embodied experience as the very means and medium through which the world comes into being and is experienced. He demanded an account of the 'actual body I call mine,' that is, the body as 'an experienced phenomenon ... in the immediacy of its lived concreteness,' and 'not as a representable object ... for the abstractive gaze' (Schrag 1969:130). He thereby rejected mind–body dualism, and (re)claimed the centrality of the body and embodied experience as the locus for 'experience as it is lived in a deepening awareness' (Levine 1985:62). For Merleau-Ponty, the focus of philosophical inquiry shifted from 'I think' to an examination of the 'I can' of the body, that is, sight and movement as modes of entering into inter-sensory relationships with objects, or the world (1964:87).

Acting as a process of 'I can': an enactive view

When Merleau-Ponty shifted from an examination of 'I think' to the 'I can' of the body, he laid the philosophical foundation for a more processual account of how our relationship to the worlds we inhabit is constituted by our inter-sensory and inter-subjective engagement with those worlds. As noted earlier with reference to Aristotle, the actor, like other skilled practitioners, ideally gains the ability to inhabit a particular world of the 'I can.' Among other scholars, Francesco Varela, Evan Thompson, and Eleanor Rosch have argued for viewing experience and its relationship to cognition as processual – a view which challenges a static, essentialist, representational model:

> We propose as a name the term *enactive* to emphasize the growing conviction that cognition is not the representation of a pregiven world by a pregiven mind but is rather the enactment of a world and a mind on the basis of a history of the variety of actions that a being in the world performs. (1991:9)

Expanding on his earlier work with Varela and Rosch, Evan Thompson explains how living beings are 'autonomous agents' for whom 'cognition is the exercise of skillful know-how in situated and embodied action' (Thompson 2007:13).

Implicit in Merleau-Ponty's theory of the body as an 'I can' is a theory of perception. Western philosophy has long viewed perception and action as distinct. As Maximilian de Gaynesford explains:

> On this old view, the mind receives sensory information from its environment, information which is then given structure by various cognitive processes and fed into the motor cortex to produce action. This view seems erroneous for numerous neurophysiological, behavioral and philo-sophical reasons. We should, instead, treat perception and action as constitutively interdependent. (2003:25)

Anthropological ecologist Tim Ingold explains how psychologists in the 1960s and 1970s assumed that

> the mind got to work on the raw material of experience, consisting of sensations of light, sound, pressure on the skin, and so on, organizing it into an internal model which, in turn, could serve as a guide to subsequent action. The mind, then, was conceived as a kind of data-processing device, akin to a digital computer, and the problem for the psychologist was to figure out how it worked. (2000:3)

James Gibson rejected the notion that the mind is a separate organ that operates on the data the bodily senses provide. He argued that

> Perception [...] is not the achievement of a mind in a body, but of the organism as a whole in its environment, and is tantamount to the organism's own exploratory movement through the world. If mind is anywhere,

then, it is not 'inside the head' rather than 'out there' in the world. To the contrary, it is immanent in the network of sensory pathways that are set up by virtue of the perceiver's immersion in his or her environment. (Quoted in Ingold 2000:3)

One proponent of this new view of the interdependence of perception and action is philosopher Alva Noë whose work is discussed further in Chapter 6. Noë's thesis is that 'perceiving is a way of acting. Perception is not something that happens to us, or in us. It is something we do ... the world makes itself available to the perceiver through physical movement and interaction' (2004:1; see also Stewart et al. 2010). If perception is not something that unfolds in the brain, neither is it like the sense of sight which makes it seem as if we are passive to the world. Noë argues that perception is like the sense of touch. Perception is active and relational.

Paralleling Noë's perspective, the anthropologist Tim Ingold takes an 'ecological approach to perception' in which the sentient, perceiving person is considered an organism like other organisms (2000:3). For Ingold the 'whole-organism-in-its-environment' is not a bounded entity, but rather is constituted by an ongoing *process* in real time: a process, that is, of growth or development' (ibid.:19–20). This process of growth or development consists of the acquisition of perceptual skills. For Ingold the notion of skills incorporates, but should not be reduced to, bodily based skills; rather, perceptual skills are 'the capabilities of action and perception of the whole organic being (indissolubly mind and body) situated in a richly structured environment' (ibid.:5).

Indeed, the content of our perceptual experience is acquired through psychophysical skills that we come to possess. '*What we perceive* is determined by *what we do* (or what we know how to do; it is determined by what we are *ready* to do ... [W]e *enact* our perceptual experience; we act it out' (Noë 2004:1). An enactive approach is therefore counterintuitive in that it rejects the overly simplistic view of an input and output model where 'perception is input from the world to mind, action is output from mind to world, thought is the mediating process' (Noë 2004:3). Unfortunately, this overly simplistic input–output model is too often assumed in conventional, textually based acting where the actor analyses and scores a script (input), and then acts the score (output). Rather than this computer model of perception and the mind, perception is 'a kind of skillful activity on the part of the animal as a whole' (Noë 2004:2).

For the actor/doer as a sentient perceiver on stage, perception should not be reduced to merely having subjective feelings. Perception occurs when we experience sensations sufficiently that make a certain sort of sense to us, that is, *we understand that the sensations we experience are constitutive in some way.* Perceptual knowledge is practical knowledge. *One knows how* and *one comes to know the 'feel' of the how.* There is a certain quality of relationship to the act of doing. Over time one gains a 'practical grasp of the way sensory stimulation varies as the perceiver moves' (ibid.:12). We develop a battery or repertoire of sensorimotor skills and ways of being attentive and aware which are the foundation for our perceptual encounter with the world.

What we *can* say about actors is that they are like others skilled in embodied practices. The actor is ideally trained towards an ever-subtler awareness of the shape or feel that is intrinsic to a specific psychophysical practice. As Rolf Elberfeld explains:

> Sensuality is the standing open of a world. The more that humanity develops this area of the open, the richer the possibilities of world reference become. The necessary condition of sensuality is humanity's embodiment. The body is the point of junction of all individually sensual experience. Bodily being is the zero point, from whence both 'fundamental sources' of knowledge – sensuality and understanding – unfold. (2003:478)

The shape and feel of a practice is not derived from or intrinsic to the sensations per se, but rather are gained from what becomes via training and/or experience an implicit embodied, sensory form of knowledge of the organization, structure, as well as 'the feel' of sensation-in-action.

The implications of an enactive view for acting

When we construct an acting score appropriate to a specific dramaturgy and aesthetic during rehearsals, as for *Ohio Impromptu*, through repetition the score comes to constitute a form of embodied, psychophysical, 'sensual'/sensorimotor knowledge for the actor. From my perspective as the actor playing Reader, my kinaesthetic knowledge of the score consists of the 'feel' of my body in the chair as Reader, the 'feel' of the fingers of my left hand as they touch the pages of the book before me, or the 'feel' of the words in my mouth when reading aloud the opening line, 'Little is left to tell.' These forms of sensory/perceptual knowledge are not present somewhere in my brain, but rather, the content of this (past) perceptual experience is virtually present to me, the actor, as available. I make adjustments in the moment as necessary. The form or structure of the acting score is available for inhabitation at the moment we initiate entry into embodying/expressing each action in the score. The structure/ form is available as a horizon of possibilities. Noë explains how

> I experience the world as present even when the detail is hidden from view... My experience of all that detail consists in my knowing that I have access to it all, and in the fact that I do in fact have this access. (Noë 2004:67)

When one enacts an acting score, one's relationship to each specific repetition of that same form or structure is similar, yet different. Optimally, in the present moment of doing one does not think about the form/structure or draw upon some mental representation of it or try to reproduce the experience of the last repetition; rather, one *enters a certain relationship* to the form/structure in the present moment of doing through one's cultivated perceptual/sensory awareness. As one learns to inhabit a form or structure of action, one is gradually attuned to an ever subtler experience of one's relationship to that structure.

> Experience is always of a field, with structure, and you can never comprehend the whole field in a single act of consciousness. Something always remains present, but out of view... Qualities are available in experience as possibilities, as potentialities, but not as givens. (Noë 2004:135)

Therefore, experience is a process of engaging the dynamic possibilities of the particular form or structure as it happens within a specific context or environment. As one continues to repeat a particular form or structure over time, a larger field of experience accumulates as an expanding field of possibilities. Ideally one is able to improvise within this larger field of possibilities for movement/action.

The actor engaged in certain forms of training and/or through cumulative experience builds a repertoire of sensorimotor skills which afford various possibilities of action and which possess a 'sensual' feel/ familiarity within the theatrical environment. There is the potential affordance available within the forms of training in which an actor becomes virtuosic in terms of the generation of a particular kind of embodied/sensory awareness and/or way in which training is enlivened by one's energy; however, the training also exists with a second set of affordances – those for application, that is, how one might apply and adapt specific modes of embodied knowledge to various performance structures or dramaturgies (see Zarrilli 2001).

If we consider the actor as a gestalt – a human animal inhabiting a specific performance environment such as Andy Crook and I as Listener and Reader in *Ohio Impromptu* – then actor training (whether 'formal' or 'on the job') can be thought of as providing a practical, experiential means of attuning one's perceptual attention and awareness so that they are able to be more immediately responsive and sensitive to the performance environment shaped by a particular dramaturgy. This type of preparation can take place on two levels – the preparation of the actor's perceptual and sensory awareness necessary for any/all performance environments, and the preparation of the actor's perceptual and sensory awareness specific to a particular performance environment shaped by each specific dramaturgy and the need of each specific performance score. The attunement of the actor's awareness ideally provides a heightened, non-ordinary ability to inhabit one's body-mind and stay sensorially and perceptually alert in the moment to the acting tasks at hand, such as *Ohio Impromptu.*

To summarize this discussion of acting as enactment, human perception is enactive, relational, and specific to an environment. Viewed from the perspective of the actor inside the performance of an acting score, we have considered acting not in terms of how the actor constructs a character or how the actor makes a performance believable, but rather in terms of *acting as a phenomenon and a process.* Stage acting may therefore productively be considered as one among many extra-daily skilled modes of embodied practice requiring the performer to develop a heightened attunement of sensory and perceptual awareness of a certain sort in order to be fully responsive to theatrical environments and dramaturgies. According to this alternative paradigm of acting, rather than considering acting in terms of representation, it may be much more useful to consider acting in terms of its dynamic, psycho-physical, embodied, enlivening processes – the actor-as-actor and actor-as-human-being senses, perceives, imagines, feels, and remembers in the moment of performance. This understanding of acting allows us to examine acting and performance not as a 'theater [...] of meaning but of "forces, intensities, present affects"', that is, as an 'energetic' theatre (Lyotard, quoted in Lehmann 2006:37; see also Hornby 1992:10 and Pavis 2003:95ff). Of course, meaning and representation may present themselves to the viewer or critic of a performance, but they are a result of the actor's immediate embodiment and deployment of her energy, sensory awareness, et cetera in the act of performance and the spectator's experience of that performance. In this view the actor practically negotiates interior and exterior via embodied/sensory perception-in-action in response to an environment.[16]

As we shall see in Chapters 2 and 3 respectively, Indian and Japanese paradigms for understanding the embodied phenomenon and process of acting provide culturally specific articulations of the "'forces, intensities, present affects'" of an 'energetic' theatre. Chapters 4 and 5 are likewise culturally specific and reflect on contemporary cosmopolitan/Western attempts to articulate and actualize these "'forces, intensities, present affects'" sometimes making use of insights, concepts, or techniques from non-Western cultures. Before examining these paradigms and examples of acting practice, in the final two parts of this introduction, I first examine the complex set of issues that arise when considering acting (and theatre) from an intercultural perspective. Finally I will focus on how to reflect upon the actor's complex process of deploying her senses, awareness, memory, and imagination – issues of the actor's 'consciousness' encountered in all culturally specific paradigms of acting practice.

Acting: an intercultural perspective

An introduction to 'inter'-cultural interaction

The prefix 'inter' points to that space between where something has the potential to happen. This 'space' in-between peoples, groups, cultures, and nations has often been a contested and fraught place. In his seminal 1994 book, *The Location of Culture*, Homi K. Bhabha began to theorize and examine these spaces between, that is, the 'interstices – the overlap and displacement of domains of difference' where 'intersubjective and collective experiences [...] are negotiated' (1994:1–2). Bhabha is one of a number of important scholars to interrogate in-depth how 'subjects [are] formed "in-between", or in excess of, the sum of the "parts of difference [...]"'? (1994:2). Obviously, the historical context, specific circumstances, and type of interaction 'between' – invited, mutually agreed, uninvited, imposed from outside – determines whether an exchange is experienced or perceived as positive/beneficial, benign, demeaning, damaging, or destructive.

One way of reading the history of world theatre and performance is in terms of the ongoing processes of re-formation of theatrical content and practices as specific genres/approaches to performance have been influenced by intra-cultural exchange taking place within a culture, and intercultural exchange taking place between. The resulting changes in theatrical practice have ranged from subtle shifts to alteration, borrowing, quotation, re-interpretation, or outright stealing and appropriation of every aspect of theatre – content, dramatic form, design, aesthetics, approaches to acting, context of performance, or approaches to creating a performance. [For those readers not familiar with issues of the history of theatrical interculturalism, please see Appendix I for a contextual overview of key issues and examples.]

Modernist forms of Western theatrical interculturalism

From the late nineteenth century well into the twentieth-century Western modernism as well as the rise of an avant-garde and experimental theatre movements prompted new waves and forms of intercultural exchange. To take but a few examples of East to West exchange, the Irish playwright William Butler Yeats developed a series of 'dance plays' based on English translations of Japanese *nō* dramas in order to re-imagine Irish drama and theatre. Many of the most important twentieth century visions and/ or approaches to Western acting have been influenced by non-Western principles, concepts, or techniques – yoga had a substantive impact on Stanislavsky as well as Michael Chekhov;[17] Antonin Artaud articulated his radical vision of the actor as an 'athlete of the heart' after experiencing Balinese dance (Artaud 1970; see Cohen 2010:140ff); and Bertolt Brecht's theory of 'alienation effect' (*verfremdungseffekt*) was in part shaped by his (mis-) interpretation of how the great female impersonator Mei Lanfang performed female roles on the *jingju* (Beijing Opera) stage (see Tian 2008:39–60).

These examples are part of a complex set of often unequal, trans-national, global, cultural flows between and among cultures. They are part of what the anthropologist Arjun Appadurai and historian Carol Breckenridge long ago described as 'public culture', that is, that they constitute one of many

> zone[s] of cultural debate...characterized as an arena whereother types, forms, and domains of culture are encountering,interrogating and contesting each other in new and unexpectedways. (1988:6)

By the twenty-first century, interculturalism and the global flow of ideas, concepts, techniques, practices, et cetera have become ubiquitous. While now commonplace, global intercultural flows nevertheless still need to be analysed, historicized, and questioned.

During the late twentieth century these global flows in theatre were most visible in the attention given to a limited set of problematically iconic productions by Western directors exemplifying a specific form of often ahistorical interculturalism, for example, Peter Brook's controversial adaptation of one of India's two great epics into an all-day performance – the *Mahabharata*;[18] some of the productions of Ariane Mnouchkine with Théâtre du Soleil in Paris where she has made use of elements of *kabuki* in performances of Shakespeare (*Richard II, Twelfth Night, Henry IV, Part 1*) and of *kathakali* in her cycle of Greek tragedies;[19] and some of the intercultural performances organized by Eugenio Barba when he has brought together virtuosic performances from many different cultures and performance traditions as part of his International School of Theatre Anthropology (ISTA). These iconic productions also captured much of the critical attention and discourse surrounding interculturalism at the time. But as Haiping Yan points argues, one of the major problems with Western forms of interculturalism has been 'the operative rubric of universalized humanism and ontologized individualism [...]' (1994:109). In some cases, in the artistic work itself and/or in the process of its making aesthetic concerns would completely transcend any concern with 'the political', 'the individual' would transcend 'the social [... while] the historical is abstracted into the universal' (Yan 1994:109).

Models for understanding and analysing intercultural theatre

Unfortunately, an overly simplistic Western model of interculturalism was articulated by Patrice Pavis (1990, 1992) which focused on the iconic East to West productions of Brook, Mnouchkine, et cetera. Pavis' binary 'hourglass' model of exchange between a 'source' and 'target' culture long dominated analysis and discussion of intercultural theatre. As Ric Knowles observes, 'Pavis's hourglass model posits a one-way flow and filtering of information from source to target culture than any kind of fluid interchange' (2010:26). Numerous critiques and alternative models of intercultural theatre theory and exchange have followed (for example, Holledge and Tompkins 2000; Watson 2002; Lo and Gilbert 2002, 2007; Tian 2008; Knowles 2010).

Among the more recent analyses of intercultural theatre, Tian's *The Poetics of Difference and Displacement* (2008) breaks promising new theoretical and historical ground.[20] Tian *treats equally* a series of historically/context-specific examples of Chinese-Western as well as of Western-Chinese intercultural exchanges and interactions. Tian's main analytical premise is that central to all 'intercultural knowledge and understanding' are specific forms and modes of 'displacement and re-placement of the Other by the Self' (2008:7). He argues that this intercultural space 'between' is always 'a site of displacement' where there is the potential for both positive and negative, 'constructive and deconstructive' contestation and negotiation between different 'theatrical forces' (2008:11). New theatrical concepts, ideologies, ideas, content, conventions, as well as techniques and practices displace and modify, and/or replace what already exists. In Part I he examines in separate chapters the different nuances and types of Chinese-to-the-West displacements and replacements in the work of Bertolt Brecht, Vsevolod Meyerhold, Edward Gordon Craig, Eugenio Barba, and Peter Sellers. In Part II Tian then analyses a series of displacements and replacements from the West-to-the-Chinese – how Chinese actors negotiated a historically complex intrusion and insertion of Stanislavsky's approach to acting in the Chinese context, how concepts of the European avant-garde displaced and/or replaced concepts and approaches to Chinese performance, and how specific adaptations/ stagings of Greek tragedies and Shakespeare in China have been negotiated.

Intercultural perspectives on acting as an embodied, psychophysical process

Given that most theories and analyses of interculturalism in theatre have focused on production and reception of the iconic Western performances directed by Brook, Mnouchkine, Barba, et cetera, discussion and analysis have been limited by the limited set of productions often discussed and by the dominance of the 'outside' perspective of the critic/spectator. Insufficient attention has been given to a number of key areas of intercultural exchange and interaction relevant to acting, including

- the role played by our human imagination in the process of intercultural exchange and (re)conceptualization of acting processes;[21]
- examination of intercultural performances and modes of interaction/ exchange that are *not* part of the iconic set of productions mentioned above;

- in-depth description and analysis of intercultural exchange taking place in training studios among actors/performers at the micro-level of transmission of embodied performance techniques, devising processes, the exercise of the imagination, et cetera;
- discussion of the underlying paradigms of psychophysical embodiment unique to specific cultures and of the elements and principles informing specific modes of embodied practice;
- analysis of processes of translating or transposing elements, principles, and techniques between cultures.

Regarding the imagination, it is clear that if the imagination is stimulated when you experience something new, you may begin to re-consider or re-imagine the familiar.[22] For example, one's assumptions about how to act may no longer be sufficient to encompass that practice when considered in light of a new or alternative dramaturgy that makes different demands on the actor's repertory of skills; therefore, the existing model of acting is displaced as it is being adjusted or re-imagined. What *is* a problem is not so much the re-imagining of acting per se, but the fact that too often the individual doing the re-imagining may be naïve about what has influenced them, that is, an individual may have little or no in-depth knowledge of the specific cultural, socio-political, and/or historical context that has shaped the content, or acting that causes one to reconsider. This was the case with Brecht and Artaud in particular. As Tian explains about Brecht,

> Chinese acting's 'A-effect' is eventually 'prised loose' from itshistorical, cultural, and artistic contexts and studied 'profitably'as 'a piece of technique' by Brecht, who needed such a technique for'quite definite social purposes' [...] in Brecht's interpretation, Chinese *xiqu* was clearly displaced and used as a means to valorize andlegitimize Brecht's own theoretical desires, investments, and projections. (2008:58–59)

Perhaps the first point to be made when addressing acting from an intercultural perspective is how important it is that whenever possible we attempt to understand precisely how both embodiment and psychophysical practices like acting are understood, talked about, and practised from cultural perspectives other than our own. This means addressing embodiment and acting in non-Western contexts. To that end, Chapters 2 and 3 in this book focus specifically how the embodied practice and experience of acting is selectively understood in the Indian and Japanese contexts.[23] These chapters focus first on deeply embedded cultural notions of embodiment in specific traditional forms of performance, articulate the aesthetic principles that inform these genres, and finally turn to a discussion of contemporary practitioners who are mixing intra-cultural practices from within their culture with intercultural models, content, et cetera from outside their culture in innovative ways.

Most attention has been given to influences from Asia on Western approaches to acting, that is, how Stanislavsky, Michael Chekhov, Brecht, Artaud, and Barba have been influenced by non-Western, especially Asian concepts and techniques. A second important point to be made about intercultural acting is that a next-to-invisible exchange history exists of how non-Western actors and directors have negotiated their encounters with realist drama and Stanislavskian-based techniques, and/or with the legacy of Grotowski's approach to acting (see Lendra 2002). While beyond the scope and remit of this book, thankfully recent publications have begun to address the complex set of intercultural negotiations, displace-ments, and replacements that began to take place in the twentieth century between Stanislavsky and Chinese acting (Tian 2008:159–174) and Stanislavsky and Indonesia (Winet 2010:134–140).

Ethnographic historian James Clifford observed as long ago as 1988 how 'the world's societies are too systematically interconnected to permit any easy isolation of separate or independently functioning systems. Twentieth-century identities no longer presuppose continuous cultures or traditions' (1988:231, 14). Early in the twenty-first century, I would argue that contemporary theatre practices are shaped within the crucible of a global, (largely) urban, cosmopolitan context, which is inherently multi-cultural and intercultural. For example, as Kay Li explains, 'Hong Kong is a globalized city' with a 'long history of cosmopolitanism and capitalism'; therefore, 'theatre in Hong Kong captures the city's response to the challenges of globalization' and as 'a meeting place between Eastern and Western cultures' (2007:440–442). In addition, mass media and the internet allow immediate (if mediated) access to the multiple 'worlds' of performance and performer trainings available today. Global mass/higher education means that – whether we like it or not – most young people today aspiring to become actors have received an education shaped in part by Western pedagogy and Western institutional models. Therefore, any consideration of acting today must address our global, urban, multi-cultural, intercultural realities.

Among many traditional forms of non-Western performance such as Japanese *nō, kabuki,* Beijing Opera, or Indian *kathakali* and *kutiyattam* actor training begins by engaging the young actor's body-mind in gradually developing a virtuosic actualization of a particular mode of embodied practice shaped by the conventions of that genre of performance and its guiding aesthetic principles. The initial 'point of entry' or 'beginning place' for the actor is *not* reading a dramatic text, or thinking about analysing the text to understand a character or the motivations driving a character. These actors first engage their bodyminds in an immersive, intensive, and complete psychophysical process that only much later in their development – after achieving maturity and mastery of all the basic movement/voicing techniques of the genre – invites certain forms of reflection and analysis on their art and its practice. An intercultural perspective on acting suggests that we examine acting as an embodied process which fully engages the actor's body-mind.

Finally, we need to consider the role that discursive/explanatory paradigms play in shaping how acting is framed, viewed, and practised. Ever since the seminal work of Stanislavsky, the dominant commonplace paradigm informing how Westerners usually think and talk about acting is psychology – a discipline invented in the nineteenth-century at the same time theatrical realism and naturalism focused attention on the individual self. An intercultural perspective on acting invites us to re-frame discussions of contemporary acting by displacing psychology from its primary explanatory position and replacing it with alternative paradigms for understanding the interior/inner processes and possibility of acting as an embodied phenomenon and process. Psychology in its various sub-disciplines retains tremendous explanatory power especially with regard to questions of the individual self and character manifest in realist drama; therefore, psychology needs repositioning as a secondary paradigm to be applied to acting processes when appropriate to a specific dramaturgy.

Towards alternative, intercultural paradigms for contemporary acting

However important the most visible forms, modes, and discourses of intercultural theatre exchange and interaction have been in the late twentieth century, I would argue that it is time to move beyond the limitations of these previous models of interculturalism in relation to acting and production. Indeed, it could be said that both theatre practices and the discursive frameworks for understanding acting as an intercultural process *have already moved on.*

There are many unacknowledged pioneers – both East and West – who have explored intercultural acting processes. In the West this is the generation of practitioners/artists/scholars who between the end of World War II and the 1960s/70s immersed themselves in learning, practising, and writing about *specific forms of non-Western performance within specific cultural contexts with master teachers*. Major figures include James Brandon (*kabuki, nō,* and Southeast Asian performance), Leonard Pronko (*kabuki*), A.C. Scott (*taiqiquan*), Andrew Tsubaki (*nō* and *kyogen*), John Emigh (Balinese *topeng*), Don Kenny (*kyōgen*), Richard Emmert (*nō*), Kathy Foley (Indonesian puppetry and dance), and Phillip B. Zarrilli (*kalarippayattu* and *kathakali*) among many others. For practitioners who work with specific techniques from another culture, the critic Daryl Chin expresses the double-edged prospect and problem of intercultural practice:

> Interculturalism is one of the ways of bringing previously suppressed material into the artistic arena, by admitting into a general discourse other cultures, cultures which had previously been ignored or suppressed or unknown. But the general discourse (which we must define in terms of the dominant culture) must not deform other cultures by making them speak in the language of the dominant culture. (1991:95)

James Brandon pointedly states the case: 'The problem is having superficial knowledge and applying Western standards to everything' (1989:37).

Growing out of their immersive in-depth experience in non-Western approaches to performance, some of the practitioners noted above have developed alternative models of acting and actor training that *do not rely solely on psychology* (for example, see Scott 1993; Foley 2002; Zarrilli 2009). Although of the same generation as Grotowski and Barba, A.C. Scott's (1909–1985) approach to Asia and intercultural acting was quite different from Grotowski and Brook. Scott's approach to Asia was immersive. Fluent in Chinese and Japanese, Scott trained in *taiqiquan* Wu style under Master Cheng Yung-Kuan in Hong Kong between 1947 and 1952. Inspired by Jacques Copeau (1879–1949) and Michel St. Denis (1897–1971) to explore an intercultural approach to training actors, it was in 1963 when Scott established the Asian-Experimental Theatre Programme at the University of Wisconsin-Madison that he began to use *taiqiquan* in training American actors. Scott explains why he did so:

> I was worried by the casual naturalism [American acting students] regarded as acting, impressed by the vitality they needlessly squandered, staggered by their articulate verbosity on the psychological

nature of theatre, and dismayed by their fragile concentration span, which manifested itself in a light-hearted attitude toward discipline that seemed to arise from an inability to perceive that a silent actor must still remain a physical presence on both the stage and the rehearsal floor. (1993:52)

For directorial as well as pedagogical reasons, Scott chose to displace the then stereotypical, psychologically driven approach to acting assumed by American actors at the time in order to challenge his students to learn in a completely new way to act, that is, how to be 'a silent actor' yet 'remain a physical presence' on stage and in the studio. Scott replaced the Western acting vocabulary and discourses drawn from psychology and Stanislavsky with daily practice of *taiqiquan* and applied what was being learned from *taiqi* to specific Western dramaturgies in production. The co-founder of Mu Performing Arts in Minneapolis, Martha Johnson, explains how Scott was experimenting with taking the deepest principles of Asian performance and applying them to the staging and acting of contemporary plays. He was

[n]ot doing 'Kabuki' versions of anything; he was working with underlying artistic principles. . . . It is, actually, this work that has had the deepest influence on me as an artist and teacher. (Quoted in Liu, 2011:420)[24]

An increasing number of non-Western practitioners have also immersed themselves in intercultural acting practices combining elements, principles, and techniques from their own cultural heritage with practices and principles encountered in the West. I noted at the beginning of this introduction the work of Yoshi Oida who originally trained in *kyōgen* and whose publications on acting exemplify how essential Asian principles and practices have been to developing his own approach to acting as an embodied, intercultural practice.

Another example is the Balinese performer I. Wayan Lendra who spent over twenty five years as an actor-dancer performing both *keybar* as well as *topeng* masked performance before pursuing a PhD at the University of Hawaii, and becoming part of Jerzy Grotowski's Objective Drama Project at the University of California Irvine between 1983 and 1986. Lendra has reflected at length on his intercultural experience between Balinese principles (such as *kundalini* and *taksu*) and practices, and the principles informing Grotowski's 'the motions' (2002).

More recently a new generation of practitioner/scholars – many from Asia – have been practising, reflecting upon, and proposing alternative, non-psychologically based understandings of and approaches to acting and actor training. They all view acting as a psychophysical process and phenomenon. Those from Asia draw primarily on concepts, principles, and practices from their own 'home' cultures in their encounter with the West. The Korean actress/director/teacher Jeungsook Yoo has reflected at length on developing a Korean language and psychophysical process for approaching acting. Yoo explains the context for her new approach as follows:

> As an individual brought up in the cosmopolitan atmosphere of Seoul, I have been exposed to and assimilated aspects of traditional Korean culture, and simultaneously received an education and training largely derived from Western paradigms. When training as an actor at the Korean Academy of Performing Arts (March–November, 1994) I experienced both contemporary Western actor training methods and several traditional Korean modes of training and performance either as part of the official programme of study or undertaken later on my own initiative – voice training in *Pansori* [traditional Korean form of solo performance] and practice of *DahnHak* – a form of Korean meditation discipline. This environment affected me, as a contemporary Korean actor, to search for a way to reconcile my 'Korean-ness' with my equally important contemporary sensibilities [...] I attempt to develop and articulate a theory and practice of contemporary acting and actor training from a Korean perspective by utilizing the principles and practices based primarily on *DahnHak.* (2008a:9–11)

Developed by Seung-Heun Lee in the 1980s and central to both the philosophy and practice of *DahnHak* are certain key traditional Korean principles including *ki, Tao, Te,* and *Kungfu,* among others. Yoo's published essays involve a philosophical and linguistic examination of these key principles that inform how the body, mind, their relationship, and experience inside a practice of acting are understood and explained from a Korean perspective. Yoo's research examines these principles at work as they inform her practice of *DahnHak* as well as her practice as an actress from inside productions of Ionesco's *The Bald Soprano* and Ōta Shōgo's *The Water Station* (see Yoo 2007, 2008b). Importantly, Yoo has taught at the Korean National University of the Arts (KNUA) and is currently course leader of the B.A. in World Performance course at East 15 Acting School in the UK where she has taught her approach to intercultural psychophysical training.

Paralleling Yoo's important approach to practice and analysis as a Korean is the work of master Western voice teacher, Tara McAllister-Viel currently teaching voice at East 15 Acting School. After obtaining her MFA in acting/voice at the University of Wisconsin-Madison, McAllister-Viel continued her professional work as a director and voice teacher before taking up a teaching position in Western voice practice at Korean National University of Arts (KNUA). While teaching at KNUA, in order to better integrate Western voice practices into the intercultural curriculum at KNUA where the students learned both Western voice as well as Korean *Pansori* vocal techniques. In a series of essays based on her PhD research, McAllister-Viel has begun to address key issues of intercultural voice practice that equally addresses practical training and problems with exclusively Western concepts and techniques of voice production (2009a, 2009b, 2009c, 2007). In her own practice McAllister-Viel draws on both her expertise as a Western-trained voice teacher and on her experience of practising *pansori* with master teachers in Seoul.

As a part of his current practice-based/pedagogical research, Grisana Punpeng from Thailand has been exploring how principles drawn from Buddhism and Asian philosophy might articulate with psychophysical processes and procedures of acting that will address contemporary acting in a Thai context. Punpeng describes how in Thailand an actor training programme should be responsive to

> the broad range of non-realist dramaturgies, emerging and gaining recognition in Thailand...In Thailand, the conventional psychological realist character, studied in the exercises and productions within the university acting courses, are *now rarely seen in theatrical venues in Bangkok, such as Thailand Cultural Centre and Patravadi theatre, and even in the annual Bangkok Theatre Festival, in which more than 40 live performances from professional and amateur theatre groups are staged every year.* (Emphases added, 2012:35–36)

Punpeng is therefore developing a psychophysical training process for contemporary Thai actors which will utilize a number of Buddhist concepts as the discursive constructs through which to contextualize the training. Punpeng explains that these concepts are 'not new to Thai people' because they are 'embedded in everyday life'; however, unlike the concept of the psychological realist paradigm that has been developed in and for Euro-American theatre and which has dominated the teaching and practice of contemporary actor training in Thailand, the concepts will nevertheless be 'new' to the context of acting. The young Thai actors 'may not have realized before how these concepts [and the practices from which they arise] could relate to acting' (ibid.).

Concluding discussion of interculturalism

Whether acting practices originate within one specific cultural context, or are generated intra-culturally or inter-culturally, because acting is an embodied process and practice, each actor's living/breathing/experiencing body-mind is always present as a beginning point for understanding and analysing acting as a psychophysical phenomenon and process. Drawing on Merleau-Ponty's work, the philosopher Rosi Braidotti provides the following definition for what she calls 'corporeal materialism' where

> the body is seen as the inter-face, a threshold, a field of intersection of material and symbolic forces; it is a surface where multiple codes of power and knowledge are inscribed; it is a construction that transforms and capitalizes on energies of a heterogonous and discontinuous nature. The body is not an essence and therefore not an anatomical destiny: it is one's primary location in the world, one's primary situation in reality. (1991:219)

The 'material' forces to which Briadotti refers are the specific sensory and experiential entailments of the one's embodied encounter in the acting studio – whatever the approach and techniques being utilized. In their chapter on 'intercultural bodies' Holledge and Tomkins draw upon Briadotti's 'corporeal materialism' to argue that

> the *body of the performer* is the subjective body of corporeal materialism located in a specific historical time and geographical space, embodying the ethics and beliefs of a particular place [...E]very act of performance also requires that the performer heighten or alter her state of consciousness. These inner states are acquired through the study and practice of techniques designed to shape and concentrate thoughts processes, emotions, and energies. (2000:111–112)

As anthropologists and sociologists have long noted, bodies, experience, consciousness, and the senses/emotions are shaped in different ways in different cultural contexts (see Kasulis et al. 1993; Howes 2004; Guerts 2002; Hahn 2007; Turner and Yangwen 2009; Brownell 2009). There simultaneously exist culturally distinct 'traditions of embodiment' producing often 'profoundly different traditions of corporeal experience and expression', and a 'very deep process of globalization' which is resulting in an 'increasingly hybrid' mixing of modes, techniques and paradigms of embodiment across cultures (Turner and Yangwen 2009:7–8). For example, in the West the five senses of touch, taste, smell, hearing, and sight are 'naturally' assumed to constitute the 'normal' range of human sensory awareness, and among the five, sight has always played a dominant role in 'the philosophical interpretation of reality in European culture' (Elberfeld 2003:478–479). But in other cultures, such as the Anlo Ewe-speaking people of southeastern Ghana, balance or kinesthesia is considered a sense, and physical/psychological balancing are essential processes shaping one's process of embodiment and experience (Guerts 2002). The auditory sense was given priority in ancient Chinese culture, while in Indian classical philosophy eight senses are identified rather than five (Elberfeld 2003:479, 483). Culturally variable modes and paradigms of embodiment, the body-mind relationship, and sensory awareness will be further addressed in Chapters 2 and 3.

Drawing on further insights from phenomenology, in the final section of this chapter, I turn my attention to how specific modes of psycho-physical practice articulate acting as an embodied phenomenon and process and shed light on the question of the actor's body-mind awareness and 'consciousness' in performance.

Acting as an embodied phenomenon and process

Sensing is this living communication with the world that makes it present to us as the familiar place of our life. The perceived object and the perceiving subject owe their thickness to sensing.[25]

(Merleau-Ponty 2012:53)

Having considered an enactive model of acting and having considered acting from an intercultural perspective, I return to a consideration of acting as a specific phenomenon and process, that is, to the actor as a living, breathing, sentient being who psychophysically embodies and enlivens a performance score in the moment of its enactment. This is the territory Martin Sheen was pointing to in his observation that he must be physically present to what I do,' and to which Ingmar Lindh referred as the *'other dimension'* of the actor's work. It is the territory where, as we shall see in Chapters 2 and 3, the work of the Asian actor always begins – embodied practice which ideally engages the actor's body-mind completely in the task-at-hand. As revealed especially in Jean Benedetti's recent translation of Stanislavsky's monumental publications on acting, *An Actor's Work*, it is the territory to which Stanislavsky also pointed – 'experiencing' (Part I, 2008) and 'embodiment' (Part II, 2008).

It is revealed in Stanislavsky's wise reminder that

> all our acts, even the simplest, which are so familiar to us in everyday life, become strained when we appear [...] before a public[...] That is why it is necessary to correct ourselves and learn again how to walk, move about, sit, or lie down. It is essential to re-educate ourselves to look and see, on the stage, to listen, and to hear. (1980 [1936]:73; see also Benedetti's translation of the same passage, 2008:93)

Acting and actor training are all about 'experiencing', 'embodiment', and finding a way to a fully focused/concentrated sensory engagement in the phenomenon of performance, as will be discussed in Chapter 4 in relation to Stanislavsky and his 'legacy'.

Earlier in this chapter we briefly addressed the vexing issue of body-mind dualism that has historically been so trenchant in Western thought and that has plagued how we think and talk about acting. Having introduced a post-Merleau-Ponty phenomenology, my purpose here is to briefly tease out two aspects of the 'lived' experience of the actor – embodied consciousness and sensory awareness. We will return in Chapter 6 to a further reconsideration of these issues of embodiment, perception, sensory awareness, and experience from the perspective of the new sciences.

As Donald A. Landes explains in the introduction to his recent translation of Merleau-Ponty's seminal first book, *Phenomenology of Perception*, Merleau-Ponty's project was to establish once and for all 'the body's unity [... as] a lived integration in which the parts are *understood* in relation to the meaningful whole, and in this sense the body's unity is comparable to the unity of a work of art' (Merleau-Ponty 2012:xlii). This embodied synthesis is accomplished 'not through an intellectual act, but because together the body-mind in all its parts "*perform*(s) a single gesture"' (2012:xlii). For Merleau-Ponty, 'mental states and activities are constituted by *bodily* engagement with the world', that is, 'the body *is* a form of consciousness' (Romdenh-Romluc 2011:2–3).

As discussed in detail in Chapter 3, the co-founder of Japanese *nō*, Zeami Motokiyo (1363–1443) described how it is necessary for the young actor to learn how to deal with our 'squirrel-like' human minds that are constantly racing here and there. In one of his recent books, James Austin, M.D. and cognitive neuroscientist, asked virtually the same question: 'how can one escape from that restless monkey mind, let go of discursive thoughts, settle down to clear, base awareness' (2006:33). Both Zeami and Austin point to the importance of cultivating a state of non-dual consciousness/awareness. This type of awareness is required in meditation and similar modes of psychophysical training where one is learning how to be attentive while not 'thinking' (see Blackmore, 2003). Certain specific modes of non-Western and Western modes of psycho-physical training each in their own way awaken, shape, focus, and concentrate an individual's attention, awareness, and 'energy' (*ki/qi/prana-vayu*).

Ned Block's nuanced discussion of the differences and relationship between *phenomenal* consciousness and *access* consciousness (1995, 1997:380ff) provides one useful model for describing aspects of the performer's non-dual consciousness discussed here. Block explains that 'phenomenal consciousness is experience; what makes a state phenome-nally conscious is that there is something "it is like" to be in that state' (1995:227). P-conscious states 'are sensations, whereas the paradigm A-conscious states are "propositional attitude" states like thoughts, beliefs, and desires, states with representational content expressed by "that" clauses' (1997:384). Access consciousness serves more of a functional process than phenomenal consciousness because it carries specific types of information generally available for the organism. These are not absolute categories since thoughts may be P-conscious and sensa-tions/experiences 'often have representational content' (1997:384). Performances and modes of performer training may be understood as practices which shape culturally and historically specific forms of extraor-dinary, non-dual phenomenal consciousness that are different from one's ordinary states of consciousness.

While the performer's phenomenal consciousness is shaped to embody/enact the performance at an optimal level of attainment such as in the example of the *nō* actor, since a performance score is a repeatable structure when the performer is not performing the score, one can self-consciously *review* that score mentally. That is, the performer can choose to use his access consciousness to review and reflect upon the performance of a score or structure, or to reflect more generally on his artistry as an actor/dancer/doer.

When performing, a specific score is available as representational content at the periphery of one's phenomenal consciousness even as one embodies/enacts that score. The representational content of the score in its entirety and of each task/action that constitutes the whole is 'available'; however, the performer ideally *does not use access consciousness* during a performance to become directly conscious *of* a task or action within the score as it is being performed.

Block also calls our attention to what he calls 'monitoring consciousness' – the notion that there is 'some sort of inner perception', that is, 'P-consciousness of one's own states' (1997:390). Because performer training techniques and performance are highly repetitive modes of embodiment, P-consciousness may be characterized as conscious awareness where an embodied, sedimented relationship to the performance or doing is experienced as a residue, an echo, or resonant 'shadow'. At the periphery of P-consciousness in the act of doing is an inner perception, sensory awareness, or consciousness of the doing – what is sometimes described by performers as the feeling of the form. As discussed in detail below, there is often a 'what it is like for me' state viewed from the first-person perspective inside the process of embodying a specific performer training process and when enacting a specific performance score. Performer training and performing can therefore be described as a special form of 'P-consciousness with awareness',that is, the performer inhabits an awareness of the doing at the same time the actor remains completely *inside* the 'feeling' of the doing. The 'feeling of the doing' is the additional layer of resonance within the performer's consciousness. For actors it is the 'listening' or 'hearing' within oneself in the act of speaking. It is the saidness of the said. It is the feel of the touch of the finger tips to the lips. It is the 'more than' the ordinary. It is what makes a performance which may look like everyday life 'more than' everyday life.

Two caveats are in order. First, the description provided above is the optimal ideal assumed in virtuosic performance and therefore is often not achieved during initial training, or in performance. Second, in this process the performer ideally never becomes *self-conscious*. The actor should not think about what he is doing, but remain within the 'flow' of phenomenal consciousness as appropriate to the training or the dramaturgy of a specific performance.

The actor's phenomenal consciousness has often been described as a 'double consciousness' or 'multiple consciousness' – apt descriptions of the 'feeling of the form' and the presence of the score/structure at the periphery of phenomenal consciousness. For the performer 'inside' phenomenal consciousness enacting the score, the performer constantly adjusts each specific performance to the stimuli (sensory, imaginative, mnemonic) in the performance environment moment by moment (Yoo 2007; Zarrilli 2009:41–60). Perception, attentativeness, memory, imagination, feeling, and the engagement of our various sensory awarenesses – listening, visualizing, tasting, smelling, touching (along with other senses central to specific cultural formations) – are all present to be attuned and engaged as appropriate by the performer to her dramaturgy and score. From the performers' perspective *inside* this embodied process, as one practices, performs or 'plays' within the structure of a process, there is often a strong autotelic element to that engagement, that is, actors usually enjoy the practice/act/experience of performing.

Systems of and approaches to actor training like those discussed in this book are designed to shape the performer's phenomenal consciousness in order to achieve an extra-ordinary discrete alternate state of non-dual consciousness different from one's ordinary perceptual consciousness. In Chapters 2 and 3 we turn to a specific examination of psychophysical paradigms and practices of acting as they are understood, articulated, embodied, and enacted in India and Japan.

Notes

1. For further discussion of Johar and Rao's work see the concluding section of Chapter 2.
2. For further information on Yoshi Oida's approach to acting see his books (Yoshi Oida with Lorna Marshall 1997, 1992). Issues of intercultural performer training are explored in Appendix I and later in this chapter.
3. Hans-Thies Lehmann uses the term 'post-dramatic' to denote the diverse range of alternative scripted and devised performances produced since the 1970s in which there is no longer a central story/plot or character(s)/ subjectivity(ies) forming the center of the theatrical event (2006:26–27). In 'post-dramatic forms of *theatre*, staged text (*if* text is staged) is merely a component with equal rights in a gestic, musical, visual, etc. total composition' (ibid.:46). Since post-dramatic texts and performances are not necessarily organized around a plot or recognizable individual characters, a variety of alternative 'aesthetic logic(s)' (ibid.:18) inform the structure and type of action, as well as the tasks of the performers. However important psychology has been to shaping the dramaturgy of realist and naturalist plays from the late nineteenth through the twentieth centuries, conventional realist approaches to acting and/or textual analysis may be inadequate or even inappropriate to the realization of the dramaturgy and acting tasks that constitute an actor's performance score in a post-dramatic text or performance. It is important to note that the term 'post-dramatic' does not really apply to non-Western performance since the notion of 'drama' in the Western, Aristotelian sense, never existed in the history of most world performance cultures. Indeed, Lehmann's definition of post-dramatic above applies to many or even most forms of non-Western performance where the authored, dramatic text is really only the beginning point in the creation of a performance.

4. 'Theories of acting' is most often used with reference to specific *approaches* to acting, and/or preparation of the actor. Later in this introduction I offer a more general account of acting as a phenomenon and process. Such a general theory of acting can also be thought of as a 'meta-theory' in the sense that it attempts to provide an overarching account of the phenomenon of acting regarding of the specific *approach* an actor takes to her preparation and training.

5. For a broad range of contemporary approaches, see the following three edited collections of essays: Alison Hodge's *Actor Training* (2010), Ian Watson's *Performer Training: Developments Across Cultures* (2002), and Phillip B. Zarrilli's *Acting Reconsidered* (2002) as well as Routledge Press' journal, *Theatre, Dance, and Performer Training.* For an earlier set of interviews with acting teachers in the US, see Eva Mekler, *The New Generation of Acting Teachers* (1987).

6. The UK playwright/dramaturg Kaite O'Reilly began to use the term 'alternative dramaturgies' a number of years ago with reference to plays and performances exploring the aesthetics and dramaturgies of work inspired by and making use of devices and conventions from deaf/disabled performance such as text projection, sign-interpretation, etc. In O'Reilly's plays, such as *peeling* – specifically written for three actresses with disabilities – she incorporates the access devices directly into her dramaturgy creating an alternative aesthetic.

7. Confronted with the 'vast array of training methods and types of theatre' I have outlined above, John Lutterbie addresses a similar concern in his recent book, *Toward a General Theory of Acting* (2011:10). Lutterbie phrases the question as 'what it is that makes acting possible' (2011:6), and answers it by reflecting on acting through insights and findings from contemporary cognitive science and Dynamic Systems Theory in particular (2011:77–102; passim). In Chapter 6 which focuses on the 'situated' body-mind, Rebecca Loukes provides her own account of perspectives on acting from cognitive science.

8. The word 'perform' derives from the Latin '*per-*, thoroughly + *fournir, fornir,* to complete' (Partridge 1983:485). The actor/performer is a doer who brings tasks/actions to completion in the moment of their doing.

9. Stanislavsky described how actors had to develop a 'physical score' which, once perfected through extensive rehearsals, would allow a 'deeper' level of experience 'rounded out with new feeling' and that is 'psychophysical in quality' (1961:66). In his recent book, Lutterbie devotes a full chapter to 'The Actor's Score' (2011:181–210).

10. For an example see Zarrilli's description of his performance score and discussion of that score for *Told by the Wind* (2012).

11. The Swedish born actor/teacher, Ingemar Lindh was first a student of and then assistant to Etienne Decroux before going on to an illustrious career as a master teacher of acting whose emphasis lay on improvisational processes

of creation. For an account of Lindh's work see *Stepping Stones*, edited and introduced by Frank Camilleri (2010).

12. For a full account of the enactive approach to considering acting and embodiment on which this version is based, see Zarrilli (2009:41–60). Zarrilli's full 2009 version and the shorter summary here is similar to Lutterbie's (2011) account. As explained below in more detail, both accounts make use of the branch of cognitive science called 'embodied dynamicism' (Thompson 2007:4–13), also known as Dynamic Systems Theory (Lutterbie 2011:9). Lutterbie's book makes use throughout of this branch of cognitive science while my account combines elements of 'embodied dynamicism' with phenomenological methods. On the relationship between embodied dynamicism and phenomenology see Thompson (2007:13–15). Evan Thompson's *Mind in Life* (2007) is his long-awaited follow up his co-authored book, *The Embodied* Mind, with Varela and Rosch (1991). See also John Stewart, Olivier Gapenne, and Ezequiel A Di Paolo's recent collection of essays, *Enaction: Toward a New Paradigm for Cognitive Science* (2010). This collection of essays presents a comprehensive argument for and overview of 'enaction' as a 'new paradigm' in cognitive science as an alternative to the earlier, still dominant paradigm of Computational Theory of Mind (CTM). Although not identified within the framework of 'enaction', James Austin's research has many parallel arguments (1998). For a cogent critique of 'enaction' as a paradigm, and for alternative arguments and assessments, see Lawrence Shapiro's *Embodied Cognition* (2011:55, and throughout). Responding to Shapiro's critique is beyod the scope of this introduction.

13. Given that both accounts make use of embodied dynamicism, not surprisingly Lutterbie's view of acting as an enactive response to our immediate environment is similar to this account, that is, he 'sees the actor as thinking, feeling, moving, speaking, perceiving, and continuously engaged in the rehearsal hall, on stage, and in everyday life [...] It is by seeing the actor as embodied that we can begin to rethink how we talk to and train actors [...]' (2011:24).

14. See Noë (2004), Leder (1990), Nagatomo (1992a, 1992b), and Yasuo (1987, 1993).

15. See Lakoff and Johnson (1999, 1980); Johnson (1987).

16. In the second half of my discussion of an enactive approach to acting in *Psychophysical Acting*, I provide an alternative four-fold model of the actor's embodied modes of experience: (1) the ecstatic surface (sensorimotor) body; (2) the recessive (visceral) body; (3) the aesthetic inner (subtle) body-mind; and (4) the aesthetic outer ('fictive') body (Zarrilli 2009:50–60). This model is important for a full understanding how the actor's work interweaves the psychophysically embodied self with the aesthetic/fictive.

17. Yoga is a set of body-mind practices originating in India that have since the late nineteenth century gone 'global'. Various forms of yoga or

yoga-based practice are arguably as ubiquitous today in the studio throughout the world as is Shakespeare on the global stage. Both have been and are being constantly remade and marketed to achieve and sustain their international status. Scholars are currently rewriting the history of the most popular forms of yoga – usually called 'modern postural yoga' – in the late nineteenth and early twentieth century in the intercultural space between the introduction by the British of YMCA models of 'body-mind-spirit' as well as 'harmonial gymnastics' and Indian yoga practices (Singleton 2010:119).

18. Two of many critiques of Brook's *Mahabharata* include those of Rustom Bharucha (1993) and Una Chaudhuri (1991). See also Williams (1991). Regarding Peter Brook's *Mahabharata*, Bharucha points to how 'the implications of interculturalism are very different for people in impoverished, "developing" countries like India, and for their counterparts in technically advanced, capitalist societies like America, where interculturalism has been more strongly promoted both as a philosophy and a business' (1993:1). Chaudhuri argues that 'well-meaning intercultural projects can unwittingly perpetuate a neo-colonialism in which the cultural clichés which underwrote imperialism survive more or less intact' (1991:196).

19. See for example Ariane Mnouchine discussion of her work in *The Intercultural Performance Reader*, ed. Patrice Pavis (1996:93–98).

20. In *Asia as Method* Kuan-Hsing Chen tracks the concurrent processes of decolonization and deimperialization taking place in studies of Asia. Tian's new perspective is part of this shift undertaken by Asians studying Asia from within Asia. See also Pankaj Mishra's *From the Ruins of Empire* (2012).

21. Alexander C.Y. Huang in his excellent study of *Chinese Shakespeares*, describes how Shakespeare's *Hamlet* 'captured the Chinese imagination of a modern nation-state' (2009:9ff).

22. I first addressed the question of how actors come to 're-consider' their practice of acting in *Acting Reconsidered* (Zarrilli 2002:1–2).

23. Far too few in-depth studies have focused on issues of the embodiment and experience of acting from the performer's perspective within specific cultural/aesthetic contexts. For a few exemplary studies see Jo Riley's *Chinese Theatre and the actor in performance* (1997); Tomie Hahn's *Sensational Knowledge: Embodying Culture through Japanse Dance* 2007); and Phillip B. Zarrilli '*Making the Body All Eyes*': *Paradigms, Discourses, and Practices of kalarippayattu* (1998), *The Kathakali Complex: Actor, Performance, Structure* (1984), and *Kathakali Dance-Drama: Where Gods and Demons Come to Play* (2000). Much more scholarly attention needs to be given to African and South American modes of embodied practice in performance.

24. When A.C. Scott was about to retire, I was invited to replace Scott as Director of the Asian Experimental Theatre Programme. We worked together as co-directors during 1979–1980. During that year together I learned *taiqiquan*

from Scott, and his uncompromising attitude towards the importance of daily psychophysical training in the studio. From Scott's perspective, what has always been a commonplace in traditional Asian modes of training – daily training – had to become a necessity if contemporary actor were to have any chance of embodying fully body-mind awareness and focus on stage. In my own way I have tried to extend Scott's legacy utilizing a combination of *kalarippayattu,* yoga, and *taiqiquan.*

25. Donald A. Landes in his recent translation of Merleau-Ponty's *Phenomenology of Perception* notes that he has chosen to use the 'more active "sensing"' rather than the less active '"sense experience"' to translate *le sentir* (2012).

2 Psychophysical Acting in India

Phillip B. Zarrilli

[b]reathe through the eyes whenever there is a point of emphasis…It is like 'looking' as in yoga. [Usha Nangyar, *kutiyattam* actress]

Introduction

This chapter provides a detailed account of psychophysical approaches to and practices of acting in India with special reference to Kerala State – the Malayalam-speaking southwestern coastal region of India. This account is based on extensive ethnographic research and interviews with actors and practitioners undertaken in Kerala between 1976 and 2003, and on the author's in-depth immersion in several of the training processes described. As discussed in Chapter 1, India has often been perceived and represented in the West as 'timeless'. But, as Lewis Rowell explains, while 'Indian thought relies upon authority' and although '"oldest is best!"', thought and cultural practices in Indian are thoroughly 'dynamic, not static' and emphasize 'processes and transformations rather than permanent certainties' (1992:25).

This chapter begins by describing a specific example of psycho-physical acting in the *kutiyattam* tradition of staging Sanskrit dramas.[1] The chapter then addresses a series of key questions raised by this example, providing insights into India's unique way of understanding psychophysical processes, and of articulating the relationship between 'inner' and 'outer' processes of embodied 'being' and 'doing'. It concludes with a discussion of how traditional modes of psychophysical acting are informing new and changes approaches to creating performance in India today.

What does it mean to 'breathe through the eyes': one example of psychophysical acting in the kutiyattam tradition

Usha Nangyar is an accomplished actress/dancer and teacher within the *kutiyattam* style (Figure 2.1) of staging Sanskrit dramas whose earliest origins date from as early as the ninth century A.C.E. *Kutiyattam* is a unique form of staging Sanskrit dramas found only in Kerala. Within the *kutiyattam* tradition of 'solo acting', one important set piece takes place when an actor playing a specific character visualizes, and/or transforms into a different character not present on stage. This process of visualization is known as 'head to foot' (*padadik-shesham*) acting, and can take the form of remembering a lover or seeing a god or goddess.

Figure 2.1 Usha Nangyar in performance (Photo by Kunju Vasudevan Namboodiripad with permission)

Kutiyattam: originally known as *kuttu* (drama); *kutiyattam* literally means 'combined' or 'mixed' acting. *Kutiyattam* is a unique, regional style of staging dramas written in Sanskrit that began to develop from earlier forms of Sanskrit drama under the patronage of King Kulasekharavarmam (978–1036 A.C.E.) in the southwestern coast region of India known today as Kerala State. The early history of Sanskrit theatre dates to between the 2nd century B.C.E. and 2nd century A.C.E. when all aspects of theatrical practice were recorded in the *Natyasastra*. This encyclopedic collection included information on the mythological origins of drama, types of plays, theatre buildings, music, psychophysical training, how the actor embodies a character's states of being-doing (*bhava*), et cetera. It outlines a complete theory of aesthetics (*rasa*) and explains how pleasure is brought to an audience in performance. The distinctive style of *kutiyattam* developed very late in the history of Sanskrit theatre at a time when Sanskrit theatre and drama were on the decline elsewhere in India (see Paulose 2006:65–101). By the fourteenth century *kutiyattam* had developed its distinctive style and began to be performed on a regular basis in specially constructed temple theatres within the compounds of high caste Hindu temples as a 'visual sacrifice' to the primary deity of the temple. The performance tradition has been sustained by the three sets of temple-servants who traditionally have the right to train in and perform *kutiyattam* – Cakyars who play male roles, Nambiars who provide percussion accompaniment on large copper drums (*milavu*), and Nangyars who play the female roles. The Cakyars and Nangyars are highly learned actors with a vast knowledge of Sanskrit and Malayalam literature. They traditionally perform both solo performances in which the actor elaborates stories from encyclopedic collections of traditional tales (*puranas*) as well as the 'combined acting' of *kutiyattam* in which they stage selected acts of important plays in the repertory. The example given here exemplifies an approach to solo acting where the actor playing a character elaborates the story by seeing and/or becoming another character in the story.

In 2004, Usha Nangyar was approached by the dancer/choreographer Gitanjali Kolanad for instruction in this unique approach to visualizing and 'becoming' another character. Gitanjali was researching and preparing a new solo performance/adaptation of an Indian folk tale, 'The Flowering Tree.'[2] In 'The Flowering Tree' Gitanjali plays/dances the role of a sister who, after meditating upon and visualizing the goddess, transforms herself into a tree; therefore, she sought instruction from Usha Nangyar on visualizing and transforming into the goddess (Figure 2.2). Usha instructed Gitanjali to

Figure 2.2   Gitanjali Kolanad in the process of visualization as she transforms into a tree in *The Flowering Tree* (Photograph by Riaz Mehmood)

breathe through the eyes whenever there is a point of emphasis, as in this solo acting when visualizing the goddess. Close off all other avenues of breath – do not use your nostrils, but inhale/exhale through your eyes. Hold all the orifices closed, and close your ears. It is like 'looking' as in yoga.

Usha Nangyar's instructions reveal a uniquely South Asian understanding and approach to the inner and outer dimensions of acting.

A series of questions arise from or are implied by Usha's instructions:

- What does Usha mean when she says the actor must 'breathe through the eyes'?
- How does one close off all venues of the breath *except* the eyes, and what does it mean to 'close the ears'?
- What do these instructions reveal about a South Asian approach to acting and embodiment? More specifically, what assumptions are made about the inner (psycho) and outer (physical) dimensions of embodied experience, and the relationship between inner and outer, mind and body?

• How does the practitioner train to become virtuosic in the psycho-physical task of visualization and transformation?

The purpose of this chapter is to answer these questions. To do so, we will expand our discussion beyond *kutiyattam,* examining what we know about acting and actor training in the early history of staging Sanskrit dramas, and focusing at length on two other arts unique to Kerala – the martial art, *kalarippayattu,*[3] and especially *kathakali* dance-drama.

Kalarippayattu: is a compound technical term that refers to the traditional martial art and physical therapy healing techniques unique to the southwestern coastal region of Kerala, India – the same region in which *kutiyattam* is performed. The first half of the compound term, *kalari,* refers to the place of training – a five foot deep earthen pit, covered by thatched palm. The second half of the compound term, *payattu,* is derived from the Tamil *payil* meaning "to become trained, accustomed, practice," and refers to the psychophysical exercises practiced in the training space. The *kalari* was a centre for psychophysical exercise, martial arts training, and physical therapy treatments in villages throughout Kerala. As revealed in India's vast literary traditions, Indian martial arts have existed on the subcontinent since early antiquity. *Kalarippayattu* as the distinctive Kerala martial art emerged by the twelfth century A.C.E. out of two earlier source traditions – ancient Tamil martial practices indigenous to the far South of the subcontinent, and the Dhanur Vedic ("science of the bow") brought to the south as part of the Aryan migration from north India (see Zarrilli 1998:24–60).

Kathakali: literally 'story play' is a genre of dance-drama dating from the late sixteenth century also indigenous to Kerala. It enacts stories from the two great Indian epics, the Mahabharata and Ramayana, as well as stories about Krishna from the *puranas.* When *kathakali* emerged as a new form of dance-drama, its first actors were Nayars – a particular Hindu caste many of whom were practitioners of *kalarippayattu.* Therefore, *kathakali*'s well-known intensive system of psychophysical training and massage originated in *kalaripappayattu.* Its aesthetic form, hand-gestures, plastic use of facial expression, and its understanding of acting were all based upon and influenced by the much earlier techniques and aesthetics of *kutiyattam.* In both *kutiyattam* and *kathakali* easily distinguishable make-up types allow the audience to identify and understand each character. But unlike *kutiyattam* where the actors deliver the lines of the

Sanskrit text they are performing, in *kathakali* onstage vocalists deliver the entire dramatic text in a unique form of singing (*sopanam*). The actor/ dancers speak the entire text with the complete language of hand-gestures (see Zarrilli 2000).

Embodied modes of practice in South Asia: shared patterns and assumptions

Usha's instructions focus on the actor's relationship to and use of the breath. As discussed in detail below, in South Asia the 'breath,' 'wind' or 'vital energy' (*prana* or *prana-vayu*) refers to 'any kind of vital current' (Rowell 1992:233; see also Chakravarty 1988:97–115). It is the conceptual and practical link between the gross, outer, physical body and inner experience. Working *through the breath*, the *kutiyattam* actor 'sees' and absorbs each specific aspect of the goddess that appears before her – from the goddess' head and hair, all the way down to her feet. Taking the goddess 'in' through the breath awakens, enlivens, and communicates the connection between the actor/character and the goddess before her. Likewise, when Gitanjali transforms from the sister into the tree, her breath serves as the psychophysical vehicle through which she 'becomes' this 'other.' A major aspect of the audience's pleasure with this type of acting is witnessing the actor's embodied visualization and subsequent transformation *into the other* as it happens.

The centrality of the breath in South Asian modes of embodied practice is also reflected in interviews conducted with masters of *kalarippayattu* and *kathakali* dance-drama. One martial arts master summed up the importance of controlling the internal 'wind' and developing 'wind power' as follows:

Prana-vayu is the basis of all other powers, and only by increasing one's wind-power will that person's mental power and physical power increase. The various steps, poses, and applications in martial arts practice need strength (*balam*); however, this strength can only be acquired when one has control of the vital energy. Only by taking the breath in and training it at the root of the navel (*nabhi mula*) can the practitioner spread the 'special' power situated in the inner parts through the external organs.[4]

The *kathakali* actor/master teacher Padmanabhan Nayar (1928–2007) makes explicit what is usually implicit:

Anything physical requires control of the *vayu*. All the arts... have their own specific ways of using the *vayu*. In *kathakali*, each of the inner states of being-doing (*bhava*) require the specific development and proper use of the *vayu*... I systematically train the actor in all the body movements for a role, and how to bring the *vayu* through the whole body...

The teacher should know how the *vayu* moves around within the body for each specific *bhava,* and then utilize the basic poses and movements of the training which help to train the student in the circulation of the *vayu*... So you must make the student practice until he is perfect through repetition, and then the *vayu* will come. I won't stop until the student gets it correctly. The students will get bored, and I too will get bored, but I won't stop until the student gets it correctly! (Interview 1 July 2003).

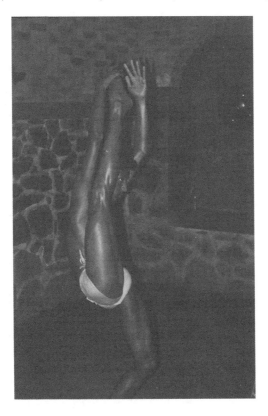

Figure 2.3 Mastering the 'body' in *kalarippayattu* begins with basic exercises, like this straight leg kick in which the is leg so flexible that it can be easily kicked so that it touches the hand raised above the body. Pictured is Sathyan Narayanan Nayar of the CVN Kalari, Thirvananthapuram, executing the first leg exercise. (Photo by Phillip B. Zarrilli.)

Figure 2.4 A *kathakali* performer demonstrates the kind of body flexibility gained through the intensive psychophysical training process. Pictured is a rehearsal (*coliyattam*) of the *kathakali* drama, *Lavanasuravadham* by the playwright Palakkatt Amritta Sastri (1815–1877). The actor-dancer shown here is playing the role of Hanuman – the chief of the monkeys. Hanuman is depicted showing off his great psychophysical prowess using a high kick with his left foot taken into the dance-drama directly from *kalarippayattu*. (Photo by Phillip B. Zarrilli)

From the interviews cited thus far, it is clear that practitioners of *kutiyattam, kalarippayattu,* and *kathakali* assume that learning to awaken, control, and circulate the wind/vital energy (*vayu*) throughout the body is central to mastery in all three arts.

But how does the practitioner learn to awaken and circulate the inner wind in order to become a virtuosic actor/dancer or martial artist? The *kathakali* actor M.P. Sankaran Namboodiri explained that 'first, perfection of the body is most important' (interview, 1978). Echoing this observation, a Muslim master of *kalarippayattu* explained how any student 'who wants to become a master must possess complete knowledge of the body'. Therefore, training begins with 'body-control exercises' (*meyyarappatavu*) (Figures 2.3, 2.4). The first step in preparing, perfecting, or gaining complete knowledge of the body is by repetition of the basic exercises and forms that constitute a specific mode of embodied practice.

The earliest description we have of this type of training for the actor/dancer is recorded in the *Natyasastra* (dated between the second century B.C.E. and second century A.C.E.). An intensive, rigorous 'method of exercise' involving preparatory psychophysical exercises and complete massage of the body is prescribed as follows:

> One should perform exercise … on the floor as well as (high up) in the air, and should have beforehand one's body massaged with the (seasamum) oil or with barley gruel. The floor is the proper place (lit. Mother) for exercise. Hence one should resort to the floor, and stretching oneself over it one should take exercise. (Ghosh 1967:209)

Traditionally training began at an early age under the guidance of a master-teacher (*guru*), and in some traditions, students lived in their master's house from childhood. As one masters basic preliminary exercises, the neophyte goes on to learn more advanced techniques – in *kutiyattam* and *kathakali* this includes learning dance steps/choreography, movement patterns necessary to play various roles in the repertory as well as an entire system of hand-gestures (*mudras*) and facial gestures (*rasa-abhinaya*).

Whether learning the preparatory exercises or more advanced techniques, the student mimics the master and/or senior students, repeating over and over each day the basic techniques until they become part of one's body knowledge – ready-at-hand to be used 'unthinkingly.' For the young boys going through this type of training, the process is anything but romantic. It is difficult, hard work. Masters are strict, correcting the student in performance of each detail. Over time, this process or repetition has the potential to shape and transform the neophyte into a mature, accomplished, virtuosic practitioner.

Exercises for the body at first appear to simply be physical, that is, they seem to be 'that which is external.' But as the forms are practiced assiduously and as they 'come correct,' students begin to manifest physical, mental, and behavioural 'signs' (*lakshana*) that indicate change and effect a gradual transformation not only of the body, but also of one's relationship to doing the exercises. The exercises gradually become 'that which is internal' (*andarikamayatu*). The relationship between the doer and what he does has been qualitatively transformed from an external process that only engages the gross physical body, to a psychophysical one in which the practitioner's inner experience, awareness, attentiveness, and perception are ideally engaged and altered.

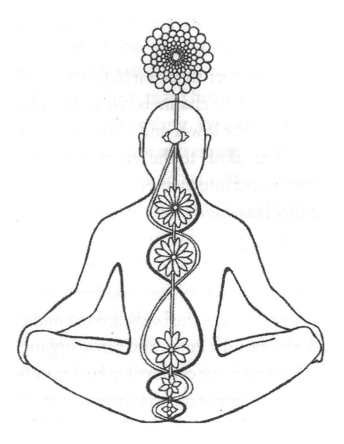

Figure 2.5 The seven *cakras* of the subtle body. Each *cakra* is represented by a flower with petals. The number of petals indicates the respective frequency of a vibration once a *cakra* is activated. The lowest *cakra* at the root of the navel has the smallest number of petals and least vibration, while the *cakra* at the top of the spine (top of the head) has most. The cosmic energy (*kundalini* or Sakti) is understood and represented as coiled within the lowest centre where it sleeps until awakened. Pictured here is a schematic drawing of one typical 'map' of the subtle body with each of the *cakras*, arrayed along the spine, represented by a flower. To either side are the two main channels (*nadis*)

One of the central 'signs' marking this transformation from external form to internal action is when the teacher observes how 'the *vayu* [wind] comes' fully into a student's practice. In order to understand both this process of transformation of 'the body' as well as what is meant by 'that which is internal', we will briefly examine two key South Asian paradigms that inform psychophysical processes and acting.

When Usha Nangyar compared the process of 'looking' by inhaling/exhaling 'through the eyes' to that of yoga, she makes explicit the fact that a yogic paradigm and understanding of embodied experience informs embodied practice. What Usha does not explicitly mention is the second paradigm of the body and experience that informs training and embodiment throughout South Asia – India's traditional system of medicine, Ayurveda (literally, the 'science of life'). Possessing 'complete knowledge of the body' traditionally meant gaining knowledge of *three different but closely related* 'bodies' of practice:

1. the fluid body of humours and saps;
2. the body composed of bones and muscles (and for the martial arts practitioner the vulnerable vital junctures or spots of the body); and
3. the subtle, interior body (Figure 2.5).

The first two bodies are based on Ayurveda and together constitute the gross, 'physical/exterior body' (*sthula-sarira*). The third – the subtle, interior body (*suksma-sarira*) – is most explicitly identified with Kundalini/Tantric yoga, but this map of interior experience informs all systems of embodied practice in South Asia. Since the yogic and Ayurvedic paradigms are ubiquitous in South Asia, informing how 'the body', the 'mind', their relationship, and experience are traditionally understood in yoga, martial arts, and performing arts, we will briefly examine these two paradigms before continuing our discussion of psychophysical acting.

The 'physical/exterior body' explained by Ayurveda

Ayurveda is a compound term literally meaning 'the science' or 'knowledge' of 'life'. Ayurveda is the indigenous form of medicine that seeks to establish harmony with the environment by maintaining equilibrium in a process of constant fluid exchange. The art of this traditional medical system is meant to establish

'junctions' or 'articulations' between man and his environment, through the prescription of appropriate diets and regimens ... Equality, balance and congruous articulations are meant for the conservation and restoration of these precious fluids ... By means of ['restraints'] (*brahmacarya*) ... and various other psychosomatic disciplines, one should establish congruous junctions with the surrounding landscapes and seasons, and thus one should protect one's powers, one should husband one's vital fluids. (Zimmermann 1983:17–18)

The daily practice of psychophysical disciplines is understood to establish congruence among the three humours: wind (*vata*), phlegm (*kapha*), and fire (*pitta*). The role of exercise and massage in maintaining inner fluidity and articulation among the humours was explained in antiquity in a medical text attributed to Susruta:

The act born of effort (*ayasa*) of the body is called exercise (*vyayama*). After doing it, one should shampoo (*viMRD*) [massage] the body on all sides until it gives a comfortable sensation. Growth of the body, radiance harmonious proportions of the limbs, a kindled (digestive) fire, energy, firmness, lightness, purity (*mrja*), endurance to fatigue, weariness, thirst, hot and cold, etc., and even a perfect health: this is what is brought by physical exercise... It is especially beneficial to him in the winter and spring. But in all seasons, every day, a man seeking his own good should take physical exercise only to half the limit of his strength, as otherwise it kills. When the [wind] *vayu* hitherto properly located in the heart (*hrdi*) comes to the mouth of the man practicing physical exercise, it is the sign (*laksana*) of *balardha*, of his having used half of his strength. (*Cikitsasthana* xxiv, 38–49) (Zimmermann 1986)

To maintain heath, one's diet as well as massage and vigorous exercise (as depicted in Figures 2.3, and 2.4) should be adapted to the cycles of the seasons. Therefore, the rainy season from June through August is considered the best season for intensive psychophysical training and massage. During these cool months the heat produced by vigorous exercise and massage is counterbalanced by the seasonal accumulation of phlegm. By contrast, the very hot summer season from March to the onset of monsoon is characterized by accumulation of the wind humour; therefore, exercise should be either cut back or avoided altogether. Exercise and massage are understood to increase the circulation of the wind humour throughout the body, and this, too counterbalances the accumulation of phlegm during monsoon.

The fluid humoral body is supported by the body as a frame of bones, muscles, ligaments, vessels, joints, as well as their junctures and vital spots. This body must be exercised daily to achieve flexibility and fluidity – a process assisted by massage and application of special oils to the entire body.

The interior, subtle body of yoga

The specific term *yoga* is derived from the Sanskrit root, *yuj,* meaning 'to yoke or join or fasten ... make ready, prepare, arrange, fit out ... accomplish' (Monier-Williams 1963:855–856). Yoga encompasses any ascetic, meditational, or psychophysiological technique which achieves a 'binding', uniting or bringing together of the body and mind or consciousness. A wide variety of yogic pathways developed historically in South Asia including *karma yoga* or the law of universal causality; *maya yoga* or a process of liberating oneself from cosmic illusion; *nirvana yoga* or a process of growing beyond illusion to attain at-onement with absolute reality; and *hatha yoga* or specific techniques of psychophysiological practice. The most popular and visible form of yoga practised today are versions of classical *hatha* yoga. It includes repetition of breath-control exercises, forms/postures (*asana*), combined with restraints/constraints on diet and behaviour. These practices are understood to act on both the physical body (*sthula sarira*), as well as the subtle body (*suksma sarira*) most often identified with Kundalini-Tantric yoga.

The physical body and subtle body of yoga are *not absolute categories.* Exercise of one body is understood to naturally affect the other. They are fluid conceptual and practical counterparts. Specific parts of the subtle body are thought to correspond to specific places in the physical body. These are analogous/homologous correspondences and are never exact. The two are so fundamentally related that what affects one body is understood to affect the other.

As early as the *Rg Veda* (1200 B.C.E.) ascetic practices (*tapas*) are mentioned.[5] By the time of the composition of the Upanisads (600–300 B.C.E.), specific methods for experiencing higher states of consciousness and control of the self were well developed. The earliest use of the term 'yoga' is in the *Katha Upanisad* where the term means 'the steady control of the senses, which, along with the cessation of mental activity, leads to the supreme state' (Flood 1996:95).

Philosophical assumptions informing yoga vary widely, and range from monist (all is one) to dualist (all is two) to atomist (all is many). Yoga's psychophysical practices have never been 'confined to any particular sectarian affiliation or social form' (Flood 1996:94). As a consequence, both yoga philosophy and practices are found throughout South Asia and inform all modes of embodied practice as well as the visual and plastic arts.[6]

From the earliest stages of its development, yoga developed as a practical pathway towards the transformation of both the body as well as consciousness (and thereby 'self'). The ultimate goal was spiritual release (*moksa*) through renunciation by withdrawal *from* the world and the cycles of rebirth. Some yogic pathways provide a systematic attempt to control both the wayward body and the potentially overwhelming senses/emotions that can create disequilibrium in daily life. Rigorous practice therefore *can* lead to a sense of detachment (*vairagya*) through which the *yogin* withdraws completely from daily life and its activities, and is understood to achieve a state where he transcends time (*kalalita*).

However, yoga philosophy and its practices have also always informed and been directly adapted by non-renunciants as well, that is, those who keep their feet firmly *within* the spatio-temporal world. Traditionally this included India's martial castes (*ksatriyas*) who served as rulers and/or those martial artists/warriors in the service of rulers, as well as a wide variety of artists – actors, dancers, musicians, painters, and sculptors. Rulers, martial artists, and performing/plastic artists had to live and act very much *in* and *upon* the world and/or its social order. Rulers/*ksatriyas* were required to govern, maintain the cosmic order mirrored in the microcosm of worldly kingdoms, and be able to use well-honed martial skills to maintain order. Artists/performers were expected to bring pleasure and aesthetic joy to the diverse gods of the Hindu pantheon and/or those one was serving and entertaining.

In contrast to the 'classical' yoga practitioner-as-renunciant who withdraws from everyday life, for martial artists and actor/dancers 'yogic' practices do not lead to renunciation and/or disengagement from daily life. Rather, as the practitioner engages in yoga-based psychophysical practices, ideally the ego becomes quiet and the emotions calm. One is better able to 'act' within their respective socio-cultural domain while still *in* the world. The martial or performing artist who practises yoga-based psychophysical techniques does so to transcend personal limitations to *better* 'act' rather than withdraw from the world. In the South Asian context, later in life when one's duties and social obligations have been fulfilled, the individual might choose to become a renunciant and follow the radical, ideal pattern of the yogi who withdraws from life.

Of most relevance to our discussion of psychophysical acting is the relationship between the physical and subtle bodies. They are integrally related. The concept and specific inner alchemy of the subtle body historically developed separately from Ayurveda as part of ascetic and yogic practice and appears fully developed after about the eighth century A.D. The essential elements of the subtle body usually identified in these later texts include structural elements known as wheels or centers (*cakra*), channels (*nadi*), and dynamic elements including the vital energy or wind (*prana*, *vayu*, or *prana-vayu*) and the cosmic energy (*kundalini* or Sakti) sleeping coiled within the lowest centre (Figure 2.5).

Through the channels or conduits (*nadi*) flows the vital energy or inner wind. The channels usually range in number from ten to fourteen. Of the three most important channels two (*ida* and *pingala*) reach from the lower end of the spinal column (*muladhra cakra*) to the left and right nostrils. Between and intertwined with them is the central channel (*susumna-nadi*). It too originates at the 'root' of the spinal column and stretches to the top of the head. All the channels originate at the lower end of the spinal column and form an intricate network through the body linking *muladhara cakra* with the various limbs and sense organs.

The wheels or centres (*cakra*) number from five to eight and take the form of a stylized lotus (*padma*). They are arrayed vertically from the base of the spine (along the corresponding central *susumna nadi*) up to and through increasingly refined and more subtle centres. These centres are places within the subtle body where latent functions, often represented as half-opened buds, await the invigorating exercise of the internal energy. The number of petals indicates the respective frequency of vibration once a *cakra* is activated.

Moving from 'that which is external' to that which is 'internal'

The 'breath' or 'vital energy' within is the conceptual and practical link between the physical and subtle bodies of Ayurveda and yoga, and the key to understanding the 'internal'. The natural form that the wind humour took in classical Ayurveda was its form in nature as wind or breath.[7] Wind is understood to spread throughout the body and to be responsible for all activity, just as atmospheric wind is thought to be responsible for all activities in the natural world. Within the physical body, specific activities are identified with specific forms of wind or breath (see Zarrilli 1998:131; Filliozat 1964:210–211). The term *prana* or *prana vayu* is used generically to refer to any type of wind activity within the body, whatever its form, as well as to the specific wind/energy/life force of the breath. *Prana* as the 'vital breath' is also the source of human vocal sound which is traditionally understood to take shape as the original sacred syllable, *om* (or *a-u-m* where *a* is 'the "primal sound" as well as the first letter of the Sanskrit alphabet)' (Rowell 1992:36).

This equation of breath or wind as the vital energy or 'life-force' (*jivan*) was explained to me by *kalarippayattu* master-teacher, Gurukkal Govindankutty Nayar when he asked rhetorically:

> Who am I? My hands, legs, nose, etc.? Who am I/ My hands, legs, breast? That, all of these is *prana*. Just to close your eyes – that is one *prana*. Yawning is another *prana*. Therefore, life itself (*jivana*) is *prana*.

In interview, another martial arts master who requested anonymity similarly explained how *prana* is

> [t]he *vayu* which rules the body as a whole. *Prana* is the controlling power of all parts of the body. *Vayu* is not just air, but one power (*sakti*). That is what rules us completely. *Prana* means *jivana* – 'life', individual soul.

In *kutiyattam, kathakali,* and *kalarippayattu* trainings, the *vayu* is gradually awakened, controlled, and spread throughout the body in one or more of the following three ways:

1. By overt practice of special breath-control exercises as taught by some but not all specific teachers;
2. 'correct' daily practice of preparatory body-control exercises such as yoga *asanas,* or *kalarippayattu* and *kathakali* training exercises; and
3. 'correct' practice of other psychophysical forms – such as the circulation of 'vital energy' to enliven hand or facial gestures in *kutiyattam* and *kathakali,* or in use of voicing/sounding text in the *kutiyattam* tradition.

When done fully and 'correctly', psychophysical exercise and forms of embodied practice – including vocalization of text – operate at both the physical level and on a subtle, interior level as the bodymind is 'vibrated'. The practitioner gradually frees himself from the flux of the body's agitation, and/or the everyday psycho-mental stream of consciousness. The 'interior' affected by psychophysical training includes consciousness, awareness, and perception as they are deployed in doing the exercise/ form and/or in delivering text.

This process reflects a general cultural assumption that *long-term* practice of psychophysical disciplines leads to discoveries. Discussing what one learns through yoga practice, the *Bhagavad Gita* (4.38) tells us, 'he who attains perfection through the practice of yoga *discovers of his own accord, with time,* the brahman present in his soul' (Varenne 1976:58, italics mine). Varenne cites the *Amritabindu Upanisad* as further illustration of the idea that 'knowledge' in a discipline of embodied practice is assumed to be 'already there', hidden, waiting to be discovered:

> And knowledge is hidden in the depth of each individual just as in milk the butter we cannot see is hidden; this is why the wise practitioner must carry out a churning operation within himself, employing his own mind without respite as the churning agent. (Varenne 1976:59)

What is meant by the term 'mind' here? In South Asia there are three important Sanskrit terms which can be translated as 'mind'. The term *buddhi* specifically refers to the rational mind, that is, such mental processes as judgement, evaluation, inference, deliberation, conducting systematic research, et cetera. The term *mana* or *manasa* may be translated (as in the passage above) as 'mind', however, it actually

> means both mind and heart, as well as mood, feeling, mental state, memory, desire, attachment, interest, attention, devotion, and decision. These terms do not have a single reference in English, and must be understood through clusters of explicit and implicit meanings ... [T]he terms of emotion and though, mind and heart are not opposed. (McDaniel 1995:43)

Another Sanskrit term, *cittam*, means thinking, mind, intelligence, will, or heart. When used in relation to martial arts, yoga, or acting, both *mana* and *cittam* are understood as consciousness itself, that is, awareness, perception, or the attunement/direction of one's attention-in-action. Unlike the term *buddhi* (rational mind), the use of *mana* or *cittam* assumes that the 'mental' element engaged in *doing* a psychophysical practice is *not* rational thought 'in the head', but an operation of the mind/awareness/consciousness-itself in-the-body as it engages a specific psychophysical task. As Haridas Chaudhuri explains, in yoga-based psychophysical disciplines such as *kalarippayattu, kutiyattam,* or *kathakali*

> ...mind and body are not heterogeneous but homogeneous. They are different evolutes or modes of manifestation of the same fundamental creative energy ... In the same way, the outside physical environment and the mind-body evolves of the same primal energy, too. Since there is

homogeneous and existential continuity here, the fact of interaction between mind and matter causes no problem. The dualism of mind and body is a product of our discursive understanding. It is a division inserted by dichotomous thinking within the continuum of our multidimensional experience. (Chaudhuri 1977:255–256)

In terms of the distinction between phenomenal consciousness and access consciousness introduced in the final section of Chapter 1, *buddhi* or the rational mind at work is access consciousness where there are propositional attitudes with representational content, or access consciousness. *Cittam* and *mana* are forms of phenomenal consciousness where the 'feeling' dimension of embodied engagement is an essential part of these modes of experience-in-action.

The goal of all virtuosic psychophysical systems in South Asia is reaching a state of masterly 'accomplishment' (*siddhi*) in which the doer and done are one. At the highest level, a master's practice seems 'effortless'. The practitioner reaches a state of being/doing within which one is free to practice 'the principle of non-action in action ... ,' that is, one is in a position to practise '"I act, yet it is not I but Being acts through me"' (Chaudhuri 1977:252). This is a self-actualized mode of realization that is egoless in its action. The dancer is danced; the song sings the vocal artist; the *kalarippayattu* practitioner's body is so flexible it 'flows like a river'. The yogi is freed for meditation; the martial artist is freed to fight; the actor/dancer is freed to perform.

The actor enters into an optimal' relationship with an action, that is, the relationship is one of unmediated, fully embodied being/doing. The actor does and/or apprehends in each present moment. In performance, the actor 'is that' which he does. As one *kathakali* actor explained, the actor 'becomes one with the character' ('*natan kathapathravumai tadatmyam prapikanam*') in a psychophysical sense.[8]

One way of understanding this optimal state of awareness and actualization in acting is through a key passage in Nandikesvara's *Abhinayadarpanam* – a Sanskrit text usually dated somewhere between the tenth and thirteenth centuries. The passage describes the optimal state of being/doing from the actor/performer's perspective. It explains how the actor realizes India's *rasa/bhava* aesthetic in performance:

> Where the hand [is], there [is] the eye;
> where the eye [is], there [is] the mind;
> where the mind [is], there [is] the *bhava;*
> where the *bhava* [is], there is the *rasa.*

From the actor's point of view 'inside' a performance, the ideal state of awareness one inhabits is a non-conditional state of being/doing/consciousness. The use of the state-of-being verb ('is') clearly indicates that there is no intentionality or conditionality in this optimal state. It is an emergent state – wherever the actor's attention (eye) is directed, the actor's mind/heart/awareness is fully present. With the actor's mind/heart/awareness fully present in the moment, the actor embodies the state of being/doing (*bhava*) specific to the dramatic context in each moment. Simultaneously, when the actor is fully present embodying a specific *bhava*, then the audience will experience aesthetic bliss (*rasa*).

Drawing upon principles of yoga, the Indian actor's body is traditionally trained through a long-term process to become a suitable vehicle through which this ideal aesthetic experience might be actualized. Conventions guiding acting and movement ranged from *lokadharmi* – the 'ordinary' and 'concrete' – to *natyadharmi* – that which is 'extraordinary' and 'ideational'. The 'concrete' is what is easily recognizable, such as a gesture mimetically representing a deer. The 'ideational' is that which elaborated, abstracted, transformed, or distilled and therefore is more decorative, abstract, and stylized. As genres of performance, *kutiyattam* and *kathakali* both possess 'ordinary/concrete' and 'extraordinary/ideational' aspects in similar but different proportions.

To more specifically understand psychophysical acting process in India, we examine in detail the *kathakali* actor's training and approach to actualizing 'the interior' when acting/dancing roles within the *kathakali* repertoire.

The psychophysical actor at work in kathakali dance-drama

Intensive training of the *kathakali* actor/dancer traditionally began from the age of seven or eight. [Today's students may be ten or much older.] Formal instruction is a long and arduous process that traditionally lasts eight hours a day, six days a week, for between six and ten years. When their formal training is complete, young actors at first dance preliminary dances and/or play minor roles and only gradually work their way into medium-sized and major roles. It is generally agreed that *kathakali* actors usually do not reach maturity as performers until about the age of forty.

The formal years of training are understood to gradually reshape the actor's bodymind. Basic techniques must first be mastered, including preliminary body preparation exercises and massage, meticulous isolation exercises for the eyes and facial muscles/facial mask, a complete vocabulary of hand-gestures (*mudras*) and facial expressions (*rasa-abhinaya*), rhythmic patterns, and set dance steps and choreography. All these elements are woven into the fabric of a complete performance of a dance-drama text.[9] In addition, the young student must grow and mature as an individual, engage in study and reflection of the dramatic texts and the collections of stories and epics on the basis of which specific dramatic texts have been authored, develop his embodied imagination, and integrate all the above into shaping and playing small, medium-sized, and large roles in the repertory.

The specific techniques of training, as well as the application of those techniques to playing roles combine to render the entire body flexible, balanced, and controlled. Over time these techniques help the individual to awaken, discover and creatively embody and utilize the inner 'wind/breath/life-force' (*prana, prana-vayu*) in performance.

Preliminary body preparation and exercise[10]

With the onset of the cool, seasonal monsoonal rains, beginning as well as advanced *kathakali* students start their annual cycle of training by undergoing the same process of 'body preparation'. Based on Kerala's martial art, *kalarippayattu*, daily training begins with the repetition of a rigorous physical regime of body-control exercises and oil massage – given with the teacher's feet and hands.[11] Together the exercise and massage gradually render the body flexible, balanced, controlled, and reshaped to suit *kathakali*'s aesthetic style and stance – a grounded, wide stance with splayed knees and full turn-out, arched back, use of the outsides of the feet, and up-turned big toes. After applying oil to his entire body, the student pays respects with his body to Lord Ganesha – the elephant-headed incarnation of Lord Vishnu who is prayed to before any new undertaking – by prostrating himself on the floor. He then performs a series of jumps (*cattam*) as well as jumping steps, and finally progresses through an elaborate series of body-control exercises. Either before or immediately following massage additional exercises are performed including the splits (*suci,* literally meaning 'needles'), circling the body, body flips, foot-work patterns (*kalsadhakam*). Another essential part of the early morning training regime designed to develop the young actor's expressivity is repetition of eye exercises (*kannusadhakam*) performed in nine different directions and three different speeds.

The most obvious expressive means through which the actor conveys a character's states of being/doing (*bhava*) within the dramatic context

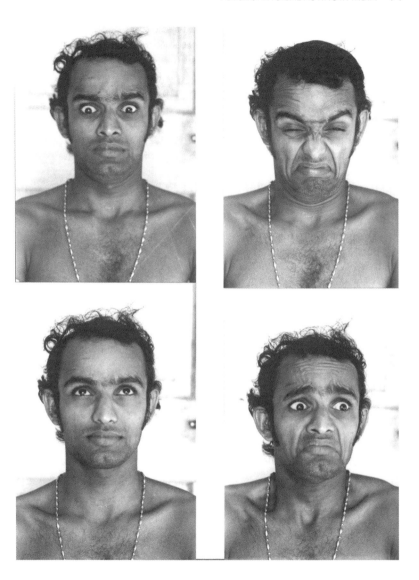

Figure 2.6 Four of *kathakali*'s nine basic facial expressions (*rasa-abhinaya*). Pictured are (top left) fury, anger, or wrath (*krodha bhava*); (top right) disgust or the repulsive (*jugupsa bhava*); (lower left) peace or at-onement (*sama bhava*); (lower right) fear (*bhaya bhava*). When embodying 'fury' (top left) the actor's 'wind' is pushed into the lower eyelids. (Photo by Phillip B. Zarrilli)

of a story include not only the eyes, but hand-gestures and facial expressions. Therefore, the young actor must technically master hand-gestures and the complete set of facial expressions. This means exercising the fingers, wrists, hands, as well as each set of facial muscles (cheeks, lips, et cetera) required to fully embody each expressive state.

Kathakali's language of gesture and expressive use of the eyes is part of its inheritance from the *Natyasastra* via *kutiyattam*. Both *kathakali* and *kutiyattam* base their gesture language on twenty-four root *mudras* (Figure 2.6) on a regional text, the *Hastalaksanadipika* – a catalogue of basic hand poses with lists of words which each pose represents (see Prekumar 1948; Venu 1984; Richmond 1999). The two terms, *mudra* and *hasta*, refer to the twenty-four root gestures performed with a single hand, combined hands, or mixed hands. Meanings are only created when the actor uses the basic alphabet to literally 'speak' with their hands.

The *kathakali* actor's face is a pliant vehicle for displaying the constantly shifting manifestations of a character's inner states of being/doing (*bhava*) through which he serves as a vehicle for the audience's aesthetic experience of *rasa*.

The nine basic states include the erotic, love, or pleasure; the comic, mirthful, or derision; the pathetic/sadness; fury (Figure 2.6), anger or terrible; repulsive or disgust; the wondrous or marvelous; and peace or at-onement.

The nine basic *bhavas/rasas* and their facial expressions

bhava	*rasa*
(states of being/doing the actor embodies)	('tasted' by the audience)
1. pleasure or delight (*rati*) corresponds to	the erotic (*srngara*);
2. laughter or humor (*hasa*)	the comic (*hasya*);
3. sorrow or pain (*soka*)	pathos/compassion (*karuna*);
4. anger (*krodha*)	the furious (*raudra*);
5. heroism or courage (*utsaha*)	the heroic/valorous (*vira*);
6. fear (*bhaya*)	the terrible (*bhayanaka*);
7. disgust (*jugupsa*)	the odious (*bibhatsa*);
8. wonder (*vismaya*)	the marvelous (*adbhuta*);
9. at-onement (*sama*)	at-onement/peace (*santa*).*

*The twelfth-century commentator Abhinavagupta identified this ninth state of at-onement/peace.

At first, each expression is learned technically through continuous repetition and correction. Beginning instruction in how to assume the basic facial expression for *rati bhava* – the erotic, love, or pleasure – is usually very technical, much like the following:

> Open the upper lids as wide as possible. Keep the lower lids slightly closed. With the lips make a soft, relaxed smile, but do not show the teeth. Keep the gaze focused straight ahead. Having assumed this position, begin to flutter the eyebrows. Keeping the shoulders still, and using the neck/head, move the head first to the right, and then to the left – back and forth. While keeping the external focus fixed ahead on one point, move the head to a 45-degree angle to the right, continuing to flutter the eyebrows. Repeat to the left.

Similar instructions for assuming the comic or mirthful (*hasa bhava*) are as follows:

> Slightly raise the upper bridge of the nose between the eyebrows and slightly turn down the outsides of the eyebrows. Keep the eyelids slightly closed, and the lips drawn down on each side. Indent the upper lip muscles on the outsides.

Vasu Pisarody explains how at first many students simply 'move [their] facial muscles'. It is only after six to ten years of training that a 'fuller understanding of the states of expression' arise through the training as well as further reading and personal experience. Eventually the student 'realizes what he had done at first [i.e., simply moving his facial muscles] ... wasn't enough' (1993, interview).

The subtler, 'inner' art of kathakali acting

As students progress through the training process, a subtler process of 'internal' connection is gradually realized. Each hand-gesture 'spoken' and each state of being/doing embodied is enlivened via circulation of the breath (*prana-vayu*) – that inner energy or life-force assumed to be present and available for deployment in performance. There is the external form – the appropriate use of the hands and/or engagement of the facial mask – and the internal dynamic that animates the form – the enlivening action of the *prana-vayu*. At the periphery of his awareness, the mature *kathakali* actor senses or feels the form as it is animated and as it takes shape. He fully embodies the erotic state with his entire bodymind. He *is* that state of being/doing at the moment it is brought to actualization. Actualizing 'free' circulation of the vital energy (*prana-vayu*) within allows the practitioner to dynamically release and shape this 'energy' for performance of each nuance of a role. As the vital energy circulates within and is shaped through training exercises and performance techniques, there is the 'felt' experiential quality to the flow of *prana-vayu* throughout the entire body (palms, feet, top of the head, et cetera). Optimally, the *kathakali* actor attains a state in which his bodymind is fully and constantly 'energized' as/when he moves as appropriate to the dramatic context.

For example, when performing the erotic state (*rati bhava*) the actor animates his external facial mask via this specific breathing pattern:

> Beginning with a long, slow and sustained in-breath, the eyebrows move slowly up and down. The eyelids are held open half-way on a quick catch breath, and when the object of pleasure or love is seen (a lotus flower, one's lover, et cetera), the eyelids quickly open wide on an in-breath, as the corners of the mouth are pulled up and back, responding to the object of pleasure. (Author's description)

Throughout this process the breathing is deep and connected through the *entire* bodymind via the root of the navel (*nabhi mula*); that is, it is not shallow chest breathing, nor is the activity of the breath only in the face. The characteristic breath pattern associated with the erotic sentiment is slow, long, sustained in-breaths with which the object of love, pleasure, or admiration is literally taken-in; that is, the sight, form, et cetera of the beloved or a beautiful lotus flower is 'breathed in'. This dynamic and intricate process is exemplified in Usha Nangyar's instructions to Gitanjali about how to psychophysiologically take in the goddess she sees before her with/through her breath.

The amount of force brought into the direction and circulation of the *vayu* depends on the specific state of being-doing actualized. For the erotic sentiment, much less overt force is given to the breath than, for example, when actualizing 'fury' and sending the breath/wind into the lower lids. Each expressive state has its own unique pattern and strength in use and circulation of *vayu*.

Students are instructed to breathe *only through their nose, and not the mouth* – a simple instruction which, when adhered to along with maintenance of correct spinal alignment when performing a variety of exercises, develops breathing which originates at the root of the navel. Correct instruction also comes from the hands-on manipulation of the student's body by the teacher. As the *kathakali* teacher M. P. Sankaran Namboodiri explains, 'Without a verbal word of instruction the teacher may, by pointing to or pressing certain parts of the body, make the student understand where the breath/energy should be held or released.' When a student assumes *kathakali*'s basic position with the feet planted firmly apart, toes gripping the earth, it creates a dynamic set of internally felt oppositional forces as the energy is pushed down from the navel through the feet/toes into the earth, while it simultaneously pushes up through the spine/torso, thereby supporting and enlivening the upper body, face, hands/arms.

This centred groundedness is behind all aspects of *kathakali* performance including delivery of elaborate hand-gestures. Psychophysiologically, each gesture originates in the region of the root of the navel (*nabhi mula*) as the breath/energy extends outward through the gesture, optimally giving it full expressivity appropriate to the dramatic moment.[12] When teaching some of the basic facial expressions, some teachers instruct students to literally 'push the breath/energy' from the root of the navel *into* a certain part of the face. When creating the furious sentiment (*krodha bhava*) the teacher may ask the student to push the *vayu* into the lower lids in order to create the psychophysiologically dynamic quality necessary to fully actualize 'fury' (Figure 2.6).

During my 2003 interview with actor, master-teacher Padmanabhan Nayar, he demonstrated and explained some of the myriad ways in which the *vayu* is present throughout the body of the *kathakali* actor-dancer, and how it moves through and supports the actor's embodiment and delivery of all aspects of performance including the hand-gestures (*mudras*, Figure 2.7) and facial expressions. Taking the basic stance of the *kathakali* actor/dancer learned at the beginning of training – the feet are just beyond shoulder width, knees are splayed, and the feet turned onto the outside with the big toes pointing up. Padmanabhan Nayar explained how to sustain this position correctly the actor/dancer must engage the *vayu* in four places:

- Through the four toes (except the big toe) as they 'grip' the floor;
- the knees as they open wide to the sides;
- the small of the back which is constantly lengthened and flat and on the opposite side of the body, the 'root of the navel' (*nabhi mula*);
- and the neck as the chin is tucked in.

'The *vayu* should never be held in the chest as that will push the chest forward and shoulders back.' From this basic foot parallel position, the

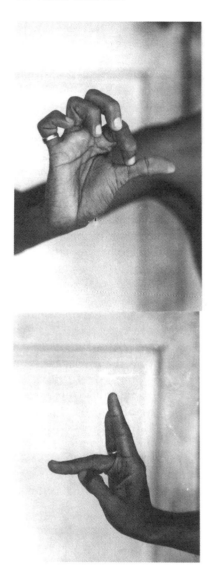
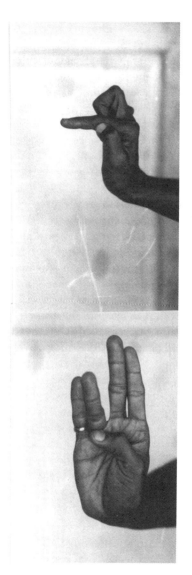

Figure 2.7 Four of *kathakali*'s twenty-four root hand-gestures (*mudras*). Each gesture animates/activates the actor's energetic connection to/ through his hands/fingers and throughout the entire body. (Photo by Phillip B. Zarrilli)

vayu sustains the left foot as it slides across the body and extends upward with the big toe extended.

Padmanabhan Nayar also described how proper awakening and circulation of the breath is developed in the fundamental training of the *kathakali* actor/dancer through the repetition of the beginning body exercises (*meyyurappadavu*). For example, 'you must be doing jumps (*cattam*) twenty-five times. But when you finish these twenty-five, the student should not open his mouth, but be breathing only through his nose. Through exercises like this, correct use of the *vayu* will come'. As we talked, Padmanabhan Nayar demonstrated how, when embodying the lotus flower, the actor's fingers open as the petals. Here the 'actor should bring the *vayu* into the fingers as the petals so that the vibration of the petals is there.'

According to Padmanabhan Nayar, the result of the presence of such a deep, yogic, psychophysical connection through the *vayu* is that the actor becomes a 'musician inside. He then 'plays' the psychophysical score of each role. Just as the original sounding of the Sanskrit *aum* is understood to 'vibrate' the universe, so ideally at a micro level within the actor when *vayu* is 'correctly' circulated and fills out the external expressive form there will be an inner 'vibration' which moves within the actor. Therefore, if the actor plays the 'right note inside, then the *bhava* comes out from the inside ... Then only will the movement be according to the character' (Padmanabhan Nayar interview).

The process of the *kathakali* actor begins not with the personal, the behavioral, or the motivational aspects of playing an action, but rather with the psychophysiological forms through which aesthetic emotion is eventually expressed as the student grows and matures. The student actor's personal feelings are not the point of origin for the creation of a facial or hand-gesture, or for the full realization of a state of being-doing; however, one's experience of life, the feeling behind 'emotions', and imagination are all used to fill out the outer forms. As he enters the process of embodying the hand-gesture for lotus, the *kathakali* actor momentarily 'becomes' a lotus flower as he 'sees' its beauty, and 'smells' its fragrance. He 'is' that, i.e., the flower itself as it opens to the sun to show its petals, as well as the appreciation of the beauty and fragrance of the flower. He simultaneously 'is' the flower from inside, and observes/appreciates the flower that he is. Constantly in the background is the actor's 'real-life' pleasure encountering the beauty and fragrance of the lotus.

Some teachers also prompt their young students to engage their imagination in the specific process of embodiment. K. Kanan Nayar explains how he asked his students when practising the heroic state to

[i]magine an elephant. For the erotic state, a lotus. For the furious, imagine a lion. For wonder, imagine a sudden action. I then ask them later in training if they are, for instance, performing wonder, imagine being in a big city. Or imagine being in a forest, seeing elephants, snakes, etc. (1976, interview)

Vasu Pisharody asks his students to 'show the feelings of an experience he can understand'. Vembayam Appukoothan Pillai explains the actor's expression of *bhava* as

how we feel toward a person or thing. For example, *srngara* is the emotion we feel towards a thing or a person we like. When we see this person or thing, our mind is enlarged. Similarly, for *hasya*, it is the feeling we get when we see a funny thing. Sorrow is the feeling we have when we experience difficulties, et cetera. (1993, interview)

Along with the circulation of the inner wind, engaging the young actor's imagination, perceiving/phenomenal consciousness, or 'mind' contributes to the full embodiment of each expressive state.

Each moment the *kathakali* actor uses to create a character is always shaped by what is considered 'appropriate to the action'. The performer's engagement in this process is part of an aesthetic that is culturally shaped and identified as 'acting'. Therefore, the actor's engagement in his work is clearly differentiated from both the experience of emotion in everyday life, and from other activities such as that of the ritual performer who enters a state of trance or possession. Trance/possession are a different type of work and experience from that of the actor.

As one actor explained when differentiating between everyday experience and his work as an actor:

It is not right to have real tears on stage: it does not fit our stylized type of theater. But the emotion of crying must be there and it will affect the audience. As an actor you must always use your emotions, knowing that you are onstage. There must be balance. After the long period of training, the gestures, the technique become automatic. You don't have to concentrate on them; then you can really fill in the role, add the emotion, and so on.

Enacting an aesthetic state of being/doing in *kathakali* is a fully physicalized and embodied psychophysiological task which ideally engages the actor's bodymind completely.

The kathakali actor in performance: King Rugmamgada's Law[13]

Kathakali's dramatization of stories from the *puranas* and epics place at centre stage a variety of idealized, but usually flawed, epic heroes. One heroic figure is King Rugmamgada. The playwright Mandavalapalli Ittiraricha Menon's (c.1747–1794) *King Rugmamgada's Law (Rugmamgada Caritam)* dramatizes a test of the king's devotion to Lord Vishnu. The full text has ten scenes. Today, only the final three scenes (8–10) are performed.[14] The play focuses on how a holy day of fasting and meditation known as *ekadasi*, became central to worship of Lord Vishnu. On *ekadasi* devotees of Vishnu are supposed to remain pure and chaste while fasting and meditating.

The three scenes usually performed today begin when Brahma – one of the three main deities in the Hindu pantheon along with Siva and Vishnu – sends the enchantress Mohini to test King Rugmamgada's devotion to Vishnu by having Mohini obstruct his observation of *ekadasi*. When Mohini first arrives at Rugmamgada's court, he does not know that she has been sent by Brahma to test him. When he sees Mohini, he immediately falls in love with her, and invites her to join his court as one of his consorts. [As was typical in the distant past, along with consorts King Rugmamgada had a primary wife to whom a son, Dharmamgada, and heir to the throne was born.] Mohini agrees, but on condition that he never deny her anything she desires. Rugmamgada agrees by taking an oath that he will indeed never deny her anything she desires.

In Scene 10 of the play, it is *ekadasi* day. After undergoing the necessary purification rites, King Rugmamgada is seated on stage meditating on Vishnu. Mohini enters in an amorous mood, dances, and then addresses Rugmamgada as follows:

O my lover,
one whose body is as handsome as Kama,
(and) one as deep as the ocean;
One who resembles Kama in (your) amorous games,
please come to me with delight!
[Today] I haven't yet had the slightest gratification from love play.
(Zarrilli 2000:164)

As Mohini is about to touch him, Rugmamgada draws away from her, explaining

> O young lady,
> I will do everything you desire, (but) today is the auspicious *ekadasi*
>   day.
> All Kama's [the god of love] sports are prohibited.
> O young lady, my life-blood, my life-blood.
>
> O auspicious one, (today one) must avoid rich foods,
>   Oiling the body, and other pleasures.
> (One) should only meditate on Vishnu. (Zarrilli 2000:164)

Mohini insists on being pleased, but Rugmamgada resists. She asks him, as a King, whether it is 'proper to break a vow like this?' For a King to break any vow would mean his failure to 'uphold the truth' and therefore uphold the world on which his truthfulness is founded.

Rugmamgada continues to refuse, insisting that he must complete his day of fasting and meditation. Mohini is adamant, but offers Rugmamgada a way out of his moral dilemma:

> You may observe this great rite if (you meet one condition):
> Place your son, Dharmamgada, on his mother's lap and gracefully
>   cut (his neck) with your sword. (Zarrilli 2000:165)

King Rugmamgada is shocked, and becomes angry.

> Alas! O wicked one! How can you make such hideous demands?
> Given up such cruelty and state what you want. (Ibid.)

Mohini responds:

> If both father and mother freely do (as I have asked) without
>   shedding a single tear,
> Then you may observe (the rites) without hindrance. (ibid)

King Rugmamgada's test of devotion to Vishnu means that he has no choice but to cut off his son's head as Mohini demands. The climactic, highly dramatic scene[15] of the play-in-production is one in which the senior actor playing the role of King Rugmamgada enacts his inner conflict between three emotions: anger at Mohini for her demand to cut off his son's head; pathos at the potential loss of his only son and heir to the throne; and the heroic recognition that he cannot transgress a vow he has taken, that is, as a king he *must* uphold the truth by cutting off his son's head. Throughout the scene his heroic duty is represented by the sword he holds in his hand – a symbol of kingly power and authority.

Kathakali's approach to psychophysical acting is clearly and simply demonstrated when a master actor, such as Kalamandalam Gopi, plays the role of Rugmamgada in this scene (Figures 2.8, 1.2). The dramatic and performative focus is on Rugmamgada's mental state of torment – an excruciating roller-coaster ride as Rugmamgada attempts over and again to eradicate both the 'fear' he has at having to execute his duty and the tremendous 'pathos' he feels over the forthcoming death of his son at his own hand. Rugmamgada attempts to summon up the heroic courage necessary to do his duty. As a king, he must erase this personal 'fear' and personal anguish, and regain the mental equilibrium and 'mental power' necessary to sacrifice his son.

But just as he raises the sword and is about to 'cut the boy's neck and maintain the good fame of our dynasty,' he loses his inner resolve when

Figure 2.8 Kalamandalam Gopi Asan in a performance of *Rugmamgadacaritam*. Rugmamgada sits in a state of disbelief over what has been asked of him. (Photo by Phillip B. Zarrilli)

he sees the boy lying on his mother's lap before him, drops the sword, and falls to the ground, fainting. This is anything but 'heroic' behavior; however, it makes tremendous (melo)drama. Desperate, Rugmamgada turns to Lord Vishnu, and demands that Vishnu provide him with the 'courage to sacrifice my son, thus protecting the truth, in order to maintain the good fame of our dynasty.' For *kathakali* connoisseurs in the audience, this particular moment in the performance is the highlight when the actor sequentially enacts in quick succession the three conflicting states of being/doing which have produced Rugmamgada's mental confusion and inability to act. The actor moves deftly from a full, psychophysical embodiment of anger as he gazes, eyes blazing, at Mohini, to pathos as he looks at his son, to the heroic as he looks to and takes courage from his sword. Each of these immediate changes from one 'emotional' state to another is achieved through the circulation/ manipulation of the *vayu* – that which fully animates/activates the actor's bodymind and produces *bhava* – each state of being-doing.

Finally, in a moment of realization of what is demanded of him in the moment to fulfill his overriding duty, Rugmamgada leans forward, loosening his long hair, and draws its strands to either side of his head. As he raises himself up, Rugmamgada's eyes are wide open, revealing the fact that he has now entered a fourth state of being/doing – 'fury' (*raudra*). In this transformative state (see Figure 1.2), he has transcended his personal emotional confusion and reached a state beyond fear in which he *will* be able to cut off his son's head. It is only in this state that he can announce:

I have no fear. What you see with your naked eye is perishable. The truth is the only thing that is imperishable. Therefore, now what should I do? Cut the boy's neck and protect the truth itself! (2000:168)

In this transformed state, just as Rugmamgada lifts his sword to 'sacrifice' his son as required, Vishnu intervenes and reveals to Rugmamgada the fact that Lord Brahma had sent Mohini to test his devotion.

Returning to Usha Nangyar's instructions to Gitanjali with which we began this chapter, it should by now be clear what Usha meant for the actor to 'breathe through the eyes'. By undergoing extensive, in-depth psychophysical training, the inner breath/wind is circulated throughout the actor's body and allows the actor to fully inhabit and embody each state of being-doing – such as Rugmamgada's transformative state of 'fury'. This is especially manifest in the actor's use of his eyes and facial expressions; however, the actor's entire bodymind from the soles of his feet through the tips of his fingers fully engages each expressive state and each 'image' in one's acting score. The beginning point is never analysis, but rather embodied actualization. The actor's complete engagement in psychophysically engaging these states – of 'breathing through the eyes' – exemplifies the embodied imagination at work.

Psychophysical acting in contemporary Indian performance

During the nineteenth century the British brought Western drama and theatrical practices such as the use of the proscenium stage to India along with English education and financial/industrial practices.[16] The arrival of English drama in India was part of the expansion of the British empire via the activities of the British East India Company – at first in the three cities where the company established its bases, that is, Kolkata (Calcutta), Mumbai (Bombay), and Chennai (Madras). The earliest theatrical activity was by the British for the British.

By the mid-to-late nineteenth century English plays were being translated into Indian languages and Indian language dramas were written and performed by amateur Indian actors for Indian audiences. But as Erin Mee explains,

> the spread of English drama was part of colonizing Indian culture; it was designed not only to shape artistic activity but to impose on Indians a way of understanding and operating in the world and to assert colonial cultural superiority. (2008:1)

In response to this process of colonization, from the late nineteenth through the mid-twentieth century, there ensued a lengthy period of political struggle for social reform and Indian Independence (achieved in 1947). Throughout this period Indian reformers wrote and produced a wide variety of modern text-based dramas that promoted social and/or political reform and even revolution.[17] The use of drama techniques for social reform and educational purposes has remained an extremely important part of contemporary theatre practice in India to the present.[18]

The 'Roots' movement: a return to indigenous Indian models and psychophysical practices

The models for the vast majority of the very early modern Indian plays and productions were Western; therefore, processes of acting these modern dramas were usually not informed by the types of indigenous Indian psychophysical principles and techniques discussed earlier in this chapter. Indeed, during the late nineteenth and very early twentieth century many of the traditional genres of Indian performance were looked down upon by English-educated Indians. Western sports were preferred over indigenous practices like yoga. In contrast to Western models of text-based spoken drama, *kathakali* was sometimes called a 'dumb-show'.

This began to change in the post-Independence period when – in response to the dominance of Western models guiding the writing and producing of modern drama, theatrical practice, and aesthetics – a number of contemporary Indian theatre artists searched for indigenous paradigms, techniques, and stories that could create distinctively 'Indian' modes of contemporary theatre. As Erin Mee reports in her book-length study of this movement, *Theatre of Roots: Redirecting the Modern Indian Theatre*, these impulses

> became known as the theatre of roots movement – a post-Independence effort to decolonize the aesthetics of modern Indian theatre by challenging the visual practices, performer-spectator relationships, dramaturgical structures and aesthetic goals of colonial performance. (2008:5)

Three of the most important figures in this movement were the playwright/actor, Girish Karnad (b. 1938) of Matheran (near Mumbai), playwright/director, Kavalam Narayana Panikkar (b. 1928) of Kerala, and Ratan Thiyam (b. 1948) of Manipur.[19]

Girish Karnad's seminal dramas such as *Hayavadana* (1971), *Nagamandala* (1988), and *Agni Mattu Male* (*The Fire and the Rain*, 1994) drew upon some elements of Western drama, but intermingled Indian structure, form, content, and aesthetic considerations. The main plot in *Hayavadana* was drawn from an eleventh-century collection of Sanskrit stories – *The Ocean of Stories (Katharsarisagara)* – but also drew elements from the German author Thomas Mann's *The Transposed Heads*. Karnad also drew upon elements of Karanataka's *Yaksagana* performance tradition since he was creating 'a hybrid theatre that reflects the complex subjectivities of post-Independence reality' (Mee 2008:142).

When Kavalam Panikkar began working in theatre he wanted to create a theatre that was a distinctively Indian form of 'visual poetry [*drishya kavya*] – poetry for the eyes as well as the ears' (Mee 2001:6; see also Singleton 1997). For inspiration he turned to Sanskrit theatre and drama and numerous indigenous Kerala performance traditions that he had experienced since childhood – vocal music (chanting of the Vedas and the unique Sopanam style of singing), and the psychophysical techniques and systems discussed earlier in this chapter (*kalarippayattu, kathakali, kutiyattam,* as well as *Mohiniattam* [Kerala's dance tradition performed by women]). When he established his company, SOPANAM, Panikkar wanted his actors to be fully trained in *sarirabhinaya* – acting with/through their entire bodies; therefore, early in the company's history, Panikkar had members of the company train in *kalarippayattu* with Gurukkal Govindankutty Nayar of the CVN Kalari, Thiruvananthapuram.[20]

A second highly visible and important contemporary theatre director to have made extensive use of indigenous regional traditions in creating his unique theatre aesthetic is Ratan Thiyam of Manipur. When he established his cooperative ensemble – the Chorus Repertory Theatre – Thiyam began to make extensive use of a variety of distinctive local Meitei arts to train his acting ensemble – traditional forms of dance (Pung-cholum and Raslila), storytelling (Wari leeba), and the martial art, *thang-ta*. Similar to the way in which *kalarippayattu* provides a complete training of the individual's bodymind, *thang-ta* practitioners 'learn to activate and use each and every body part' as they simultaneously develop an 'inner awareness' in which they constantly adjust and readjust 'energy and body movement...rather than sight' (Mee 2008:256).

The rediscovery of the value of indigenous Indian psychophysical principles of embodiment through traditional systems of training led India's major actor training institutions such as the National School of Drama in New Delhi (founded in 1958 and originally named the Asian Dramatic Institute at Delhi; renamed NSD in 1962 when Ebrahim Alkazi became the Director) (Chandradasan 2010:46) and the Calicut School of Drama (Trissur, Kerala) to eventually introduce traditional genres of performance (*kathakali, yaksagana, kutiyattam*) and/or practice of yoga and martial arts like *kalarippayattu* into their curricula alongside their originally almost exclusive use of Western modes of acting, voice, and movement to train contemporary Indian actors.[21] However, too often there has not been an attempt to integrate the elements and principles of these disparate practices into a clear, practical, and coherent methodology through which it is clear to acting students precisely how to apply what they are learning to specific dramaturgies whether Indian, Western, or hybrid.[22]

The 'roots' movement has not been restricted to contemporary theatre practice. Among contemporary Indian choreographers, Chandralekha (1928–2006) was the first major dancer/choreographer to utilize yoga and *kalarippayattu* training as she reinvented *bharatanatyam* – the 'classical' form of dance practised in the South Indian state of Tamil Nadu – for the contemporary proscenium stage. Chandralekha began to take into her company young men who were highly accomplished *kalarippayattu* practitioners. Given their years of training in *kalaripayattu,* they were easily assimilated into Chandralekha's company and choreography – some of which used *kalarippayattu* sequences such as the salutation with the body known as *vanakkam* as part of the choreography. When the *kalarippayattu* practitioners joined Chandralekha's company the entire group began to use yoga and *kalarippayattu* as their basic psychophysical training.[23]

Performers trained in traditional psychophysical disciplines

In the final section of this chapter, I focus on an exciting, relatively recent development. Rather than examine institutions and companies, we explore a younger generation of individual actors, dancers, and performance makers who, having been trained in-depth in traditional psychophysical disciplines such as *bharatanatyam*, *kathakali*, et cetera, have expanded their artistry and performance vocabulary beyond the traditional genres in which they originally trained. As noted in Chapter 1, arguably the best known among internationally recognized theatre actors who originally trained in a traditional Asian performing art before becoming a well-known contemporary stage actor is Yoshi Oida – a long-time member of Peter Brook's company based in Paris.

This younger generation of Indian performers began their training during the 1970s/80s. They have brought the elements, principles, and techniques of their traditional psychophysical trainings into an encounter with alternative, new forms of theatre and performance. For example, Navtej Johar originally trained as a *bharatanatyam* dancer at Rukmini Arundale's, Kalakshetra (Chennai), and with Leela Samson at the Shriram Bharatiya Kala Kendra (New Delhi). Johar is also a long-time student and practitioner of yoga, having trained in Patanjali yoga at the Krishnamacharya Yoga Mandiram (Chennai), under the guidance of Sri T. K. V. Desikachar. He began teaching yoga in 1985 and in his teaching today freely merges yoga postures (*asana*), breathing exercises (*pranayama*), visualization, mediation and Vedic chanting.

As a dancer Johar has performed at venues throughout the world, and has worked with a number of well-known international companies and choreographers – The Bill T. Jones/Arnie Zane Co., The Chandralekha Group, Yoshiko Chuma, the New York City Opera, among many others. Johar's choreographic work includes solo and ensemble works – both 'classical' *bharatanatyam* as well as contemporary performance pieces, street theatre, performance-installations, site-specific events, musicals, and spectacles. One particularly striking piece of solo performance is 'Never Failed Me Yet' (1999) which clearly makes use of Johar's extraordinary ability to inhabit both inner and outer worlds of performance.

As a final example I will discuss the work of Maya Krishna Rao who creates her contemporary work out of her years of training and performance of *kathakali,* her interaction with a wide variety of contemporary approaches to performance making, and most recently her encounter with new media. Trained at the International Centre for Kathakali in New Delhi from a young age beginning in 1961, Maya Krishna Rao learned *kathakali* from such excellent traditional masters as Guru Madhava Panikkar who came to the New Delhi Centre on its creation in 1960 (see Zarrilli 1984:304–8). These master teachers introduced Maya Krishna Rao to *kathakali*, not through the female roles, but rather through training her in the strong male roles, providing her with a firm foundation in the 'strong' (*tandava*) aspects of playing *kathakali* characters such as the demon-king Ravana. Only later in her training did she begin to learn and discover the joys of the repertory's female roles. Throughout her years of performance and teaching, often at the National School of Drama in New Delhi, Maya Krishna Rao's work has been inspired by and based on her *kathakali* training.

During her career as a performer and performance-maker, Rao's work has ranged from performing traditional *kathakali* to highly political street theatre performances focusing in particular on women's issues in India, to a growing repertoire of solo performances as well as stand-up comedy, to her work in theatre-in-education. Manifest in all her performance work are the deep psychophysical skills and engagement of the imagination that originate in her deep, long-term *kathakali* training.

One example of her creative application of her psychophysical training in *kathakali* to her contemporary performance work is her solo performance, *Khol Do*, first performed in 1993 (see Figure 1.3). Inspired by the short story by Saadat Hasan Manto, in a programme note Rao explains the context which led to her adaptation of the story for performance:

> *Khol Do* is set in the riots that ended the division of India and the creation of a new state, Pakistan. Millions left their homes to cross the new border to make a new home. Sirajuddin was one such who left India and traveled by train to Lahore [in what became Pakistan]. By the time he got off, he was nearly unconscious. For days he sat on the platform staring at the dusky sky. Where was his daughter Sakina? When had he got parted from her? He could only remember the running crowd and Sakina's *dupatta* or veil, falling to the ground. When he turned to pick it up she had urged yelling in the melee, 'Don't bother with it.' In the refugee camp, the heavily armed eight young male volunteers had been solicitous. 'If Sakina is alive we will find her for you,' they had said reassuringly. How was old Sirajuddin to know they had already found her but they were not through with her, yet? (Rao 1999)

While inspired by this story, her performance – the first of a series of solo performances she began to create in 1993 – is neither an exercise in storytelling nor a *kathakali*-style enactment of the story. In this sense it is *not kathakali* per se. Rao's work is a radical departure from traditional *kathakali* or experiments done in '*kathakali* style'. In an interview Maya Rao explains how she has been 'looking for a physical language, where every action may set off different signals of experience. The eventual form is not *kathakali,* yet it is inspired by it' (interview, 1999). Maya Krishna Rao's performance is an hour-long unrelenting, forcefully embodied physicalization that communicates through her bodymind the complete and unrelenting pathos and terror of the experience of dislocation. It is not a literal telling of this horrific story, but rather a suggestive/performative embodiment of elements that communicates the violence and horror of this experience.

As part of *Khol Do*, Rao occasionally uses specific *kathakali* gestures facial expressions, and choreographic elements, but these are woven into the fabric of this totally psychophysical performance score developed out of a lengthy process of improvisation and devising. During the creative process of devising the performance, Rao

> kept trying physical actions to generate that range of thought and emotions that are part of the atmosphere of the story. The result is, single gestures may have no particular meaning, but resonances that create multiple meanings. (Rao 1999)

At the core of her creative process are *kathakali*'s interior modes of acting – the total engagement of her bodymind through the breath/ energy in physicalization of specific states/tasks/actions, and thereby the engagement of her embodied imagination in the present moment of performance as she embodies each image/action in her score. Her process in one intended to discover how 'to shift dance energy to a moment in a person's life when words are not being used to signal the tradition' (Rao 1999) – an approach to creation that is psychophysical, not psychological.

Khol Do was created by Rao as a member of the theatre group, Vismaya. Founded in 1993 under the Chairpersonship of the late Shri P. N. Haksar, Vismaya draws upon India's diverse traditions of dance, music, literature. and the other arts to create new forms of theatre, and in using the arts as a means of education. The company's work has increasingly incorporated elements of live camera feed and multi-media design by Amitesh Grover. The company's productions include *The Job* based on Bertolt Brecht's story (1997), *Rainmaker* (1998), *The Four Wheel Drive* (comedy, 1998), *Departures* (1999), *A Deep Fried Jam* (2002), *Lady MacBeth Revisited* (2010), *The Non-Stop Food-Clothes-Feel Good Show* (comedy, 2011), and *Ravanama* (2011).

Performed in its most recent version as part of the 2010 Bharat Rang Mahotsav Festival, New Delhi, *Lady MacBeth Revisited*, one day, in the midst of rehearsals, *kathakali* encountered Shakespeare in the form of the demon-king Ravana. As Rao explains in a programme note,

> Ravana entered...probably to meet his kindred spirit, Lady M. Yes, in many ways these two seem alike – both, often, have very little notion of the consequences of their actions. And so, to honor both, I have used a sequence of *mudras* and the music with it from a celebrated Ravana piece of a *kathakali* play. They seemed just right for Lady Macbeth as well. (2010:157)

And in Rao's work stand-up comedy also meets *kathakali* in that Rao's larger than life caricatures – such as her send up of an American-returned non-resident-Indian woman – are fully embodied through her training in the semi-comic near caricatures of female demonesses such as Simhika as performed in the *kathakali* repertoire (see Zarrilli 2000, *The Killing of Kirmmira*). What is significant about Rao's work is that 'even though she does not use the code of *kathakali*, she is clearly influenced by the principles of the form' (2010:156) and the deep, intensive psychophysical engagement of her inner/imaginative life in acting process which is produced by years of *kathakali* training. In Rao's new forms of artistry, *kathakali* is constantly present, but remains in the background. This is intercultural/intracultural work in the most fundamental sense – an exploration of the meeting-ground between her own Indian content/ traditions/social-realities and ideas/forms/realities experienced in her cosmopolitan education both within India and in the UK where she took an MA in Theatre at Leeds University.

In a recent talk, Rao described how her process has been one of 'preparing the inner work with the breath', that is, how she utilizes quick shifts of breath to create sharp juxtapositions between 'the small and the big' in a performance score, or when she utilizes a long-sustained inhalation or exhalation to breathe into and sustain an action (Rao 2012). This subtle but central use of *kathakali* points to how traditional modes of psychophysical training provide the individual actor/performer with a process that addresses simultaneously both the subtle, interior processes of working with 'energy' as it 'fills out' each action in a performance score, the full engagement of a performer's imagination in the moment of playing, and the ability to design and shape a performance score through use of the entire body.

The diverse body of work being created today by traditionally trained contemporary performers such as Johar and Rao are helping to change the complexion of the Indian performance scene today. Crucially for such performers, they have spent a significant period of time immersing themselves in one or more traditional modes of psychophysical training which have provided them with a solid foundation for their ever-evolving creative work.[24]

Concluding discussion

In this chapter I have focused attention on the underlying psychophysical paradigms, processes, and practices which inform the traditional embodied acting practices of Kerala, and which inform the work of an increasing number of contemporary Indian performers and theatre-makers. I have focused in particular on articulating and explaining the paradigm and process through which the *kutiyattam* actor 'breathes through the eyes' as she engages and activates her entire bodymind in performance. Beyond India itself, the influence and impact of Indian paradigms of psychophysical practice discussed here have been evident in the influence of yoga on Stanislavsky (Chapter 4), in Jerzy Grotowski's ideal vision of the actor after travelling to Kerala and seeing *kathakali* actor training and performance (Chapter 5), and in the continuing development of alternative modes of pre-performative training for today's performer such as my own process of psychophysical actor training through Asian martial arts and yoga (Zarrilli 2009).

To conclude this chapter, I return to Padmanabhan Nayar's description of how the actor ideally becomes a 'musician inside'. Through extensive training and on-stage experience as the actor is psychophysically awakened inside and out, and comes to engage each image/action within his score with a deep, yogic, psychophysical connection through the circulation of *prana-vayu*, he becomes a 'musician inside'. Just as the original sounding of the Sanskrit *'aum'* 'vibrates' the universe, so ideally at a micro level within the actor experiences an inner 'vibration' when he fills out each image/action in his score. Ideally the actor 'plays' the psychophysical score of each role, as he is 'played' by that score. If the actor plays the 'right note inside, then the *bhava* comes out from the inside … Then only will the movement be according to the character' (Padmanabhan Nayar interview). We see this inner musician at work in Rao and Johar's contemporary experiments as they 'play' their inner life in new ways with new forms of performance.

Having focused much of our attention in this chapter on embodied practice and the 'inner' animation of the actor and having only touched briefly on the *kutiyattam* actor's process of vocalization/sounding in India, I begin Chapter 3 with a discussion of the psychophysical dimensions of vibration/vocalization at the heart of the Japanese *nō* actor's process, and open out from voicing to embodiment, phenomenon, and process.

Notes

1. For readers unfamiliar with the genres of theatre and martial arts discussed in this chapter – *kutiyattam, kathakali, bharatanatyam,* and *kalarippayattu* – or with the contemporary work of Kavanalam Narayana Panikkar or Ratan Thiyam, it is highly recommended that you complete a search of YouTube for current videos that might be viewed. As always on YouTube, some of the performances posted will be of excellent quality, while others may be of poor quality.

2. Gitanjali Kolanad is a well-known *bharatanatyam* dancer-choreographer who trained at Kalakshetra in Chennai. She and the author were researching, adapting, and co-creating a new solo *bharatanatyam* dance-theatre performance based on A. K. Ramanujan's translation of the traditional tale, 'The Flowering Tree.' The performance premiered in Chennai and Toronto in 2004.

3. Similar to other Asian cultures, the martial arts of South Asia were historically diverse and regionally specific. We focus here on *kalarippayattu* of Kerala. Other extant Indian martial arts still practised today include, among others, *thang-ta* (Manipur), *ati-tata* (also known as *ati-murai*, *varma-ati*, and (incorrectly) as southern style *kalarippayattu* [Tamil Nadu]); *silambam* (Tamil Nadu); and Indian wrestling (throughout North India).

4. This master requested anonymity.

5. For further information on the history and diversity of classical yoga practices and philosophy, see Flood (1996:75–102), Varenne (1976), Filliozat (1991), Feuerstein (1980), and White's exhaustive study of siddha yoga traditions in medieval India (1996). For the best study of modern yoga see de Michelis (2005).

6. Although we are focusing in this chapter on yoga philosophy in particular, as Lewis Rowell explains, it is important to note that that all six systems of Indian philosophy 'stress that which is latent – pure potential, dormant energy, an infinite well of subtle life force – whether conceived as the primal waters, the reservoir of vital air situated at the center of the human body, or the continuous vibration of all creation' (1993:29).

7. Filliozat traces both the organic sense of breath and the association between wind and breath from the period of the Vedas through the classical Ayurveda of Susruta and Caraka and the psychophysiology of yoga. As early as the Vedas breath (*prana*) and wind (*vayu* or *vata,* from Indo-Iranian pre-history 'the principle of activity') were assimilated to each other (1964:184–185). The technical vocabulary of the Vedic texts was later developed into a full 'system of pneumatic cosmo-physiology' in which the animating power of wind took the shape of breath or Atman (ibid.:65–66). The *Atharvaveda* affirmed the identity of breath and wind: 'it is the wind which is called the breath; it is on the breath that all that was and all this is, all is based' (ibid.:64–65).

8. A fundamental assumption of Indian thought is the Upanishadic statement, *tat tvam asi,* 'you are that' (*Chandogya Upanisad* 6.1 6:12–13). Indian philosophy, cosmology, and everyday life are played out against the underlying assumption that one might 'become one with'. Rather than dualities, it reflects the fact that microcosm and macrocosm, self and universe, subject and object are not set against one another, but are correlative.

9. See Zarrilli (2000) for a complete account of *kathakali* dance-drama texts and translations of four plays from the repertory.

10. For a complete description of all the exercises and training summarized here, see Zarrilli (1984:107–143).

11. When *kathakali* began to emerge as a distinctive genre of performance in Kerala under the patronage of rulers of small principalities, its first performers were Nayars trained in the traditional Kerala martial art, *kalarippayattu*. These *kalarippayattu*-trained Nayars were pledged to serve their ruler/patron. At first their annual training would have simply been their

traditional, rigorous *kalarippayattu* training. As different styles of *kathakali* developed, the training evolved from *kalarippayattu*'s preliminary body-training into a distinctive form of *kathakali* training based on the earlier *kalarippayattu*. For further information see Zarrilli (2000:19ff).

12. This deep, inner, psychophysiological connection to the 'root of the navel' (*nabhi mula)* is a commonplace assumption in *kalarippayattu* practice. As Mohammedunni Gurukkal explained about the performance of breath exercises, when performed correctly, 'your mind is simply on what you are doing. There is a grip or power at the base of the navel (*nabhi mula*) at the full point of inhalation.' During vigorous practice sustained breathing is maintained so that there is a constant 'gripping' (*piduttam*) which comes naturally to the lower abdomen. This is where the traditional loin cloth (*kacca; lengoti*) is securely wrapped and tied to 'hold in' the life-force.

13. See Zarrilli (2000, Chapter 8, pp. 159–174) for a translation of *King Rugmamgada's Law* by V.R. Prabodhachandran Nayar, M.P. Sankaran Namboodiri, and Phillip B. Zarrilli and for more detailed commentary. The play is based on the story of King Rugmamgada found in Chapter 21 of the *Padma Purana*.

14. Many plays still in the active repertory have been edited to shorten them to three to four hour performances. It is commonplace for an all-night performance today to include three shortened plays focusing on scenes of most interest to connoisseurs. Since 1930 when the best-known Malayali poet, Mahakavi Vallathol Narayana Menon, founded the now well-known Kerala State Arts School (Kerala Kalamandalam), *kathakali* has been adapted both by practitioners from within the tradition and by artists and entrepreneurs from without. These experiments have included *kathakali* for tourist audiences, writing and staging new plays based on traditional epic/puranic sources, transforming *kathakali* techniques and choreography into modern forms of Indian stage dance and/or dance-drama, and writing and staging new plays based on non-traditional sources and/or current events, such as the 1987 leftist production of *People's Victory* which pitted the personified hero (World Conscience) against the personified villain (Imperialism). Non-Hindu myths or non-Indian plays have also been adapted for *kathakali* style productions, such as the stories of Mary Magdalene, the Buddha, Faust, as well as the *Iliad* and *King Lear*.

15. This scene is actually a performative 'interpolation' or elaboration on the dramatic text invented by *kathakali* actors at some point in the history of the play's production. What distinguishes such interpolations from the original dramatic text is that they are not sung, but simply enacted without repetition by the actor or actors, through action and hand gestures.

16. It is beyond the scope of this chapter to provide a complete history of the emergence of contemporary Indian theatre. See Chatterjee (2007), Dharwadkar (2005), Mee (2008), Solomon (1994, 2004), and Chapter 12 in Richmond, Swann, and Zarrilli (1990). For a diverse collection of contemporary Indian plays in English translation see Mee, editor (2001).

17. For one historical example see Zarrilli (2006:391–399) and Bhaasi, T. (1996).

18. For two of many examples, see Eugene van Erven (1992:114–139) and Zachariah and Sooryamoorthy about the work of Kerala Sastra Sahitya Parishad (KSSP) which uses drama as one of its primary tools for education (1994).

19. Mee provides detailed information in a chapter about the practices of Panikkar (Chapter 2), Karnad (Chapter 3), and Thiyam (Chapter 5) in the context of the 'roots' movement.

20. The author regularly trained and practised *kalarippayattu* with Sopanam actors at the CVN Kalari during the 1980s.

21. See Chandradasan (2010) for a discussion of the shift in training at NSD. While Ebrahim Alkazi was still Director of the National School of Drama during the 1970s, the author introduced students and staff at the NSD to *kalarippayattu* and its potential for training contemporary actors.

22. See my *Psychophysical Acting* (2009) for a book-length discussion of these issues and one attempt at integration.

23. For a book-length account of Chandralekha's life and choreography, see Bharucha (1995).

24. Yet another model is that provided by Sajeev Purushothama Kurup. Kurup originally trained for six years as a *kathakali* dance-drama actor-dancer. After several years of professional performance experience in Kerala within the *kathakali* tradition, he decided to seek out new forms of training so that he could expand beyond traditional *kathakali* and enter into contemporary performance practice. Sajeev was admitted to the Theatre Training Research Programme (now called the Intercultural Theatre Institute or ITI) in Singapore and undertook an intensive three-year professional actor training programme which combines traditional Asian psychophysical disciplines of training (*jingxi, noh, wayang won, kutiyattam*) with contemporary Western approaches to acting, movement, and voice.

3 Psychophysical Acting in Japan

Phillip B. Zarrilli

[The actor] attunes [himself] with his 'activating force' [*ch'i/qi/ki*] [in order to establish and maintain his tone center], then closing his eyes and inhaling, he vocalizes. [Zeami (Hada no Motokiyo, 1363–1443), *Kakyō* ('A Mirror of the Flower' [written in 1424], Nearman trans. 1982a:343]

Introduction

In Chapter 2, I examined how key principles such as *prana-vayu* ('vital breath' or 'energy') and the paradigm of the subtle body of yoga inform acting and the experience of acting as embodied and understood in India. As noted in the epigraph above, in Japan and throughout East Asia (China/Korea), a similar animating principle – *ki* ('activating force'; in Chinese *qi* [*ch'i*]) – is central to understanding embodied practices such as acting/vocalization, medicine (acupuncture), and the martial arts. In Chapter 2 I also examined the underlying aesthetic (*bhava/rasa*) paradigm which informs Indian acting from the perspectives of both actor and audience. In this chapter I examine selected key principles, metaphors, aesthetic principles, and psychophysical processes informing acting in Japan.

This chapter begins with a brief overview (see boxed text below) of what today is called *nō* theatre and the closely allied tradition of short, humorous plays, *kyōgen*, performed between *nō* dramas.[1] I focus on *nō* for two reasons: (1) embedded in the practice of *nō* are distinctly Japanese/East Asian psychophysical principles which continue to inform contemporary approaches to Japanese acting, and (2) Zeami, one of its founders, authored a series of acting treatises in which he elaborates the practical and aesthetic psychophysical 'secrets' of the actor, and which, as we shall see, collectively constitute the first 'phenomenology of acting' (Nearman 1978:300) still highly relevant to actors today.

In the fourteenth and early fifteenth centuries, *nō* (with *kyōgen*) were known as *sarugaku-nō* ('monkey music'). We begin our discussion of *nō* with an historical examination of how this genre of performance began to develop and evolve under the leadership of Kan'ami (1333–84) and his son Zeami (1363–1443) from early forms of popular entertainment into what eventually became a refined, courtly genre of performance that is still performed today – albeit in some ways very different from fourteenth/fifteenth century performances. Recognizing that *nō* theatre as performed today has changed substantially from *sarugaku-nō* as performed in the late fourteenth century, the primary discussion and analysis of *nō* acting as a psychophysical process, past and present, is written as a dialogue between Zeami's treatises with special reference to *Kakyō* ('A Mirror of the Flower'), contemporary accounts/reflections by professional Japanese *nō* actors and others with in-depth *nō* training, and scholarly accounts of selected key elements, principles, and metaphors that inform, shape, and animate the embodied psychophysical practices of the of *nō* actor such as *keiko* ('training'), *shugyō* ('cultivation'), *ki* ('activating force'), *onkan* ('tonal [or vibratory] feeling'), *ma* (interval in space and time), *mushin* ('no-mind'), *yūgen* ('elegance and grace' or that which '"lies beneath the surface"' [Hare 2008:472]).

Following the discussion of acting in the *nō* tradition, I examine the principles and psychophysical practices of three post-World War II approaches to embodiment in performance. I provide an in-depth account of *butoh* ('dance of darkness') and very brief summary discussions of the actor training and theatre practice of Suzuki Tadashi and 'theatre of quietude' (Boyd 2006) as practised by Ōta Shōgo.[2] All three manifest the tensions between Westernization and modernization in post-World War II Japan. All three are intra-cultural as well as intercultural in that each has interacted with and/or responded in some way to the principles/practices of 'traditional' Japanese performance whether *nō* or the popular, flamboyant artistry of *kabuki* actors, as well as to Western influences, literary/philosophical sources, content, music, and/or genres of performance.

A brief introduction to contemporary nō and kyōgen performance

Nō and *kyōgen* exist today as two distinct, but inextricably linked performing arts that are known together in Japan as *nōgaku*. Since the early evolution and development of *sarugaku-nō* by Kan'ami and Zeami in the late fourteenth and early fifteenth centuries, *nō* and *kyōgen* continued to evolve until they separated, and then assumed something close to their present forms of performance during the Edo period (1603–1867). Dance and chanting came to assume primary roles in *nō* performance.[3] *Nō* dramas are traditionally performed by an all male ensemble of actor-dancers who specialize in each role-type, accompanied by musicians. The performance company includes:

- *shite*: actors who play the primary 'doer' or 'figure' that is the focus of a drama. *Shite* actors perform across a tremendous range of role types from youth to female roles of any age, and also play gods and demons. In many plays the lead *shite* actor plays one figure in the first part of the performance, and after a costume change performs what can be an extremely different figure in the second part of the play. For example, in a performance of the play, *Fujito,* the primary actor takes the role of a grieving/angry mother in the first part, and then appears as the spirit of her dead son in the second half. [See Figures 1.1 and 3.2 for examples of the female figure in Part I of *Hashitomo* and *Aoi no ue*.] *Shite* actors may also appear as the companion (*tsure*) to the *shite,* or appear as a member of the chorus (*jiutai*), act as an on-stage attendant (*koken*) or backstage assistant to the *shite.*
- *waki*: actors who play the secondary role or 'side-man', often a Buddhist priest. *Waki* actors also appear as the *waki-tsure* or companion to the *waki.*
- *kyōgen*: actors playing the roles of local commoners, and who also perform separate short, humorous, comic interludes traditionally performed between five *nō* dramas in a full day of performance.
- *hayashi*: the instrumental ensemble of four musicians accompanying a performance, including: a transverse flute (*nōkan* or *fue*) player and three drummers playing *shime-daiko* (stick drum), *ōtsuzumi* (hip-drum), and shoulder drum (*kotsuzumi*).
- *jiutai*: the chorus of six to eight *shite* actors who chorally chant specific sections of the dramatic text, sometimes in first person as the 'doer' or 'primary figure' (*shite*). Once the chorus enters before the beginning of a *nō* performance through a special small door upstage, they sit in *seiza* position – with legs folded under the thighs, resting the buttocks on the heels – to the audience's right throughout the performance.

The contemporary repertoire of *nō* plays includes approximately 240–250 dramas, mostly written during the Muromachi period. By the Edo period (1603–1867) the plays were organized into five types or categories defined by the *shite* role: god, warrior, women (most often young women or those at court), miscellaneous (various distraught souls, wandering spirits, or mothers whose children have died), and demons. Whatever the category of play, the texts are highly poetic and suggestive in their use of language. A programme of completely *nōgaku* during the Edo period came to include five *nō* dramas separated by four short *kyōgen* interludes, with the entire programme of five plays ordered to actualize the structural progression identified by Zeami as from

* *jo:* the 'preface', opening or initiation which is generally 'smooth and even' (Hare 2008:481),
* through *ha:* meaning to 'break', and indicating a shift or change of tone and/or structure,
* to *kyū:* meaning 'fast', i.e., the culmination, conclusion, or 'the play's finale or climax' (Hare 2008:481).

A performance of a *nō* drama begins in silence. There is an accumulation or thickening. After the culmination/climax, there is again silence.

Today, a *nōgaku* programme usually includes only two *nō* dramas with one *kyōgen* interlude between them. Complete programmes of *kyōgen* without *nō* performances have also become popular.

In published English translation, *nō* dramas of approximately five to seven pages in length take approximately one hour to perform. Today's performances are considerably slower than during Zeami's life-time. The slowing-down of the overall tempo-rhythm of *nō* is one of the many changes that have developed over the past six centuries.

Exquisitely carved by specialist mask-makers from blocks of cypress wood, *nō*'s highly expressive masks are utilized for many but not all *shite* roles (Figure 1.1; 3.2; 3.3). Occasionally if a *tsure* role is female, the actor also wears a mask. Masks are especially used for nonhuman (demons, gods, animals) roles, female roles, young males (under twenty), and old men (over forty). Male *shite* roles in their twenties through forties do not wear masks. The female masks in particular are noted for being highly expressive of key emotional states a character may experience such as the fury of the Hannya-*nō* mask (Figure 3.3).

Today's elaborate, rich, brocaded silk costumes are an important part of contemporary *nō,* adopted beginning in the late sixteenth century (Figures 3.1; 3.2).

[To see images of Japanese *nō* stages, visit on-line sources as follows: (1) http://www.the-noh.com/en/plays/photostory/ps_006.html; (2) the outdoor *nō* stage at Chuson-Ji temple. Built in 1853 to replace the stage destroyed by fire in 1849 on commission of Date Yoshikuni, head of the Sendai clan. Performances of *nō* have been held since 1591, and continue to be performed at both the Spring and Autumn Fuijiwara Festivals. [Image accessed via: mw2.google.com/mw-panoramio/photos/medium/74618265.jpg]; (3) conduct a general 'google search' for 'noh theatre stage'.]

The relatively small stage (approximately 5.5 metres square) on which *nō* came to be performed evolved into a roofed pavilion constructed of Japanese cypress wood in an architectural style based on the *kagura* stages found in Shinto shrines. The main playing area is open on three sides. The four pillars supporting the roof of the pavilion above the main playing area are especially important for the orientation of the actor in performance, especially for the *shite* when wearing a mask which considerably limits sight. A narrow bridgeway (*hashigakari*) connects the 'green room' or 'mirror room' from which *waki* and *shite* actors enter the playing space. The floor of highly polished wood allows the actors to slide their feet on the floor. Beneath the floor are giant pots set at an angle which enhance the resonance of the wooden floor, especially when actors stamp while dancing. The entire stage is raised approximately three feet above the audience ground level. At the very back of the main playing area, a stylized, ancient pine tree is painted.

The 'school' system for organizing actors and musicians was formalized during the Edo period. Today there are five *shite* schools (Kanze, Hōshō, Komparu, Kongō, Kita), three *waki* schools, two for *kyōgen*, plus multiple schools for musicians. Each school has developed its own performance style and is headed by the *iemoto* who licenses and controls performance rights.

Nō performances usually take place after a single rehearsal; therefore, there is a sense of spontaneity and difference as each performance is a unique blend of the performance ensemble gathered for that specific performance. Prior to the rehearsal, and once scheduled for a performance, individual performers prepare chanting of the text, dances, and movement for a role on their own under the tutelage of a master within their lineage for the specific role they will play. Performance of specific major roles *may* only take place for particular *shite* actors *once in a lifetime*.

As *nō* developed during the generations following Zeami, he passed on the techniques and principles of his specific lineage to his successor, Zenchiku (1405–1468/70?). The direct 'influence' of Zeami and his treatises after Zenchiku's generation has been minimal. It was only during the lifetime of the infamous *nō* actor Kanze Hisao (1925–1978) that Zeami's treatises and their key principles began to be studied, critiqued, actively discussed and utilized by some up of today's *nō* actors (see Rath 2003).

Today, a large number of amateurs study *nō* chanting and dancing with master teachers from the traditional five schools, and attend professional performances often with their 'chanting books' in hand to follow the text during a performance. At certain stages in their training as amateurs they also commission their own performances.

Zeami and the development of sarugaku-nō

The religious, socio-cultural context

As a unique theatrical tradition, the sources that shaped *nō* include elements drawn from indigenous Japanese Shinto ritual and shamanic practices; a variety of earlier performance traditions; Japanese forms of Buddhist practice and its philosophical principles; key literary master-pieces such as *The Tale of Genji* (written by the court lady Murasaki Shikibu around 1000 CE, and often considered to be the world's first novel); and historical accounts of clan warfare such as chronicled in *The Tale of the Heike*. All these elements were adapted, transformed, and crafted by the creative genius of Kan'ami, Zeami, and their descendants. For example, when masks were adopted as part of the early development of *nō,* it was 'a practical move by performers, intended to increase the credibility of, and give poignancy to, their performances in the role of supernatural beings and ghosts' (Ortolani 1984:179). As the *nō* stage evolved, it began to be modelled on the architecture of Shinto shrines.

In order to understand both the development of *nō,* as well as Zeami's texts and the underlying psychophysical principles of acting practice assumed by those texts, I begin with a brief examination of the religious, cultural, historical milieu within which *sarugaku-nō* developed.

Shinto is an indigenous Japanese set of utilitarian ritual practices intended to harness the natural forces of the environment in which it is assumed that everything – trees, birds, seas, animals, mountains, wind and thunder, et cetera – has its own soul or spirit (*kami*). *Kami* are the natural energies and agents understood to animate matter and influence human behaviour, and are sometimes identified as gods or goddesses. Shinto-inspired forms of shamanistic propitiatory ceremonies and dances predate Buddhist and Chinese inspired forms of Japanese performance.

After Japan invaded Korea, from 370 CE Chinese literature and writing were introduced to the Japanese court by Korean scholars brought to educate the crown prince. Chinese literary, poetic, aesthetic, and religio-philosophical forms had a tremendous influence on the development of Japanese culture and performance. When Chinese Buddhism became the official religion of Japan during the mid-sixth century A.C.E., Chinese writing and culture became even more influential in Japan. Chinese Buddhism did not displace the earlier practices of Shintoism; rather, Buddhas and *kami* are often worshipped side by side. Interaction with China also brought the religious and philosophical influences of Confucianism and Taoism to Japan. Confucianism emphasizes that social harmony is maintained through hierarchical relationships in which a subordinate person is obedient and loyal to the higher-ranked person such as a husband, father, or older brother – a hierarchical legacy most evident when *nō* 'schools' were legislated in the Edo period. The influence of Taoism in Japan is seen in both the underlying principle of metaphysical balance of complimentary opposites (*yin-yang*), and the inclusion of Taoist practices into the structure of the state. One of the most significant Buddhist practices for the majority of Japanese became rituals honoring one's family ancestors, and one of the primary issues in *nō* dramas eventually became issues of the resolution of the pain or agony of restless, wandering spirits, both living and dead.

Along with Buddhism, Confucianism and Taoism, contact with Chinese culture in the sixth century brought the introduction of proto-theatrical court performances including several types of masked dance dramas such as *bugaku* and *gigaku* (mentioned in Chapter 1). The musical structure and terminology informing *gigaku* was to influence Zeami's thinking about *nō* chanting. Some *gigaku* and *bugaku* masks depicting warriors, gods, and semi-mythical beasts dating from as early as the Nara Period (710–84) may have influenced the design of some masks carved for *sarugaku-nō*.

Along with *dengaku* ('field music') and *sangaku* (a type of variety entertainment), *sarugaku* was one of several types of travelling entertainments popular throughout the country and whose troupes vied for affiliations with specific temple complexes and to curry favour with audiences at performances where multiple troupes performed. James Brandon explains how at that time 'the term *nō* probably indicated a plotted, dramatic performance within the repertory' of any of these three styles of performance (1997:94).

Kan'ami, Zeami, and the evolution of the Yamato style of sarugaku-nō

Kan'ami was head of a *sarugaku-nō* ('monkey music') troupe of actors that included his young son, Zeami. Their original home was in the countryside near the old ecclesiastical capital of Nara, and their company was one of four in Yamato Province in central Japan. Yamato style *sarugaku* troupes were best known at the time for their excellence at role-playing or dramatic imitation (*monomane*). In contrast, the performances of rival troupes from the region of Ōmi were noted for their 'elegant, romantic, formal, and largely visual beauty' – or *yūgen* (Hare 2008:492). By the twelfth century *yūgen* had become a key concept in the practice of Japanese poetry, 'designating a mysterious and dark profundity not apparent on the surface of a poem but crucial to its understanding' (Hare 2008:492), and came to have a major influence on the development of Zeami's artistry.[4]

In 1375 when Zeami was twelve years of age, after his father's troupe performed for the shogun Ashikaga Yoshimitsu (1305–1358), they were offered patronage north of their original home at Imagumano in Kyoto:

> As a result of winning Yoshimitsu's patronage, Kan'ami and Zeami broadened their base of activity from the temple grounds and the provincial circuit to the shogunal palace and mansions of elite audiences in the Kyoto capital. (Quinn 2005:29)

Kan'ami's troupe began to live at court, and under the leadership of Kan'ami and Zeami their specific lineage/troupe style of performing shifted towards incorporation of a more refined style that incorporated more elegant, Ōmi *yūgen* elements into their performances. Kan'ami's greatest innovation was the combination of popular mimetic drama for which his company was known, with new dance forms such as the *kusemai*, and for developing more refined forms of chant and dance within their style.[5]

Tom Hare describes how once at court the young Zeami would have been exposed to and absorbed

> *waka* poetics and arcana, Buddhist philosophical speculation, aesthetics, Pure Land devotionalism, myths and legends, Chinese anecdotes, a modicum of Confucian philosophy, views of the material world formed by Chinese rationalism, and so forth. (2008:4)

Part of Zeami's aesthetic and religious/philosophical education is attributed to the well-known court poet Nijō Yoshimoto who tutored the young man. In a letter written in 1376, Yoshimoto 'praises Zeami's *waka* and *renga* verses on the grounds that they have interesting artistic effects (*kakari*) and a style having *yūgen*' (Quinn 2005:30).

Among the diverse influences on Zeami's intellectual, aesthetic, and artistic development, there is no doubt that the Buddhism of the medieval period played a central role; however, overemphasis has been given to Zen Buddhism per se as an influence on Zeami and the development of *nō*.[6] As Royall Tyler has convincingly argued, the Buddhism to which Zeami was exposed in the medieval period, and within which *nō* acting and its repertory of plays first developed was the commonplace Buddhism of the period which was a highly syncretistic, pre-formal-school mix of Shinto/Buddhist beliefs and practices (1987).[7] Some scholars have argued that when Nijō Yoshimoto tutored Zeami at court, he also introduced him 'to the complex teachings of *Yuishiki* ("consciousness only") ... associated with the Hossō sect of Buddhism ... in the Kōfuku Temple, with which Kan'ami and Zeami had a long relationship' (Ortolani 2001:125). In 1384 after his father's death, at the young age of twenty-one, Zeami both assumed leadership of his troupe, and 'became a student/monk at the Fuganji, a Sōtō Zen temple' (Ortolani 2001:126).

As head of the family/troupe Zeami continued to refine the company's artistic practice and transform the social reality of formerly outcast actors. *Nō* came to be considered an elegant, refined, and philosophically self-reflexive set of artistic practices. Zeami was equally a great actor/performer, a renowned playwright authoring between thirty and forty plays (Hare 2008:1), an acting theorist steeped in the nuances of poetic and aesthetic theories of the time, a shrewd manager of a company of actors always with an eye on how he and his fellow actors had to constantly reinvent their practice of acting in order to attract and hold the attention of their contemporary audiences, and a teacher who authored twenty-one highly sophisticated treatises on the arts of acting and playwriting written over the course of forty years from his mid-career to the end of his life (see Quinn 2005:footnote 39, p. 329; Hare 2008:451–459).[8]

Shelly Fenno Quinn credits Zeami-the-playwright with originating what recent scholars describe as phantasmal (*mugen*) *nō* – dramas which in performance 'create a highly poetic, multisensory stage event that did not depend for its coherence on the representation of the story' but rather utilized 'poetry, music, and dance' to allude to a story whose primary figure (the *shite*) is already known to the audience (2005:118). In phantasmal dramas, Zeami was '"moving away from descriptions and representation"' to construct narratives that operated by suggestion and allusion (Quinn 2005:119).

Let us consider one play, *Aoi no ue (Lady Aoi*, c. fifteenth century as revised by Zeami) [Figures 3.1, 3.2, 3.3]. *Aoi no ue* was inspired by a chapter in *The Tale of Genji*. There are traces of early shamanic practices reflected in the play. As the performance begins, the audience sees an elaborate folded robe in the middle of a highly polished wooden-floor stage (Figure 3.1). The empty robe represents the prostrate figure of the mortally ill Princess Aoi, the pregnant wife of Prince Genji. She

Figure 3.1 Lady Aoi, exhausted by a vengeful spirit, takes the form of a *kosode* (a specific type of women's kimono) – lying on the floor in her state of exhaustion. The character holding a set of beads next to Lady Aoi is Teruhi – a shamaness, who by plucking her catalpa bow identifies and calls out the vengeful spirit.

Figure 3.2 Responding to the call of the catalpa bow played by the shamaness and her repetition of a *mantra*, the living spirit of the regal, beautiful, elegant, and noble, Lady Rokujō appears along the bridgeway played by the primary actor (*shite*) in the female Deigan mask.

Figure 3.3 In the second part of *The Lady Aoi*, the actor playing the elegant Lady Rokujō in the first part is revealed as the vengeful spirit of Lady Rokujō. Having covered her head with her outer garment, when uncovered she reveals her true nature in a Hannya-*nō* mask – women who have transformed into demonic form. Carved to capture both the sorrow and fury of a jealous woman, its features include open/angry eyes and an open, gaping mouth. The mask's name '*hannya*' is taken from the golden pigment used to paint the whites of the eyes. Notice the strands of hair across the hair line and forehead showing the disheveled state of mind of the figure. Here the mountain ascetic fights with and eventually pacifies the vengeful spirit by utilizing his prayer beads. As the play concludes, Lady Rokujō can now become a Buddha. (Figures 3.1, 3.2, 3.3: Three images from performances of *Aoi no Ue* (*Lady Aoi*) by Zeami. Photos 3.1, 3.2, 3.3 @ Toshiro Morita. By permission of the-noh.com. For a fuller set of photographs of *The Lady Aoi* in performance, visit http://www.the-noh.com/en/plays/photostory/ps_006. html. This excellent website offers copious information on *nō*, provides summaries and translations of a number of *nō* dramas, and sets of photographs of specific plays in performance.)

has been possessed by the angry, restless spirit of Lady Rokujō, Genji's former mistress, whose living spirit leaves her body when she sleeps. A Shintō shamaness known as a *miko* performs a ritual to call forth the spirit that is possessing Lady Aoi.[9] At the far end of the bridgeway (*hashigakari*), the curtain is lifted by stage attendants as from the green room emerges the spirit of Lady Rokujō, performed by a male actor in an exquisitely carved female mask (Figure 3.2). Lady Rokujō eventually reveals her identity:

> In this mortal world ephemeral as lightning,
> I should hate nobody,
> nor should my life be one of sorrow.
> When ever did my spirit begin to wander?
> Who do you think this person is
> who appears before you now
> drawn by the sound of the catalpa bow!
> I am the vengeful spirit of Lady Rokujō. (Goff 1991:135)

Since the shamaness only has sufficient power to call forth but not exorcise this invading spirit, a male Buddhist mountain priest (a 'warrior priest' or *yamabushi*) is summoned to perform the exorcism. In Figure 3.3 Lady Rokujō's true nature as a vengeful spirit is revealed when she appears in the Hannya-*nō* mask – a mask worn by women who have transformed into demonic form. The play concludes as the Buddhist mountain priest pacifies her vengeful spirit. Once pacified, the actors leave the stage in silence.

The period during which Kan'ami and Zeami both lived and developed *sarugaku nō* is generally known as the Muromachi period of Ashikaga rule (begun in 1336 continuing to 1573).[10] Although the company was taken into court patronage, Janet Goff describes how 'the Muromachi period as a whole can be summed up as a time of chronic warfare in which the chaos and destruction were offset by a remarkable burst of cultural activity' which included not only the development of *nō* but also of tea ceremony and flower arranging (Goff 1991:5). The vagaries and uncertainties of court patronage which first took Zeami into court patronage and produced *nō* are revealed in the fact that in 1434 when his patron-shogun died and was replaced by his successor, Yoshimochi, Zeami (then in his seventies) was banished to the island of Sado. In the end, Zeami was granted an amnesty in 1441.

Zeami's treatises or 'notes' on acting and performance

Quinn describes Zeami's treatises as constituting 'a nuanced and comprehensive phenomenology of the stage informed by a lifetime of artistic practice' (2005:1). Written to transmit the unique 'secrets' of the evolving art of acting he learned from his father as well as the discoveries he continued to make in his own experience as an actor and teacher, his texts cover key principles such as finding ways to continuously engage the interest of an audience; the rhythmic development of the actor's work both in a specific performance and in plays (*jo, ha, kyū*, 'introduction', 'intensification', and 'rapid close'); analysis of mask/character types with advice on how to play each; metaphysical reflection on the path of the actor; treatises on writing plays; and often complex discussions of aesthetic and psychophysical principles of the actor's art. Zeami's texts are often written in an 'elliptic style' and have a rich, 'technical vocabulary' with numerous Taoist, Confucian, and Buddhist references, allusions, or direct quotations found, especially in the treatises written later in Zeami's life (Nearman 1978:300–301).

As was common at the time, Zeami's twenty-one treatises were kept secret. They were written for transmission *only to those within the lineage of practice of the family's style of performance* in order to

- preserve the integrity of their insights and approach to actor training;
- maintain their edge over other companies as a successful company; and
- ensure that their lineage 'might attain [the] highest level of artistic realization'. (Nearman 1978:300).

When Zeami began to author his treatises, no similar texts existed within the lineage of Zeami's practice of *sarugaku-nō*. With the exception of his immediate successor, Komparu Zenchiku who authored his own set of treatises, 'nothing remotely equivalent appeared again' (Pinnington 1997:204).[11] As Noel Pinnington argues, Zeami's notes were probably modeled on collections of notes as *aides-memoires* within esoteric Buddhist traditions (1997:204). Within esoteric traditions, written notes were 'copied, collected, and passed down, and their possession was treated as proof of authority' (Pinnington 1997:204). Secret knowledge was to be passed on to heirs within one's lineage of practice. As a result, the treatises did not come to public attention until 1908 when Yoshida Tōgo discovered a trove of Zeami's texts which had come into the collection of the Matsunoya Library (Hare 2008:451) – published in 1909.

Tom Hare titled his recent translation of Zeami's treatises 'performance notes' – a recognition of the diverse nature of these often cryptic, elliptical, and difficult-to-decipher notes on the principles and practices of acting and dramatic writing (2008). The nature of the treatises as a series of notes is exemplified in the text known variously as *Fūshikwaden* or *Kadenshō* (*Transmitting the Flower Through Effects and Attitudes* or *Teachings on Style and the Flower*) which Zeami assembled as a series of notes on acting over a period of approximately twenty years. The full title above was probably only given after the first five sections of the text were gathered together in 1402 (Hare 2008:252).[12]

The constant goal of Zeami's well-trained actor 'was first of all to hold the interest of the audience by his performing' (Nearman 1978:332); therefore, all of Zeami's texts focus not on aesthetic appreciation but on psychophysical training, principles, problems actors face in performance, and the further artistic development of the actor in order to attain the highest, subtlest level of actualization of the actor. This ideal is fully expressed in Zeami's *Kyūi* ('A Pedagogical Guide for Teachers of Acting') written when Zeami was approximately 65 years old and probably after he had become a Zen monk (Nearman 1978:301). In the *Kyūi* Zeami describes nine different levels (*kurai*) of acting arranged into three groupings: the lower, middle, and upper levels. The lowest, most obvious level is associated with creating an appeal for the audience that is visually attractive, that is, where emphasis is on the 'concrete, physical, sensual aspects such as dancing, singing, costumes, et cetera …. [the] visible' elements of performance (Nearman 1978:304). The middle level is less obvious than the visual and is associated with hearing. The appeal at this middle level 'derives from a perception of relationships, such as the rhythm in singing and dance', that is, 'elements of form created by the deployment of the actor's energy, which transcend the simply material and physical aspects' (Nearman 1978:304). The upper three levels Zeami associates with the actor's ability to hold the spectator's attention with ever subtler modes of bodymind concentration, that is, the actor attains at the highest levels a type of consciousness that is 'not the analytical-conceptual intellect, but an open, perceptive awareness that has put aside critical functions in order to experience directly' (Nearman 1978:304).[13] At the very highest level of attainment, the actor's technique per se disappears or is burned away completely. Here, the actor creates an inexplicable state of wonder and astonishment in the audience. Zeami describes this as 'The Mark of the Miraculous Flower' where 'In Silla, at midnight, the sun is bright' – a level of accomplishment and mastery that 'transcends praise', is 'beyond … critical analysis and judgment', and where 'its external mark is No-Mark' (Nearman 1978:324).

Assumptions about practice (keiko), training and cultivation (shugyō)

Zeami assumes that for the *nō* actor to attain even the lowest of the middle levels of accomplishment as an artist, he must undergo assiduous, continuous in-depth psychophysical training (*keiko*). If one undergoes assiduous training whether in a martial art, tea ceremony, or *nō* under the guidance of a master teacher, it is assumed that there will be a progressive cultivation (*shugyō*), alteration, and refinement in the body-mind relationship which will be different from the normative, everyday body-mind relationship that existed prior to training. The neophyte will eventually go 'beyond the standards of normality in its everyday (ontic) sense', that is, 'cultivation means pursuing a way of life that is *more than* the average way of life' (Yuasa 1987:208).[14]

Similar in some ways to the process of transformation described in Chapter 2 within Indian psychophysical modes of training, in *nō* training one begins with the external forms of training and progresses from the outside 'inward' towards realization of an ever more subtle and refined bodymind relationship in practice. A different order and quality of bodymind relationship is 'cultivated' and arises through sustained training. The repertoire of movements constituting a specific mode of 'form' training is to be practised by 'using the whole body' (*karadagoto*) (Cox 2003:59). One's experience of the quality and nature of that relationship has the potential to change, and therefore one's relationship to what one does and the lived experience (*taiken*) of that process fundamentally changes.

> Buddhist methods of self-cultivation were based on a somatic philosophy in which there was no distinction between body and self. The Japanese word for body, *mi*, can also mean self or I and there is a saying which illustrates this: *mi o suttee koso, ukabu se mo are:* 'One can help oneself only when one leaves one's body – that is, gives up the small egotistical I'. (Cox 2003:59)

It is only *after* undergoing a process of cultivation through sustained training that one begins to reflect upon the nature and quality of that lived experience. Speaking about Zeami's theory of acting in his *Transmission of Stylish Form and the Flower*, Yuasa explains how all artistic practices are not 'mastered merely through the conceptual understanding, but *must be acquired*, as it were, through one's body. In other words, it is a bodily acquisition by means of a long, cumulative, difficult training (*keiko*)' (emphasis added, 1987:104–105).

Zeami uses two metaphors to describe the optimal state of the actor when he reaches a virtuosic level of effectiveness in his artistry and is able to 'constantly adjust to inevitably changing contexts' in each immediate performance environment for each specific audience (Quinn 2005:281) – the actor as a 'vessel' and the notion of the actor's artistry as 'the flower' (*hana*) (Quinn 2005:281). Given his emphasis on the actor's development as a process of cultivation, it is likely that the notion of transmission of 'the flower' refers to how teaching, guidance, reflection, and a constant process of surprise and discovery on the part of the actor has the potential to produce a flower that is appropriate to specific performances at specific stages in one's life and career.[15]

How does the actor become 'a vessel', able to constantly adjust, and thereby to 'flower' in performance? Zeami eventually arrived at a point where the training of the actor focused first on mastering the two foundational modes of performance – dancing and chanting – which are the technical basis for one's further development when learning 'the three styles' or three basic role types: 'the "venerable style" (*rōtai*)' [older figures], '"feminine style" (*nyotai*)' [female roles], and '"martial style" (*guntai*)' [warriors] (Quinn 2005:6).[16] Through the embodied repetition of basic dance/chant techniques it is assumed that the actor not only assimilates a basic set of psychophysical forms and patterns through which performances will be created, but even more importantly is offered the opportunity to 'empty his mind of conscious striving' in that process of repetition' (Quinn 2005:282) – a process of skill acquisition.

Psychophysical principles and practices in nō) acting/vocalization

What constitutes the sensorial field of the *nō* actor from 'inside' his experience of performance? What 'felt' stimuli are offered by each element of the performance? In what ways is the actor's experience shaped by these 'felt stimuli'? To answer these questions, I will 'map' some dimensions of the *nō* actor's psychophysical process utilized by actors as they progress towards Zeami's ideal.

In 1424 when Zeami was sixty-one years old, he authored *Kakyō* ('A Mirror of the Flower') in which he provides what is arguably his most comprehensive view of the underlying psychophysical principles of *nō* acting. In the first part of the treatise, he provides pithy aphoristic statements of six key principles, each of which is followed by a brief commentary [see boxed text below]. The remainder of *Kakyō* discusses tactics for how to best achieve 'the performative ideal *yūgen*' (Hare 2008:96), including an extended discussion of the *jo-ha-kyū* progression.

Six Fundamental Principles from Kakyō ('A Mirror of the Flower')[17]

1. First, the Key; Second, the Activating Force [Ch'i/qi/ki]; Third, the Voice (Nearman 1982a: 350)

   Zeami's commentary on the first principle begins:

   The modal key is what the [performer's] *ch'i* maintains. [The actor] attunes [himself] with his 'activating force' [*ch'i/qi/ki*] [in order to establish and maintain his tone center], then closing his eyes and inhaling, he vocalizes. (Nearman 1982a:343)

2. Work the Mind Ten-Tenths, Work the Body Seven-Tenths (Nearman 1982a:350).
3. When the Torso Moves with Emphasis, the Foot Steps with Calmness [or restraint]; When the Foot Steps with Emphasis the Torso Moves with Calmness [or restraint] (Nearman 1982a:352).
4. First, Hearing; Then, Seeing (Nearman 1982a:354).
5. First Become the Thing, Then Imitate the Way It Acts (Hare 2008:100).
6. Make Movement a Voicing of the Fundamental [Creative Energy] (Nearman 1982a:360).

The six principles outlined above are all concerned with one or more of what Zeami considered 'the three mysteries of human life': embodiment, vocalization, and 'the Mind' of the actor (Nearman 1978:301). For Zeami, acting was a life-long project and process through which the actor might 'plumb the depths' of these three closely interwoven 'mysteries' (Nearman 1978:302).

But before turning to a specific discussion of embodiment, vocalization, and 'the mind' of the actor, it is essential to examine the 'activating force' *ki/qi/ch'i* to which Zeami refers in his commentary on the first principle above. As noted in the introduction to this chapter, throughout East Asia *ki* is assumed to be the animating/activating force of life, and therefore of all arts and practices. *Ki* is manifest, deployed, and manipulated in acting, movement, vocalization, as well as in 'mind' (or bodymind). As *ki* is activated and utilized in practice, there is a 'felt' quality to the movement of *ki*. Shigenori Nagatomo describes this type of embodied attunement as having a 'felt inner resonance (*kannō dōkō*)', a sense of 'calm immovability', accompanied by 'no-mind' (*mushin*) (1987:227, 232).

The 'activating force' (*ki/qi/ch'i*)

The philosopher, linguist, and East Asian scholar Rolf Elberfeld explains how the Sino-Japanese word *ki* can be translated as

> 'vapor, spirit, finest influence, breath of life, gaseous expansion, ethereal matter, fluid, breath, or power of life.' It is used in Japanese … in the following ways: *ki ga aru* (to have *ki*: if a man, for example, should be interested in an activity or a woman), *ki ga kiku* (*ki* works: when one attentively and thoroughly senses what the situation requires), *ki ga shizumu* (*ki* sinks: when one becomes melancholy and depressive), *ki ga haru* (*ki* stretches: when one feels uptight and tense) … *Ki* is invisible and inaudible, but present, like a scent that envelops one completely and swallows one. (2003:481)

In both China and Japan it is assumed that through certain psychophysical practices – calligraphy, painting, poetry, the Chinese martial art *taiqiquan*, Japanese tea ceremony, flower arranging, archery – *qi/ki* can be actively cultivated and developed in its own way (Elberfeld 2003:487).

For example, the painter does not 'portray' a landscape, but rather, *qi/ki* is the animating force that moves the painter or the calligrapher's brush. The calligrapher, for example, does not move the brush, but rather could be said to learn to listen to the brush for the moment when *ki* arises. The artist must learn to be open and to enter a state of receptivity.

The calligrapher says that the 'brush runs', while the carpenter claims that the 'plain advances'. These expressions, in which the person is never the subject, describe work done…spontaneously. (Noguchi 2004:22)

The assumption that *ki* is an animating force of life, meant that Japanese culture assumed a 'worldview in which all things possess life' (Noguchi 2004:14). For master craftsmen, the materials used in creating his art is 'alive'.

The dye maker says that cloth is alive; the potter says that the clay is alive; blacksmiths maintain that the steel they hammer is alive. (Noguchi 2004:14)

In traditional modes of architecture and construction with wood in Japan, since timber also was 'alive', it was weathered for ten years before being used in construction so that 'its ability to breathe' would be sustained in the transition from living tree to living in its new form as part of a home or temple. Traditional architecture took into account the 'life force of the timber' as of 'utmost importance in achieving the desired balance' (Noguchi 2004:14–15). These assumptions about craftsmanship inform the carving of wooden masks used in *nō* perform-ances, many now considered national treasures.

Ozawa-de Silva observes that *ki* is understood as '"spiritual energy"' – which 'suggests an underlying unity to phenomena…as an organizing force-field' or '"dynamic unity"' (2002:28). '*Ki* pervades nature'; an imbalance in *ki* caused by diet, a failed relationship, or bad habits can bring about illness; and it 'can also be understood as "atmosphere", "air", "feelings", "intention", "will", "mind" and "heart"' (ibid.). As discussed by Yuasa, *ki* has both psychological and physiological dimen-sions as a phenomenon and as experienced (1993). Cox therefore defines *ki* as

an extraordinary state of consciousness arising from the 'sensations of the body' (*shintai kankaku*). To realize this state of consciousness which is tied to the body's condition and not simply a somatic theory, [is] referred to…by the expression *sokushin jobutsu* meaning ('enlightenment of this very body'). By engaging the body in the practice of the physical forms (*katachi*) we find in activities like the martial ways, it is possible to mani-fest mind-body complex (*ki*) of which, in terms of Buddhist metaphysics, we are already a part. (Cox 2003:59)

Within East Asian cultural contexts, Thomas P. Kasulis explains how traditional medical research and modes of embodied practice all focused on 'living subjects, living mind-body complexes' (1993:305). Unlike Western research which came to focus on 'the body as hydraulic and electrical systems' where autopsies were performed, historically

> the East Asians studied [the mind-body complex] as a system in which flows a matter-energy or life-force called *ch'l* [*qi*] in Chinese or *ki* in Japanese. Given this context, it is not surprising that acupuncture has proven to be particularly effective in managing pain, for examples. Corpses do not feel pain; only living mind-body complexes do. (Kasulis 1993:306)

Ki is utilized in a wide variety of contexts and with a variety of shades of meaning. *Ki* as one's inner energy is treated through acupuncture. In addition to *ki* as 'the life-force flowing in the mind-body complex', Kasulis offers the following examples: one can 'have *ki*', 'become *ki*', 'lose *ki*', or 'draw *ki*', and *ki* can be 'long' 'rough', or 'strong' (1993:306). For some Japanese thinkers, such as Ito Jinsai (1627–1725) and Kaibara Ekken (1630–1714), *ki* as life-force is 'continuous with the life-force in the universe in its spirit-matter complex' (Kasulis 1993:308).

Kasulis goes on to explain how it is through embodied practices that

> we become what we are. And what are we? A mind-body complex that is in internal relation with the mind-body or spirit-matter complex of the universe. (1993:311)

From the perspective inside a specific practice such as *nō* acting, for some assiduous practitioners, pursuing their practice becomes a 'path to enlightenment' as well as 'the expression of enlightenment' (Kasulis 1993:312). As discussed earlier, this is exemplified in Zeami's *Kyūi* ('A Pedagogical Guide for Teachers of Acting') where at the very highest level of attainment, the actor's technique per se disappears or is burned away completely.

Practically for the actor, *ki* should be understood as that 'activating force' that the actor (as mover/vocalist) experiences within himself, and is able to manipulate, shape, and animate his creative process for aesthetic ends. The circulation and animating force of *ki* within the actor is what allows the potential to 'blossom' appropriately to the dramatic context. *Ki* reveals itself to the young actor in the process of psychophysical training through which he discovers/awakens, and then 'attunes' his *ki*. With experience and training, one is able to modulate *ki*-in-action because there is the 'felt' quality of its presence-in-action.

Trained as both a *nō* actor and musician, Richard Emmert has observed how one of the most fundamental aspects of contemporary *nō* practice is an 'underlying and very controlled sense of energy, a kind of constant yet quiet tension' achieved through a long 'internal' training in both movement and vocalization (1997:25). Emmert describes the training process as a cumulative one through which the performer develops 'a level of energy that builds and subsides but is always maintained' (Emmert 1997:25). As the actor begins to awaken *ki* through the patterns of movement and vocalization to which he is introduced, there is a felt sense of the inner movement of this energy in movement and vocalization.

> For the Japanese, the body was not merely a tool to be utilized for daily life. It was a place in which the abstract was to be received...it was not something that could be managed by the person's will, but could be brought to a state of harmony through the focusing of *ki*, which occurs when one breaks away from a state of volitional concentration...By nature, it can only improvise its every movement. It fluctuates in resonance with the vibrations of life, in a world where everything is alive. (Noguchi 2004:14)[18]

This *ki* energy optimally becomes constantly present and available to the performer to be shaped in/through the movement and vocal patterns learned. Repetition of physical forms and voicing gradually produce an inner, felt quality and sensation of vibration or inner movement to be shaped in performance.

Training the bodymind

Unlike the South Asian pre-performative trainings examined in Chapter 2 which begins with the preliminary preparation of the actor's bodymind for performance through pre-performative training exercises, Japanese *nō* training consists of repetition of the actual basic patterns actually used in performance. In *nō* training, the master-teacher performs a section of a play, and the students at first attempt to reproduce as exactly as possible over and over again the 'shapes and movement of the body and the tonal patterns and qualities of the voice through that section' (Brandon 1997:106). This process is repeated until an entire play is learned. The outer (physical) and inner processes and psychodynamic principles underlying embodiment are embedded within and absorbed from the systemic repetition of a progressive set of whole performance scores.

The two beginning, most fundamental forms of body-training for the *nō* actor embedded in the performance sequences are the 'at ready' standing position known as *kamae* [Figure 3.4] and the flat 'sliding feet' (*suriashi*) [Figure 3.5] used to propel and move the actor on the polished wooden floor of the stage. Richard Emmert provides the following description of the dynamic physical and internal processes of the basic *kamae* and how the actor sustains this form (see also Berberich 1984):

> Even though the posture itself is still, it is made very much alive by the fact that strength is focused in the lower abdomen. Rather than lifting the rib cage high, which in the case of Western classical ballet creates its floating, upward quality, in *nō* the lower abdomen is pushed out, giving a downward earth-centeredness. The weight of the body is slightly forward on the balls of the feet. The upper torso is kept straight and erect by slightly pushing in the lower back, which forces the chest out. The arms are slightly curved with the elbows turned out (the exact height of the arms differs from school to school, from role to role, and from actor to actor). *Kamae* is a position of relaxed strength that gives a sense of expectancy. From this position all other movement is generated... It easily leads to all movement and is the position that the actor-dancer returns to after completing a movement. Although still, it is not static, but rather suggests a great amount of energy flowing through the body generated from the lower abdomen. It is quiet energy whose flow should not be hampered by an unnaturally tense quality. It takes several years of training before an actor feels confident in its execution. (Emmert 1997:25–26)

This *kamae* position requires 'firm pelvic support (*koshi o ireru*), enabling a smooth transfer of weight when moving through space' (Berberich 1984:211). Master actor Nomura Shirō describes how from this basic position

> energy pulls the body in all directions, and the pelvis stays in the center of this dynamic balancing of the overall body. The energy pulling the body outward is counterbalanced by the energy drawing it inward toward the pelvis. (Berberich 1984:211)

Figure 3.4 Omura Sadamu of the Kita School, demonstrating the basic patterns which constitute part of the underlying process of the psychophysical preparation of the *nō* actor for performance – basic 'at ready' standing posture (*kamae*). (Photograph by Richard Emmert.)

The sense of 'expectancy' or energetic readiness generated in *kamae* should not dissipate when the actor-dancer begins to move across the stage as he slides his feet in the basic 'walking' pattern (*suriashi*).

> It appears to be a simple technique; but what may seem very simple and graceful with the body of an experienced *nō* actor-dancer can be extremely awkward for the beginner ... As the word implies, the feet are not lifted from step to step, but rather slide across the floor. The foot is flat and toes and heels are in constant contact with the floor until the end of the step, at which time the front of the foot is raised slightly. Throughout, knees are slightly bent to absorb the leg action in such a way that the torso remains at a level height. There must be no bobbing up and down. The strongly held basic posture established in the *kamae*, particularly in the hips, continues in *suri ashi* and prevents the upper

Figure 3.5 Omura Sadamu of the Kita School, demonstrating the basic patterns which constitute part of the underlying process of the psychophysical preparation of the *nō* actor for performance – the flat 'sliding feet' (*suri ashi*). (Photograph by Richard Emmert.)

> body swaying from side to side with each step. The *kamae* and *suri ashi* determine how the basic energy of the actor will be conveyed to the audience. Is it strong, yet relaxed, flowing, and graceful? Or is it tight, static, and awkward? (1997:26)

Nomura Shirō has explained how the sliding walk is 'like plaining a board – much strength is required. By plaining the floor with the feet... motion through space takes on an energized quality' (Berberich 1984:211).

As the *kamae* and *suriashi* forms come to be embodied by the actor and serve to awaken his energy, the student brings the 'same sense of energy and quiet tension' (Emmert 1997:26) discovered in the *kamae* and sliding steps into work on *kata* – form patterns or units of choreography such as the stylized 'crying' gesture known as *shiori* where the two hands, palms upward, are raised towards but never touch the eyes of the slightly bowed head. With a few exceptions, these basic patterns or units of choreography are most commonly used to perform plays throughout the *nō* repertoire. The feel and quality of the performance of a pattern is determined by the role and context within a specific drama and therefore what is communicated can be vastly different. Although *nō* often possesses a surface quietude, there is always a manifestation of *ki*-energy as dynamic vibration which should be palpably present in performance (see Berberich 1984, 1989).

The basic *jo-ha-kyū* progression identified earlier in this chapter should inform all movement and dance performed by the actor.[19] In relation to movement the qualities suggested by the progression the sequence might be translated as 'slow/initiation, gradual build/acceleration, climax/finishing'. Through extensive, repetitious training in the basic movement forms that constitute *nō,* the actor comes to embody this progression as manifest in the quality and relationship of his *ki*-energy to movement. Nomura Shirō explains how 'stopping forward movement' in this progression 'at the peak of energy is very difficult'; therefore, when one takes six steps forward, 'one should imagine taking ten steps. By doing this, the last four "imagined" steps are transformed into energy projecting itself further forward' (Berberich 1984:212). Thereby the actor projects '"one's mind"' and releases '"it into the space beyond you"' (Berberich 1984:212). Furthermore, when walking forward and then backward, the actor works with projecting the energy forward and then pulling the energy back, creating a strong inner dynamic quality shaped according to the context of the specific drama. Berberich describes how 'the *jo-ha-kyū* pattern in *nō* movement employs energy spatially as well. The energy which is carried in one direction is also simultaneously counterbalanced in the opposition direction, further enhancing the three-dimensionality of *nō* performance' (1984:216). As discussed in more detail below, the projection of the actor's *ki*-energy and awareness through the body and into the performance space necessarily engages the actor's 'mind'. The 'mind' is an essential, integrated extension of embodied training.

In addition to these fundamental movement forms, there are specific set pieces of choreography/dance that are a central part of the training process as they are performed at the culminating dimension of most performances of *nō* dramas. In the Yamamoto *nō* theatre in Osaka reconstructed during the 1950s after the war, it was built in the traditional manner with twelve huge empty pots set under the stage to create the appropriate vibratory/resonating quality of the stage floor.

This phenomenon means that the *nō* dancer's performative energy is in direct physiological dialogue with the stage floor as it vibrates in response to his dance. Emmert observes that while movement in *nō* may be abstract and stylized, it nevertheless conveys 'the feelings and emotions behind the poetry being sung by the chorus or the actor-dancers', that is, 'the *kata* serve to heighten the emotion felt through the poetry' (1997:27).

Vocalization/chanting and 'vibratory feeling' (onkan)

The second 'mystery' the actor explores in training and development is the realm of embodied vocalization through modes and styles of chanting. Here, as in movement, the inner movement of *ki* within the *nō* actor is 'felt' in relation to vocalization/chanting. 'Zeami's term for this vocally created feeling is *onkan*, "tonal [or vibratory] feeling"' (Nearman 1984:44). As Mark Nearman explains,

> [t]he emotions that the portrayed character appears to experience and that are attributed by some spectators to the actor's personal feelings are seen by Zeami to be the product of the trained actor's use of his voice, particularly through his manipulation of the tonal properties of speech. Hence, the appearance of these emotional effects is directly dependent on the actor's understanding of the dynamics of vocal production. (1984:44)

According to Richard Emmert there is a 'physicality' to *nō* music that is of equal importance to the development of the *ki*-energy, strength, and 'quiet tension' informing *nō* movement (1997:27). Vocal production in *nō* performance today includes two 'distinctive modes: *utai* (chanting) and *kotoba* ("words" – speech)' (Serper 2000:129) – both clearly delineated in the texts of *nō* plays known as *utai-bon* or 'chanting book'(s). Although in the early stages of the development of *nō* there was only one mode of chanting, towards the end of the seventeenth century a dynamic chanting style called *tsuyogin* – '"strong chanting," (or "hard chanting" – *gōgin*)' began to develop (Serper 2000:130). This mode of 'strong chanting' contrasts with the earlier (single) mode, which came to be called '*yowagin* – "weak chanting" (or "soft chanting" – *jūgin*)' (Serper 2000:130).[20]

The 'strong chanting' style (*tsuyogin*) is 'dynamic' and 'masculine' (Serper 2000:130), exhibits a great deal of energy and intensity, produces a 'wide frequency of vibration(s)' which are 'irregular', and is therefore considered appropriate for battles and ceremonial scenes (Tamba 1981:42). In contrast the 'weak chant' style (*yowagin*) is 'melodic feminine' (Serper 2000:130), initiated with 'a slow, ascending *glissando*,' characterized by a softened articulation used to create connections between syllables, and therefore is utilized for lyrical scenes (Tamba 1981:42). Some *nō* plays only utilize one of these two modes, while in performance of other plays the contrasting modes are both used. In *Kanawa* (*Iron Crown*) strong and weak modes are used 'to create two different aspects' of the same character – a deserted woman who, by turning into a demon, attempts 'to take revenge on her former husband and his new wife' (Serper 2000:131).

Unlike Western 'singing', modes of vocalization in *nō* are not set to a specific pitch and do not follow a specific scale of notes; rather the range of pitches (diapason) fluctuates depending on the individual vocal range of each individual performer. However, the performer takes his initial register from what is offered by the flute player. Another major difference in vocal techniques is that in Western vocal production pitch is kept constant and does not fluctuate; however, in *nō* vocalizing there is some fluctuation of tone when voicing a particulate note (Tamba 1981:39). It should also be noted that, whether or not *nō* actors wear a mask in a particular performance, the same vocal techniques are utilized.

In his extensive study *The Musical Structure of Nō* Tamba Akira provides an extensive account and analysis of vocal and musical production in *nō* (1981). As Tamba explains, all vocal production results from simultaneous use of the lungs, larynx and three cavities – nasal, oral, and pharyngeal [that part of the throat located immediately below the mouth and nasal cavity, and just above the esophagus and larynx] (1981:33). Tamba describes how French vocal technique

> utilizes the nasal cavity and the oral cavity, trying to use them both simultaneously to the maximum in order to obtain resonance in the upper sinuses ... [while in *nō* vocalization one] ... utilizes the cavity of the pharynx much more than the other two cavities in lowering and drawing in the chin. One employs the nasal cavity to resonate the nasal consonants: (n), (m), and (g). One tries to modify the anterior vowels to posterior vowels ... (a) tends towards (o), (i) tends towards (u), et cetera. (1981:37, 36)

This method of vocalization produces what Tamba describes as 'a somber coloration and a fullness giving a sensation of dramatic intensity, of... energy' (1981:36), and 'a timbre that is somber and grave'.[21]

A range of vibratory stimuli are offered to the *nō* actor-dancer by the musical ensemble as well as the resonant wooden stage itself: the playing of the flute; the rhythm patterns and accents of the three drums sounding; the 'strange, guttural' calls (*kakegoe*) vocalized by the drummers (Ortolani 1984:177); and the vibrations of the wooden floor itself when the actor-dancers stamp their feet. Each musician and technique offers its own mode of sounding/vibration to the actor-dancer for his sensorial experience and response at particular moments in a performance – whether the piercing initiation of a sound from the transverse flute, the rhythmic accompaniment of the culminating dance within a performance as dancer/drummers create what might be described as a 'vibratory dialogue' with each other through the foot stamping of the dancers and the striking of the drums, or a drummer sounding a call such as 'yo, ho, yo-ii, ii-ya'.

The centrality of *nō*'s soundscape should be understood in the context of how a Japanese sense of sound historically developed. Noguchi Hiroyuki explains how a Japanese sense of sound suffused traditional religious practices in Japan.

> Sound created through deep and focused intensity was considered to have the power to cleanse impurities. The *ki-ai* techniques handed down by Shinto priests and mountain ascetics, the chanting of Buddhist monks, and even the act of cleaning were all religious practices, or music, based on the mystery of sound. The use of the *hataki* – a duster made of paper and stick – and broom originates from Shinto rituals, which invited the Divine by purifying the surrounding environment through the use of sound...the sound of the...bamboo flute used in *nō* drama was for resting the dead, the...reed flute for inviting the dead to visit this world. The sense of depth held by sound in traditional Japanese culture was based on a sensitivity towards sound that was entirely different from that found in Western music. (Noguchi 2004:10–11)

Although the visual plays an important role in *nō*, Zeami's principle of 'First, hearing; then, seeing' points to the centrality of the vocal and auditory dimensions of *sarugaku-nō* and its reception.[22] Zeami explains how:

> To begin with, when [the actor] performs so that what strikes the spectator's ear comes first and the physical expression [of the emotions implied by the words] is delayed a little, a feeling is [generated in the spectator] of the full realization of the visual and auditory [elements] at that juncture

where [the spectator] shifts his attention from what he hears to what is seen. (Nearman 1982a:354)

The actor's first task is to open the audience's ears to the auditory/ vibratory quality of a performance. In his treatise *Fūgyoku shū* Zeami describes the ideal, optimal attainment of the actor in vocal production as follows:

> When chant seems to have no ornamentation, yet the impression it creates just seems more and more singular, and, at the same time, there is no limit to its interest, you will indeed know that this is non-ornamentation that has reached the ultimate [stage] of ornamentation and gone beyond it. This is the level of the wondrous voice of supreme accomplishment. (Quinn 2005:262)

'The Mind' (*ma* and no-mind)

As suggested in the analysis offered thus far, 'mind' (or the third 'mystery') has already been a key element in the modes of embodiment and vocalization central to the *nō* actor's development. The realm marked by 'mind' is already complicit and implicit *in* movement and vocalization as embodied processes. They are a means to exploring the nuances of 'mind'. As noted above, repetitious psychophysical training under the tutelage of a master teacher optimally takes the practitioner 'out' of himself, that is, one is so focused on the embodied process that one suspends subjectivity itself and moves beyond ego. One is so absorbed in the immediate state of being/doing that arbitrary thoughts simply do not arise. Embodied practices are understood to cultivate 'a new mode of mindfulness in which his cognitive activity is hidden even from himself' (Quinn 2005:282). For the *nō* actor, 'this is a condition that allows him heightened spontaneity and attunement with his audiences' (2005:282) as *hana*, or flowering.

As noted earlier, during his career Zeami shifted the Yamoto style 'away from advocacy of lifelike semblances for their own sake' and developed a training in which the stage figure is created on a combination of superb physical/vocal technique and development of 'a state of mind that counterbalances his physical expression' (Quinn 2005:106). In *Fūshikaden* Zeami provides one very specific example of this counterbalancing between a 'state of mind' and 'physical expression', or what contemporary *nō* actor Haruo Nishino describes as 'the relation between bodily expression and mental attitude' (2001:149) – the outer and inner dimensions that shape the actor's underlying, constantly present *ki*-energy.

> When... you perform in a manner expressive of anger, you must not forget the gentleness of mind. This will give you a method of acting as angry as you wish without becoming coarse. To maintain a gentleness of mind when angry is the principle of rarity. Again, in dramatic imitation requiring *yūgen*, you must not forget the principle of strength... Also, there must always be intent in making the use of the body. When you move your body strongly, you should hold back in stomping your feet. When you stomp your feet strongly, you should carry your body quietly. It is difficult to convey this in writing. It is something for face-to-face oral instruction. (Hare 2008:69).

While in the above translation Tom Hare uses 'mind' to begin his translation of the key term *kokoro*, Rimer and Masakazu translate *kokoro* as 'heart' (1984:58). *Kokoro* is a commonplace term throughout East Asia, and is usually translated as 'mind', 'heart', or 'intent'. Tom Hare goes on to explain that

> *kokoro* (or *shin*, in its Sino-Japanese pronunciation in compounds) is the seat of cognition, perception, and emotion in the body. And it also is the internal organ that pumps blood. In Japanese *kokoro* may also mean 'meaning' or 'essence' or the disposition of intent. (2008:467)

Mark Nearman explains how from a Japanese perspective 'thinking (both rational thought and mind images) and feeling (emotional responses) are not viewed as discrete functions but rather as two related types of mind-created responses to sensory awareness or to some previous content (thought, image, or feeling) in the consciousness' (1984:474).

Both translations above attempt to capture the actor's process of embodying and shaping his energy appropriately so that in his embodied expression of anger there is a dialectic between the physical expression of anger and a quality of tenderness or gentleness that affects that physical expression of anger. The 'inner' tenderness modulates the physical expression/manifestation of anger. The actor's process must remain nuanced and subtle so that it not become 'coarse' or rough' in expressing anger in an obvious way. Because it is not obvious or coarse, this inner psychophysical dialectic or tension between the inner state of the heart/mind and the outer expression of anger creates more interest in the audience.

[T]he actor's mind forms the ground out of which an interplay of linguistic, vocal, kinetic, and visual elements find expression, but the 'meaning' of this interplay of elements is something that the spectator must create. (Quinn 2005:109)

Explaining the actor's 'mental' process, Zeami observes how

members of the audience often say that the places where nothing is done are interesting. This is the secret stratagem of the actor...The gap between is where, as they say, nothing is done...the mind bridges the gap...you maintain your intent and do not loosen your concentration in the gaps where you've stopped dancing the dance, in the places where you've stopped singing the music, in the gaps between all the types of speech and dramatic imitation...This internal excitement diffuses outward and creates interest. (Hare 2008:115)

Through his psychophysical process of development, the actor ideally obtains a state of bodymind integration, or 'no mind' (*mushin*) – a state which Richard Pilgrim describes as an 'instinctual, *a-priori* mind' (1969:398).

This state of 'no mind' is the ideal state of awareness through which to evoke the 'flower' in performance since that flower must remain fresh and full of surprise; therefore, the actor works against what is obvious, and works unthinkingly and without premeditation. 'The experience of novelty depends, at least in part, on what, for the audience, is unpredictable' (Quinn 2005:106). Rather than creating an obvious 'demonstration of emotion' in playing a demon that is rough, through 'suggestive complexity' the actor opens an imaginative space for the audience (Quinn 2005:106).

Benito Ortolani has (controversially) argued that the tremendous 'intensity and depth' characteristic of *nō* performance can be ascribed in part to the legacy and influence of both early shamanistic practices as well as various forms of Buddhist spirituality in *nō* (1984:180). Both have contributed to the sense that in *nō* performance the actor visits a very different 'other world'' from the everyday where one experiences 'the thrill of direct contact with the "other dimension" in a time outside of our time' in an altogether pristine 'sacred space set apart for that journey-encounter' (1984:180). He also argues that in his 'flower of the miraculous' Zeami points the actor to an experience 'rooted in the heart (*kokoro*) of everything – rooted in a special spontaneity and unity with the source of all, which is ultimately the Buddha Nature' (1984:181).

Contemporary nō

I will conclude this discussion of *nō* with the contrasting views of a contemporary Japanese critic and a contemporary *nō* actor. The scholar/critic Kitazawa Masakuni has argued that the traditional arts in Japan today exist in the 'shadow of cultural decadence' (1995:106). In Kitazawa's view,

> the actors and performers have neither the power of eyes which can penetrate the audience nor the fullness of *ki* (breath of inner energy) in their bodies, which can overwhelm spectators. Moreover, there is no *ma* (silence accentuating dialog), which can make a play vivid and enable the characters to display deep expression. Although *ma* is one of the central concepts of traditional theatre, the actors execute it as if it is a patterned measurement of time. (1995:106)

Nomura Shirō – a contemporary master actor/teacher of *nō* – has explained his own view of contemporary *nō* as 'introspective, contained, an art of circumspection' which requires the actor to express its

> internal qualities...through *nō*'s absence of action...in absolute stillness...Even though *nō* is an interior art based on the least possible movement, it must be highly expressive. It is a paradox. *Nō* is a paradoxical art. (1997:205)

For Nomura Shirō this paradox is exemplified in how the *nō* actor works with the mask when playing those primary *shite* in which a mask – just smaller than the size of the human face – covers the actor's face and thereby denies the actor use of facial expression. As Nomura Shirō explains:

> Expression lies in the mask, which is never expressionless. The mask is only a small portion of the body. If you act with the mask alone, you are acting from the neck up. In fact, the *nō* actor expresses with the entire body, incorporating the mask into it...[A]cting in *nō* is highly physical and in my view each part of the actor's body – the costumed torso, the hands, the feet, and the masked face – are equally expressive. At the same time, the body is bound, restricted by inaction and the actor must project the character's feelings. What I think is *nō* is an unusual art of 'nearly expressionless expression'. The mask is complex in its effect, but it allows the actor to express not merely the outer form of a human being, but the interior spirit as well. (1997:202)

Whether at the time of Zeami, or today, for Nomura Shirō learning *nō* requires each individual undergoing the training to absorb and assimilate the fact that the training is not simply a set of exercises or techniques, but is part of

> a path or way (*michi, dō*) to reach one's art... *Nō*'s true nature reveals itself only to the artist who undertakes that journey. That is rather philosophical. But... this special spirit of *nō* [is] not just intellectual knowledge but some-thing naturally and directly absorbed through the bodily training. And that [takes] time. Intellectual ideas can be learned much faster than body knowledge. (1997:205; for an historical discussion, see also Pinnington 2006)

Contemporary psychophysical performance in Japan

The devastation wrought by World War II created a heady-mix of political, social, and artistic upheaval in post-war Japan. Particularly acute was the tension between Westernization and modernization, as well as between whether a future might be created that was somehow 'Japanese' but that did not copy the worn out ways of the past. This led to a search for new modes of expression within the arts that reexamined all aspects of artistic practice, processes of training, making, embod-iment, and aesthetic form. To conclude this chapter we discuss three examples of performance – an in-depth look at *butoh*, and brief glimpses of the theatre work of Suzuki Tadashi and Ōta Shōgo – all of which are both intracultural as well as intercultural in that each has interacted with and/or responded in some way to the principles/practices of 'tradi-tional' Japanese performance as well as to contemporary Western influences.

Butoh

> The body in *butoh* is already the universe dancing on the borders of life and death. (Ohno Kazuo, quoted in Fraleigh and Nakamura 2006:35)
>
> *Butoh* is a dead body standing desperately upright. (Hijikata Tatsumi, quoted in Fraleigh and Nakamura 2006:51)

The Japanese word *butoh* (*butō*) consists of two characters – *bu* meaning dance and *toh* (*tō*) literally meaning to step. During the mid to late nineteenth century *butoh* referred in general to dance in Japan, but later was used in a more restricted sense to refer to "'ancient dance'" (Stein 1986: 110). The primary founder and architect of Japanese *butoh* in the late 1950s and early 1960s was Hijikata Tatsumi (1928–1986). Among his many collaborators over the years, he soon began to work with a dancer much his elder, Ohno Kazuo (1906–2010), and eventually with Ashikawa Yōko during the 1970s.[23] It was Hijikata who began to use *ankoku butoh* or "'dance of darkness or gloom'" (ibid.) or 'darkness dance' (Fraleigh and Nakamura 2006:1) to refer to his own emerging, ever-evolving style of dancing as it 'explored the darkest side of human nature' (Kurihara Nanako 2000a: 12).

As the two epigraphs above indicate, death as a phenomenon was central to the work of Hijikata, Ohno and *butoh* from its inception; however, the two epigraphs suggest the quite different qualities, textures, and tones that Hijikata and Ohno each brought to their encounter with 'death' in their performances. There is a suggestion of fragility in Ohno's *butoh* bodymind as it becomes 'the universe [itself] dancing on the borders of life and death'. In contrast, there is great tension in Hijikata's 'desperate' 'dead body standing...upright'. Hijikata's early work was overt, assertive, shocking, and often filled with sexual/erotic/psychophysical tension, while Ohno's work always possessed an inherent lyricism.

Hijikata and those who joined or followed him – Ohno Kazuo, Ashikawa Yōko, Akaji Maro (of Dairakudakan), Tanaka Min, Sankai Juku, Waguri Yukio, among many others – created a movement so diverse that it was and remains in many ways both uncontainable and indefinable in that it can be any/all of the following:

Shocking ... provocative ... physical ... spiritual ... erotic ... grotesque ...
Violent ... cosmic ... nihilistic ... cathartic ... mysterious. (Stein 1986:110)

When *butoh* began to emerge in the late 1950s and early 1960s it was a response in part to the post-war chaos in Japan, as well as a rebellion against what had gone before. It was a movement seeking a new pathway that would never become settled as 'a' way. If at first *butoh* was so rebellious and radical that the artists were described as "'crazy, dirty, and mad'" (Stein 1986:125), over the years *butoh* gradually has became a global, intercultural phenomenon and set of distinctive if very diverse psychophysical practices. This diversity of styles, approaches, and politics means that *butoh* is many things: an approach to embodiment and its immediate experience which demands total psychophysical commitment with its dynamic/expressive forms and striking, transformative images; a sometimes radical, local, communal practice linked to farming, landscape, and nature and open to people from all walks of life (as in the work of Tanaka Min and others);[24] a compellingly visual, highly choreographed, technically polished performance – such as in the work of Sankai Juku and Dairakudakan – invited to perform on the world's most visible stages.[25]

Butoh emerged in Japan as a uniquely and decidedly Japanese invention in the transitional period of Japanese history after the end of World War II. But given its roots and its radical difference as an approach to live performance in which the performer's bodymind constantly confronts, morphs, and transforms between and among our human fragility, nature itself, and death as a process of decay/dying, it has 'translated' and been embraced by practitioners and audiences first in Japan, and then across cultures. I focus this discussion of *butoh* primarily on the formative work of Hijikata Tatsumi and Ohno Kazuo.

Hijikata Tatsumi

Hijikata Tatsumi was the stage name taken by Yoneyama Kunio in 1958. Raised in Tōhoku in the far northern, rural prefecture of Akita on the main island of Honshu, at eighteen, Hijikata began his study of German expressionist *Neue Tanz* at the Masumura Katsuko Dance School. As discussed at length in Chapter 5, the German 'new dance' movement was in many ways radical, and was led by the innovative work of Rudolf Laban and Mary Wigman. Hijikata's first teacher, Masumura studied with Takaya Eguchi and Miya Misako, both of whom had studied with Wigman in Dresden, Germany from 1931–33. Wigman and others in the *Neue Tanz* movement had been in part inspired by East Asian sources. For her *Hexentanz* (*Witch Dance* 1926) Wigman wore a special mask created for her by Victor Magito, a *nō* mask maker. In the dance

> Wigman sat and turned in a hunched-over minimal pattern, pounding the floor percussively with her feet, while her hands morphed from tense claws to delicate flutters grazing the still mask. (Fraleigh and Nakamura 2006:21)

Kurihara Nanako describes how when Hijikata left Tōhoku and arrived in Tokyo in 1952 at the age of 23, he

> experienced a great shock … Postwar confusion prevailed and the dramatic postwar economic growth hadn't started yet. People were far from affluent, especially young artists. But they were free and full of chaotic energy. World War II destroyed Tokyo physically, but had

liberated it artistically. The society's quick change in values – from the restriction of unquestioning obedience to the emperor-god to the 'free choice' brought by 'democracy' made people suspicious of everything'. (2000a:18)

After his move to Tokyo among other influences deeply affecting Hijikata was the Western surrealist movement, and the literary work of Jean Genet and the writings of Antonin Artaud.

Hijikata's *butoh* gradually developed *not* as *a* model, style, or technique intended to replace something/anything that had come before it; rather, as *butoh* dancer/choreographer Tanaka Min explains, Hijikata's *butoh* was a declaration: "'We ARE different," not "What we DO is different'" (quoted in Tanaka 2006).

> Hijikata wondered about its aesthetics, and questioned if movement is the essence of *butoh*. He was skeptical about the then prevailing concept of dance, and that is why he sought another name. I think the best way to describe *butoh* is that it is a name for an activity, not dance itself. So Hijikata's *butoh* is a result of a new way of thinking, new kinds of activities. He would often say something is *butoh-teki, butoh*-like. "Look, isn't he *butoh-teki?"* he would say or, looking at a dog, "You see, this dog is *butoh*!" (Tanaka 2006)

> [For photographic images of Hijikata Tatsumi's *butoh* conduct a 'Google' search and also visit youtube for video clips. For example, to see excerpts of 'Hosotan' visit http://www.youtube.com/watch?v=3xYsO7OpQkQ]

Hijikata's *butoh* was equally a response to the chaos of the period and the legacy of World War II, including the American use of nuclear bombs and the devastation wrought in Hiroshima and Nagasaki; an attempt to find new modes of embodied/corporeal expression that would not reproduce Western modern dance or a bourgeois Western mentality; a reaction against the perceived ossification of Japan's traditional arts in the modern era, as well as against Westernization and increasing Americanization.[26] Hijikata wanted to (re)discover a body that was his own body – a body that did not need to conform, that was alive and animated, and that related to his own sense of where he belonged and how he was shaped by his rural childhood. As we shall see, even as *butoh* was finding a new way, some of the elements, principles, and metaphors which have always been formative for Japanese arts and practices, such as the flower (*hana*), and the space/interval between (*ma*), and no-mind (*mushin*) have continued to inform the interior processes of the *butoh* performer.

In 1959, a year after taking his stage name, Hijikata performed *Kinjiki* (*Forbidden Colors*) at the 'New Face Performance' of the Japanese Dance Association. The title is taken from Mishima Yukio's 1951 homoerotic novel (*Kinjiki*), 'but the feeling and content were taken from Genet' (Nanako 2000a:18). Kurikara Nanako explains how this early work 'was quite different from what we consider *butoh* now' (ibid.). Alongside Hijikata onstage performing 'Man' was Kazuo Ohno's thirteen-year-old son, Ohno Yoshito (born 1938), performing 'Boy'. Fraleigh and Nakamura describe *Kinjiki* as

> a dance of darkness in several ways. The stage itself is darkened: Yoshito, Ohno's young son, dances in dim light with Hijikata, and they mime sexual attraction at points – looking deeply in to each others' eyes…Nario Goda…describes the dance as a ritual sacrifice…After the boy appears on stage, the man, holding a chicken, enters and runs in a circle. The boy stiffens, and walks to a narrow illuminated area…where the man is waiting in the darkness. Breathing hard, they face each other, and the man thrusts the chicken into the light with the white wings fluttering 'stunningly.' The boy accepts the chicken, turns his head, and holds it to his chest. Then placing the chicken between his thighs, he slowly sinks into a squat, squeezing it to death while the man watches from the darkness. (Fraleigh and Nakamura 2006:79)

The second half of the performance takes place in darkness. Fraleigh and Nakamura report how in *Kinjiki* there are also 'beautiful episodes of slow restrained movement…Eternally slow continuously morphing movement' – elements that mark the lyrical dimension of *butoh* (2006:80).

Some in the audiences for Hijikata's early work were outraged. Others were stunned, electrified, and transfixed by the strong, erotic, muscular, rebelliousness of his emerging form of *butoh* – also evident for example in Hijikata's *nikutai no hanran* (*Rebellion of the Body* or *Revolt of the Flesh*, 1968; see Hijikata's 'To Prison' first published in 1961 [2000b]). Tanaka Min describes how in Hijikata's early work:

> His body was always like a weapon, like a knife. People couldn't close their mouths watching him. They were amazed and afraid – something like enormous tension. He was always attacking the audience…provoking…I thought, 'This is truth'…He wanted to uncover what is hidden by ordinary society. (Tanaka 1986a:146)

But Hijikata's work was ever-evolving. During the 1960s he worked primarily with male performers where the work centred around themes at the time seen as '"sexual perversion": homosexuality and transvestism' (Kurihara Nanako 2000a:19). From the late 1960s Hijikata's work was marked by a literal (if momentary) and artistic 'return' to his rural home in Tōhoku. His work began to intensely examine 'his own body, specifically a male body that grew up in Tōhoku, probably to liberate himself from the body' (Kurihara Nanako 2000a:20). In Tōhoku, during spring 'the abundance of mud taught [Hijikata] how to dance' (Kurihara Nanako 2000a:24).

In the 1970s Hijikata began to focus on working with women performers, in particular Ashikawa Yōko, and by 1973 Hijikata himself stopped dancing to focus solely on choreographing. With Ashikawa Yōko and Tomiko Takai, Hijikata explored of a series of 'forms' (*kata*) such as 'the smiling flower', 'the wafting smoke of incense', 'the female demon's smile' (Holledge and Tomkins 2000:140). Although these '*kata* gave *butoh* form' they 'were never allowed to become fixed or repetitive'; rather, Hijikata told the dancers that '"Forms exist so that we can forget them"' (Holledge and Tomkins 2000:140). In this period Hijikata produced a new style of *butoh*

characterized by concentrated, contained movements for female performs. The incredible transformation of Ashikawa into a bowlegged midget-like figure and the complete changes in her masklike facial expressions were striking and surprised the audience. What Ashikawa showed was the result not only of practical work on the body, but of the words Hijikata bombarded her with as they worked alone in the studio. His words were metaphors for his body … Ashikawa even said that an exchange of bodies occurred … His words – her actions. (Kurihara Nanako 2000a:22)

Hijikata's words and metaphors provided an inner stimuli for Ashikawa's bodily modes of transformation. And towards the end of his life, Hijikata's work shifted again as it focused on '"*suijakutai*" (the emaciated body)' such as Ashikawa Yōko's 'ghostlike figure' in 'Tōhoku Kabuki Project 4' (1985):

In a man's kimono, Ashikawa moved as if she were floating, her eyes almost closed, as if her body was disappearing … [Hijikata] ambitiously attempted to erase the body and go beyond it, beyond anything with a material form. (Kurihara Nanako 2000a:25)

Ohno Kazuo

In 1949 – prior to his permanent move to Tokyo in 1952 – Hijikata had witnessed Ohno Kazuo's debut dance performance in Tokyo – a performance Hijikata described as 'overflowing with lyricism' – a lyricism so intoxicating that for Hijikata it became 'a deadly poison ... one spoonful of it contains all that is needed to paralyze me' (quoted in Fraleigh and Nakamura 2006:21). The seed for their eventual collaboration during the late 1950s and 1960s in the creation of this completely new form of radical dance, *butoh*, had been sown.

Ohno Kazuo was born in Hokkaido – the northernmost island in Japan in 1906. After graduating from the Japan Athletic College in Tokyo where he studied the Denmark and Rudolf Bode modes of corporal expression and exercise, he started his teaching career in physical education. Originally inspired by a performance of the Spanish dancer Antonia Merce (known as La Argentina) in 1928, in 1933 he began to study contemporary dance at the Baku Ishii Dance school, and in 1936 studied German *Neue Tanz* with Takaya Eguchi and Misako Miya. His early dance work focused on modern expressionist dance. Between 1938 and 1946 he served in the Japanese army throughout World War II. After the war, he returned to teaching and continued to pursue dance.

His first public dance performance was in 1949 in Tokyo. Although Hijikata saw Ohno's debut dance, they apparently did not meet until 1954 – two years after Hijikata moved to Tokyo. They first worked together in 1956 when Ohno 'participated in *Ballet Pantomime,* along with Hijikata and Mamako Yoneyama at the Haiya-za Theatre, Roppongi, Tokyo' (Ohno and Ohno 2004:310).

From the very late 1950s, Ohno joined Hijikata in collaborations that further developed *butoh.* Hijikata choreographed many of the pieces that eventually thrust Ohno Kazuo into the international limelight. In 1977, at the age of seventy-one, Ohno premiered *Admiring La Argentina* – his signature performance directed by Hijikata which brought him recognition throughout the world. After Hijikata's untimely death in 1986 at the age of fifty-seven, Ohno Kazuo began to work with his son, Ohno Yoshito, who took over directing his work and often performed with his father onstage. Other notable pieces in his repertoire have included *The Dead Sea* (1985 premiere directed by Hijikata) and *Water Lilies* – a duet with his son (1987). [For images of Ohno Kazuo's *butoh* conduct on-line searches for Ohno Kazuo images, and on youtube search

Ohno Kazuo 'The Dead Sea' (visit: Ohno Kazuo 'The Dead Sea' (http://
www.youtube.com/watch?v=ZUjhQLB0hXY). For a series of video
clips of Kazuo Ohno on youtube, visit (http://www.youtube.com/
channel/HC8PbBNDYaE8o). Also visit (http://www.youtube.com/
watch?v=2gqukIxf8oM)].

In an interview with Richard Schechner when he was seventy-nine
years old, the butoh dancer Ohno Kazuo describes how for him there are
no lines separating dancing from daily life, that is, he 'doesn't commute'.
Nearing his eightieth birthday, he described how 'Everyday I am
constantly developing' (1986:169). Describing his process, Ohno
explained how:

> [T]he costume is the cosmos. I must wear the cosmos and move within
> it ... I dance at the place where the large cosmos meets the small cosmos.
> I stand in the large cosmos and everywhere my hand reaches is the small
> cosmos. I understand where the meeting place is ...
>
> I want spectators to say, 'I am so glad to be alive. Watching this gives me
> the power to go on living.'
>
> (Ohno Kazuo 1986a:165, 164, 169)

Improvisation is central Ohno's practice; but that improvisation is as
much in his internal processes of 'heart and mind, sitting and writing'
as in actual movement in the studio (1986a:165).

> I practice every day. Like this: [Ohno demonstrates a mother holding a
> child by one hand.] I respect studio practice, but movement in the womb,
> for example, I do not need to practice. I have experienced it. Daily, all day
> long, I try to remember. I remember what my mother did – I remember
> some great feeling coming from my mother, but then when I look back,
> the world was collapsing. I think until I understand-then that comes to the
> stage as a technique, not a dance technique but something of my own.
> Isn't that like practicing? And I improvise. Everyday I live in practice.
> (1986a:165)

Entering a world of remembrance for Ohno is clearly a place where his
embodied imagination actively operates. It is not a fixed place in
which a stereotypical memory as an image appears in the chrono-
logical past, but a point of entry into what was described earlier in
this chapter as *ma* – that empty place of possibility where 'movement'
arises. *Kokoro* – his heart/mind – is activated and animated in the
moment of recollection and re-membering. This is clearly *not* a
'mental' exercise, but rather a complete, embodied engagement in a

psychophysical experience that arises in the moment of re-membering. Inner movement moves him.

Ohno Yoshito describes how his father constantly stimulated 'his imagination by reading poetry and haiku, studying paintings and other visual artists' work during the long gestation period required in his creative process' until the point where there was 'a blueprint of his inner universe on paper' (Ohno and Ohno 2004:9). But this blueprint is always rediscovered and remade in a process of free interaction with that universe in the moment. Ohno 'attains a level of consciousness that allows him to forget the self' thereby freeing 'him from certain strictures – such as rigid choreography – and ... enable him to flow with all that surges forth from his interior life' (Ohno and Ohno 2004:18).

For example, the published performance score of 'The Dead Sea', choreographed/created by Ohno Kazuo and danced by Ohno Yoshito and Ohno Kazuo (1986b:170), is one-page long. It consists of an evocative prelude and a series of six titled sections, each with annotated activating images and/or music, and notation of a few actions/reactions. Specific images and music are provocations within that empty space (*mushin*) where the self has been completed divested so that what arises in the moment spontaneously 'surges forth from his interior life' (Ohno and Ohno 2004:18).[27]

The Dead Sea
Vienna Waltz and Ghost
Dancers: Ohno Yoshito and Ohno Kazuo
Choreographer; Ohno Kazuo

Steps of the dead carrying love;
Bewilderment of the dead searching for love.

1. *Greeting*

I feel crushed and want to cry, want to play, want to die, want to live. I think that 'the shape of the sou' is one undifferentiated mass, that cannot be divided into parts.

2. *The Dead Sea*

(music: Josquin Des Pres, *Royal Fanfare*, Tokyo Brass Quintet)
A resounding fanfare: many small animals scurrying over the mountains; a middle-aged woman walking towards her death. At some point these two overlap and become the mountains surrounding the Dead Sea. They have both received life from their mothers' wombs, and naturally grow close to each other. It seems that the animals feel a bewildering love for this woman who is eternally dying. I have to pull up my skirt to answer them.

3. *Requiem*

(music: Johan Strauss, *March of the Gypsy Baron, Voices of Spring*)
Joyful cry of the dead, march of the living.

4. *Episode in the Creation*

(music: The Great Litany, Orthodox Church of Osaka)
Not being able to help in even a small way in the creation of Heaven and Earth, I fall on my back, feet Heaven-pointing, as if standing upside down.

5. *Deserted Garden*

(music: W.A. Mozart, Piano Sonata No. 11 in A Major, K. 331)
Dead angel.

6. *Vienna Waltz*

(music: Johann Strauss, *Artist's Life*)

I imagine ghosts streaming from the long-abandoned fortress, like overflowing flowers. When I danced to this music in Europe, I felt strange spirits staring at me – but in that horror I saw beauty and goregousness suddenly blossom.

Note: During the performance, from time to time an unknown being appears and disappears, casting a light like salt, or like a pillar of salt.
(Ohno Kazuo 1986b:170)

Given the centrality of 'the flower' (*hana*) in Japanese poetry, Japanese gardens, and in *nō*, it is not surprising that Ohno Kazuo in his workshops invites participants to work in/with/through flowers. In his aesthetic 'a flower is constantly cited as the ideal mode of existence' to which the dancer aspires (Ohno and Ohno 2004:89). In a transcription of a workshop in which 'becoming a flower' was the central point of entry into the work, Ohno explained how:

Just because you admire flowers or find them attractive is no reason to imitate them. What's to stop you from becoming a flower? If those eyes of yours, your soul, your way of looking at the world were to burn as much energy as you've so far consumed here at the workshop, you could burst into bloom right here before our very eyes. There's nothing stopping you from becoming a flower. It blossoms for all time by pushing itself to the edge, by offering all it has to give. We're now getting to the heart of the matter of today's workshop. It's absolutely immaterial how you twist or contort your body. That's not going to create a flower. As soon as you offer your eyes, as soon as you offer all that you have to give, I'll see you bloom before me. Offer all you have so as to create a flower. (Ohno and Ohno 2004:218)

In this passage it should be clear how transformation of both mind and body are central to Ohno's work process. Only a process of emptying and divestment of the inner-self creates the opportunity for an 'offering' to be made as a form of psychophysical becoming.

In his performance of *The Dead Sea*, Ohno clasps in his right hand the long stem of a paper flower.

Speaking in relation to his own dance, Kazuo insists that his physical presence must at all times be flowerlike ... By becoming an integral part of the body's nervous system, a flower functions much in the same way as an insect's antennae do: constantly palpitating the air. Not only does it receive and respond to incoming stimuli, it also acts as a natural extension to the hand, and, in doing so, becomes a point of contact with the outside world. It functions independently, as though it were an external eye detached from the trunk of the body. In that respect, it exists both as an autonomous entity and as a sensory organ. (Ohno and Ohno 2004:89)

The 'speaking', all-seeing, 'astonished' butoh body

Although Ohno Kazuo and most *butoh* performers do not include speaking or overt use of the voice in their performances, nevertheless the dancer's body should still project one's 'inner voice', that is, 'dance is the body's voice objectified' (Ohno and Ohno 2004:21). The theatre critic and scholar Tamotsu Watanabe witnesses in Ohno Kazuo a 'body mak[ing] itself heard' (ibid.). Although Ohno's 'voice' is 'muted' and no sound is literally uttered, the body nevertheless speaks. From Yoshito Ohno's perspective his father's 'speaking' body is part of *butoh* as an 'art of suggestion', where much of what is experienced by the audience remains implicit and suggestive in the performer's embodiment. 'We find ourselves perceiving his inner world unravel before our very eyes' (Ohno and Ohno 2004:21).

One example of the process of activating the bodymind Ohno Kazuo utilizes is working with how one 'sees' and where one locates 'the eyes'. For Ohno 'the entire body must become a receptor organ for light', that is, the eyes are not restricted to their fixed physiological location in the head; but rather, 'the entire body, from head to foot, is capable of visually assimilating our immediate surroundings' (2004:24). In workshops, Ohno 'repeatedly stresses the necessity to start looking with the underside of the foot' so that one can eventually 'see with our feet' (ibid.). Therefore, the eyes 'migrate throughout the body' allowing perception to move out to the world or to explore within (ibid.). Indeed, all the senses must be fully embodied, and the dancer should be able to morph awareness from its physiological location, such as the ear, into any other part of the bodymind. Optimally one becomes all seeing, all hearing, et cetera. The bodymind of the *butoh* dancer becomes an open conduit between inner and outer, able to transform and morph in an instant.

We have already seen examples of the *butoh* performer's process of transformation in the example of 'The Dead Sea' and in Ohno's workshop exercises. Psychophysical transformation is evident in the *butoh-fu* first developed and recorded by Hijikata from 1970 as a form of notation chronicling the performance scores he developed and created in workshops and rehearsals. *Butoh-fu* are a series of poetic, visual, onomatopoetic images which serve to animate, astonish, and evoke a psychophysical response from the performer as she moves into/through embodying, becoming, and living within each specific image. They are a system of notation that constitutes a repeatable performance score within which there is a constant process of transformation from one image to the next. In her essay, 'Hijikata Tatsumi: The Words of Butoh,' Kurihara Nanako explains how central words, language, and writing were to Hijikata's process. 'For Hijikata the body is a metaphor for words and words are a metaphor for the body' (2000a:16).

One of Hijikata's *butoh-fu* recorded by Waguri Yukio – a student and performer with Hijikata between 1972 and 1986 – and utilized in the teaching of *butoh* by Australian choreographer/dancer, Fran Barbe [Figure 3.6], her version of 'You Live Because Insects Eat You':

A person is buried in a wall.

S/he becomes an insect.

The internal organs are parched and dry.

The insect is dancing on a thin sheet of paper.

The insect tries to hold falling particles from its own body.

And dances, making rustling noises.

The insect becomes a person, who is wandering around.

So fragile, s/he could crumble at the slightest touch.

(In Fraleigh and Nakamura 2006:136; see Waguri 1998).

Figure   3.6 Australian *butoh* dancer/choreographer Fran Barbe's
'Palpitations'.

Barbe explains how the performers should in no way attempt to literally
mime each image; rather, working from the inside-out, each image
ideally 'act(s) on and change(s) your body'/mind (ibid.). The *butoh*
dancer sees/experiences things from the perspective of being/becoming
an inanimate object – the person buried in a wall; an insect; an insect
experiencing one's organs as they parch and dry; an insect attempting to
hold the particles falling; as insect dancing on such a thin sheet of paper;
as a person ... wandering ... . fragile ... .crumbling. The moments of transformation from one state or image to the next is crucial as it is in this
space between the dancer's experience of being/becoming/inhabiting/
embodying is manifest over time, and in the experiential changes that
can be palpable to the audience.

As evident in this *butoh-fu*, there is a sense that everything/everywhere
is 'alive' and a potential source of enlivening animation *at this moment in
time*. Fraleigh describes how Hijikata 'wanted to uncover the dance already
happening in the body', while one of his successors, Takenouchi, assumes
that '"everything is already dancing"' (quoted in Fraleigh and Nakamura

2006:1). If everything *is* already animated and in movement then every-thing is potentially open to constant transformation and change.

In *butoh* performances which are exceptional, as Holledge and Tomkins note,

> Audience members not only see, but *sense* and *feel* the presence of the body... There is a kinaesthetic dimension to live performance that inte-grates body-to-body awareness'. (2000:135)

Turning to Deleuze and Guattari and their 'concept of desiring machines', Holledge and Tomkins argue that

> [w]hen this model is applied to the theatre, flows become sensations, as well as words and information. Of course, there is an inscribed surface of the body that is read visually, but in addition there are sounds, affects, and the invisible, but palpable, energies and intensities... Tomiko Takai... describes the relationship between the audience and the per-former as a 'united space' in which 'one breathes out, and the other breathes in'. (2000:135)

Transformation and metamorphosis are central to the operation of this '"desiring machine"' (2000:137). Hijikata assumed bodyminds were completely transformational and could learn to morph into any kind of matter – organic or inorganic since '"there is a small universe in the body"' (Holledge and Tomkins 2000:137). *Butoh* as a constantly morphing radical project of embodiment and awakening in/to embod-iment is summed up in Tanaka Min's 'Stand by Me!':

I begin to dance:

> so that I restore the sense to the intellect.
> so that I may not perfect myself.
> so that I re-encounter my old emotions.
> so even the woman next door will know
> that I am a dancer.
> so again and again to be born into the world.
> so I run through the sceneries I picture in layers.
> so I summon myself a dizzy spell.
> so I expel from my soul my conservative thoughts.
> so I let my body be the abode of images of others.
> I know well the moment when the body forms sweat.
> I now want to create instinct
> to howl the mystical antiquity.
> I am always sensing someone's body.

> (Tanaka Min 1986b:152)

[To see an example of Tanaka Min's *butoh*, visit Tanaka Min: 'The Rite of Spring' (http://www.youtube.com/watch?v=E9QrTA-Q4Xg).]

Paying homage in 1986 to the primary founder of *butoh*, Hijikata Tatsumi, Tanaka described '*ankoku butoh*' (darkness dance) as 'a joyous despair' in which 'the body does not exist unless one is astonished with its ingenuous state' (Tanaka 1986c:153). For many *butoh* artists, their dancing *is* an embodiment of the paradox of 'joyous despair'. *Butoh* performance is often a matter of holding in embodied tension/suspension this type of paradox. *Butoh* dancing as a way of life is for many *butoh* performers a pathway – if not to enlightenment (*satori*), then towards a lived bodymind that is in as constant a state of 'astonishment' as is possible. Min Tanaka announces that his 'actual work is to awaken emotions of the body sleeping in the depth of history' (1986c:154). He chooses the word '*shin-tai* ("mind-body")... to describe the body' he dances and lives as he attempts 'to become an artist who shoots an arrow into everyday life' (1986c:155). Hijikata's long-term female collaborator/ dancer, Ashikawa Yōko, explained how

> *Butoh* is not something you can do casually. The body must be in a constant state of change. I want the body to be reduced to a single core of spirit, to disappear, to be beautiful even in contortion. I believe you must be very harsh, very disciplined in finding the body's ideal expression. (quoted in Holledge and Tomkins 2000:142)

At the point of Hijikata's untimely death in 1986, *butoh* 'was an ongoing process' that for Hijikata 'never could be finished or achieved' (Nanako 2000:25). That is still the case today. *Butoh* continues to be a set of psychophysical processes on a pathway towards embodied astonishment both within Japan and in an international/intercultural context. Many non-Japanese performers, such as Fran Barbe, have trained with Japanese *butoh* performer/choreographers, and are choreographing/creating new *butoh*-inspired work throughout the world.

A brief glimpse into the psychophysical processes of Suzuki Tadashi and Ōta Shōgo

In the section on intercultural performance in Chapter 1 and in Appendix I – an historical/contextual introduction to intercultural theatre – I briefly introduced a few examples of Japanese encounters with other cultures, including the 'new drama' movement (*shingeki*) which developed in Japan early in the twentieth century.[28] For Osanai Kaoru who founded the Free Theatre in Tokyo in 1909 and the other

Japanese inside the 'new drama' movement, their fascination with the West was so complete that

> it was only natural that all the tenets of realistic theatre were swallowed whole: the dramaturgy based on the dialectics of conflicting powers, the acting style aimed at the lifelike portrayal of individual characters, the belief in the psychological motivation of human behavior, and the underlying assumption that the ultimate standard of reality is logically explicability. (Takahashi 2004:1)

So devoted was Osanai to reproducing European realist theatre as precisely as possible to the Japanese contemporary stage that when he returned to Tokyo from Russia in 1912 after observing Stanislavsky directing at the Moscow Art Theatre, he attempted 'to reproduce every detail he had jotted down' in his notebooks in his own production (Takahashi 2004:2). As discussed in Chapter 1, *shingeki*'s direct imitation of Europe was, ultimately, a dead end artistically and aesthetically.

With the new opening to the West and America in particular on the conclusion of World War II, new forms of politically leftist *shingeki* flourished for awhile. But as Takahashi Yasunari explains, *shingeki* ultimately took too much for granted from Western theatrical/dramatic paradigms – the priority of the dramatic text, the actor and director as servants of the text, and 'the simplistic mimetic doctrine of realism that the actor had only to try to imitate and reproduce the lifelike and lifesize reality of the ordinary world,' that is, *shingeki* had 'failed to establish its own theatrical esthetics about the ontological identity of the actor' (2004:2–3).

Within the wider context of the world-wide student political movement and responses to American involvement in Vietnam, Japan's 'Little Theatre' movement was launched as a direct response to *shingeki* as a bankrupt, outmoded mimicking of the West. The theatre work of both Suzuki Tadashi and Ōta Shōgo were part of this new movement.

It was in 1972 that Suzuki began to develop a method of psychophysical training – an approach to training actors not only used by Suzuki and his own theatre company, but throughout the world. Suzuki provides his own account of the training in 'The Grammar of the Feet' in *The Way of Acting* (1986). Other accounts include those by James Brandon based on his early description of the training at the Waseda Little Theatre in 1976 (published in 1978), Paul Allain (2002:95–135, 2009) and Ian Carruthers (2007:70–97). Suzuki's training was independently developed and is not a direct copy of any traditional training; however, it is clearly informed in many ways by the underlying elements and principles of Japanese bodymind work discussed thus far. Suzuki has explained how

> [w]e don't copy the forms (*kata*) just as they are. We aren't learning to perform Kabuki. It's the feeling of the particular form that I try to teach so the actor can revitalize that marvelous physicality that comes from *nō* and from Kabuki. (Quoted in Carruthers 2007:71)

Suzuki emphasizes that the training he has developed over the years is not simply a set of physical exercises for muscular/physical development.

> These are *acting* disciplines [*kunren*]. Every instant of every discipline, the actor must be expressing the emotion of some situation, according to his own bodily interpretation … The actor composes … on the basis of … sense of contact with the ground. (Suzuki quoted in Carruthers 2007:71)

Similar to the discussion of *nō* movement earlier in this chapter, Suzuki's training emphasizes the area between the hips (*koshi*) known as

> *hara* (the psycho-physical centre) just below the bellybutton. To create a sense of 'presence,' the actor needs at all times an artificial sense of 'resistance' in the *hara*. It is the home of the breath, the platform on which we place our torso, the center of gravity. (Carruthers 2007:80)

Carruthers calls attention to how Suzuki training emphases 'body and mind' as a 'psycho-physical unity' and how Suzuki's 'stop' during training where the actor momentarily suspends overt physical action while sustaining the completely and full 'inner' life behind the 'frozen' posture, is similar to moments of 'no action' (*iguse*) discussed with regard to *nō*.

Given the availability of so many published accounts of Suzuki's training and how his own creative process is embedded in the training, we will turn our attention to the less-known work of Ōta Shōgo.

Ōta Shōgo's 'theatre of divestiture' and nō

The Japanese playwright/director Ōta Shōgo (1939–2006) and his company, Theatre of Transformation (Tenkei Gekijo) are particularly noted for the development and refinement of what Mari Boyd describes as 'theatre of quietude' (2006). Ōta and his company are best known for the trilogy of non-verbal performances (the 'station plays') created from 1981 when they created and premiered, *The Water Station* – a remarkably suggestive, poetic, non-verbal piece of theatre. The published ' "script as document"' is a record of the psychophysical score that resulted from the initial rehearsal process (Ōta 1990). *The Water Station* was devised and created from a diverse set of source materials gathered from plays, novels, paintings, poetry, film, as well as some scripted dialogue initially authored and/or selected by Ōta for possible use in some scenes (Boyd 2006:107–109) [Figure 3.7]. The two main premises guiding the company's development of the performance score from these source materials included 'acting in silence, and to make that silence living human time, acting at a very slow tempo' (Ōta 1990:150). According to Ōta, it should take an actor five minutes to walk a distance of two meters (1990:151).

The artistic process that crystallized for Ōta while working on *The Water Station* has been described by Mari Boyd as one of 'divestiture' (2006, *passim*), that is, the discarding or paring away of anything

Figure 3.7 Ōta Shōgo's *The Water Station* (Scene 3): Melissa Leung (foreground) as Woman with Parasol, and Jeungsook Yoo as Girl (background). A TTRP production directed by Phillip B. Zarrilli (2004: Esplanade Theatre Studio, Singapore). Photo by permission of Phillip B. Zarrilli and Intercultural Theatre Institute.

unnecessary from the performance score and theatrical environment so that actors and audience alike are taken out of their everyday world and focus on the irreducible elements of our shared existence – what Ōta calls 'the "unparaphrasable realm of experience"' (1990:151). As a result of this working method, Ōta's body of work – especially his trilogy known as 'station' plays (*The Water Station* (*Mizo no eki*, 1981), *The Earth Station* (*Chi no eki*, 1985), and *The Wind Station* (*Kaze no eki*, 1986) – are 'dominated by silence, slow movement, and empty space' (Boyd 2006:x).

When members of an audience enter a theatre for a performance of *The Water Station*, they immediately encounter the sound and sight of a constantly running, broken water faucet. As the thin stream of water from the spout hits the surface of the pool gathered in the basin, it creates a constant, base-line sound in an otherwise silent theatre. To the audience's left and upstage of the broken faucet is a pathway – similar to that of the traditional *nō* stage – along which a series of travelers enter. The pathway leads them to a place near the 'water station' centre stage. Upstage centre and behind the pathway is a huge pile of junk – shoes, tyres, dishes, bicycles, birdcages, crates, et cetera, that have been discarded (or abandoned?). From the junk pile to the audience's right, the pathway continues – the way taken by each traveler as s/he departs.[29] In a series of nine scenes travelers enter the pathway from the audience's left alone, in pairs, or in a group. First the Girl, and each traveler in turn, encounters and interacts with the water before continuing their journey. For the duration of the approximately 100 to 120-minute performance the base-line sound created by the constantly running water is shaped into a dramatically variable soundscape in two ways. Each time a traveler interacts with the running water by touching it, taking a drink from the tap, filling a canteen, bathing, et cetera, the type of sound produced by the water changes. The soundscape is also shaped by Ōta's strategic scoring of occasional incidental music, such as Erik Satie's *Three Gymnopédies*, no. 1 which is heard in the background in the transition between the Girl's encounter with the water at the end of Scene 1 and the entrance of the Two Men at the beginning of Scene 2, or the growing presence of Albinoni's Oboe Concerto during much of the group scene.

While working on *The Water Station*, Ōta and his company were exploring the process of how to 'stage living silence' (Ōta 1990:151). In a programme note to the 1985 Tokyo production, Ōta asked:

Is it not possible to construct a drama from the nature of human existence itself rather than from elements of human behavior? I feel this question lies behind my search for appropriate dramatic experiences and my approach towards silence as a dramatic expression in itself...To me...silence is not so much a thing but a very realistic situation. In the course of one day, I wonder how much time we spend uttering words (i.e., we are out of silence)?...[W]e spend almost 90% of our lives in silence...[S]ilence is not a kind of irregular behavior which belongs to special circumstances; rather it is the reality of our normal state. To exist, therefore, means to be mainly in silence...The silence may spring from the great amount of words that fills that human being's existence...The 'Drama of Silence' which I am trying to construct is not designed to exalt human beings to some mystical height, but rather to root them in the fact of 'being there.' I want to explore the depths of the silence which occupies 90% of all our lives. (Quoted in Sarlos 1985:137–138)

If, as Ōta states, silence is the human norm, then it can be argued that 'verbalization does not deserve the prominence granted it by a drama of activity' (Boyd 1990:153).

Ōta's 'drama of silence' is first and foremost a divestiture of (unnecessary) words. Given the soundscape described above, Ōta's 'living silence' is not the absence of any sound per se, but an attempt to turn down the volume of everyday life by abandoning the noise and clutter of our constantly wagging tongues and squirrel-like, busy minds. Ōta's theatrical silence is equally created by slowing the actors down so that each everyday action they perform is divested of anything unnecessary.

Ōta's process of divestiture de-emphasizes 'the functions of the playwright and director' and 'return[s] the stage to the actor,' that is, 'the physical presence of the actor in the here and now of the stage' becomes the focus (Boyd 2006:97). Drawing inspiration from traditional nō acting during the 1970s and 1980s, Ōta and the Tenkei company evolved their own rigorous actor training process as a means of paring down the actor's overt modes of expression – 'words, speech, gestures, and facial expressions' (Boyd 2006:98–99) – to that fundamental relationship and confrontation in the moment between 'the doer and done'. Tenkei's training regime eventually included four important elements: '(1) running to build endurance, (2) practicing yoga asana to develop dynamic stillness, balance, and concentration [...], (3) doing Suzuki-method centering exercises to strengthen the lower body' and at many rehearsals (4) the repetition of 'the slow walk' which forced the actors to work on 'slowness, balance, and the preservation of the natural arc of each step' (ibid.:127). The result of slowing down the actor's respiratory system through deep abdominal breathing is to distil the actor's relationship to each impulse and action so that this fundamental relationship becomes the focus of the audience's attention. Given the centrality of yoga to Tenkei's training regime, it is not surprising that Ōta emphasized 'the importance of the spine' and verticality in the development of his actors (Boyd 2006:99–100).

> On the level of practice, Ōta notes that our sensitivity to the outer world depends partly on the condition of the spine as a metaphoric antenna, and wants acting to be done on the highest level of receptivity. (Boyd 2006:100)

The kind of heightened *ki*/sensory awareness required of the actor to fully sustain slowed-down actions is a result of deep psychophysical training which engages the spine and thereby the lower abdominal region (*dantian/hara*) as emphasized in *nō* training.

From the perspective of the actor, slowing down allows the actor to constantly maintain 'the still centre of reality' (Boyd 2006:153) within oneself while embodying each state of being/doing that constitutes the score. The actor's dynamic inner energy (*ki*) thereby resonates with and between the actor *qua* actor and the actor's fictive body as one inhabits each action and state of being/doing.

Robert K. Sarlos describes the quality and affect of this process of divestiture with regard to the Girl's entrance during the 1985 production of *The Water Station* in Tokyo as follows:

> My body has hardly adjusted to the cramped space, my eyes to the dim light, when I grow aware of Young Girl [Tomoko Ando]…on the stage left walkway. Is she standing still? No, she is moving. Slower than I have ever seen a human being move, she lifts one foot, places it with control and grace in front of the other, and repeats this movement with her second foot. Her entire torso moves along almost imperceptibly. In about eight minutes, she traverses the dozen feet that brings her near enough to the tap to notice it. (Sarlos 1985:131)

In this slowed down, non-verbal world, time itself slows down to a point where 'silence breathes as living human time, not as form' (Ōta 1990:150). Without the constant chatter of talking heads, for actors and audience alike the visual and auditory senses of observing and listening open up and are heightened. '[B]y reducing the tempo…Ōta breaks the dynamic propulsion of activity and enables the attention to linger on seemingly trivial events, leading to a new perception of life' (Boyd 1990:153).

Given the stark, barren landscape and the length of time the audience has to observe each figure's relationship to each moment they inhabit that landscape, 'stark images of divestiture, wandering, and bare survival are presented in their unrelenting entirety' (Boyd 1990:153). Ōta has been quoted as saying, the play is located '"anywhere and everywhere, [in] a place out of time … There are words here … you just can't hear them"' (Montemayor 1998:5).

In contrast to the overt activity and conventions of realist drama which provide motivations and actions for individual characters within a narrative structure that guides an audience towards making a particular interpretation or gaining a specific meaning from what they observe, Ōta intentionally explores 'the power of passivity' (Boyd 2006:3). The audience is passive in that the stripped down *mise-en-scène* and the actors' engagement with the slowed-down performance score do not guide them to a specific interpretation, meaning, or conclusion; rather, there is space and time to allow associations to arise as shaped by the actors' qualitative deployment of their inner energy to each action in the score.

The development of Ōta's minimalism

Because of the development of his unique aesthetic of quietude achieved through divestiture, Ōta Shōgo is considered one of the most notable playwrights and directors to have emerged during the 1960s from the Japanese experimental little theatre (*shogekijo*) movement. If, as Mari Boyd argues, *The Water Station* is the 'play that best illustrates Ōta Shōgo's aesthetics of quietude' (2006:167), his aesthetic and work did not materialize overnight. Rather, there was a lengthy process of experimentation and gestation that eventually produced both. Ōta co-founded the Theatre of Transformation (Tenkei Theatre Company) in 1968 with Hodojima Takeo, Shinagawa Toru, and others in Akasaka, Tokyo. During the early years of the company Ōta served as playwright, assistant director, and then director. By 1970 Ōta was designated head of the company, and provided leadership as its director and resident playwright until the company was disbanded in 1988.[30] During the first decade of its existence, the company mainly produced works by Ōta as he and the company struggled to discover their own 'alternative theatre code'. (Boyd 2006:73)

When Ōta and the Tenkei actors decided to stage their next project on a traditional *nō* stage in 1977, Ōta's search for a means of divesting everything unnecessary from a live performance crystallized, and the company reached a turning-point in its development. Drawing on the well-known Japanese legend of Komachi as well as Kan'ami's (1333–1384) *nō* play, *Sotoba Komachi*, based on the legend, Ōta authored *The Tale of Komachi Told by the Wind* (*Komachi fuden*).[31] Once rehearsals of the play began on the actual *nō* stage, Yasumi Akihito reports how Ōta and the cast felt that the space itself and its history

> rejected their contemporary language. Confronted with the cosmic quality of the time-space of the *nō* stage, Ōta was forced to strip the actors of their social attributes. The task of rewriting or deleting lines began. By the time the actors reached their final rehearsal, the Old woman (Komachi) had been silenced. (Yasumi 2004:217)

By the premiere, during the two-and-a-half hour performance, no lines were spoken for approximately two-thirds of the time. In terms of Ōta's script, more than half of the dialogue was suppressed and not spoken on stage.

An unkempt Old Woman (Komachi) appears on the bridgeway 'dressed in a bedraggled "twelve-layered" court kimono' bleached and faded white 'by the passing years' (Ōta 2004:220–221). Shuffling along with 'peculiar slow steps' (Senda Akihito 1997:74), she enters 'as if searching for the whereabouts of the breeze or as if abandoning herself to the whims of a gentle wind.' It takes her five minutes to reach the stage proper where she comes to 'a halt ... sway[ing] as the wind penetrates her kimono and caresses her body' (Shōgo Ōta 2004:221). 'We in the audience, pulled in by this slow method of movement, which surpasses any category of realism, seem to enter into an unreal, a dream world' (Senda Akihito 1997:74).

The Tale of Komachi Told by the Wind follows the aesthetic logic of the phantasmal type of *nō* play in which there is a 'rereading of a past event through a dream' and where 'multiple time-spaces' simultaneously exist (Yasumi Akihito 2004:218).

> 'Fuden,' in the original Japanese title, usually means 'to be transmitted from somewhere, somehow,' 'fu' is wind (and can also refer to 'inner landscape' or the 'movement of the heart'). The fragments of the story, like leaves dancing in the wind, gather on the stage and then scatter. (Yasumi Akihito 2004:217)

The process of working on *The Tale of Komachi Told by the Wind* propelled Ōta and his Tenkei actors towards the full realization of Ōta's aesthetic of quietude achieved through divestiture in *The Water*

Station and the company's subsequent work.[32] It also first called to the attention of critics and the international theatre world Ōta's unique aesthetic.

The impact of *nō* theatre, Ōta's 'theatre of divesture', and elements of *butoh* are all evident in the work of a number of contemporary theatre directors in Japan and in the West. As discussed in Chapter 1, this includes the influence of *nō* and *kyōgen* on the seminal acting, directing, and teaching work of Yoshi Oida. In her recent essay Mari Boyd (2012) traces the impact of specific approaches to the notion of 'quietude' in performance on the contemporary work of Okamura Yojiro, Artistic Director of Ami Theatre (Tokyo), and my own work as Artistic Director of The Llanarth Group (Wales).

> Intercultural theatre has spawned many different kinds of hybrids. Recently the interweaving of different cultures and theatrical styles has become extremely subtle. Among those who devise such complex inter-cultural theatre are creator-dramaturg-director Phillip B. Zarrilli and play-wright-director Yojiro Okamura. They use primarily Asian aesthetic principles and training methods in combination with non-Asian ideas and dramatic content to construct highly experimental performances…[They both employ] quietude as a central concept in their respective work. (2012:43)

Boyd goes on to examine in detail Okamura's recent *Aminadab*, and The Llanarth Group's *Told by the Wind* (co-created by Kaite O'Reilly, Jo Shapland, and Phillip B. Zarrilli) as examples of these new intercultural hybrid performances.[33]

Concluding discussion

In this chapter I examined in depth the psychophysical elements and principles that inform Japanese *nō* and *butoh*, and briefly examined the psychophysical training and work of Suzuki Tadashi and Ōta Shōgo. I discussed how although there are continuities between today's *nō* and the *sarugaku-nō* developed by Zeami, there were major changes to the performance of *nō* over the centuries.

Even though historically in the post-World War II period there was resistance to and reaction against the ways and forms of the past, it is striking to note the degree to which many of the underlying psycho-physical elements and principles which informed the writing of Zeami's treatises and the development of *nō* continue to inform, albeit in different ways from, the practices of *butoh*, Suzuki, and Ōta, legacies in Japan and internationally. For example, there is a shared assumption within Japan and increasingly outside of Japan that psychophysical practices are a process of cultivation, even if/when those processes are *not* strict forms. There is assumed to be a continuing process of refinement and engagement of the (body)'mind' (*kokoro*) through these processes of psychophysical cultivation.

Whether *nō*, *butoh*, Suzuki training, or Ōta's approach to 'quietude' in his theatre, all share certain common assumptions about there existing a space (*ma*) into which one's artistry might open. This is not a literal, pre-determined place, but that unknown space where experience and consciousness are constituted in the moment of doing and therefore where something might happen.

Contemporary Japanese philosophers of the body, Ichikawa Hiroshi and Yuasa Yasuo have been exploring alternative Eastern approaches to understanding the nature of lived experience or the lived body beyond Cartesian body-mind dualism. For Yuasa there is 'no sharp demarcation between the metaphysical and physical dimensions. The two are mutually permeating regions in a continuum; cultivation is a process in which one's soul progresses gradually from the physical to the metaphysical dimension' (1987:217).

Ichikawa 'stresses that human beings are physical existence, and cannot exist apart from the "lived body"' (Ozawa-de Silva 2002:24). For Ichikawa artistic practices are understood to organize 'bodily forces or energies that are manifest in various concrete dramatic, physical or material forms' (Ozawa-de Silva 2002:36). When human experience of the lived body has been cultivated by certain psychophysical practices, this can lead to an increasingly subtle, heightened level of bodymind integration and unity.

> When the level of unity is high, we experience spiritual existence and feel ourselves as the centre of freedom ... [Ichikawa] concludes that the body is spirit: spirit and mind are nothing but two names given to the same reality ... When we achieve a certain level of unity 'the body truly becomes the human body', and the distinction between spirit and mind disappears'.
> (Ozawa-de Silva 2002:27)

This is the territory of Zeami's 'highest level' of attainment. It is an ideal-typical model of attainment that the artist cannot willfully strive to attain.

Looking ahead to the discussion in Chapter 6 of 'The Situated Body,' along with the work of Ichikawa and Yuasa, some of the most compelling recent research in cognitive neurosciences is that focused on Zen Buddhist practices, such as the in-depth research by James H. Austin, *Zen and the Brain* (1998), Alan B. Wallace, *Contemplative Science: Where Buddhism and Neuroscience Converge* (2007), and Francisco Varela and Natalie Depraz collaborative research (Varela and Depraz 2003; Depraz and Varela 2003). Austin describes what Zeami identified long ago, and what is clearly witnessed in contemporary Japanese psychophysical practices:

> Meditators discover a surprising fact when they finally arrive at moments of 'no-thought': *they do not have to think to be conscious.* For consciousness starts with *being aware.* The awareness has a receptive flavor. (Austin 1998:296)

We return to this discussion in Chapter 6.

Two of the constant underlying assumptions about a psychophysical understanding of acting as a phenomenon and process across the inter-cultural set of examples discussed thus far is the importance of viewing acting as a mode of 'experiencing', *and* as a deeply engaged process of 'embodiment'. In Chapter 4, Jerri Daboo focuses on the psychophysical dimensions of acting practices generated by Stanislavsky and those who followed him. Significantly, in Jean Benedetti's recent new translation of Stanislavsky' seminal *An Actor's Work*, he translates the two year cycle of training as 'Year One: Experiencing' and 'Year Two: Embodiment' (2008:vii). 'Experiencing' and 'embodiment' point directly to the common psychophysical territory of the actor's work as an enactive, embodied, experiencing 'doer' seeking to develop one's artistry to a virtuosic/ideal level of performance.

Notes

1. As recommended for Chapter 2, for readers unfamiliar with the genres of theatre and performance discussed in this chapter – *nō, kabuki, butoh,* and the work of Suzuki Tadashi and Ōta Shōgo, it is highly recommended that you complete a search of You Tube for current videos that might be viewed. As always on You Tube, some of the performances posted will be of excellent quality, while others may be of poor quality. For example, a short video extract from Ohno Kazuo's 'The Dead Sea' is posted on You Tube at the time of publication.
2. While Chapter 2 was based on the author's extensive periods of training, practice, and field research in Kerala, India, this chapter is based primarily

on analysis of translations of key treatises by Zeami and Zenchiku, and sources available in English on *nō*, *butoh*, Suzuki Tadashi, and Ōta Shōgo. Some of the sources are interviews with contemporary *nō* and *kyōgen* actors (Nomura Shirō 1997; Nomura Mansaku 1997; Richard Emmert 1997). In addition some observations are based on intensive training the author experienced under the guidance of Matsui Akira of the Kita *nō* school as part of a Japan Foundation sponsored residency between the University of Wisconsin-Madison and Farley Richmond at Michigan State University. He was also introduced to *kyōgen* by Don Kenny and Andy Tsubaki. In 1984 he had an exchange with Suzuki Tadashi while Suzuki was in residence with his company in Milwaukee. In 2000 he met with Ōta Shōgo in Seoul, Korea while Ōta was in Seoul directing a production of his play, *Sarachi*. The author has directed two productions of Ōta's seminal non-verbal performance text, *The Water Station* (Zarrilli 2009). He has also regularly participated in *butoh* workshops for actors led by dancer/choreographer/teacher Fran Barbe.

3. For an excellent discussion of *kyōgen*, see Berberich (1989).
4. Ever since at least the discovery and general publication of Zemi's treatises on *nō*, the aesthetic principle of *yūgen* has been considered central to understanding *nō* and its aesthetic. But as Arthur Thornhill explains, it is impossible to 'arrive at a universal definition of *yūgen* … because the term is used in so many different ways by poets and performers from the tenth century to the present' (1997:36). Thornhill explains that *yūgen* joins two Chinese graphs – the first meaning '"faint" or "distant," the second "dark," with overtones of "mystery"' (1997:36). The second graph possesses a 'strong Taoist flavor' as suggested in the Chinese philosopher Lao Tzu's representation of this aspect of the Tao as 'the nameless, formless realm antecedent to the differentiated world of light' (1997:36). As the Japanese compound *yūgen* it first appears in 'Buddhist commentaries, meaning "difficult" or "obscure"' (1997:36). Thornhill's study of *yūgen* provides a careful articulation of how this key aesthetic principle developed historically within the *nō* tradition. Zeami's earliest utilization and adaptation of *yūgen* was to his style of *nō*. His successor, Zenchiku, made nuanced use of *yūgen* as a dynamic principle of the actor's 'penetration' of his art. The use of the term lessened after Zenchiku's period. In the most recent period there has been a modern revival of use of *yūgen* in contemporary *nō*.
5. For a comprehensive account of these changes over time, see Quinn (2005).
6. In the Western popular imagination and for some Japanese as well, Zen has come to be identified with a range of Japanese artistic practices, often collectively known as 'Zen Arts' – *nō* theatre, the 'way of tea' (*chadō*), calligraphy (*shōdō*), and Japanese martial arts or 'ways' (*budō*). This is part of an historical and sociological process of creating a certain version of 'Japanese-ness'. For a balanced and nuanced ethnographic and historical account see Rupert A. Cox's, *The Zen Arts* (2003).

7. For a specific reading of the 'Buddhist orientation' of the *nō* play, *Seiganji* – a play ascribed to Zeami, see Foard (1980). Foard includes a translation of the play.

8. Rimer and Masakazu translate nine of the treatises (1984). Hare's more recent translation of 2008 includes nineteen complete texts plus two letters by Zeami. See also Nearman's translations of three of Zeami's most important texts regarding actor training and accomplishment in performance (1978, 1980, 1982, 1983). Nearman's translations include astute commentary written from his perspective as a theatre practitioner which will be of particular relevance to those reading this book. Quinn's sustained analysis of Zeami's texts includes translation of many key passages from Zeami's texts, plus a complete annotated translation of *Sandō:* 'The Three Techniques of Nō Composition' (2005: Appendix I).

9. On *miko* see Blacker (1975) and Meeks (2011). See also Ortolani (1984) on shamanism in *nō.*

10. The majority of the approximately 240 *nō* plays still performed today were written during the Muromachi period.

11. See Mark Nearman's four-part introduction to and translation of Zenchiku's *Rokurin Ichiro* treatises (1995a, 1995b, 1995c, 1996).

12. The text is also problematically known as *Kadensho* – the title given to this text when first published in 1909 (Hare 2008:252).

13. As discussed at the end of Chapter 1, the optimal state of the actor for Zeami is inhabiting 'phenomenal consciousness' not 'access consciousness'.

14. The Japanese philosopher Yasuo Yuasa has explained how Western philosophy begins with the question, '"What is the relationship between mind-body?"' whereas an Eastern approach begins with very different questions: '"How does the relationship between the mind and body *come to be* (through cultivation?" or "What does it *become?*"' (1987:18). The Eastern philosophical tradition "starts from the experiential assumption that the mind-body modality changes through training of the mind and body by means of cultivation (*shugyō*) or training (*keiko*)" (Yuasa 1987:18, emphasis added).

15. Zeami's use of the metaphor of 'the transmission of a flower' derives from its previous use in Zen and various other forms of Buddhism. Hare cites the 'celebrated and eloquent kōan from *Mumonkan*' as the source (2008:253).
'Figured as a flower, aesthetic achievement has the potential to provoke a smile (a smile of pleasure, a knowing smile, a smile of acknowledgement or collusion)' (Hare 2008:253).

16. Early in his career Zeami discusses nine rather than three types of characters or stage figures. The reduction from nine to three types represents a 'refinement … suggestive of human prototypes' (Quinn 2005:6).

17. In the list of six principles that follows, some are from the translations of Nearman (1982a) or Hare (2008). It is useful to compare the two.

18. For discussions of the body and experiencing the body in Japan, see Yuasa (1987), Cox (2003), Hahn (2007), Ames and Kasulis (1998), and Kasulis (1998).

19. For Zeami's main account, see *Kakyō* (Nearman 1984b:463–468).

20. *Nō* chanting may have developed in part from or been influenced by shamanic rituals (Ortolani 1984:177) and/or Buddhist *shōmyō* (literally meaning 'bright voice') – a mode of half-spoken, half-sung intonation/chanting of Buddhist texts (either in Sanskrit, Chinese with Japanese pronunciation, or in Japanese) introduced to Japan as early as the mid-sixth century. *Shōmyō* is usually *a capella,* but sometimes rhythmic accompaniment is provided by the hollow wooden instrument known as *mokugyo* or bells. For a discussion of Shingon Shōmyō, see Hill (1982).

21. In Zeami's 'Articles on the Five Sorts of Singing' he addresses vocal styles and describes five types of songs/singing practiced in *sarugaku-nō* of the period (Hare 2008:224–237), while in 'Five Sorts of Singing' he provides a large and diverse 'anthology of songs' providing model songs for training young actors in the various important types/styles of vocalization required of to become a virtuoso performer (Hare 2008:238–415). To give some sense of the range of these types, '*shiugen* means the sound of peace and contentment… [T]he delivery should be straightforward, proceeding with a light touch, in a tone that reflects the voice of order in the world' while in '*yūkyoku*' there should be an added 'grace' so that here 'the singing has a beautiful, yet correct surface'; '*reno*' adds an element of 'tenderness to what is already gentle and quiet'; '*aihyau*' should possess a 'melodic appeal' that 'should come from a sound that makes one aware of impermanence' (Hare 2008:224–226).

22. As Rolf Elberfeld has explained at length, the 'the auditory sense' and 'musical patterns of interpretation' have always been central to Chinese culture (2003:479–480). Elizabeth Wichmann explains how 'the aural dimension of Beijing opera is so fundamentally important to the identity of this theatrical form that attending a Beijing opera performance is traditionally referred to as "listening to theatre" (*tingxi*), and acting in a play is termed "singing theatre" (*changxi*)' (1991:1).

23. For a thorough introduction to Hijikata's work and for translations of some of his most important writings across his career from 1960 through 1985 into English, see the special issue of *TDR* with the lead essay by Nanako (2000a), and Nanako's translations of Hijkata (2000a, 2000b, 2000c). Kurihara Nanako discusses Ashikawa Yōko's important contribution to Hijikata's work in the 1970s, and describes her as that individual 'who could bring into danced reality what Hijikata desired' (2000a:21). See Ohno and Ohno's *Kazuo Ohno's World: from without and within* (2004), with 154 striking photographs of Ohno at work and with Ohno Yoshito's commentary.

24. Tanaka Min was born in 1945. Although he never trained with Hijikata, he sees his work as a development of Hijikata's. For many years he

developed his own unique approach to body-work as part of *butoh*. His early work emphasized extremely slow movement as the dancer connects deeply to the space/landscape they inhabit in the moment. He established 'Body Weather Laboratory' in 1978, and 'Body Weather Farm' in 1985 – an experimental in communal living, farming, and dance, located in the mountain village of Hakushu outside Tokyo. Body Weather work is now taught and practised worldwide. In Body Weather, the body must be in direct contact with and responding to weather, landscape, and nature on a daily basis. Body Weather welcomes people from all walks of life as well as trained dancers.

25. Akaji Maro was a disciple of *butoh* co-founder Hijikata and a member of his company, Jokyo Geiko before founding Dairakudakan. He is sometimes credited with establishing what has become the stereotypical *butoh* 'look' – with white body paint and shaved heads. Dairakudakan gave its first performance in 1972 at the Ushigome Theatre in Tokyo with *Dance Apricot Machine*, and in 1979 presented *People Like Poor Pole*. The company was based in Tokyo. Their work was first seen in the US in 1982 at the American Dance Festival, and the company became one of the most visible on international stages.

26. There had been a long term, radical process of Westernization in Japan from 1853 in the wake of the enforced opening of Japanese ports to Western trade and the concomitant beginning of the Meiji Restoration. The 'opening' of Japan prompted what Noguchi Hiroyuki has described as nothing less than the systematic 'dismantling' of much of Japanese traditional culture from architecture to education (2004). From Noguchi's perspective, many of the underlying elements and principles (*ma*, *ki*, *kata*, etc.) informing modes of embodiment in Japanese *nō* and other traditional arts and that shaped a distinctly Japanese way of life, experience, and consciousness were systematically destroyed leaving Japan a thoroughly 'modern' state.

27. John Barrett notes that 'Both Yoshito and Kazuo Ohno frequently use the term '*mushin*' to describe their working approach to performance' (Ohno, 2004:173).

28. For readers unfamiliar with the history of 'new theatre' or modern spoken drama in Japan at the turn of the twentieth century, it would be useful to read Appendix I which discusses the historical example of interculturalism (West to East) in Japan.

29. In the *nō* theatre all actors exit by the same bridgeway on which they entered to the audience's left. Having all travellers exit to the audience's right extends their world out into and through that of the audience, suggesting the necessity of having to continue their travels.

30. For a chronology and complete discussion of Ōta's life and career, see Boyd (2006:67–80, 255).

31. According to the legend, Komachi was beautiful and possessed superb skill as a poet. While young she had numerous suitors, but she was heartless

and mocked the pain they all suffered. Shii no Shosho, one of her many lovers, travelled a great distance to win her favour. Responding, she said she would not listen until he had made the trip from his house to hers for one hundred nights without interruption. Accepting the challenge he made the long journey each day. On the last night before reaching her, Shii no Shosho died. Growing old, Komachi became a beggar and went mad as she was possessed by the spirit of Shii no Shosho. Kan'ami's *Sotoba Komachi*, is one of a number of *nō* plays based on the legend. In *Sotoba Komachi*, Komachi is a restless spirit unable to die until Shosho's spirit is exorcised by a Buddhist priest.

32. It is important to emphasize that even while Ōta was developing his aesthetic of quietude and process of divestiture he continued to write plays with dialogue. Boyd's full-length study of Ōta's work provides a description and analysis of his plays with dialogue (2006, *passim*).

33. For a discussion of performing *Told by the Wind* from my perspective as a performer inside the performance, see Zarrilli (2012).

4 Stanislavsky and the Psychophysical in Western Acting

Jerri Daboo

The previous two chapters have explored paradigms of psychophysical acting from India and Japan. This chapter moves the discussion to Western approaches to acting, focusing in particular on the work of Konstantin Stanislavsky, and his legacy. What can be seen is that the influence of 'Eastern'[1] practices also played a part in the development of Stanislavsky's work, as did interdisciplinary considerations with his reading of aspects of Western science. Therefore, ways in which the notion of the 'psychophysical' began to emerge within Western acting in the modern period are based in the intercultural and interdisciplinary concerns of this book, and this chapter focuses particularly on areas of the body-mind relationship, consciousness, emotion and scores for the actor, and how these developed in the work of the practitioners discussed.

Introduction

The influence and legacy of Stanislavsky on Western acting is without question. However, the issue for the purpose of this book is about how he developed an approach to acting that is labeled as 'psychophysical', and what might be meant by that in his work. Additionally, this chapter questions how this notion of the psychophysical has been furthered, altered or rejected by subsequent practitioners, teachers, and directors who say that they have based their work on that of Stanislavsky. The current online prospectus for the acting programme at RADA states that the training includes 'Stanislavsky-based rehearsal exercises and project work' (http://www.rada.ac.uk/courses-at-rada/acting-and-performance/ba-hons-in-acting/ba-acting-overview

[21 July 2011]), but the idea of what is 'Stanislavsky-based' has come to mean many things. This chapter will examine common themes throughout the book: of the body-mind relationship, training, emotion, and character, taking Stanislavsky's ideas as a starting-point, and questioning how the notion of the psychophysical has been understood and utilized by actors and directors in different contexts.

There are, inevitably, problematic issues to be acknowledged. The potential for the reification and mystification of Stanislavsky might well lead to the question of why he plays such a key position within this chapter, and the book as a whole. Certainly the intention is not to state that he was either the 'father' or starting-point of investigating acting in this way, nor the sole founder of actor training systems as they are used today. However, his influence within the overall field is such that an investigation of areas of his work cannot be overlooked. There are also the many difficulties encountered with Stanislavsky's work to do with translation, interpretation, adaptation and historical contextualisation which have been discussed thoroughly elsewhere (see Carnicke, Benedetti, Merlin, Whyman). While this chapter takes these issues into account, it does not intend to offer an historical approach to the work of Stanislavsky, but rather to draw out elements related to a psychophysical understanding of the process of acting which can allow for a wider exploration of these areas in relation to the themes raised throughout the book.

There are other questions to be raised in examining issues of actor training in this way. Issues of lineage and transmission are obviously key, and Jonathan Pitches in particular has examined this in relation to Stanislavsky and traditions of Russian actor training (Pitches 2012). Directors such as Grotowski, Barba, and Brook have stated they feel themselves to be part of a direct lineage to Stanislavsky; the American Method practitioners including Strasberg, Adler, and Kazan have used the name of Stanislavsky as being the inspiration for their work, even with the vast changes that they made in their own interpretations of Stanislavsky. Contemporary directors continue this trend, with Katie Mitchell in her recent book on directing stating that 'Most of the tools described in this book come from Konstantin Stanislavsky's teachings, mediated by a secondary interpreter, and then test-run in my own work' (Mitchell 2008:2). The version of Stanislavsky in her book draws on certain areas of his work and overlooks others. It certainly begs the question: 'Whose Stanislavsky is this?' when examining the ways in which subsequent practitioners have declared their allegiance and heritage as stemming directly from the 'Russian master', and why it continues to be important for them to indicate a lineage back to Stanislavsky in this way.

It is also interesting to note that the developers of the different approaches to actor training have tended to be directors. The figure of the director in Western theatre has undergone many developments, with Georg II, Duke of Saxe-Meiningen, generally being acknowledged as the 'first' in the model of contemporary Western directors. Both Georg, in association with Ludwig Chronegk, and then Antoine in Paris, developed their own methods of working with actors in order to fit the aesthetics and forms of productions and plays that they were staging. Stanislavsky was strongly influenced by both Chronegk's and Antoine's approaches in working with actors, and creating an aesthetic that was influenced by a shift towards realism, and in the case of Antoine, based in the principles of Naturalism. These 'early' directors created different approaches to actor training and performance to shape the actors to the style of performance they wanted. This emphasis on directors as the developers of forms of actor training has continued throughout the twentieth and into the twenty-first centuries. This raises the question of whose voice is heard in the articulation of each specific form of a psychophysical approach: is it the actor, the director, the theatre critic, the academic?

Other questions in relation to examining traditions of actor training include those of culture, and the influence of the socio-cultural and political contexts in which new ideas and methods of training were developed. This is certainly important in understanding Stanislavsky's shift towards the development of a psychophysical approach. Additionally, problematic issues of culture and cultural appropriation are an inherent part of investigating the way in which a psychophysical approach developed. The issue of forms that draw on aspects of techniques and aesthetics from other cultures, particularly those from Asia, has been much debated. Our focus in this book in articulating an intercultural approach to the psychophysical makes this debate significant in understanding the way in which these forms have been used and integrated into Western systems. One more point to make is that in the history of the lineage and transmission of these forms, there is a clear focus on men, and a general absence of women. Not only is this due to an imbalance of gender in relation to directors, but also that the statement of heritage is often a patriarchal one. For Eugenio Barba, his spiritual and theatrical 'grandfathers' are Stanislavsky, Michael Chekhov, Jerzy Grotowski, and Antonin Artaud. There are, of course, many women directors who have made a major contribution to the development of actor training, but it is not possible to deny the story has mainly been centred around male lines of descent.[2]

Finally, it is important to acknowledge that this chapter can only be a limited discussion of a selection of psychophysical issues in relation to

Western acting, with an exploration of Stanislavsky and a small number of other practitioners. Rather than providing an overview of many practitioners, it is more appropriate to explore aspects of practice which the reader can then examine in relation to specific practitioners and practices. The focus in this chapter will be primarily on text-based acting, with some inevitable cross-over to devising practices discussed in Chapter 5.

Stanislavsky and the psychophysical in acting

Alison Hodge suggests that two of 'the key factors of the early twentieth century interest in actor training are partly a knowledge of Eastern traditions, partly the influence of objective scientific research' (Hodge 2000:3). Certainly Stanislavsky was influenced by both these factors, which became integral parts of his thinking and practice in relation to the notion of the psychophysical. Although there had been a marked separation between mind and body in Western science since the Age of Enlightenment there was, at the beginning of the twentieth century, a 'growing scientific belief of the inseparability of the mind and body [which] interested Stanislavsky greatly, as did the proposition of the French psychologist Théodule Ribot, who claimed that emotion cannot exist without a physical consequence' (Hodge 2000:4). As well as Ribot, Stanislavsky drew on the work of other scientists and psychologists including Pavlov, William James, and Carl Lange (see Whyman 2008 for a fuller discussion of these and other influences). In addition, Stanislavsky was also fascinated by Eastern practices, particularly yoga. Both these approaches require a shift in the perception of the body-mind relationship from a dualistic to a unified view, and this led Stanislavsky to develop a new approach to actor training and performance, where body and mind are part of an integrated whole. The following section examines some of Stanislavsky's key concepts and exercises that are relevant for this chapter by firstly examining the way he saw the relationship between body and mind, and secondly the influence of 'Eastern' practices, particularly yoga, in his work. This is followed by ways in which they have been adapted and re-framed by subsequent practitioners in the field of acting.

The 'Creative State' and the psychophysical

Sharon Carnicke states that the 'first, and most pervasive of [his essential ideas] is Stanislavsky's holistic belief that mind and body represent a psychophysical continuum' (Carnicke 2000: 16). This emphasis on the unity of body and mind is reflected throughout this examination of Stanislavsky's core views on the nature of acting, and in his exercises. The imagination in his work is not a disembodied process, nor the means for a purely psychological device for creating a character. Instead, it can be trained and utilized as a bodymind tool to assist in understanding the potential for conditioning and reconditioning of the 'self' of the actor and aligning the bodymind with the specific patterns of a 'character' in a given moment of a situation in a play. This can create a unity of actor-character, which Stanislavsky describes as the need to 'feel the role in yourself and yourself in the role' (Stanislavski and Rumyantsev 1975: 57).

The system which Stanislavsky developed over his many years of work, involved specific exercises for training body, imagination, and consciousness, as well as a range of rehearsal methods culminating in the Method of Physical Actions and Active Analysis. These exercises and methods have produced an integrated, interconnected system of bodymind cultivation for the actor. This section will explore a selection of key ideas and exercises from the system, rather than attempting to discuss the whole.

Stanislavsky believed that one of the main obstacles for an actor is their 'self', that is, being 'self'-conscious, which can lead to being distracted by the awareness of the presence of the audience. This results in excess physical and mental tension, leading to restrictions in psychophysical action and spontaneity on stage. In order to move away from the self-consciousness, where the sensation and awareness of 'I' blocks their ability to enter into the role, the actor must be mentally and physically engaged with each action they are performing in and as the part. He stressed the importance of the imagination which is absorbed and focused with the action, acknowledging and working within the interconnectedness of mind and body:

> Our art demands that an actor's whole nature be actively involved, that he give himself up, both mind and body, to his part. *He must feel the challenge to action physically as well as intellectually* because the imagination, which has no substance or body, can reflexively affect our physical nature and make it act. Therefore: *Every movement you make on the stage, every word you speak, is the result of the right life of your imagination.* (Stanislavsky 1980: 70–71)

For Stanislavsky, the process of acting is inherently psychophysical: body and mind interrelate and affect each other, and the imagination is completely embodied. It is in the merging of action and imagination that an actor can forget their 'self', and be absorbed in the creative process of act-ing. The merging of the bodymind of the actor with the life of the role was described by Stanislavsky in *An Actor Prepares* as follows: '*Our type of creativeness is the conception and birth of a new being – the person in the part*' (Stanislavsky 1980:312).[3] He wanted to find the creative state for the actor through his understanding behaviour, conditioning and training of the bodymind of the performer. He describes this state as, in Russian, *ja esm'*, or 'I am Being'. According to Jean Benedetti, '[t]his is a case of Stanislavski inventing or rather revising a lost word. The verb to be now only exists in Russian in the infinitive, *est'*. Stanislavsky uses the first person singular, *ja esm'*, which no-one would normally use. 'I am being' is a way of conveying this usual message' (Benedetti 1998:6, fn). This state of 'I am being' is the 'actor's sense of being fully present in the dramatic moment. A term that functions in the System as a synonym for "experiencing"' (Carnicke 1998:174). *Ja esm'* was Stanislavsky's ultimate aim for the actor, which all of the training and rehearsal exercises are leading them towards. Through development of both outer action and inner life, the actor can, as Benedetti suggests, enter into a heightened, creative state of being:

> By following this process methodically I become involved in the action. The situations take on a reality for me, I believe in them, my mind begins to accept them as true. There comes a point when the borderline between me and the 'character' is blurred. I am in the state Stanislavski called 'I am Being'. At that point a kind of creative spontaneity occurs. The subconscious takes over. I behave with the same immediacy as I do in life but with the difference that my behaviour is selective, shaped, aesthetic and transparent. (Benedetti 1998:9)

This merging, or absorption of the actor and character, results in what Benedetti describes as when the 'Third Being, the actor/role begins to emerge, the combination of my own life, experience and imagination, physical characterisation and written script' (Benedetti 1998:10). The notion of the merged 'Third Being' allows for the paradox of the actor both being and not-being the character. The character is manifested through the 'self', the psychophysical reality, of the performer; as Stanislavsky said: '[t]he actor really acts and lives his own feelings: he touches, smells, listens, sees with all the finesses of his organism, his nerves' (Toporkov 1998:156). This places the actor firmly within the present moment: they are here, now, on the stage, being them-selves in/

as the character through action and imagination. Carnicke states that Stanislavsky describes this as 'experiencing':

> He compares it to the sensation of existing fully within the immediate moment – what he calls 'I am' and what Western actors generally call 'moment-to-moment' work. ... [It is] the term he chooses to describe what actors feel when his 'entire set of exercises' successfully releases their full creative potentials'. (Carnicke 2000:17, 1998:107)

The Russian word for 'experiencing' is *perezhivanie*, from *perezhit*, meaning 'living through'. Carnicke explains that there have been problems with this word being translated into English by Hapgood as 'feeling', or 'to feel', instead of 'to experience'. Likewise, Whyman cites from Stanislavsky's *The Art of Experiencing* where he states 'it is necessary to experience the role, that is to have the sensation (*oshchushchat*) of its feelings every time and on every repetition of creativity' (*Collected Works*, vol. 6:80 in Whyman 2008:40). Whyman states that Stanislavsky did not define either feeling or emotion, but that he tended to use the word *chuvstvo*, or 'feeling', rather than *emotsiia*, or 'emotion' (Whyman 2008:51). It is not about feelings in terms of emotions, but instead the experience that is a complete psychophysical engagement with the action, the 'actor's deep concentration on stage and absorption in the events of the play during the performance' (Carnicke 1998:110). To experience is to live, to be present, to be fully in the moment. This can be compared to other models and paradigms of 'emotion' which have been presented in this book.

The manifestation of the 'Third Being' happens as a result of the training process of body and mind. Bella Merlin states that the 'combination of relaxation, imagination, a sense of truth regarding inner actions and the actor's faith in those actions, should arouse a sense of 'I am' at which point the actor imperceptibly merges with the character' (Merlin 2003:79). The 'I am being' state was described by Stanislavsky in *An Actor Prepares* as arising from the 'ocean of the subconscious'. He believed that the subconscious is reached through the conscious, that is, through the psychophysical training, which leads to the point where the actor is absorbed in the action, and is 'experiencing', or 'living through' this action. He describes this experience in an exercise performed by the student Kostya in *An Actor Prepares*. The Director, Torstov, had been giving Kostya instructions in improvising a scene, and suddenly Kostya finds himself in the creative state:

I heard all of these remarks [the Director's instructions and observations], but they did not interfere with my life on the stage, or draw me away from it. At this point my head was swimming with excitement because my part and my own life were so intermingled that they seemed to merge. I had no idea where one began or the other left off. ...I do not know what happened from then on. I know only that I found it easy and pleasant. ...I was in a state of ecstasy... because I had again felt creative inspiration. (Stanislavsky 1980:290–1)

But Torstov warned Kostya that

[t]he coming of inspiration was only an accident. You cannot count on it. But you rely on what actually did occur. The point is, inspiration did not come to you of its own accord. You called for it, but preparing the way for it. ...The satisfying conclusion is that you now have the power to create favourable conditions for the birth of inspiration. (Stanislavsky 1980:292)

Stanislavsky is highlighting the fact that the state of 'I am being' can be reached through a systematic training which encourages the removal of the blocks and hindrances of the 'self' to a forgetting of the 'self', which is the moment where there is simply action being performed.

Although great concentration is needed for the absorption process to lead to the 'I am being' state, Stanislavsky also stressed that an obstacle to this occurring was the potential for too much attention. The experience of the state is one of ease, leading to the feeling of the action 'just happening' with no 'self' doing it: literally, getting the 'self' out of the way, or 'self' forgetfulness. If the actor is trying too hard to achieve this state, then they – their 'self' – is in the way, blocking the natural ability of the bodymind. Kostya describes the state as being one of '"ecstasy": that it is easy, effortless and pleasurable. The merging of actor and character feels like being "seized" by the role' (Carnicke 2000:17). However, if the actor is trying too hard, or thinking too much about what they are doing which can lead to over-focusing of attention, then this can impede their performance. Many of Stanislavsky's training methods are about trying – or rather not-trying – to be as relaxed, free, and 'natural' as possible in order to have the best psychophysical foundation to establish the state of 'I am being', which is one of ease and effortlessness. The system of training and rehearsal exercises which Stanislavsky developed was leading the actor towards this state of 'I am being': the 'Third Being' of the merged actor/character, absorbed in the here-and-now of the psychophysical action.

Training exercises

Imagination

The imagination, for Stanislavsky, is not something that is separate from the body, but is rather rooted in the bodymind, and gives inner life to an action in a given circumstance, a particular moment in the life and situation of a character, which creates a mode of behaviour in that moment appropriate to the circumstance. The actor can explore the environmental Given Circumstances of the play, and the bodymind response of the character in that situation, to develop and embody the psychophysical state suitable to the character in a specific moment. The imagination provides the route into the process of realigning the patterns of the bodymind, which creates the merging actor/character in a given moment of experience.

Stanislavsky's exploration of the imagination is bound up with action. This action is not purely physical, but rather psychophysical: it must be filled with the life of the imagination engaged with the movements of the body. Stanislavsky's student Kedrov stated that 'Konstantin Sergeyevich used to say that when we say 'physical actions' we are fooling the actor. They are *psycho*-physical actions, but we call them physical in order to avoid unnecessary philosophising' (Toporkov 1979:205). If the action is not filled with the inner life of the imagination, then it would be a meaningless, empty movement. In working with opera students, Stanislavsky

> did not recognize any beauty in gesture or pose for its own sake; he always insisted on some action behind it, some reason for a given pose or gesture based on imagination. . . . [He said:] 'If you are trying to make beautiful movements in space by using your softly curvaceous arms whilst your imaginations are fast asleep and you do not even know it, then what you are indulging in is empty form. Try to fill it up with something out of your imagination. (Stanislavsky and Rumyantsev 1975:6, 7)

Imagining is not passive by nature, but instead, '[a]ctivity in imagination is of utmost importance' (Stanislavsky 1980:58). Imagining has to be an active process, embodied in physical action, and based in a specific reason or circumstance for that action. It cannot be unfocused, for to 'imagine "in general", without a well-defined and thoroughly founded theme is a sterile occupation' (Stanislavsky 1980:70). In this way, the imagination is awakened and focused through the action of the body, and the action of the body is given life by the imagination. This creates the psycho-physical experience, where

> thoughts are embodied in acts, [as] Stanislavski taught us, and a man's actions in turn affect his mind. His mind affects his body and again his body, or its condition, has its reflex action on his mind and produces this or that condition. (Stanislavsky and Rumyantsev 1975:4)

This relationship between mind and body was explored by Stanislavsky in exercises designed to stimulate the imagination. In initial body training, he would ask actors to perform an action such as lifting an object and examine which muscles were being used. The next stage with this is to perform the same action but with an imaginary object. These exercises encourage kinaesthetic awareness within the body, as well as focus and concentration in using the appropriate muscles. In addition, they begin to stimulate the embodied imagination in relation to action. Stanislavsky devised a number of exercises designed to help awaken and train a psychophysical approach to the imagination for the actor. The next section will focus on two of the most important: the 'Magic If', which relates to the Given Circumstances, and the complex area of affective memory.

'Magic If'

Stanislavsky developed the technique of the 'Magic If' with actors at the First Studio of the Moscow Art Theatre (MAT). He related this to the importance of naiveté in the work, which led to a 'child-like' sense of belief in the action of the play. According to Carnicke:

> Stanislavsky learned much about 'belief' in imaginary circumstances from his six year old niece. Her 'what if' game inspired his 'magic if'.... Stanislavsky's replacement of 'playing' with 'doing' does not reject the fictional level of acting so much as it focuses on theatre's special means of communication. (Carnicke 1998:148)

The most basic child-like quality of simply playing, of making-believe in the game, is one that Stanislavsky felt could allow the imagination to find the way into 'believing' in the circumstances of the play. For Mel Gordon, it 'is the ability and desire to believe fully and truthfully in the unseen. To enter into a play's circumstances, the actor must relearn and develop his child-like powers to completely believe in imaginary stimuli' (Gordon 1987:64). In order to do this in a way that is convincing for the imagination, it is necessary to be precise about the Given Circumstances of the situation. One way of defining these Circumstances is to ask six basic questions about the character:

- Who [am I]?
- Where?
- When?
- Why? (past circumstances that have led to present)
- What reason? (in the present moment, i.e., what is the present task)
- How? (what is the action necessary to fulfill that task)

By creating as concrete an answer as possible to these questions, the actor can enter into the Given Circumstances of the character with the 'Magic If'. Through asking the questions in the form 'Who am I?', this places the actor firmly at the centre of the action in the present moment. The answers must always be 'in the present, in what Stanislavsky called the *Here, Today, Now.* The more precise my understanding of the situation, the more precise my response to it, my behaviour, will be' (Benedetti 1998:7). This encourages the playful state of naiveté in the actor, to allow them to 'believe' in the circumstances of the situation. Stanislavsky explained that

> [a]s a means of extending your imaginative powers you will have to invent all sorts of 'given circumstances'. Using the magic formula 'if things were so and so', surround yourself with imaginary objects and always answer for yourself the questions: 'Where, when, for what reason or purpose is this?' When you create an imaginative life for a part, when you know all the facts concerned with it and you enjoy this – then it becomes a reality. (Stanislavsky and Rumyantsev 1975:10)

Stanislavsky encouraged the actors to explore their imaginations from the present moment, in order to find truth in what they were doing. Some exercises would begin with the current situation in the room in which they were working, and gradually change one element of that reality at a time by asking 'what if?', in order to create a completely different situation purely through the psychophysical imagination reacting to that imaginary impulse: 'Take an object and change your relationship to it' (Carnicke 2000:21). In this way, it is not the objects that change, but the relationship to them, which has been transformed by the imagination. For Benedetti, 'what is important is not the object itself but my *attitude* to it. That is what creates the 'reality' of the situation'

(Benedetti 1998:5). The imagination creates a new situation, a new reality, by seeing it differently. The actor can use the 'Magic If' to alter their reality of the present moment, to believe it to be a new situation, and so be/become the bodymind of the character defined through the Given Circumstances.

Another means for assisting the imagination in this process of belief, is by creating a logical or 'organic' sequence of actions for the 'self' to believe in. This is not so much believing it to be true, but in the truth of it. Stanislavsky devised a series of exercises to help train the imagination to create this logical sequence of actions, with the aid of memory. This imaginary sequence of actions can be used to find the actual physical sequence in rehearsal. In exploring the Given Circumstances, the actor might ask what their objective is: what it is that they want, always expressed as a verb, and then discover what the obstacles are to achieving this. In this way, these 'physical (outer) and psychological (inner) obstacles provoke a series of actions, albeit imaginary at this point, which he [the actor] has to undertake if he is to achieve his objective. ... There is a logic and a coherence' (Merlin 2003:132, 133). This logic gives credibility to the sequence, and so allows it to be believable in terms of the possibility of it taking place. As Merlin further states:

> With any imaginary exercise, Stanislavsky stresses the importance of a logical sequence of actions. You mustn't miss out a single step, or your imagination won't believe in what you're doing and your whole sense of faith in the scenario will collapse. Stanislavsky suggests that it's a good idea to imagine the props and furniture as well: feel the cold of the door handle, heave the heavy oak door open, trip up on the rug. If you can connect with an imaginary object in this way, at the same time as developing a score of actions, you can provoke your emotion memory and increase your personal sense of 'I am' in the role. (Merlin 2003:131)

This comment on the creation of the inner life of the actor/character aligned with the outer physical action, which can provoke an 'emotion memory', will lead into a discussion of that most misunderstood of psychophysical exercises.

Sense/emotion/affective memory

The development of this area of Stanislavsky's work has been misinterpreted, misused and abused by directors and teachers from Stanislavsky's day through to contemporary training and performance. In exploring this vast area for the purposes of this chapter, this discussion will be limited to the way in which Stanislavsky intended these exercises to be a process of the bodymind and, as with the exercises discussed before, to show how the actor can transform themselves in each moment through physical actions and the imagination to create a merging of actor/ character in the situation of the play.

Stanislavsky's exploration of affective memory began in the early 1900s, and was originally influenced by the French psychologist Théodule-Armand Ribot (1839–1916). Ribot's assertion was based on the interconnection between mind and body and that 'concrete' or specific memories have a physical affect: 'an emotion which does not vibrate through the whole body is nothing but a purely intellectual state' (Carnicke 1998:132). The memory of a particular event can recreate similar physical reactions in the present moment. An examination of habitual physical tension patterns can lead to an understanding of condi- tional reactions based on the memory of past circumstances. The resulting physical patterns can provoke the same feeling as the original memory which, rather than being described as an 'emotion', could be labelled as 'sensation'. As stated earlier, Stanislavsky used the word *chuvstva*, which was translated by Hapgood as 'emotions', but in fact means both 'feeling' in terms of sensation, and also the five senses (see Carnicke 1998:133). The memory is used as a device to incite and examine physical reactions, and it is these patterns of tension which can then be produced on stage to provoke the appropriate sensations in that moment. While rehearsing *Hamlet* in 1911, Stanislavsky stated that the 'assumption was that once an emotional state was represented or realized in a physical action, the repetition of that physical action would evoke the emotion' (Benedetti 1990:193).

A fundamental aspect of emotion memory is that although it origi- nates in the Here and Now of the actor, from themselves, it is not a matter of actually 'living through' the experience again in order to be subsumed in the sensations, but to understand and be able to utilize the resultant bodymind states in a performative context. This is often where subsequent uses of this technique have gone astray, and actors believe that they have to re-live the actual event again and again in order to be 'realistic' on stage. Stanislavsky instead stressed that the actor should keep a distance from the actual memory, seeing it as a secondary experience, not the 'real' thing: it is a remembered real, rather than a 'real' real. This is helped by the 'magic if', which places it in the realm of 'make-believe', so the actor can know that it is not actually happening. For Stanislavsky, this approach to the memory resulted in it washing 'feelings clean of all that is superfluous. It results in the quintessence of all similar feelings, ... it is stronger than genuine real-life feeling' (Carnicke 1998:135). Extraneous details of the incident are used initially to contact the sensation, but these need to be let go of in order to have full attention and understanding of the actual experience, to access the essence of it. Like the process in making essential oils, the memory is distilled into a small quantity which is far stronger and more potent in quality than the original.

This approach to the memories is important, for otherwise identifying with it too closely can cause mental distress for the actor. Sulerzhitzky 'warned that the actor's use of the personal can easily lead to "stage hysteria", which conveys only "the sick nerves of the actor and not the heroes"' (Carnicke 1998:130). Stanislavsky distinguished between a real-life 'truth', and a 'truth' as it is seen on stage:

> 'Living truth on stage is not at all what it is in reality,' Stanislavsky writes in one of his notebooks. 'On stage truth is whatever you believe and in life truth is what actually is'. Moreover, 'the actor's experiencing on stage is not at all the same as it is in life. ... The theatre exists to show things which do not exist actually. ... When you love on stage, do you really love? Be logical: you substitute creation for the real thing. The creation must be real, but that is the only reality that should be there.' (Carnicke 1998:120–121)

This created reality is developed through the exercise of affective memory, which came to be divided into two parts: sense memory and emotion memory. In *An Actor Prepares,* Stanislavsky 'made the distinction between sensation memory, based on experiences, connected with our five senses, and emotion memory. He said that he would occasionally speak of them as running along parallel to one another. This, he said, is a convenient although not a scientific description of their relation to one another' (Stanislavsky 1980:168). Sense memory can be evoked by remembering the sensory details of a particular event. These sense stimuli are then focused on to help re-experience similar psychophysical patterns in a specific moment on stage. This was developed in response to the views of Ribot, who wrote in 1896: 'to re-experience an emotion, one must first re-experience the emotion's imprint. By recalling the sensory atmosphere of a past activity, one can capture the past emotion' (Gordon 1987:39). Another exercise Stanislavsky developed was to present actors with objects which relate to a particular sense, for example, objects, taste or smell, and allow this direct access to the sense to stimulate an association of a memory or feeling which can again then be used in performance, with the recalling of the sense object (not the memory or event associated with it). In this way, the imagination is based in all the senses, and so completely embodied. The stimulus to the imagination is through the body, and this imaginative involvement in turn affects the physical condition.

The process of emotion memory is again designed to be psycho-physical, rather than psychological. Stanislavsky said that the actor must not '"assault the subconscious" ... *Rehearsal is not group therapy. Acting is not analysis*' (Benedetti 1998:61, fn). It is through the understanding of the relationship between body and mind, and the effect that the imagination can have in altering the physiology, that emotion memory can be utilized as a tool for actors to develop a full psychophysical presence on stage. Benedetti describes the process as being in two stages:

1. Recall a moment in your life when you experienced an emotion analogous to that which the character is experiencing – the 'then'.
2. Improvise in the present a situation which will provoke the same emotion – the 'now'. (Benedetti 1998:67)

This again places the actor in the Here and Now, with their own present circumstances included as part of the process. In addition, by acknowledging being in the present moment, and therefore that the memory is from the past, then 'the past is brought into the present and made immediate but in an imaginary situation, so that distance is created between us and our memories. They then become material out of which a character can be shaped' (Benedetti 1998:67). This is significant, as it is the embodied imagination which creates a new reality in the bodymind through recollections of the event, while at the same time knowing that the event is not repeating in the present. It is not living-through the past event again, but rather experiencing in terms of *perezhit* as discussed earlier, which is an engagement with the sensations being felt, rather than a psychological re-entering into the past event. The following exercises from the First Studio demonstrate this process:

(Note: keep the memories simple). Recall: An enjoyable part. Something disagreeable. Something that made you angry. When you had a success. When you felt ashamed. ...

Using these triggers in rehearsal:

1. [R]ecall an occasion when you experienced terror. The 'then'. A friend and I were going through a public park at night with heavy bags full of shopping. It was very dark, eerie, there wasn't a soul about. Suddenly we were aware that we could see someone stealing through the bushes. We were scared, we stopped and looked at each other. ...

2. Improvisation. The 'now'. I am alone with my sister/brother. It is late at night. The doorbell rings. I go to the door and ask who is there. No reply. But I can feel that there is someone outside. (Benedetti 1998:66–67)

The technique of remembering a past experience, then using the psycho-physical sensations in a Here and Now improvisation, can be applied to a specific moment in a scene, if an actor is having problems accessing the appropriate psychophysical response. The actual memory is not replayed nor re-lived, but used as a device in creating the state of being related to the character in that moment. Stanislavsky explained:

You can understand a part, sympathise with the person portrayed, and put yourself in his place, so that you will act as he would. That will arouse feelings in the actor that are *analogous* to those required for the part. But those feelings will belong, not to the person created by the author of the play, but to the actor himself. (Stanislavsky 1980:177)

He demonstrated this in an exercise from *An Actor Prepares*:

Imagine that you have received some insult in public, perhaps a slap in the face, that makes your cheek burn whenever you think of it. The inner shock was so great that it blotted out all the details of this harsh incident. But some insignificant thing will instantly revive the memory of the insult, and the emotion will recur with redoubled violence. Your cheek will grow red or you will turn pale and your heart will pound. (Stanislavsky 1980:187)

There is a direct physical response to the imagination, and it is this particular bodymind pattern of the response that can be used in a specific moment appropriate to the Given Circumstances of the character. The memory which is a route into the bodymind experience is only intended to spark that response, and so can be connected to any event rather than directly to the situation of the character. Stanislavsky acknowledges, in the quotation above, that while the actor's feelings correspond to those necessary for the character, they are, ultimately, created by the psycho-physical reality of the actor themselves.

This is the establishment of the Third Being of the merged actor/character, where the actor has created a specific boydmind state by aligning patterns of body and mind to those of the given circumstances of the character in a particular moment, but also acknowledging that it is the actor who is doing this through their technique cultivated during the training process. They 'become' the character through assimilating these patterns, but they are not 'taken over' or 'possessed', and 'lose themselves' in the act of so doing. Stanislavsky's training of actors through an embodied imagination can engage all systems of the body to bring forth a new world: the character in the environment of the play, which both is, and is not, the actor themselves.

Consciousness and exercises developed from yoga

Stanislavsky's exploration of exercises from yoga is also significant in an examination of the relationship between body, imagination, concentration, and the connection with subtle energies. Therefore, this section on training will focus on Stanislavsky's work with the bodymind consciousness of the actor, with particular reference to his exploration of these exercises developed from yoga. This exploration will focus on two specific exercises that were designed to assist the actor with inner life, consciousness, concentration, and connection with and utilization of the subtle energies within the bodymind.

Leopold Sulerzhitzky was a main influence on the introduction of ideas from yoga practice as part of the work at the First Studio. This was related to other significant explorations from this time, such as relaxation, concentration, and naiveté, as described by Gordon:

> Suler instructed the actors in yogic relaxation techniques, demonstrating the relationship between breath control and bodily tension. Other sessions in concentration showed how the actor could learn to focus his attention on objects and then in small and larger circles around the stage. [...] According to Suler, Relaxation, Concentration and Naiveté were the initial steps in acquiring the Creative State of Mind. (Gordon 1987:38)

Yoga was seen as a means to develop bodymind relaxation, focus, and spontaneity. Stanislavsky was familiar with the works *Hatha Yoga* and *Raja Yoga* by Ramacharaka. In *An Actor Prepares*, Stanislavsky himself appears to acknowledge that he wanted to find ways of cultivating the psychophysical ability of the actor, rather than an investigation of Eastern practices:

> I have no desire to prove whether Prana really exists or not. My sensations may be purely individual to me, the whole thing may be the fruit of my imagination. This is all of no consequence provided I can make use of it for my purposes and it helps me. If my practical and unscientific method can be of use to you, so much the better the better. If not, I shall not insist on it.' (Stanislavsky 1980:199)

It is worth bearing in mind that this quotation is from Hapgood's translation, and in the context of Carnicke's argument, could be an indication of an American view that was trying to dismiss the Eastern, 'mystical' aspect in Stanislavsky's ideas, by implicating that he himself was ultimately not so concerned with their own practice, as with how he could use and adapt them for a 'scientific' actor training. Whyman, in her reconsideration of Stanislavsky's ideas through archives in Moscow, states that he wrote about the importance of developing prana for the actor: 'Prana is the mechanism for linking "external movements…with the internal movements of emotion"' (MAT, KS Archive 834, 1919, 27, in Whyman 2008:84). He thus connects the inner movement of prana energy, with the outer physicality of the movement, creating a psychophysical unity for the actor, with the prana as a central core. This appears to contradict the statement in Hapgood's translation that he was not using such terms in his work. For the present context, it is the effect of the exercises themselves which will be the focus. The exercises discussed in this section explore aspects of concentration and prana which Stanislavsky adapted into his work on the Circles of Attention and Radiation. (For further information about yoga and prana, see Chapter 3.)

Circles of Attention

The exercise of Circles of Attention is related to the practice of concentration. Whereas the concentration/attention exercises in relation to training the body were to help with awareness of physical tensions, the Circles of Attention are designed to develop attention and concentration within all areas of the bodymind, as well as with external objects and environments, which creates consciousness of inner and outer in variable sizes of circles around the biosphere of the actor. It thus connects to ideas yoga of the practice of concentration within the bodymind, and its relationship to the idea of Will. In *Hatha Yoga*, Ramacharaka explains: 'The higher Yogis have a wonderful control over the involuntary system and can act directly upon nearly every cell in their body. … The trained Will is able to act directly upon these cells and groups by a simple process of direct concentration, but this plan requires much training on the part of the student' (Ramacharaka 2007:95). In his *Series of Lessons in Raja Yoga*, he further states in relation to *dharana*, or 'concentration', that 'concentration consists in the mind focusing upon a certain subject, or object, and being held there for a time. This, at first thought seems very easy, but a little practice will show how difficult it is to firmly fix the attention and hold it there' (Ramacharaka 2004:30).

Reflecting this practice of focusing the mind on a particular object, Stanislavsky would begin this training with making the actor focus their attention on a particular object close to them in the space, to observe and enhance their ability to keep concentrated on a fixed point. This is the Object of Attention, as seen in this exercise from the First Studio:

> Concentrate on a single point that is close to you. The corner of a table for example. Study it. Allow our body to relax. Whenever you feel your mind wavering, return to the same fixed point. (Gordon 1987:63) [This was repeated with objects at different distances.]

This helps develop single-pointedness of mind, where although there is a central focus for the concentration, there is simultaneously an awareness of the periphery around the practitioner. This is also developed by Stanislavsky in the next stage of progression from the Object of Attention, which is the Circle of Attention. This circle was explored in three sizes of circumference: small, medium; and large, and the actor is trained to shift between them. In *An Actor Prepares*, Torstov uses circles of light to help actors keep their attention within specific areas around them, gradually widening these circles from their bodies, to the area immediately surrounding them, and finally to the whole room (which on stage, would include the auditorium). The exercise would then be repeated with all the lights on, and the actor would have to use their own powers of concentration to stay within the defined circle.

Once developed, the actor can adjust their concentration between these three circles as necessary for a particular moment in a scene. Stanislavsky also pointed out that if the concentration became distracted while in the large circle, the actor can shift immediately back to the small circle, which will help regain the focus and attention:

> As the circle grows larger the area of your attention must stretch. This area, however, can continue to grow only up to the point where you can still hold it all within the limits of your attention, inside an imaginary line. *As soon as your border begins to waver, you must withdraw quickly to a smaller circle* which can be contained by your visual attention. (Stanislavsky 1980:84)

Stanislavsky explained that the actor does not need to be always at the centre of a circle: they could be observing a circle outside them. However, the actor is always contained within a small circle of attention: 'You can carry it with you wherever you go, on the stage or off. Get up on the stage and walk around. Change your seat. Behave as you would if you were alone' (Stanislavsky 1980:85). The connection between the imagination, heightened awareness, prana, and breathing is developed further in the next exercise to be discussed, that of radiation.

Radiation

Radiation, also known as irradiation or communion, could be seen as the most 'esoteric' aspect of the system, based in Stanislavsky's understanding of the movement of prana within yoga exercises. It is a device which links the visualizing and concentration of the mind with the physical body and subtle energies, and 'focuses on filling external actions with inner content... [T]he actor's attention is now outwards towards the other actors [rather than on internal memories/processes etc.]' (Merlin 2003:64). Stanislavsky believed that this could occur through the use of prana energy, which he defined as 'the vital energy... which gives life to our body' (Carnicke 1998:141). In rehearsal notes from 1919 to 1920, he wrote: 'Pay attention to the movement of *prana*. ... *Prana* moves and is experienced like mercury, like a snake, from your hands to your fingertips, from your thighs to your toes' (Carnicke 1998:141). Ramacharaka connects the idea of prana to that of the practice of Will and concentration, discussed earlier: "the Will forces the mind to all parts, and in all directions, and it directs the *Prana* or vital force likewise' (Ramacharaka 2004:43). In this way, the concentrated mind engages with the breath to help circulate the prana around the body, then out through the body to the other actors and audience, which creates communion. Bella Merlin explains:

> Despite sounding somewhat esoteric, communion is in fact incredibly simple. It is the absolute attention of one actor to another... through the exchange of energy which inevitably takes place between two or more human beings. It involves each actor getting the other actor in his or her grasp. ... If the actors are 'in each other's grasp', the audience will be drawn – like magnets – towards the on-stage action. In this way, they also become part of the communion or grasp of the live performance. (Merlin 2003:158–159)

This fills the actor with inner life, which is projected outwards to 'commune' with others around. The communion aids in the absorption process of 'self' and 'other', so allowing the establishment of 'self-forgetfulness': the 'I am being' state of the creative actor. The embodied imagination leads to awareness of the internal energies, and helps in the ability of the bodymind to circulate these around and out through the body, thus creating a psychophysical unity of body, mind, and consciousness.

The embodied imagination brings together all processes of the bodymind in a psychophysical unity of experience which is the cultivation and culmination of the training. The absorption of the relaxed, concentrated, and aware bodymind of the actor with the patterns of the being of the character in a specific moment has the potential to lead to a Here and Now reality of the Third Being of the merged actor-character, and Stanislavsky's ideal of the creative actor, based in his adaptation of ideas from yoga.

Rehearsal methods

Having explored specific aspects of Stanislavsky's system of actor-training in relation to the bodymind and his interest in yoga, the chapter will now briefly discuss applications of his techniques in the process of rehearsal, focusing on his later work of the Method of Physical Actions and Active Analysis. This is a vast subject, and has been written about in detail by Carnicke, Merlin, and Benedetti, so this section will outline specific points with reference to a psychophysical approach to action and imagination in the creation of character and the through-line of the play.

Method of physical actions

In the early 1930s, Stanislavsky felt that 'around the table' analysis of a play-text was resulting in actors thinking and talking too much, and finding it difficult to take this process into actually embodying what had been discussed. Instead, he began to focus on psychophysical action, where the imagination gives inner life to the outer movements of the body, and this became the heart of his approach to creating character and situation in the context of a play-text. The actor needs to find the appropriate psychophysical action for the character in each moment and link these actions together to create a through-line, a score, of physical actions. Every moment must be 'filled' and embodied, with the bodymind of the actor fully engaged with each action.

It is important to stress that action had always been important in Stanislavsky's work, but in 1935 it began to take on a different meaning, and 'actors were compelled by the director to decide which physical actions they would execute in the Given Circumstances of the play. Only that which could be physically performed and seen by an audience was allowed' (Gordon 1987:208). A 25-step plan for the use of the Method of Physical Actions in rehearsal was created in 1936 (this plan is given in Gordon 1987:209–211). The following is a summary of Jean Benedetti's outline of this way of working to demonstrate the through-line of the process (see Benedetti 1998:6–14).

Method of physical actions: outline and summary, based on Benedetti

- *Read the* Play – study the outline, events and actions.
- *Find the* Supertask – the main theme of the play.
- *Divide into* Episodes – these are the main sections in the play.
- *Divide Episodes into* Facts – the events that happen in the Episodes.
- *Now focus on the individual character:*
- *Within each Episode and Fact, define the* Task – what it is the character needs/wants to do.
- *Find the appropriate* Action – what specifically they need to do to carry out the Task.
- *Create the* Through-Action – joining the actions together in a line to check that they have a logic and coherence.
- *Explore the inner life of the action using* Inner Monologue *(what is being thought in each moment),* Mental Images *(the pictures in the mind in each moment), and* Emotion Memory. *As with physical actions, find the* Through-Emotion *which relates to the* Through-Action.

This psychophysical process of aligning the outer action with the inner life, means that the actor will, to repeat Benedetti from earlier,

> become involved in the action. The situations take on a new reality for me, I believe in them, my mind begins to accept them as true. There comes a point when the borderline between me and the 'character' is blurred. I am in the state Stanislavski called 'I am being'. ... 'I am' is living. 'I am Being' is acting. (Benedetti 1998:8–9)

This sense of 'belief' is cultivated through an engagement with the action. The action itself is absorbed with the imagination to give it a sense of believability within the realm of *naiveté*. The action 'denotes what the actor does to solve the *problem*, set before the character by the *Given Circumstances* of the play and production. ... Stanislavsky also advocates using the *magic if* to help identify action. "What would I do *if* I found myself in the circumstances of the scene?" The answer, expressed as a verb, suggests the action' (Carnicke 2000:24, 25).

The use of the score of actions, which are learnt and practised, allows the actor to have complete psychophysical engagement throughout the length of the play. As Stanislavsky said:

> You just learn to do a series of physical actions. Join them in one unbroken line, then you will have the scheme of the physical actions of the [play]. ... Don't *act* anything, just play each action. ... [It is] through the correct execution of physical actions, through their logic and their sequence, one penetrates into the deepest, most complicated feelings and emotional experiences. (Toporkov 1979:86. 87)

It is this line of actions, of separate moments connected together, that gives a sense of a continuous 'character'. However, these are still distinct moments, different 'Here and Now's, each of which need to be fully experienced. In this sense, there is no fixed 'self' of the character which continues unchanged from moment to moment. There is instead a line of constantly changing patterns of actions and reactions: 'Going from one episode to another, the actor gradually clarifies for himself the whole line of his behaviour, of his conflict, of his logic during the entire course of the play' (Toporkov 1979:211). Stanislavsky's systematic study and understanding of the nature and foundation of behaviour, the way in which we – and a character – create the sense of 'self' through action, offers the means by which the actor can construct that character as a series of states of being, which they both become, and yet are separate from. The imagination is not a psychological or pathological means to believe that the actor is living through exactly what the character does, night after night, but instead, in my interpretation, is a psychophysical process to help construct patterns of body and mind appropriate to the circumstances of the Here and Now.

Active Analysis

Active Analysis, the last stage of development in Stanislavsky's life, is a method whereby the actor integrates their body, imagination, and energies in a spontaneous series of improvisations to lead them into embodying the character in the Here and Now, with a real sense of *ja esm*. It is 'a holistic system ... whereby actors' emotions, imagination, body and spirit – or 'superconscious' as Stanislavsky sometimes called it – were stimulated' (Merlin 2002:4, 6). The approach to the text was through improvisation rather than intellectual study, which means that 'one activates oneself on stage through improvisation, thus obviating the need to translate imagination into actuality' (Carnicke 1998:155). The body and mind operate simultaneously in exploring the action through *doing/being* it, rather than thinking about it. Maria Knebel, who participated in Stanislavsky's last workshops, taking notes and then teaching this work in Moscow afterwards, explained that the improvisations were designed to bring the actor into the present moment, the Here and Now, and 'break down the wall between analysis and embodiment' (Carnicke 1998:156).

According to Merlin, the basic process of Active Analysis begins with reading the scene, then finding the appropriate facts of the scene by asking questions. These facts would then be taken straight into the actor improvising the scene, using their own words. They would re-read the scene, noting how their improvisation relates to the original. This four-stage process is repeated, adding more detail and lines from the play each time, until the scene is memorized. This process of the actor using their own words in improvisation and only gradually assimilating the actual text of the playwright was important for Stanislavsky:

> The words of another are alien until we have made them our own, are nothing more than the signs of future emotions which have not yet come to life within us. Our own words were needed in the first phase of physical embodiment of a part because they are best able to extract from within us live feelings, which have not yet found their outward expression. (Merlin 2002:20)

Carnicke offers a slightly more complex version, whereby the text is examined for 'clues', which suggest an 'event'. She explains that 'in this technique, the actor learns to read each line not only for semantic meaning, but also for style, literally images and rhythms, which betray the action of the scene and the personality of the character' (Carnicke, 2000:27). For each 'event' there is an 'action', which creates a particular momentum, and results in a 'conflict'. This 'conflict' is then explored, and an attempt at resolution is made through the use of 'action' (see Carnicke 2000:27).

Within Active Analysis, the imagination is not a separate, disembodied process associated with a mental state, but instead is experienced through physical action, suggested by the 'event' of a specific moment:

> Whereas imaginative visualizations may create impressionistic outlines of action, the physical reality of improvisation allows the actor no gaps in the flow and logic of behaviour. ...What do we physically do when we persuade someone, ...or challenge someone, ...or contemplate suicide ...? By persuading, challenging, or contemplating, the actor finds answers. (Carnicke 1998:156)

Improvisation is used to find the 'truth' behind the action, with the engaged imagination giving inner life to the body through the Given Circumstances and Magic If. This is an embodied, active exploration of the play, where 'the actors analysed their roles actively by using their bodies, imaginations, intuition and emotions on the rehearsal-room floor. So – just like the Method of Physical actions – the detective work on a play was carried out by the actors using their entire beings not just their intellects' (Merlin 2003:34).

In Active Analysis, the actor is always present in the Here and Now reality of the moment. With the understanding of the Given Circumstances of the character, the 'Magic If' of the embodied imagination, and other devices discussed above, there can be an alignment of the patterns of body, mind, and subtle energies to be/become the character. They both are, and are not them-'selves' and the character. The question of 'believing' in the 'truth' of the character and situation is an outcome of being fully absorbed in the process, while also knowing that it is a created situation. This is the paradox for actor and spectator; the actor is the embodied presence of the character – they *are* the character. And yet they are also the actor. The audience, too, needs to become absorbed in the psychophysical action on stage in order to have 'belief' in what they are seeing, while also knowing that it is a created reality.

Stanislavsky's psychophysical cultivation of the actor through training exercises, the exploration of the bodymind relationship, and the inner life of the imagination manifested through the outer expression of physical action, can lead to the creative state of *ja esm*, 'I am being', the singular experience of the merged actor/character. If we can understand the way in which we create our 'self' through our actions, conditionings, and behaviour, we can find how to create the 'self' of a 'character' using psychophysical techniques to manifest a state of being, which is the appropriate patterning of body, imagination, and subtle energy in that moment. In this sense, the actor is working with a sense of themselves and character as being process rather than object. With all the misunderstandings, mistranslations, and misappropriations, Stanislavsky's work is still of immense value and validity for the contemporary actor, with his own exploration of the interconnectedness of all aspects of the bodymind. He wrote: 'How astonishing a creation is our nature! How everything in it is bound together, blended, and interdependent!' (in Carnicke, 2000:33).

The psychophysical legacy

Stanislavsky's exploration of the psychophysical in acting has had far-reaching consequences on the development of training and performance within acting. For Bella Merlin, 'Konstantin Stanislavsky was without question the father of contemporary acting practice, particularly when it comes to the kind of realism which dominates Western theatre and screen today' (Merlin 2007:3). Certainly the focus on 'realism' can be traced through the way in which Stanislavsky's work was disseminated and transformed within the United States and beyond. However, this has often tended to lose the emphasis on the psychophysical, the unity of body and mind, and instead what emerges is a dominance of the psychological over the physical. There have been theatre practitioners, though, who have followed Stanislavsky's ideas and practices with regard to the connection of the bodymind, consciousness, physical training and ways of encouraging the creative state, and taken this forward in their own way to further the notion of a psychophysical approach to acting for the twentieth and twenty-first-century actor. Although there are many areas of investigation in relation to this, the rest of this chapter will focus on two issues which arise from this examination which relate to the question of the psychophysical and the shifting views of the mind-body relationship: that of the development of the emotion memory exercise in different forms, and the question of the psychophysical continuum, or the relationship between 'inner' and 'outer'. It will also essentially stay within the time period up to 1960, as the following chapter will be investigating psychophysical approaches after that time.

Emotion Memory: to re-member or to re-live

The Emotion Memory exercise has come to be one of the most contentious aspects of Stanislavsky's work which has been much adapted by subsequent practitioners and debated as to both the intention and validity of it as a way of working for actors. But even during Stanislavsky's lifetime, the exercise proved to be a point of disagreement for those who had been closest to him. Michael Chekhov, nephew of the playwright Anton, and one of Stanislavsky's star student-actors in the First Studio of the MAT, moved away from his teacher to develop his own psycho-physical approach to acting, with a focus on the embodied imagination, and an understanding of the way in which body and mind interact. From as early as 1918, Chekhov was speaking out against the use of emotion memory for actors. When he met with Stanislavsky in Germany in 1929, Chekhov tried to convince his former teacher that rather than emotion memory, an actor should instead use the abilities of their imagination in creating a part, since of 'the mind's three active phases (dreaming, thinking/remembering, and imagining), Chekhov lectured Stanislavsky, only imagination was truly effective in the creation of art' (Gordon 1987:149). It must be borne in mind that Chekhov had worked with Stanislavsky at a particular point in Russia when he placed much emphasis on the use of emotion memory. Chekhov had no connection with Stanislavsky in the development of the later work on the Method of Physical Actions and Active Analysis, and so his earlier criticisms were based on his experience at the First Studio at the MAT. At the end of his life, Chekhov did acknowledge that Stanislavsky never wanted to use emotion memory on stage, only as a means in rehearsal to find a sense of 'truth' in the feelings of the character, and ultimately he believed that their aims were the same (Chekhov 1996:Tape 4).[4] However, he developed ways of approaching the character which utilized the actor's creative imagination, rather than their real-life memories.

Chekhov believed that one of the main problems with emotion memory is that it involves the use of personal, 'egotistical' feelings, and that these are not appropriate for performance on stage. He was greatly influenced by the work of Rudolf Steiner and anthroposophy, from which he discussed what he terms the 'Higher Self' (see Daboo 2007, 2012 for further details). This Higher Self transcends the everyday and the personal, so moves beyond the person which forms the basis of the emotion memory exercise:

> I don't speak about our personal feelings. I speak about the feelings which belong to the realm which is bigger than we are. To the realm of feeling which comes from inspiration. If I say the line 'To be or not to be' as if it were my personal problem no-one would be interested in it – it is too small. In order to say these lines I must have some feelings, some

electricity which changes my whole being and then perhaps I have the right to ask 'To be or not to be'. (Dartington Archives a)

Our real-life memories do not offer enough potential in themselves for this transformation on stage. They are also, Chekhov points out, like 'ghosts' (Chekhov 1996:Tape 4) from our past, which makes them too personal and subjective for use on stage. He believes that not only does an audience find it unpleasant to see these personal feelings displayed, but also that this might encourage the actor to encounter problems in losing their mental balance, and enter into a state of negativity. He graphically describes an emotion memory as being like a 'small, dirty envelope' (Chekhov 1996:Tape 4) from the past in which the actor can potentially get 'stuck', resulting in the establishment of habitual patterns of the bodymind. In order to find creative inspiration, the actor must reach beyond their everyday lives and feelings, into the realm of their Higher Self.

In order to accomplish this, Chekhov states that instead of using personal memories, an actor should instead attempt to discover the archetype of their character, and from this, begin to add particular details to create a specific part. He gives the example of how to find the appropriate feeling in relation to the idea of 'my dying grandfather', and suggests there are two ways to approach this. One is from the perspective of emotion memory, where the actor uses the memory and image of their real-life grandfather. However this, he believes, will be

> too personal in the wrong sense. You will get certain feelings, perhaps strong ones, but they will be of a different kind than we are aiming at in our work – they are not to be shown. They will have a certain personal colour which makes us a little smaller and makes the audience suspicious whether consciously or unconsciously, and the actor can become hysterical after a certain period of time if he works in this way, because we do not allow our nature to forget the 'grandfather' drama in our life to the extent that our psychological life requires. We always take him out of his grave and cannot forget him, which makes us psychologically ill after a time, because we force our nature. (Chekhov, 1985:40–41)

An alternative approach, and the one which Chekhov advocates, would be to find the image of the 'archetypal': the universal, quintessential grandfather. This image would include

> all the 'grandfathers' in existence. We don't need any one particular image. In it are all 'Lears', all 'fathers', all everything – if the emotional life is

developed, it is there forever. ... If, for instance, we imagine King Lear, we can imagine him only because we are already rich enough inside ourselves with all the 'grandfathers' ... But we cannot imagine King Lear if we have a concrete grandfather who is still tearing our physical nerves and heart to pieces. (Chekhov, 1985:40, 42)

If the actor were to focus on their own memory of their real grandfather, they could be restricted by the bodymind patterns associated with their emotional experience. By instead focusing on the archetype of 'grand-father', they are potentially able to expand their ability to explore and encompass the feelings associated with the part. This, for Chekhov, is why the Higher Self offers much more potential for creativity and inspi-ration than the 'smaller' everyday self, bound up with personal concerns which are of no interest to the audience. It is also a much more positive and healthy experience for the actor, for instead of having to 'squeeze' an emotion out of their psyche, they can instead become the creative force of their performance by using their imagination to transform their physi-cality and psychology through the means of specific exercises to generate a new 'self', which is the psychophysical embodiment of the character. Chekhov states that he experiences 'a sense of joy when absorbed in a creative process and it is derived from the following: (1) a release from my own personality; and (2) awareness of the enactment of the creative idea which otherwise would remain out of the grasp of my everyday consciousness' (Chekhov 1983:32). This is clearly a very different type of experience to the personal torture which Chekhov believes is inherent in the use of emotion memory. His work is focused on the psychophysical unity of body and mind. In a recorded Master Class given near the end of his life, he states:

All our physical exercises will be considered and done as psychophysical exercises. We want to fill, to permeate our bodies with psychological values. Therefore, while doing all our bodily exercises, it is good to have in mind this side of the exercise. ... Everything like the development of our imagination or using of the psychological gesture, all such means makes physical exercises to psychophysical. (Chekhov, 1996: Tape 4)[5]

This interconnection between body and psychology, inner and outer, dominates his thinking and exercises. His working method is that of a synthesis of all aspects of the bodymind. Mala Powers, who trained with Chekhov in Hollywood and was the editor of several of his books, explains that his 'approach to preparation for "inspired acting" empha-sizes the use of Psycho-Physical exercises which provide the actor with simple and practical means for calling up the energy and emotions while joining the actor's psychology, body and voice with the unique character he or she is bringing to life' (Powers 2002:xxviii). His embodied approach to the imagination offers a significant contribution to the development of a psychophysical approach to acting.

Even though Chekhov had such reservations about it, the emotion memory exercise grew in popularity, most notably in the United States, through the work of the Method School of acting developed initially at the Group Theatre and subsequently the Actors Studio in New York. This is a vast subject, on which much has been written, so only relevant aspects are discussed here. One of the key points to make is that Stanislavsky's work grew, developed and significantly altered throughout his life. He worked with many actors and students at different times of this development, and what tended to happen was that each of these actors took what they had studied with him as being the 'truth' of his system as they had understood it at that point, and in turn taught this 'truth' to others. As Grotowski noted, 'Stanislavsky had disciples for each of his periods, and each disciple stuck to his particular period' (Grotowski 1975:174). This was the case with two actors who had worked with Stanislavsky in the First Studio, Maria Ouspenskaya and Richard Boleslavksy, who moved to America in 1922, bringing with them their own versions of Stanislavsky's work, which influenced the development of the Method School of acting in America. One of the most significant figures of this approach, Lee Strasberg, spoke of his response to hearing Boleslavsky talk for the first time:

> Boleslavsky said in his first talk, 'There are two kinds of acting. One believes that the actor can actually experience on the stage. The other believes that the actor only indicates what the character experiences, but does not himself really experience. We posit a theatre of real experience. The essential thing in such experience is that the actor learns to know and to do, not through mental knowledge, but by sensory knowledge.' Suddenly I knew, 'That's it! That's it!' That was the answer I had been searching for. The point is that I had already read Freud and already knew the things that go on in a human being without consciousness. I had already picked up everything Boleslavsky said, but he showed me what it meant. (Strasberg, 1966:145)

As with Stanislavsky's development of his system in Russia, the Method evolved in America by absorbing elements that were present at the time, and those that interested the practitioners who were working with it. This included the work of Pavlov, Ribot, and William James, as well as behaviourist John B Watson, who had also influenced Stanislavsky. In addition came the influence of Freud and psychoanalysis, as well as culture-specific elements relating to Strasberg, Stella Adler, and Sandford Meisner, such as Yiddish theatre (see Krasner 2000 for a further discussion). There are as many mythologizings, misinterpretations, disagreements, and transformations of the work of the Method School as there are with Stanislavsky. For the sake of this chapter, what is important to note is a shift from a psychophysical approach to one based in behaviourism and psychology. In relation to his original inspiration, Strasberg said 'It is true that the basic elements are Stanislavski's, but I hope I have gone beyond some of it and have contributed something of my own' (Strasberg 1966:40), and it was certainly the case that it became his own rendition, as much as it did for Adler, Meisner, Kazan, and many directors and actor trainers subsequently. For Strasberg, 'The actor uses real sensation and real behaviour. That actual reality is the material of our craft' (Strasberg 1966:75). In this way, the actor must find a sense of the 'real' in their behaviour. This has often been taken to imply that the actor must therefore use their 'real' and actual emotions, rather than psychophysical patterns established through the sensations of a particular memory. Krasner, however, defends Strasberg in this respect, saying that Strasberg's Method was 'fundamentally not Freudian but Pavlovian' (Krasner 2000:13), thus linking back to Stanislavsky's own use of conditioned reflexes. However the influence of the psychological became increasingly important with actor training and the approach of directors towards staging productions. Elia Kazan, arguably one of the greatest of American directors, offers the following account of Strasberg giving feedback in an acting class he was leading at the Group Theatre in 1932, where the emphasis on the actor experiencing 'real' emotions is apparent:

> He said nothing. They waited. He stared at them. His face gave no hint of what he thought, but it was forbidding. The two actresses began to come apart; everyone could see they were on the verge of tears. ... Finally one of them, in a voice that quavered, asked, 'Lee, what did you think?' He turned his face away, looked at the other actors present. No one dared comment for fear of saying the wrong thing and having Lee turn on them. Finally, speaking quietly, he asked the stricken actress, 'Are you nervous and uncertain now?' 'Yes, yes,' one actress said. 'More than you were in the scene you played?' Lee asked. 'Yes.' 'Much more?' 'Yes, much more.' 'Even though the scene you did was precisely about such nervousness and you'd worked hard to imitate it?' 'Oh, I see, I see,' the actress said,

getting Lee's point that now they were experiencing the real emotion whereas before they'd been pretending. He wanted the real emotion, insisted on the 'agitation of the essence,' as it was called, wouldn't accept less. (Kazan, 1988:63)

While there appears to be an attempt by Strasberg to encourage the actors to feel the physical sensations of the emotion, this is constructed through the inner experiencing of the actual emotion, rather than constructing a psychophysical state through understanding the task of the character at that point. For Kazan, the Method is very straight-forward: 'The essential and rather simple technique, which has since then been complicated by teachers of acting who seek to make the Method more recondite for their commercial advantage, consists of recalling the circumstances, physical and personal, surrounding an intensely emotional experience in the actor's past' (Kazan 1988:63). In this way, it is again a specifically inner response which happens first through experiencing 'real' emotions surrounding an actual event from the actor's life which sparks off the reaction. This is in contrast to Chekhov's directive, stated earlier, that an actor's own personal memories do not allow enough potential for accessing the psychophysical state necessary to have a full and flexible performance. When directing Marlon Brando in *A Streetcar Named Desire*, Kazan said that Brando was 'working "from the inside," rode his emotion wherever it took him' (Kazan, 1988:343), which is not reflecting Stanislavsky's very precise and controlled approach for the actor to play the character. Kazan's psycho-logical approach to characterization is seen in his Notebook for *A Streetcar Named Desire*, where he describes the character of Stanley in psycho-logical terms:

Spine – keep things his way (Blanche the antagonist)

The hedonist, objects, props, etc. Sucks on a cigar all day because he can't suck a teat. ...

But what is the chink in his armor now, the contradiction? Why does Blanche get so completely under his skin? Why does he want to bring Blanche and, before her, Stella *down to his level?* It's as if he said: 'I know I haven't got much, but no one has more and no one's going to have more.' It's the hoodlum aristocrat. He's deeply dissatisfied, deeply hopeless, deeply cynical. (in Cole and Chinoy, 1963: 374–375)

Despite Strasberg wanting the emotion memory exercise to be used only as a rehearsal tool and not in performance, it is possible to see how the influence of psychology overtook the elements of the psychophysical that had been present in Stanislavsky's work, and this became an established part of actor training, separating the psychological emotional state from the physical, in the attempt to create a portrayal of the 'real'.

However, as will be seen in Chapter 5, there has been a reaction against psychological realism with new forms of performance and aesthetics, and also with the introduction of Asian forms of training into actor training systems. The actor may still need to be emotionally available and engaged, but the ways that they can access and construct this through a psychophysical understanding rather than a psychological or behaviourist approach has been a significant movement in the development of the portrayal and embodiment of a character in different forms of performance.

Psychophysical as continuum or paradox

The word 'psychophysical' is central to this book, and is also the way that practitioners such as Stanislavsky and Michael Chekhov have described their work in attempting to bring together body and mind as a unified whole for training actors. However, the term itself is problematic. Given that it is a compound word, by its very nature it could be read as implying a dualistic view of body *and* mind, rather than an holistic embodying which encompasses all aspects of action, thinking, feeling, and being within it.

Another way to articulate and consider this is through the terms 'inner' and 'outer', and which comes first in relation to the actor exploring physicalisation, character, and emotion. Does the impulse come from the external world which leads to the stimulation of the internal being, or does it originate within the organism and is then given an external expression? This question has been at the heart of the investigation of acting over the centuries, not least with Diderot and his Paradox, and has sometimes been placed at the borders of science in an attempt to understand the biological process involved. The work of William James has been discussed at a number of points throughout this book, and was an influence on Stanislavsky, Boleslavsky, and Strasberg. His article from 1884, 'What is an emotion?', has been used as a key text for performance practitioners in addressing this question. In the article, James examines the way in which emotions are produced by embodied action:

> Our natural way of thinking about these standard emotions [e.g., anger, fear, rapture, lust] is that the mental perception of some fact excites the

mental affection called the emotion, and that this latter state of mind gives rise to the bodily expression. My thesis on the contrary is that the bodily changes follow directly the PERCEPTION of the exciting fact, and that our feeling of the same changes as they occur IS the emotion. Common sense says, we lose our fortune, we are sorry and weep; we meet a bear, are frightened and run; we are insulted by a rival, are angry and strike. The hypothesis here to be defended says that this order of sequence is incorrect, that the one mental state is not immediately induced by the other, that the bodily manifestations must first be interposed between, and that the more rational statement is that we feel sorry because we cry, angry because we strike, afraid because we are sorry, angry, or fearful, as the case may be. Without the bodily states following on the perception, the latter would be purely cognitive in form, pale, colourless, destitute of emotional warmth. (James 1884:189–190)

As James views this, there is a physical response to an event, which results in the emotional state. However, rather than being experienced separately, they are instead felt as part of the same psychophysical moment. It is possible to consider that James' work is not relevant in the contemporary world where there is so much subsequent research in psychology and neurophysiology. However, his work has been an influence on the development of actor training, as can be seen particularly in the avant-garde movement in 1960s and 1970s in New York, as Peter Hulton explains:

The article would have been current in New York theatre training circles in the 1960s and 1970s. Emotion arising from a physical source was clearly of interest to all the physical work coming out of Europe and moving across to the States. It would have been current to the Open Theatre [run by Joseph Chaikin] and others. One of the problems the then avant-garde in the States had to contend with was how to respond to the arrival of surrealist texts from France and elsewhere which did not rely on a psychological interpretation of behaviour. Impulses for action would come, they thought, more from the body than the mind – hence the interest in this article.' (P. Hulton, personal email 2009)

Joseph Chaikin, influenced in part by Stanislavsky in the development of his own approach to acting and performance, explored this connection between inner and outer in his exercises with actors, questioning whether the impulse is originating from the inside or outside. In response to this, Dorinda Hulton suggests:

Within the process of change and transformation, there is essentially a flow or dialogue between the two. "Don't let anyone tell you to go from the inside out – or the outside in. It's a circle" ([Chaikin in] Blumentahl 1981:56). ... It is equally clear, however, when the actor allows a particular kind of shifting balance, or dialogue, between body and mind, in listening to and watching for the emerging form, the emerging image, and is able, moment to moment, to come into alignment with it. In such a case, there is a perceptible quality of 'presence', moment to moment within the process of change and transformation. (D. Hulton 2000:160–161)

As Hulton explains, it is about 'the *quality* of engagement between subject and object' (D. Hulton 1998:27). The key point is that inside and outside are not separate, but working together, and could not operate without the other. The particular direction of working is up to the individual actor as to which suits them best in a particular context. The problem is inherent with the nature of the word, and indeed the nature of language itself as a dualistic expression of a singular experience. What we are talking about in relation to the psychophysical is not new, and perhaps in recent times, as Feste said, 'the word is over-worn' (Shakespeare: *Twelfth Night*, III, i). However, for the actor attempting to explore characterization and emotion, the inner and outer, the physical and the psychological, the word might imply a separation, but the experience of the work of such practitioners as Stanislavsky, Chekhov, Chaikin, and indeed Strasberg and Kazan, can lead to a unified approach that creates a continuum of all parts of the being, whatever the word chosen for it may be. This continuum is explored further in the Afterword to this book, taking into account the different practices and paradigms discussed.

Sonia Moore states that 'We are indebted to KSS for the materialist conception of the unbreakable bond between the psychological and the physiological, between subjective experience and its objective expression' (Moore, 1962:36 in Whyman, 2008:243). This chapter has shown that Stanislavsky did indeed develop a psychophysical approach which has influenced many practitioners since, some who have followed this psychophysical path, others who have taken it into a completely different, sometimes contradictory, means to train actors. His work is still cited as a key part of actor training and directing today, demonstrated by Katie Mitchell at the beginning of this chapter, and the use of his name in institutions such as RADA. However, it is questionable as to whether it is offering actors a psychophysical rather than psychological approach, one that could help to equip them for the range of performance forms and aesthetics that is increasingly being demanded of them. The next chapter moves the discussion on from acting to examine a selection of embodied practices within Western performance based in movement, which place the performer at the centre of the creative process.

Notes

1. The problematic duality of 'Western' and 'Eastern' is deliberately employed in this chapter to highlight the way in which this division was perceived in Stanislavsky's work, but obviously acknowledges the problems inherent with this.
2. See Rosemary Malague's 'An Actress Prepares: Women and "the Method"' as an example of a feminist reconsideration of American approaches to Stanislavsky's work.
3. Hapgood's translation and revisioning of Stanislavsky's work in *An Actor Prepares* is used in this chapter with an acknowledgement of the issues and problems with it as discussed.
4. This may have been a reference to, or indeed a direct criticism of, exponents of Method acting in America, who began to use emotion memories in performance as well as rehearsal, which will be discussed later in this chapter.
5. 'Michael Chekhov on Theatre and the Art of Acting: The Five-Hour Master Class' are recordings of talks which Chekhov gave in 1955, when he was too ill to attend the classes in person.

5 Making Movement: The Psychophysical in 'Embodied' Practices

Rebecca Loukes

This chapter is about 'making movement' in modern Western performance and the work of the actor in the process of producing and then performing this movement. As noted in the discussion of the creation of performance scores in Chapter 1 we distinguish here between the notion of an actor/performer who interprets a script or a piece of choreography and one who is the author or creator of their own material. However, as the concluding discussion to the previous chapter points out, these two kinds of work are not necessarily mutually exclusive. As we have seen, Stanislavsky's approach to training actors developed in response to a wide range of cultural and scientific influences. This chapter re-visits some of those influences at the turn of the twentieth-century as the backdrop for the development of what I am calling 'embodied theatre(s)', a term embraced by Phelim McDermott of British theatre company Improbable Theatre:

> The dream is not just of a *physical* theatre but of an *embodied* theatre that combines the body, the imagination, the emotions and the voice. The performance also has a relationship beyond its own body in-the-space and is in energetic dialogue with other performers, the design environment and light, and the audience. The whole energy field is a system in constant flux as it relates to itself and organizes the system of emotions, impulses, intellect and storytelling. (McDermott 2007:204, italics mine)

Chapter 4 concluded by asking whether Stanislavsky's work can be utilized by the contemporary actor in the range of tasks demanded of them, beyond solely the interpretation of a text. The work described in this chapter might be read in dialogue with this. What understanding of the 'psychophysical' runs through the practices explored here? How is the bodymind conceptualized in these practices? And, what relationship does that have to the movement generated and performed?

I focus in this chapter, then, on the actor/performer within this process of making or generating his/her own work – looking across several historical examples drawn from the field of European 'embodied' practice from both dance and theatre, including Mary Wigman, Francois Delsarte, Pina Bausch, Jerzy Grotowski, and Jacques Lecoq. When McDermott uses the term 'embodied' theatre he is referring to the limitations of the term 'physical theatre,' which has been used to describe a huge range of contemporary performance practice and gained particular currency in the UK in the 1980s, coming to be associated with companies like DV8 Physical Theatre (from dance) and *Theatre du Complicité* (from Lecoq). The work of these companies (among many others) developed as an alternative to the dominance of perceived hegemonies of existing theatre and dance forms. The term 'physical theatre' has become a ubiquitous part of the UK theatre landscape in recent years. Although still widely used, it has also been seen as so all-encompassing in the kinds of theatre practice it describes to become meaningless. Murray and Keefe's 2007 volume *Physical Theatres: A Critical Introduction* draws on a panoply of practice to make the point that there is no such *singular* thing as physical theatre, rather a diverse array of 'ideologies and manifestos which sought to reverse a dualism and hierarchy of word over body' (Murray and Keefe 2007:7).

This chapter uses the term 'embodied' practices rather than physical theatre to describe work that uses the body as a primary site of both the making and performance of movement material. Though, of course, one could argue that the body is such a site in any performance. As McDermott himself says, 'When was the last time you went onstage without your body?' (McDermott 2007:207). I focus here on work that uses the body as the main driver to both create and perform the work. I choose to use 'embodied' practice in this chapter as an alternative to the term 'physical theatre' for a number of reasons. Firstly, the characteristics McDermott defines as 'embodied theatre' (the body, emotions, imagination, body-in-space) mirror the focus placed on the cross-cultural and interdisciplinary investigation of acting across this book. Secondly, the use of the term retains the centrality of the bodymind in the process of making movement but perhaps gets away from the cultural, temporal specificity of the term 'physical theatre'. It has been argued, for instance, that the term physical theatre describes 'a movement of renewal in British theatre and performance' that was clearly evident in the 1980s (Chamberlain 2007:120) but that has now become redundant:

> Physical theatre was a heuristic term, useful for getting out of the gravitational pull of certain normalizing fields, but after the breakout the term becomes unnecessary, even burdensome. (Ibid.)

The way that some practitioners now resist the label 'physical theatre' certainly indicates that the use of the term may have reached saturation point. For instance, Frantic Assembly write: '"Physical theatre" is actually quite a frustrating phrase as it barely manages to describe what we do never mind the wide range of styles and influences that are clustered under its banner' (Graham and Hoggett 2009:29). Instead, it might be said that the term is now more commonly used by theatre venues and their marketing teams to label work from the outside, in order to conveniently package material for recognizable consumption by the audience.

Thirdly, and perhaps most importantly, in using the term 'embodied' throughout this chapter I am acknowledging, as we all do throughout the book, that in attempting to understand the role of the bodymind within a particular style, genre, or approach to acting it is impossible to ignore its place in contemporaneous scientific understanding.

With this in mind, I examine 'embodied' theatre through selected practices since the turn of the twentieth-century across both dance and theatre, asking, primarily, what is the psychophysical within these specific practices of making movement? This chapter begins, however, with a look at the breadth of body-based practices available in Europe during the first part of the twentieth century. I very much acknowledge, of course, that the making of any movement is as much a product of culture, society, and history as it is of an individual bodymind, and explore how the roots of much of the 'embodied' practice that is seen on contemporary European stages today can be found in this period.

As pointed out in the introduction to this book, contemporary acting is 'idiosyncratic'. Recent years have seen a marked shift from the primary role of the actor as interpreter of an existing text, usually led by the vision of a sole director, to a plethora of devised and collaborative work. Within the broader field of devised theatre, practices using the body as the primary mode of generation and communication of material have thrived:

Mime becomes popular in a transitional period when theatre is in decline and is moving towards renewal. Theatre needs a heightened sense of movement because when the spoken word cannot express itself fully, it returns to the language of the body. (Vidal 1988)

It seems that the proliferation and popularity of body-based theatre practices goes further than solely a reaction against text and is situated within a wider societal focus on the bodymind. We have certainly seen the early part of the twenty-first century aligning with what the pragmatist philosopher Richard Shusterman has coined 'the somatic turn' (Shusterman 2000:154). This renewed interest in the body, according to Shusterman, is characterized by 'a revived interest in ancient Asian practices of yoga and meditation' among other types of somatic work. Shusterman posits that 'the somatic turn may express the need to find and cultivate a stable point of personal reference in a rapidly changing and increasingly baffling world' (162) and that, as Joseph Roach also suggests, it is partly a response to our societal 'technological enslavement' (Roach 1993:157). This explanation goes hand in hand with 'the recent growth of body practices as the necessary response to an evolutionary crisis, the need to renegotiate our relationship to ourselves and our environing world' (Roach 1993:164). Shusterman is not referring specifically to theatre but it seems that a current focus of attention on 'embodied' theatres could be related to this explanation. This contemporary understanding of the actor's bodymind will be explored within aspects of cognitive studies in the following chapter.

European physical culture and the body-mind

Clive Barker observed the difficulty in assessing where devised theatre started, noting that 'it has always been there' but that over the past forty years or so the broad balance of power has shifted away from the director towards more 'ensemble'-based approaches (Barker 2002:6). Heddon and Milling note that, 'It is easy to forget that fifty years ago devising as a process of creating work was almost unknown' (Heddon and Milling 2006:221). Govan, Nicholson, and Normington acknowledge that contemporary physical practices have been shaped by 'early twentieth-century dance, mime theatre and circus practices' but focus largely on contemporary examples in their book on devising (Govan, Nicholson, and Normington 2007:158). Previous studies of making movement have not focused extensively on European creative practice in the early-twentieth-century, and by looking at this period here in some detail it might be possible to reconsider some important legacies and connections. I argue that body-based practices at the turn of the twentieth-century have informed the work of many of the seminal makers of 'embodied' practices until the present day.

The industrial revolution and the vast growth of the cities were factors that made life in metropolitan Europe highly dynamic at the turn of the twentieth century, with a wealth of diverse cultural influences within easy grasp of ordinary people for the first time. One student of the German movement pioneer, Elsa Gindler (1885–1961),[1] in the 1920s remembers:

> Positive electricity was in the air...We took part in Mazdaznan, read Laotse, heard Krishnamurti speak, admired the fabulous dancer Uday Shankar, and followed the passive resistance movement of Mahatma Gandhi. (Henschke Durham 1981:17)

This recollection also illustrates how, due to mass communication and the growth of international travel, cross-cultural influences were possible on a wide scale for the first time. The use and appropriation of non-Western forms of performance and training at this time are well known, and discussed in Chapters 1, 2, and 3. The 'orient' was seen as fertile ground for drawing 'inspiration' and dance was no exception to this. The American dancer and choreographer Ruth St Denis (1877–1968), for instance, made her career in solo dancing 'with a series of sumptuous spectacles spiced with the tang of the Orient' (Mazo 1977:61). Influenced by a trip to New York's Coney Island where she came upon 'an Indian village peopled by snake charmers, fakirs and nautch dancers' (Mazo 1977:71) she created several dances 'inspired' by 'India' – the most famous of which, *Radha*, was performed throughout her career. This appropriation of selected elements of iconography or cultural symbols without in-depth knowledge of their sources was common across Europe and the United States at that time.

The industrial European city was also 'characterised by anonymity, a sense of rootlessness, alienation and disorientation, and a standardisation of existence' (Howe 1996:4). Against this backdrop artists and scholars were turning to 'knowledge gained by intuitive discovery of underlying experience' (Howe 1996:5). Expressionist art and theatre were thriving. As another student of Elsa Gindler writes:

> It was a time of great change ... People ... were becoming interested in the discoveries of Freud, of Adler, of Montessori; a wind of freedom and humanism was stirring a new pedagogy was being created. (Aginski 1981:15)

Part of this new pedagogy was a development of the way exercise and dance were taught. Germany had had a history of involvement in gymnastic exercise by the general public. *Turnen* (exercises and gymnastics with apparatus) had enjoyed popularity since the early nineteenth century, and this developed into a *Körperkultur* movement (physical culture) in which there were numerous schools (Preston-Dunlop and Lahusen 1990:47). The German movement educators Hedwig Schlaffhorst and Clara Andersen commented on the need for this physical culture movement:

> Education in our country has never taken care of the strengths of the body and the soul, but has only thought of the education of the intellect and consequently in the whole appearance of the German there is no balance between spirit, body and soul. (Aubel 2002:5)

Körperkultur was not confined to Germany. The physical culture movement spread around Europe and across to America but many of its key practitioners and performers emerged from German expressionist dance and theatre.[2] The movement also became far more important than simply a development of the teaching of physical education. Rather, it can be viewed among the key 'life reforms' that responded to the widespread effects of urbanization at the turn of the century. It comprised both sport and dance elements, as well as nudism, the youth movement, dress reform, and gymnastics (*Gymnastik*) (Howe 1996:11). Though these activities were described partly as a 'reaction against the stultifying bourgeois existence, and indolent lifestyle that corporally terminated at the shoulder-blades' (Gordon 2000:139), they apparently also united socially and culturally diverse groups of people against 'modern capitalism' and the products of the Industrial Revolution.

Pioneers of what has been called variously New Dance, New Artistic Dance, New German Dance, Central European Dance, and *Ausdruckstanz* (Howe 1996:1) crossed over into the burgeoning *Gymnastik* movement in a desire for a 'natural', expressive system of body training.[3] The earliest use of the term 'Dance Theatre' (*Tanztheater*) has been accredited to the work of seminal choreographers Rudolph Laban and Kurt Jooss which: 'defined the trend in German modern dance that sought to integrate dance into the major theatrical circuits and adhered to a model of training which taught various techniques side by side' (Franco 2007:81). Laban wrote in 1924:

> The new dance theatre aims for finding a synthesis of all possibilities of expression and bringing these together again. This synthesis can be dance tragedy, dance ballad (song), dance comedy, or a movement symphony. (Laban 1924 cited in Bradley 2009:64–65)

This notion of 'synthesis of all possibilities of expression' could be aligned to McDermott's hope for a contemporary 'embodied theatre'. It also bears similarities to the notion of 'total theatre;' a phrase derived from Richard Wagner's concept of *'Gesamtkunstwerk* – a "collected", "united", "whole" or "total artwork"':

> We most often find this totality indicated by a list of components such as music, movement, voice, scenery, lighting, et cetera. More important, however, is the understanding that there must be an effective interplay among the various elements or a significant synthesis of them...While totality as an ideal is extensive and all-inclusive, it is this relationship between elements, rather than an accumulation of means, which actually distinguishes the form. (Kirby 1969:xiii)

The notion of 'total theatre' can be seen in the work of Appia, Craig, the Futurists, and Artaud, and it reflected the pre-occupation of Modernist theatre artists to find ways to connect, integrate, and synthesize existing forms. In the context of the 'embodied theatres' we discuss here it also meant a revolutionary attitude to the expressive possibilities of physical movement, rooted in a new understanding of the bodymind (see the discussion of the influence of Pavlov, Ribot, and James in the previous chapter as examples).[4]

Gymnastik was understood as an approach, rather than a system or a group of certain exercises, focussed on 'biological principles' but crucially:

> It assumed that a natural movement is an integrated mental-physical concept and an expression of a personality which reflects the person's individual style of performance. (Gerber 1971:239)

Gymnastik has also been characterized by its lack of use of additional apparatus and its emphasis on 'good movement' (Streicher 1970:185). What defined 'good movement' varied according to the wide range of practitioners who taught their own version of *Gymnastik*, but the emphasis was always on an awareness of the bodymind in space, breath, rhythm, and, as reflected in developments in philosophy and psychology at the time, the concept of the psychophysical. The borders between *Gymnastik* and dance training were not clearly defined, and 'many dancers opened schools geared toward laymen that emphasized the artistic potential of physical culture' (Manning and Benson 1986:32). Alternatively, many schools of *Gymnastik* catered for the needs of performers.

The notion of the psychophysical at this time was strongly influenced by nineteenth century theories that 'increasingly adopted the view that non-rational and instinctive forces in man reside in a mysterious and capacious place called the unconscious' (Roach 1993:179). Sigmund Freud famously distinguished between the ego and the id and believed that 'the ego must be understood as a bodily ego' (Freud in Reynolds 2007:24) 'presenting the structure and form of the ego as a corporeal projection' (Freud in Reynolds 2007:24). Also influenced by the theories of Nietzche and Marx, this understanding of the bodymind gave new meaning to the idea of expression, described by Mary Wigman as 'the breakthrough of unconscious spiritual processes to a state of corporeal consciousness' (Wigman in Reynolds 2007:23).

It is this notion of the psychophysical that united many diverse forms of training for performance at that time and can be exemplified by the words of Franz Hilker, the founder of the German *Gymnastik* Bund who wrote:

> The aim of the organisation is the development, dissemination and pro-
> tection of *Gymnastik*, in other words a physical education, which builds
> and develops the body in its constructive and vital forces, and in so doing
> makes it the carrier of not only physical but also values of the soul and
> spirit. (Hilker 1926:1)[5]

The bodymind as a 'carrier of the physical [and] ... the soul and spirit' was reflected in different ways through the work of various practitioners and schools who were members of the *Gymnastik* Bund some of whom became very influential in the field of performance. Founders of the Bund included seminal practitioners such as Rudolph Bode, Elsa Gindler, and Rudolph Laban.

The 'ideal' bodymind within various systems of *Gymnastik* training, then, was one in which the notion of the psychophysical was essential and this understanding of the body had a direct correlation with the type of work being made and how it was created, as I explore in a moment in relation to Mary Wigman. What is also crucial to appreciate is the extent to which these notions crossed arts disciplines between dance and theatre.

Francois Delsarte (1811–1871) was an actor and teacher of music and drama in Paris and advocated a holistic approach to the bodymind. He began exploring a new methodology for training the performer after his voice was damaged while studying at the Paris Conservatoire (Ruyter 1996:62). He proceeded by 'learning about human anatomy and recording data based on his own observations of how people react to emotional stimuli' (Partsch-Bergsohn 1994:4). What Delsarte eventually created was a very popular system for developing vocal and dramatic expression, which spread throughout Europe and to the United States in the middle of the nineteenth century. Crucially for the relevance of Delsarte's work to movement, his fundamental principles 'suggest a new (to that time) functional approach to bodily expression in contrast to prevailing formal or decorative canons' (Ruyter 1996:63). For example, Delsarte's Law of Correspondence 'concerns the relationship between tangible and intangible, outer and inner, movement and meaning'. This law states 'To each spiritual function responds a function of the body. To each grand function of the body, corresponds a spiritual act' (Ruyter 1996:63). So any thought, intention, or emotion would be manifested physically and likewise any 'function of the body' also reflects meaning.

Steele Mackaye (1842–1894), Delsarte's only known American student, developed what he first named 'aesthetic' and then 'harmonic gymnastics' (Ruyter 1996:66–67). While remaining rooted in Delsarte's basic principles, he shifted the focus of his training to pantomime and expressive motion. Mackaye's 1875 syllabus named 'Aesthetic Gymnastics: The Psychologic Training of the Human Body' states the aims of his programme as:

> to bestow upon the student an intelligent and aesthetic possession of all his physical resources of expression; to place completely under his command that marvellous instrument of emotion, the human body; to gradually develop an instinctive, spontaneous, and unconscious conformity to principles of harmony and perfection in physical motion. (Ruyter 1996:66)

Mackaye developed exercises to increase 'poise, equilibrium, flexibility, precision and what he termed the "Gamuts of Expression"'. Poise was promoted by exercises that worked from a standing centred body to shifts of weight as the torso and head adjusted to create a balance. Relaxation or 'decomposing' exercises were designed to 'develop throughout the whole organisation a flexibility and pliability which are the physical basis of perfect ease' (Ruyter 1996:68). The practice of 'statue posing', 'poses *plastiques*' or 'Harmonic Poise' was a key part of the Delsartean approach to training, developed by the student Genevieve Stebbins. Genevieve Stebbins (1857–1914) was working as a performer when she was introduced to Delsarte's work. She studied with Mackaye for two years and eventually left professional theatre to focus on the theory, practice, and development of what she called 'physical culture.'[6]

Statue posing involved replicating the physical positions from existing art works, mainly drawn from classical Greek and Roman statues and 'trains the body to move all of its agents harmoniously and without waste of energy. It establishes the centre of gravity, lifts the vital organs to their proper places, and gives us control over our muscles' (Stebbins 1977:460). Stebbins' instructions to students were as follows:

> Stand in front of a large mirror and attempt to make yourself a living duplicate of the picture...(a) There must be simultaneous movement of all parts of body, from head to toe; (b) the motion must be magnetic, i.e. slow, rhythmic, and as un-affected as the subtle evolution of a serpent; (c) every movement must be made in conformity with the principles of evolution, i.e., the movements must unfold from within to without as naturally as the growth and expansion of a flower. (Stebbins 1977:459)

One of the many criticisms levelled at the Delsartean approach can be epitomized by the following comment:

> Body spirit here means the soul expressed in the body – but as if it were crystallized, petrified within it, set up for observation rather than experienced. (Giese cited in Toepfer 1997:148)

Gesture here, argues Toepfer, is not 'grounded in experience nor even in the body; rather, it was imposed upon the body by an 'objective' spectatorial gaze that actually looked backward, into an idealized, mythical, eternal past, for guidance – not on how to feel but on how to display feelings' (Toepfer 1997:148). However, I will return to this practice later in the chapter, to look again at these questions in relation to Grotowski's work on *plastiques*, asking whether in fact the difference between 'feeling' and 'displaying' might not be as distinct as Toepfer claims.

Emile-Jacques Dalcroze (1865–1950) was also a crucial part of this new wave of training for 'embodied practices' in the early part of the twentieth-century. He wrote:

> Dancing must be completely reformed ... The art is in a state of decay, and must be rooted out, and replaced by a new one, founded on principles of beauty, purity, sincerity and harmony ... Bodies trained in the refined realisation of rhythmic sensations must learn to assimilate thought and absorb music – the psychological and idealising factor in dancing. (Dalcroze 1972:252)

Dalcroze's work relating musical rhythm to movement had a far-reaching effect within performance training, progressive education and in general education. He also studied with Delsarte, and while at the Geneva conservatory of Music in 1892 he created a new method of ear training and keyboard improvisation. Through teaching he developed his work to experiment with the effects of musical rhythm on movement and concluded that 'musical sensations of a rhythmical nature call for the muscular and nervous response of the whole organism' (Brunet-Lecomte 1950:78). The experiments led him to devise exercises to improve this relationship between rhythm and movement, and his method became known eventually as 'Eurhythmics', which means good rhythm (Brown and Sommer 1969:38). E.R. Clarke, in a 1914 article, writes of Dalcroze's method:

> When the technique of the Rhythmic Gymnastics is learnt it passes into the artistic sphere; and the body and mind are free to express by movement the emotions inspired by the music. Thus the individuality and personality of every student are trained and developed. (Clark 1914: 4)

In 1911, Dalcroze founded the Dalcroze Institute in Hellerau, near Dresden, which became an immediate success, with students from all over the world. It also attracted a wide range of prominent practitioners such as Stanislavsky, Bernard Shaw, Max Reinhardt, and Serge Diaghilev to performances (Van Maanen 1981:14).

We have focused so far on a number of practices in early twentieth-century Europe in order to provide a context for the examples of 'embodied' theatre to follow. It is clear to see that though the practices varied in form and approach they all reflect a particular understanding of the bodymind, rooted in the science of the time. Wolfgang Graesner, early-twentieth-century German cultural commentator and author of *Körpersinn* (1927), writes:

Reason and will do not undermine the pulsebeat of our blood, it is completely spontaneous and the most elementary life-rhythm which penetrates our being … We feel the breath directly. It vibrates with every feature
of our body … When we free the breath from constraining will and muscles and submit to it, we feel with all our senses the rhythm of life itself,
the 'id' within us. (Graesner in Toepfer 1997:13)

As Toepfer goes on to say, 'gymnastics … focused on locating the unconscious foundation of power and being in the irrational, in an abstract
pulse over which the rationalizing will exerted no control' (Toepfer
1997:13). I will explore this further now in relation to the work of the
dancer Mary Wigman.

Making movement in dance theatre/Ausdruckstanz

The roots of the term 'dance theatre' were planted during the early part
of the twentieth-century in what was known as *Ausdruckstanz* (expressionist dance).

I have already discussed how new approaches to the bodymind emerged
partially as a response to industrialization and societal reform as well as
scientific understanding. The new developments were also a reaction to
existing forms of classical ballet. As Mary Wigman, herself, states:

The ballet had reached such a state of perfection that it could be developed no further. Its forms had become so refined, so sublimated to the
ideal of purity, that the artistic content was too often lost or obscured.
The great 'ballet dancer' was no longer a representative of a great inner
emotion (like the musician or the poet) but had become defined as a great
virtuoso. (Wigman 1983:306)

The paradigm shift from the 'virtuoso' performer creating the illusion of
lightness, height, flight, and speed was key, and Wigman's work blazed
this trail, as we explain below in relation to her seminal solo choreography performance *Hexentanz* (*Witch Dance*). But this quote also affirms
that the benchmark of an 'ideal' performance at this time was one where
the artist is able to represent a 'great inner emotion'.

Mary Wigman's Hexentanz

Does not the power, the magnificence of all creative art lie in knowing
how to force chaos into form? (Wigman 1966:41)

Mary Wigman was born in 1886 in Hanover, Germany. She came to performance late – she began studying with Dalcroze at Hellerau in her late twenties, and met Rudolph Laban in 1913 at Monte Verita, Ascona, Switzerland.[7] She has become known as one of the founders of modern dance and for her lifelong collaboration with Laban, as well as a pioneer of solo work and of the performer as creator of their own work. Wigman's work marked the beginning of the performer as creator rather than interpreter of a previously externally choreographed score. This allowed for a particular relationship with the material and therefore a new 'task' as a performer:

> And this was … perhaps the greatest of all pedagogical achievements; to be given not only one's artistic independence, but to be forced into an absolute self-responsibility. (Wigman in Newhall 2009:161)

As we have seen, it was part of the currency of the times that this new form of performance was understood as an expression of one's inner-most soul or an opportunity to 'express [one's] very being' (Wigman 1998:37). The notion of 'forcing chaos into form' assumes that composing material is about attempting to harness some kind of internal/external creative energy or transformative power. For Pavis, this implies an understanding of movement that 'insist[s] on the expressiveness and the external translation of feelings or thoughts into a gesture of a message which seeks to find corporeal expression' (Pavis 1981:85). Or as an early-twentieth-century dance historian writes:

> In it [absolute dance] we experience for the first time a dance that … springs from primary movement impulses. We encounter for the first time the phenomenon that the modern person searches for – and finds – in dance: an artistically shaping expression for his present energies, nerves and objectives, his shocks, his mental tensions and releases. (Artur Michel in Reynolds 2007:64)

This notion understands the performance to be a psychophysical manifestation of 'primary movement impulses'. As well as aligning with a late nineteenth-century understanding of the body and emotion, this definition of performance is also intimately bound to a contemporaneous view of nature and authenticity. This was visible in the trend for dancers to train and perform naked, to work in the natural environment, and to focus on movement derived from 'daily' life rather than virtuosic technique, as in classical ballet.

The first version of *Hexentanz* was made in 1914 when Wigman was still a student with Laban. As she wrote herself, 'it had to undergo many changes and pass through many different stages of development until, twelve years later it received its definite artistic form' (Wigman 1973:36). This 1926 version (sometimes referred to as *Witch Dance II*) became in some ways the definitive performance of her career, and I examine it below.

In the opening moments of *Hexentanz* we see a figure seated on the ground in dim light.[8] Her legs are held and bent at the knees. She is wearing a loose, flowing tunic and a mask facing the audience. Her body seems to mirror the spare percussive sound of drum/symbol. The first moves see her arms dart upwards in repeating thrusting movements. Her gaze follows the arms. Movements that follow include the slow opening of knees with her hands and a rotating of the whole body around in repeated circular movements. Later she slowly presses down her hands against the inside of her knees in order to open them fully to both sides.

This 'score' epitomizes the shift from height and light in classical ballet to depth and weight. In watching film fragments of *Hexentanz* one cannot fail to be struck by both the darkness and the deliberate sense of gravity of Wigman's body. It certainly could be described as a move away from virtuosity of classical 'technique' towards a focus on 'simple' more 'daily' movement vocabulary. As Susan Manning observes:

> The dance reverses the usual relation of stillness and motion: rather than moments of stasis punctuating a continuum of motion, gestures punctuate the stillness. (Manning 1993:128)

It is in this stillness that resides the power of the work because crucially 'the gestures contain more energy than they release' Manning 1993:128).[9] In this way, as argued by Dee Reynolds, Wigman 'repositioned space, not as a passive container for the dancing body, but rather as itself a space-body [*Raumkörper*] which became an active partner in the dance' (Wigman in Reynolds 2007:68):

> In the centre of space [the dancer] stands, eyes closed, feels how the air weighs on her limbs. The arm rises, groping jerkily, cuts through the invisible space body... Then space grasps for her... The great invisible, transparent space spreads itself undulating formlessly; a raising of the arms, alters, shapes it. (Sorrell in Reynolds 2007:69)

Little is known of the detail of Wigman's devising process but it is said that she used imagery to inspire her improvisation work – drawing on 'her own life, whatever was moving her at that time' as well as the elements (fire, water, earth, and air) (Newhall 2009:160). Later accounts of the improvisation classes she taught also confirm both her pre-occupation with nature and the senses and translation of these into space, observing that 'she used images from nature to arouse tactile sensitivity, not just peripherally or in the extremities but as a specific translation of the tactile experience of hands or feet into the whole dance instrument' (Partsch-Bergsohn in Reynolds 2007:71).

The score of *Hexentanz* was refined over many years and she said that it was the only piece in her repertoire that she performed without being nervous. In terms of the devising process for *Hexentanz*, Wigman says:

> Sometimes at night I slipped into the studio and worked myself up into a rhythmic intoxication in order to come closer to the slowly stirring character. (Wigman 1966:40–41)

Again this re-enforces the notion of the body as both a container of and conduit for creativity and emotion. Wigman also says:

> My purpose is not to 'interpret' the emotions ... My dances flow rather from certain states of being, different states of vitality which release in me a varying play of the emotions, and in themselves dictate the distinguishing atmospheres of the dances ... Thus on the rock of basic feeling I slowly build each structure. (Wigman 1973:86)

Wigman does not define what emotion is in her work but her understanding of 'expression' might enlighten us a little. According to Dee Reynolds, Wigman described expression as 'the breakthrough of unconscious spiritual (*seelisch*) processes to a state of corporeal consciousness' (Wigman in Reynolds 2007:23). Reynolds goes on:

> This 'coming to consciousness' or 'breakthrough' took place in the body itself, in a corporeal awareness that no direct linguistic equivalent ... Kinaesthetically experienced tensions and energies could themselves bring to 'corporeal consciousness' ideational and/or emotional charges, which remained unspecific in terms of particular thoughts or feelings. (Reynolds 2007:23)

The idea of 'corporeal consciousness' seems to exemplify the understanding of emotion described by William James, described in Chapter 4 and unpicked further in terms of contemporary science in Chapter 6. Wigman also wanted her audience to focus on the psychophysical in response to her work rather than 'any literary-interpretative content'. She wrote that her dance 'does not represent, it is and its effect on the spectator who is invited to experience the dancer's experience in a mental-motoric [or psychophysical] level, exciting and moving (Wigman 1998:36).

To summarize, training for making movement in this period across European dance and theatre drew from an eclectic range of practices. Though the practices differed in form and execution, they shared an assumption of the bodymind as a generator of its own performance material for the first time. Training for composition of material consisted of improvisation and was followed by the solidifying of these improvisa-tions into set pieces of material. The work embraced both the notion of the psychophysical, influenced by contemporary science and philosophy, and the validity of the performer's bodymind as being in a state of 'corporeal consciousness'. (Wigman in Reynolds 2007:23)

The extent of Wigman's influence on contemporary performance is currently the subject of renewed interest (Manning 2003; Reynolds 2007; Newhall 2009) and recent scholarship has also addressed her politics and actions during the Second World War (Karina and Kant 2005). Major contemporary reconstructions of Wigman's work include Sylvie Guillem (1997) and Fabian Barba (2009). Additionally, the British performer Liz Aggiss, in 2009, recreated from archive footage some of Wigman's work including parts of *Hexentanz*, reframing them as *Guerrilla Dances*, to be performed around the fringes of other perform-ances to 'amuse, baffle and challenge audiences' (Aggiss website).

As discussed in Chapter 3, one major influence of Wigman's work was on the development of Japanese butoh. Hijikata studied German modern dance at the Masumura Kasuko Dance School with Takaya Eguchi. Eguchi was himself a student of Wigman and parallels can easily be drawn between the slow, spare, and highly charged movement vocabulary of *Hexentanz* and the style of butoh.

Making movement in Tanztheater

Tanztheater as a term may have been used by Rudolph Laban but was first consistently taken by choreographer Kurt Jooss. The bridge between what later became well known in relation to Pina Bausch as *Tanztheater* could be observed through Jooss, whose work had the same groundbreaking and paradigm-shifting impact that Wigman and Laban's had had in the 1920s. Jooss' most famous work *The Green Table* (1932) uses expressive gesture within a clear narrative framework in order to comment on contemporary events. Jooss fled Nazi Germany during the 1930s and based his company at Dartington Hall in the UK during this time. The notion of the psychophysical was also at the heart of his work:

> To train a pupil bodily and mentally until he masters a certain technique and use of his body is, however, only the first step...The more important aim is to stimulate the pupil really to feel the experience of dance-move-ment, with all its powers of integrating the mind and body. (Soelberg 1941:157)

Müller and Servos have commented, that aside from Jooss's work, a significant gap in the development of dance theatre arose between expressionist dance in the 1920s and what later became *Tanztheater* after the Second World War. It was almost as if there was a fear to touch on or comment on contemporary events; therefore, for a time after 1945 'dance sheltered under the classicism and romanticism of the nineteenth-century and rarely ventured outside this area' (Müller and Servos 1986:11).[10]

Tanztheater has been described as the 'merging of dance and theatre modes... *Tanztheater* relies on the infection and co-optation of one form by another, fully utilizing both forms' representational potential so that they are fused into a cohesive whole (Climenhaga 2009:98). There is no doubt however that *Tanztheater* has come to be associated with the pioneering work of the late choreographer Pina Bausch. Bausch was born in 1940 in Solingen, Germany, and began her dance studies at the age of fourteen with Kurt Jooss at the *Folkwang Schule* in Essen. Further training included the Juillard School of Music in New York followed by a period at the New American Ballet at the Metropolitan Opera. On returning to Germany in 1962, she worked as a soloist with Jooss at the Folkwang-Ballets and she took over as Company director when he retired in 1969. Bausch's work utilized a 'total' approach to the creation of *Tanztheater* spectacle – the use of space, the contrasts in scale, and the integral part played by music and later by text ensured a complete performance world. Bausch's work was seen as utterly revolutionary when it first began to make an impact and it divided the dance community. The extent to which she seems to epitomize McDermott's use of 'embodied' theatre shows just how much this 'dancer' influenced the field of theatre. Her work is also an

interesting contribution to a discussion of the psychophysical, particularly in relation to the tasks that she set for her dancers in both the
making and performing of her pieces and in audiences' reactions to
this material, as I detail below.

There is a sequence of movement from Bausch's 1978 piece *Café
Müller* that has become almost iconic in relation to her work and encap-
sulates many of the key characteristics of her both her style and content.[11]
A man and a woman stand facing each other. A second man enters and
places the arms of the woman one by one around the man, then lifts her
so she is held momentarily. When the second man leaves, the first allows
his arms to become loose and she falls to the ground. This sequence is
repeated several more times with increasing speed until the couple are
repeating the actions together without being 'placed'. We see and hear
the 'real' exertion of the performers as their breaths become louder.
Eventually they stand still, embracing, their exhaustion visible. The
theatre director Katie Mitchell described her reaction watching *Café
Müller* in the 1980s as 'the most lyrical, painful and beautiful thing I'd
ever seen. I just sat there and cried' (Mitchell 2010) and in reference to
this particular scene:

> [T]here's an amazing moment when a woman keeps trying to jump into a
> man's arms and he keeps dropping her again and again. Bausch seemed
> to capture in the movement that strange hinterland that sometimes exists
> between men and women when they can't quite get across to each other,
> because the differences just overwhelm. (Mitchell 2010)

The impact of the sequence, which I also felt very strongly when I first
saw the piece, comes not from the performance of a gesture in isolation,
but rather in the repetition of its key components. Its power comes not
from psychological development of characters, nor the 'pure' gesture of
Wigman, but through what has been described as a 'theatre of
experience' – emotional involvement not with characters but with
problems presented' (Müller and Servos:13). In quite a 'simple' sequence
of repeated actions where the audience's attention cannot fail to be
captured by the exhaustion of the performers as they breathe together,
one can read a great deal. Patrice Pavis, in writing on theatrical gesture,
remarks:

> The transformational process of the action is chosen in the gesture.
> However, the process is not easy to place in time; it does not culminate
> at a precise moment, but is established as a series of transitions from one
> state to another'. (Pavis 1981:81)

Likewise, this sequence, for the audience, becomes more than the sum of its parts in the accumulated effect of the repetition of the 'simple' gestures. I discuss this effect of the accumulation of gesture in the performer further in a moment.

As her work developed, Bausch's way of generating movement shifted from choreographing her own work on the dancers to them devising some of their own material. Bausch would ask questions of the dancers and their improvisation was then shaped into composition by Bausch. In this way, Bausch acted as 'provocateur' (Larlham 2010:155) as well as choreographer:

> At the beginning of each process she would pose a series of thematically related questions and her dancers would respond to these provocations in words or in action. The dancers responses were written down, videoed, revised, edited, and sometimes passed from one member of the company to another before being spliced into the final performance-collage. (Larlham 2010:155)

The aim of these questions was to generate a 'personal' connection with the subject matter of the choreography but there is a very important emphasis in what she was asking them to do:

> It is not a matter of pretending. I didn't ask you to go there and cry. I asked you to try to think about what happens when you cry, the sounds … I didn't ask you why you cry, or when was the last time you cried. I asked, 'How do people cry'. (in Fernandes 2002:27)

The focus was on the *action* rather than the emotion:

> But you must remain perfectly serious. I want to hear not *how* you laugh, but *how* you laughed, *how* you used to laugh in the past … You don't have to tell us the reason, only *how*. (Fernandes 2002:28, italics mine)

So here, in contrast with the generation of material in Wigman's work, it is not about attempting to generate or summon up 'deep' emotion, rather in performing the action, the feeling may be generated for the audience. In this respect the bodymind is 'demonstrating', to a certain degree, the movement for us. Numerous scholars have equated some of the principles of *Tanztheater* with Brechtian alienation technique in order to heighten the effect on the audience:

Or else it will be necessary, as in the Brechtian alienation effect (*Verfremdung*), to intervene from the outside – in the form of a taking over of the speaker's role of a 'personal' gesture by the actor – in order to interrupt the flood of gestures and to stress what the theatrical illusion strives to make us forget: that the gestures are the artificial product of a 'staged' body. (Pavis 1981:71)

This Brechtian interpretation of the way Bausch uses gesture is developed by Daniel Larhlam who suggests that:

In Bausch's pieces, interactional behavior is alienated (or 'defamiliarised') less by an underlying gest of demonstration than by the degree of physical organization inherent in every movement – from the quotidian to the abstract – made by her highly trained performers. (Larlham 2010:153)

Bausch's performers' training in classical technique allows them to engage the work in this way. Although much of her material is based in everyday movement it is the highly trained performers' ability to translate this into performance spectacle that creates her aesthetic. Virtuosity in terms of the performance of complex movement vocabulary has been replaced with a 'virtuosic' rendering and repetition of more recognizable 'daily' movement.

But is this so very different from what Mary Wigman was doing? Bausch has famously said she was 'less interested in how people move as what moves them' and though her dancers are not asked to 'represent' a particular emotion there certainly seems to be a transformative effect on the performer. One of Bausch's dancers recalls:

In the new piece, I have to do the second act for twenty minutes, all the time … It is totally crazy. It starts fine; it is a good sensation. But then it ends up being quite depressing; even for those who are just watching from the outside … Because when we dancers repeat the movements, at least we don't stay the same person as when we started. You change as well. And she appreciates this change with the same type of movement … the movement … is loaded with possibilities and when you repeat it so many times, these possibilities grow and accumulate on each other. (Fernandes 2002:30)

It is this accumulation, as in the sequence from *Café Müller* described above, that can have such power for the audience. The emotion is not 'acted out' but the performance of the score itself can have a particular psychophysical impact on the performer that is visible. The under-standing of the bodymind that correlates to this notion of making movement is derived from late-nineteenth-century understanding of the body and emotion which assumes that 'the voluntary enactment of the symptoms of emotion will bring forth the emotion itself' (Roach 1993:192). The work of the seminal psychologist William James alongside Carl Lange formed what became known as the James-Lange theory of emotion which used the now-famous example of seeing a bear and overturning the assumption that 'I see the bear, I feel terrified, I run' and proposing instead that 'I see the bear, I run, I feel terrified.'

> He argues that it is because we weep that we feel sad, that it is because we lash out we feel angry, and that it is because we tremble that we feel afraid. In every case perception follows expression. (Roach 1993:192)

This theory has influenced much of twentieth-century acting theory, including Stanislavsky's work on physical actions, as outlined in Chapter 4. Here, the set of actions described above by Bausch's performer that she repeated for over twenty minutes was based on hurling herself into a wall on the side of the stage. It is easy to see how a supposedly 'empty' gesture could provoke a psychophysical response in the performer and it is this response to the gesture that is interesting, rather than an attempt to 'create' an emotion. This idea is picked up again in the following chapter in relation to contemporary scientific understanding of the 'situated' bodymind of the performer.

Bausch's influence in contemporary performance is enormous. Her recent death in 2009 has prompted a global re-assessment of work in scholarship and through performance (Climenhaga 2012; Sadlers Wells World Cities project 2012). Her legacy continues through the work of such choreographers as Anna Teresa de Keersmaeker, Wim Wanderkeybus, Ultima Vez, and Akram Khan as well as countless other artists from both dance and theatre.

Making movement in Grotowski's work

> To act with the hands, begin with the spine, to act with the feet, begin in the head or the hands. (Grotowski in Wangh 2000:75)

Born in 1933, in eastern Poland, Grotowski's early influences included training at the State Institute of Theatre Arts (GITIS) in Moscow and

Asian philosophical writings combined with a trip to central Asia in 1955.[12] He established the Theatre of 13 Rows with Ludwig Flaszen in 1959 and for the next ten years focused on creating theatrical works with a close team of collaborators. Throughout his long career he continually redefined the parameters of theatre, training and acting – through his paratheatrical experiments to objective drama to his final explorations of art as vehicle, his influence on the bodymind of the performer in making movement is far-reaching.[13] He wrote:

> I believe that in all the problems of exercises the misunderstanding stems from the initial error that to develop the different parts of the body will free the actor, will liberate his expression. It's just not true. You should not 'train' and, because of that, even the word 'training' is not right. You should not train, not in a gymnastic way or in an acrobatic way, not with dance nor with gestures. Instead, working apart from rehearsals, you should confront the actor with the seeds of creativity. (Grotowski in Slowiak and Cuesta 2007:138)

Grotowski, here, could be echoing where Bausch placed her attention in terms of what is necessary to make movement. Training is not an end in itself – it is a vehicle through which the actor can create material and it is never merely physical training, rather *psychophysical*. To unpick this a little further we turn for a moment to examine Grotowski's '*plastiques*'. Lisa Wolford has described Grotowski's *Plastiques* as a detailed focus on

> the articulation of movements emanating from the spine and tracing their way outward towards the periphery of the body ... the sequence involved a number of relatively codified movements which the actors learned to perform with careful precision – eg. an impulse emanating from the spine and manifesting through an abrupt movement of the trunk, or a particular way of rotating the wrist and hand. (Wolford 2010:210)

Wolford acknowledges that the *plastiques* are influenced by 'Dalcroze, Delsarte and other European systems of actor training'. This influence is acknowledged in several places by Slowiak and Cuesta (2007) and by Grotowski himself who described in *Towards a Poor Theatre* how 'Delsarte's investigations of extroversive and introversive reactions' were developed by his actors 'in order to realize the goal of our program' (Schechner and Hoffman 1997:43). Though Delsarte's work has little visibility itself in contemporary performance practice, and, as discussed earlier, is firmly bound to a nineteenth-century idea of movement/

emotion, I wondered if his work might be at all useful to today's performers? In his book *An Acrobat of the Heart*, Stephen Wangh describes watching Ryszard Cieslak demonstrating the *plastiques*:

> At first the exercises seemed to be merely strict physical forms, movement isolations invested with a sort of 'isometric' energy, as if the body part that moved was being pulled in two directions at once. But as Cieslak performed them, the *plastiques* also drew his attention into the space around him, as if they were simultaneously exciting his imagination to see things in the empty air. (Wangh 2000:75)

In Wangh's version when the students have moved through isolations of each part of the body he initiates what he calls 'the *plastiques* river':

> To enter a *plastique* River, you begin anywhere, with any *plastique*, and then simply allow the movement of your body to lead on to the next *plastique* and the next... If a feeling or an image occurs to you, trust it. Each *plastique* is a conversation, a movement that contains a dynamic, two-way pull, a simultaneous desire to move forward and away. (Wangh 2000:80)

I describe this exercise in detail here, not because Wangh's interpretation of *plastiques* is definitive, but because the emphasis here is clearly on allowing the movement in space to provoke an internal image.

In an experiment at University of Exeter in the module, 'The Actor's Body', I gave the students Genevieve Stebbins' 'statue posing' task, derived from Delsarte's work (described earlier in the chapter). They interpreted the task within their own contemporary understanding of the body and generating resources for performance and their comments on their experience of the task were remarkably similar to the feedback they gave after being verbally guided through Steven Wangh's version of Grotowski's exercises *plastiques* (Wangh 2000). The Exeter students (some of whom had never worked in this way before) were surprised at the images that were fuelled and made manifest through the 'simple' engagement in a technical movement sequence. Grotowski writes:

> With these exercises [from Delsarte] we looked for a conjunction between the structure of an element and the associations which transform it into the mode of each particular actor. How can one conserve the objective elements and still go beyond them toward a purely subjective work? This is the contradiction of acting. It's the kernel of the training. (Grotowski in Schechner and Hoffman 1997:43)

The *plastiques* are not the only part of Grotowski's legacy that owes a debt to early-twentieth-century movement practices. The optimal state of the body for Grotowski is a state of 'passive readiness' (Slowiak and Cuesta 2007:60) 'a state in which one does not want to do that but rather resigns from not doing it' (Grotowski 1991:17). The term '*via negativa*' has a specific meaning:

> In terms of the exercises, it demanded an emphasis on the elimination of the muscular blockage which inhibits free creative reaction, rather than a positive, methodical acquisition of physical skills. (Kumiega 1997:237)

The European *Gymnastik* practitioners at the turn of the twentieth-century were also searching for a way to prevent the use of excess effort. Genevieve Stebbins advocated a reconsideration of the word 'relaxation' and Elsa Gindler's work was founded on the practice of 'allowing' rather than 'doing' movement.

Making movement in Grotowski's work was based in improvisation as 'an extremely rigorous activity that demanded the actor and the director to engage creatively in a personal confrontation with the core material' (Slowiak and Cuesta 2007:88). In the 1960s, 'devising' sessions involved the actors improvising material while Grotowski intervened, provoking them by whispering or shouting instructions, physically moving them in the space or asking them to repeat a movement phrase.[14] During this process 'the actors never cut their flow, stopped to ask questions, or surrendered to confusion' (ibid.). Following this generating process, the actors wrote down everything they had done in two columns – on one side 'actions' and on another side 'associations'. Then came a discussion of what had emerged and following the discussion, a process of 'reconstruction':

> Once the first improvisation was accomplished, the actors were responsible for remembering it in complete detail. Small bits of the improvisation might be isolated and worked and then put back into the whole. (Slowiak and Cuesta 2007:88)

In this way material was gathered for performance. The notion of recording both the 'action' and the 'association' or image provoked by the improvisation is crucial in relation to this work. As with Bausch and Wigman's work the generation of the material itself was not virtuosic in its external form but rather in the engagement with it. For both, perhaps, as Manning observed in relation to Wigman, 'the gestures contain more energy than they release' (Manning 1993:128).

The actor Roberta Carreri, a long time collaborator with Eugenio Barba, who in turn has been heavily influenced by Grotowski, writes of the process she undertook to create her solo piece *Judith*, and it is useful to consider her account in relation to this transition from training to performance material. She describes training as 'the time and space in which the actor works to build up presence and at the same time to break down mechanical or automatic reactive patterns – clichés' (Carreri 1991:137). As with the *plastiques*, Carreri had spent the previous years working intensively to devise her own form of training (developed from basic work from Odin Teatret via Grotowski) and in particular work with Japanese classical form Nihon-Buyo. She describes how one particular structure ('sit on the floor and move one joint at a time, wrist, shoulder, elbow, neck, the eyes – while keeping the rest of the body absolutely still') influenced significantly the direction her devising took:

> When I work with an exercise for months, I begin to form pictures. The body's movements create internal pictures, and I see landscapes in front of me. I experience body positions I have never before been in. (Carreri 1991:138)

Carreri describes her 'geological self' in this process:

> It is a series of tensions between different muscles in the body which I can reproduce at any time without engaging psychological memory. It is a physical memory and it is very concrete: merely moving two parts of the body and keeping the eyes on a specific point while the head is tilted forward a little, for example, changes my normal everyday presence without requiring any psychological adjustment on my part. (Carreri in Watson 2002:77)

Through the deep engagement with parts of the bodymind, images are provoked which in turn generate material for the performance. This psychophysical understanding of the bodymind confirms the notion that it is by doing the action that the image is generated, again echoing James and 'psychosomatic' theories of emotion.

Contemporary interdisciplinary research in cognitive studies and anthropology has also been probing the extent to which gesture might support thinking or as Andy Clark asks:

> Is gesture all about the expression of fully formed thoughts, and thus mainly a prop for interagent communication, or might gesture function as part of the actual process of the thinking? (Clark 2011:123)

Although contemporary science is the focus of the next chapter, it is interesting to briefly look at Roberta Carreri's words on her improvisation process in this context. *The Oxford English Dictionary* definition of gesture is 'an action performed to convey a feeling or intention'. Its origins lie in the Latin word *gerere* to 'bear, wield, perform'. But according to contemporary research we do not necessarily 'bear or wield a gesture' that is pre-made, rather the process of thought and communication may be rather more complex:

> Gesture thus continuously informs and alters verbal thinking, which is continuously informed and altered by gesture (ie. the two genuinely form a coupled system). (Clark 2011:125)

This certainly fits with the way Carreri describes her work. The 'gestures' create internal images which inform the way she continues to make movement:

> Gesture is not a form of instrumental action that takes place within a virtual or narrative space. Rather, gesture is an action that helps to create the narrative space that is shared in the communicative situation. (Gallagher 2005:117)

This idea is developed further in the next chapter with a closer look at contemporary scientific paradigms of the body.

Making movement in Lecoq's physical theatre

> Whatever the actor's gesture, it is inscribed in the relationship between the actor and the surrounding space, and gives rise to an inner, emotive state. Once again, the outer space is reflected in the inner space. (Lecoq 2002:70)

Lecoq's use of movement takes its inspiration from a range of places including sport, Copeau and George Hebert and the European *Gymnastik* movement.[15] Lecoq was born in 1921 and his early career was as a sports physiotherapist:

> The interior world is revealed through a process of reaction to the provocations of the world outside. The actor cannot afford to rely on an interior search for sensitivities, memories, a childhood world. (Lecoq 2002:30)

For Lecoq 'gesture' is about relation to world around – observing, sensing, and feeling this world and 'translating' or 'embodying' this world. It can be illustrated best, perhaps, using the example of the 'neutral mask'.

> Essentially, the neutral mask opens up the actor to the space around him. It puts him in a state of discovery, of openness, of freedom to receive. It allows him to watch, to hear, to feel, to touch elementary things with the freshness of beginnings. (Lecoq 2002:38)

The neutral mask is a part of the first-year programme at Lecoq's School in Paris and forms one of the basic tenets of his pedagogical approach.

> Wearing the neutral mask encourages students to find a pure economy of movement which is uncluttered by extraneous social patterns of habits, and which invites them to explore a sensual and physical relationship with the world and its matter. A relationship that is – as far as possible – untainted and uninformed by knowledge, emotion, anticipation or experience. (Murray 2003:73)

The quest for 'neutrality', like Grotowski's sense of 'transparency', is a useful metaphor to allow the actor to search for and implement a beginning state: 'Of course there is no such thing as absolute and universal neutrality, it is merely a temptation' (Lecoq in Murray 2003:72). Rather it is used as an active strategy to engage with the world afresh.

In *The Moving Body*, Lecoq describes his pedagogical approach to the study of gestural languages. Firstly, he describes pantomime where 'gestures replace words' (Lecoq 2002:107) and students learn how to construct gestural phrases demanding 'clarity, economy and precision of meaning' (Lecoq 2002:108). The second phase of this work on gestural language teaches how to use the body to represent 'not words but objects, architecture, furnishings' so either the actor using their own body to become a door or the body of another actor. The third phase described is the use of gesture to release 'the dynamic force contained within images' and he gives the example of character going down into a cellar by the light of a candle: 'The actors can represent both the flame and the smoke, the shadows on the walls and the steps of the staircase. All these images can be suggested by the actors movements, in silent play' (Lecoq 2002:108). Here, in these three stages of work with gesture the body is used as the ultimate creative, resource. The ability to interpret and create gesture depends on the ability of the performer to respond to and learn from the outside world – developed earlier in work on the Neutral Mask.

The final stage on the work on gesture described by Lecoq in *The Moving Body* provides a clear articulation of the state of the performing body and its relationship to emotion. This is encapsulated by the exploration of 'the hidden gestures, emotions, underlying states of a character, which we express through '*mimages*':

> These are a kind of 'close-up' on the character's internal dramatic state. Feelings are never performed or explained, but the actor produces lightning gestures which express through a different logic, the character's state at a given moment (a sort of physical aside commenting on one phase of the performance). (Lecoq 2002:109)

He goes on to illustrate this using the example of a person going to see his boss to ask him for something:

> He arrives in front of the door, and is filled with a sense of anxiety: 'What shall I say to him?' At this precise moment, gestures provide an image of his feeling. Not explanatory gestures describing his state, but much more abstract movements which allow him to exteriorize elements which are naturally hidden in everyday behaviour. (Lecoq 2002:110)

What Lecoq describes here are specific pedagogical tools which are part of a holistic education journey over the two years he describes in *The Moving Body*. They are not meant to be 'performed,' but they give a very useful insight into the 'language' of gesture that Lecoq taught, and which has become commonplace in what we understand to be contemporary physical theatre (in the work of British-based Lecoq-inspired companies such as Complicité, Improbable, The Right Size, Hoipolloi, Inspector Sands, Theatre O, Gecko). Here, in that final description, emotion is completely exteriorized through movement: 'These lightning gestures demonstrate to the spectators an 'echo' of the character's fear' (Lecoq 2002:110). As in Bausch's work, the focus is not on what the actor is feeling, but on 'feeling' for the audience. The movement itself is not even necessarily performed by one actor; it might be one, but it could be several.

I have looked at these psychophysical practices from an 'embodied' perspective; that is, not only focusing on the bodymind of the performer/creator within the work, but also on the prevailing understanding of the body within each given context. The next chapter brings this right up to date with a look at an area of contemporary cognitive studies known as 'situated cognition' but it is fascinating to consider that much of what was put in place a hundred years ago, though having been developed and revised, is continuing to play out in contemporary practice – McDermott's dream of an 'embodied' theatre that combines the body, the imagination, the emotions and the voice ... [and the] whole energy field is a system in constant flux as it relates to itself and organizes the system of emotions, impulses, intellect and storytelling' (McDermott, 2007:204).

Notes

1. Elsa Gindler was a German body-awareness pioneer. For information on Elsa Gindler's work see Gindler (1995), Loukes (2003, 2006), and publications by the Sensory Awareness Foundation, www.sensoryawareness.org.
2. For a discussion of the influence of European dance and *Gymnastik* practice on the United States, see Partsch-Bergsohn (1994).
3. Alexandra Carter and Rachel Fensham provide a fascinating collection of essays on the notion of the 'natural' in dance during this period in their 2011 book, *Nature, Neo-Classicism and Modernity in Early Twentieth-Century Dance*.
4. The notion of 'Total Theatre' cannot be separated from its political context and later appropriation in Nazi aesthetics. See Karina and Kant (2005) for an account of the interaction of German modern dance with the Nazi regime.
5. The *Gymnastik Bund* was a 'voluntary accrediting organisation' aiming to 'foster and promote the new approach to gymnastics while still allowing freedom for the methodological differences between the various schools' (Brown and Sommer 1969:57). At first, schools of dance were also members of the *Gymnastik Bund* but as the difference between movement education and dance training emerged, dance schools formed their own organization. The *Bund* had a large influence on the growth of movement education in Germany, because through teaching certificates gained from State accredited examinations new movement training could be taught in 'schools, conservatories and other private and public institutions' (Brown and Sommer 1969:57).Among the founding members of this association were the Schools of Elsa Gindler, Rudolph Laban, Hedwig Kallmeyer, Rudolph Bode, Bess Mensendieck, and Loheland, under the leadership of Franz Hilker. Rudolph Bode (1881–1971) was a graduate of Jacques Dalcroze and began his career as an assistant teacher on the summer school at Hellerau in 1911. He established his own school of *Gymnastik*, movement and dance in Munich, and called his system *Ausdrucksgymnastik* (Expression-Gymnastics). He believed that:

> The task of Physical Education should be the maintenance of the organic unity of life and the natural rhythm of the life movement against the opposing powers inimical to life through their mental and mechanical aims, internally and externally (Bode 1931:16–17).

Dr Bess Mensedieck (1864–1958) began the Mensendieck system of functional exercises, and created schools in Germany, Austria, the Netherlands, Denmark, Czechoslovakia, and New York and published books in both German and English. She was a student of Genevieve Stebbins. Bergsohn claims that Mensedieck's was the first gymnastic system for young women, and that she used no music because the class 'aimed to develop physiological rhythm' (Partsch-Bergsohn 1994: 13). She based her work on the scientific study of anatomy and physiology. In her list of the necessary components for training, Mensendieck included '(1) the saving of strength (economy of movement); (2) mastery of the total scope of movement; (3) space awareness; (4) the execution of lines; (5) rhythm (6) weight; (7) breathing; (8) energising; and (9) relaxation' (Mensendieck 1908:28). *Schule Loheland* was founded by Hedwig von Rhoden (1890–1987) and Luise Langaard (1883–1974). Von Rhoden had been a student of Kallmeyer, and Langaard worked with Mensedieck. They were both influenced by the ideas of Rudolph Steiner and created a system which included the ideas of the youth movement, art education, and existing forms of *Gymnastik*, which they called 'classical gymnastics' (Brown and Sommer 1969:53).

6. For a thorough introduction to Stebbins' work, see Ruyter 1999.
7. For a detailed survey of the development of dance in this period, see Howe (1996) and Partsch-Bergsohn (1984).
8. For a filmed extract of Mary Wigman's *Hexentanz*, see http://www.youtube.com/watch?v=Tp-Z07Yc5oQ.
9. For a discussion of the notion of compressing or distilling the energy contained within a movement, see Chapter 3.
10. For a detailed discussion of the diverging opinions around the transition from *Ausdruckstanz* to Tanztheater, see Manning (2007).
11. A filmed extract of this scene from *Café Muller* can be found on YouTube: http://www.youtube.com/watch?v=oYXjk_qn3cQ.
12. Maria Kapsali discusses Grotowski's early travels in Asia in her 2010 article.
13. For more on Grotowski's work, see Wolford (1997) as a starting point.
14. Account cited in Slowiak and Cuesta (2007), but drawn originally from Smith (1969).
15. See Evans (2012) for an account of the influence of sport on Lecoq's work.

6 Beyond the Psychophysical? The 'Situated', 'Enactive' Bodymind in Performance

Rebecca Loukes

'As long as our brain is a mystery, the universe, the reflection of the structure of the brain, will also be a mystery.' We and the world are tightly intertwined. Though we may not have a special place in the universe, the universe, as far as we can ever understand it, has a special place in us. (Santiago Ramon y Cajal and Broks in Broks 2003:102)

This chapter picks up the discussion of enactment, Dynamic Systems Theory (DST) and cognitive science begun in Chapter 1 and further examines how findings and developments in some of the 'new' sciences can shed light on acting as a contemporary psychophysical phenomenon and process. The chapter begins with an in introduction to the bodymind relationship as 'situated', 'enactive' and contextualized by these new sciences. Insights from these new sciences are then discussed in relation to specific examples of psychophysical performance as phenomenon and process.

In the epilogue of *The Player's Passion* Joseph Roach leaves the reader with a definition of the bodymind of the actor at the end of the twentieth century (Roach 1993). As Roach establishes throughout his seminal volume, and as we have shown throughout this book, our understanding and evaluation of acting styles and techniques are inextricably linked to medical and scientific paradigms of the body particular to a specific cultural, temporal moment. Put another way, 'conceptions of the human body drawn from physiology and psychology have dominated theories of acting from antiquity to the present' (Roach 1993:11).

The final paradigm of the actor's bodymind proposed by Roach in *The Player's Passion*, drawing on Jungian and Reichian psychology, is described as a tough external shell that needs to be 'therapeutically liberated from the tensions and distortions that bind it' (Roach 1993:219):

> We believe that spontaneous feelings, if they can be located and identified, must be extracted with difficulty from beneath the layers of inhibition that time and habit have deposited over our natural selves, selves that lie repressed under the rigidifying sediment of stress, trauma, and shame. (Roach 1993:218)

Roach describes how the contemporary actor makes use of 'body awareness, sensitivity training' in order to be able to engage with and make use of these inner resources. I wondered what might be the next scientific paradigm of the actor's bodymind? What has changed, if anything, since the 1990s in terms of our understanding of the actor's bodymind? Where is current scientific research intersecting with, informing, or challenging our understanding of acting? While acknowledging that the issues relating to working with physical tension, habit and stress, discussed by Roach in the conclusion to *The Player's Passion* are still central to the preparation/training of the contemporary actor, I argue in this chapter that new scientific research is pointing us beyond looking at the 'psychophysical' *solely* within the boundaries of the bodymind. Rather, new scientific paradigms of 'enaction' and 'situatedness' understand that the bodymind cannot be separated from the space around it, the environment it inhabits:

> We cannot locate meaning in the text, life in the cell, the person in the body, in the brain, a memory in a neuron. Rather these are all active, dynamic processes, existing only in interactive behaviours of cultural, social, biological, and physical environment systems. (Clancey 2009:28)

As a provocative example of a contemporary scientific paradigm of the bodymind, and to provide a hint of how far things have moved on since Roach's conclusion to *The Player's Passion*, I turn to the Foreword of Andy Clark's book *Supersizing the Mind: Embodiment, Action, and Cognitive Extension* (2011) in which the philosopher David Chalmers tells us that he has recently bought an iPhone. Having stored all his phone numbers and addresses in it when once he would have committed them to memory, and having used it to calculate the tip in a restaurant or the bills he owes, he notes that his friends have joked he should have the iPhone implanted in his brain. But, he wonders, in the context of current research in situated, embodied, and extended cognition, is his iPhone actually *already* a part of his mind? If he offsets activities into it, activities that would formerly have been the domain of brain functioning, is the body then 'extended' to include tools such as the iPhone? Although this example seems extreme, it is typical of the kinds of debates within certain contemporary scientific communities, some of which this chapter addresses. But what are the implications of this for our understanding of acting? Why is it important? Is it telling us anything new or simply re-enforcing what we already know?

In recent years, theatre scholars have wholeheartedly embraced the field of 'cognitive studies' which includes research in psychology, linguistics, neuroscience as well as philosophy, anthropology, and a range of other scholarship drawing on cognitive science (McConachie 2006:ix), demonstrated by a number of new publications (Blair 2008; Conroy 2010; Kemp 2012; Lutterbie 2011; McConachie 2006 and 2013; Soto-Morettini 2010; Welton 2010; Zarrilli 2009). The question of *why* contemporary science has been so prominent in recent theatre research is addressed by some of these authors. Bruce McConachie argues that 'cognitive studies provides a valid framework for under-standing the potential truth value of many theories and practices that we presently deploy in theatre and performance studies' (McConachie 2006:x). Rhonda Blair reiterates Roach's assertion that 'it is impossible to separate views of the actor's process from the dominant scientific views of any given historical period', and explains the importance for theatre practitioners of utilizing current science:

we must engage the science, if we are to stay true to acting's mission of embodying aspects of human experience, and of expressing both the changing and the relatively (or seemingly) unchanging components of basic human conditions. (Blair 2008:23)

Both McConachie and Blair's statements about the importance of using contemporary science to understand acting call upon the notion of 'truth' and there has been an overwhelming focus in the recent literature on the use of science in relation to character-based or psycho-logical-realist-based paradigms of acting (Blair 2008; McConachie 2103; Kemp 2012). Theatre scholars have also used cognitive studies to explore issues of audience engagement, interaction, and specta-torship (Di Benedetto 2010; Machon 2009, McConachie 2008). This chapter, following the aim of the book as a whole, focuses specifically on the performer's perspective as a phenomenon and process from *inside* the performance score.

Situation, enactment, and dynamic systems theory

Many of the most current theories of cognition, across a range of disciplines, are probing the relationship between mind, body, and the world. Research practices in Enactment Theory, Dynamic Systems Theory (DST), and 'Situated' Cognition are at the forefront of current scientific and philosophical enquiry. It is worth noting at the outset, however, that these fields are neither entirely distinct from each other nor unified behind one single perspective on how this relationship between mind, body, and world is played out. Stewart, Gapenne, and Di Paulo in their 2010 book *Enaction: Toward a New Paradigm for Cognitive Science* describe enaction rather as a '*framework* for a far-reaching renewal of cognitive science as a whole' (italics mine, xii) with this framework being rooted in the notion that:

> [a] living organism *enacts* the world it lives in; its effective, embodied action in the world actually constitutes its perception and thereby grounds its cognition. (vii)

Phillip B. Zarrilli has drawn on theories of enaction to propose an 'enactive approach to acting and embodiment', which is discussed in Chapter 1 and in Zarrilli (2009). Alongside 'enaction' has been the development of 'systems thinking', which came out of mathematics and artificial intelligence (AI) research:

> Systems thinking involves studying things in a holistic way – understanding the causal dependencies and emergent processes among the elements that comprise the whole system, whether it be artificial (ie. a computer program), naturally occurring (e.g. living systems), cultural, conceptual, and so on. (Clancey 2009:12)

Systems thinking could be understood by using the example of building a road. If a road is being constructed it needs to be considered from several different perspectives: within the broader transportation system, within the economic system, within a regional and/or city plan, and within its environmental context (Clancey 2009:12–13). John Lutterbie has already argued for the relevance of Dynamic Systems Theory (DST) as a framework for understanding theatre. He proposes that the process of acting exists within a 'dynamic system' that includes the memorized 'patterns of performance' developed through rehearsal 'lines, movements, gestures, links to emotions, cues for future actions, relationships with the space, objects, and other actors'. Crucially:

> It is not a closed system ... and the possibility of performing depends on a number of signals from the external environment ... The actor is continually responding to changes in the environment caused by herself and other forces. (Lutterbie 2011:219)

What has become known as 'Situated' Cognition is somewhat of a hot topic, or 'a new trend' with 'a lot of buzz' (Robbins and Aydede 2009:3) and it too could usefully be understood as a 'framework' for understanding the bodymind and its environment.

Current research in these areas of cognition/cognitive studies is moving incredibly fast, and boundaries between fields are being erased as terminology develops. For instance, Mark Johnson (2007), whose work I draw on extensively in this chapter, locates his work within pragmatist philosophy and Alva Noë (2004 and 2009) does not use the term 'situated cognition' within his writing, yet both Johnson and Noë have been cited in reference both to 'situatedness' and 'enaction'. For the purposes of this discussion, it is useful to understand that both 'situatedness', 'enaction', and DST emerged as part of a wider challenge to the previously held 'representational' theories of mind (that is, the mind viewed as a 'computer'), which I look at in more detail below in a moment. This challenge has been seen as a 'pragmatic turn' in cognitive studies and is usefully outlined thus:

- Cognition is understood as capacity of '*enacting*' a world.
- The subject of cognition is an agent immersed in the world (as suggested by the phenomenological concept of 'being-in-the-world').
- System states acquire meaning by their relevance in the context of action.
- The architecture of cognitive systems is conceived as being highly *dynamic, context-sensitive*, and captured best by *holistic* approaches.
- The functioning of cognitive systems is thought to be inseparable from its substrate or incarnation ('embodiment').
- Explanations make reference to agent-environment or agent-agent-interactions ('situatedness'). (Engel 2010:222–223, italics mine)

In this chapter, I am drawing from work that has emerged as part of this 'pragmatic turn' to make sense of theories that share common ground within the wider territory of cognitive studies, which can usefully further our understanding of the actor's bodymind. It goes without saying that my exploration can only be a partial one, but I signpost throughout further references in a number of areas. My emphasis here, as I stated at the start of the chapter, is to explore how current scientific research probes at the boundaries of what we understand as the psychophysical performer. An exploration of the multi-faceted meaning of the word 'context' within 'situated' cognition also seems a fitting extension to Roach's project in *The Player's Passion*.[1] As he focused on 'the nature of the body, its structure, its inner and outer dynamics, and its relationship to the larger world' through the history of theatre' (Roach 1993:11) so I address these issues through the lens of selected work from contemporary 'situated' perspectives. Where does the actor start and the space around the actor begin?

The 'Non-Situated'/dis-located bodymind

It is widely accepted that the prevailing Western view of the bodymind, as outlined in Chapter 1, has its roots in the dualistic paradigm of the seventeenth-century French philosopher René Descartes which is now 'so deeply embedded in our philosophical and religious traditions, in our shared conceptual systems, and in our language that it can seem to be an inescapable fact about human nature' (Johnson 2007:2). We have explored some alternatives to this dualistic understanding in India and Japan in Chapters 2 and 3.

The pragmatist philosopher Richard Shusterman asserts that the lived, sensing, or 'conscious' body has been largely absent from philosophical enquiry beyond the notion of the body 'as a prison, distraction, source of error and corruption' (Shusterman 2008:ix). In Descartes' own words:

> On the one hand I have a clear and distinct idea of myself, in so far as I am simply a thinking, non-extended thing; and on the other hand I have a distinct idea of body, in so far as this simply an extended, non-thinking thing. And accordingly, it is certain that I am really distinct from my body, and can exist without it. (Descartes 1984:54)

If, following Descartes, 'I' am distinct from and can exist without my body, 'I' am clearly dislocated from not only my flesh, but also, therefore, from the environment this flesh inhabits. Or, in other words, in normal daily life 'our bodies hide themselves from us in their very acts of making meaning and experience possible' (Johnson 2007:4).[2]

Exercise: Body Map

Get a piece of paper large enough to lie on full-length. Have a partner draw around the outline of your body. Spend some minutes marking on your Body Map (either by drawing images or writing words or phrases) memories of previous injuries, illnesses, or accidents. You can focus on both past and present sensations arising from these experiences. Discuss the map you have made with your partner. Observe the language that you use when talking about your Body Map.

When teaching undergraduate students on the BA Hons. Drama programme at University of Exeter, during my module *The Actor's Body*, I asked them to draw a Body Map (as described above). We had already been discussing the 'psychophysical' in a range of contexts. They fed back some of the effects of past injuries and experiences on their bodies but what was fascinating was when I asked them to observe and think about the language they were using to report these experiences. They all referred to '*my* body'; '*my* body was this ... *my* body was that ... *it* felt like this ... *it* felt like that.' What surprised them greatly was the extent to which the language they use to describe experience is still very much rooted in Descartes' assertion that 'I am really distinct from my body, and can exist without it', and that they were unaware of how deeply embedded this dualism is within the way we process and communicate our experiences. As I proposed earlier, both 'situated' and 'enactive' approaches to cognition, though having philosophical and psychological antecedents stretching beyond the last century, have developed primarily since the late 1970s as 'an alternative to, or a modification of, the then-predominant paradigms for exploring the mind in the cognitive sciences' (Wilson and Clark 2009:55). These existing paradigms can be understood as variations on representational theories of mind where 'perception and thinking, and other mental processes, consist of building internal representations and manipulating them according to definite rules ... what we are conscious of is these internal representations or mental models' (Blackmore 2003:185). These representations take various forms and draw on a range of metaphors and images. Much of the work of 'first-generation cognitive science' was being conducted within Artificial Intelligence research in the 1950s where the 'mind is a computer' metaphor was born:

> The derivative information-processing metaphor of the mind tended to equate data (ie. inputs) with information, models (represented in the stored programs) with knowledge, logical deduction with reasoning, word, networks with conceptual systems and problem solving with all human activity. (Clancey 2009:14–15)

Another dominant representational metaphor, proposed by the eighteenth-century philosopher David Hume, was that the mind is, in fact, 'a kind of theatre, where several perceptions make their appearance; pass, repass, glide away and mingle in an infinite variety of postures and situations' (Hume in Blackmore 2003:65). This model was disputed by Daniel Dennett and termed the 'Cartesian Theater' (2002) or 'Cartesian Materialism' because 'this is the view you arrive at when you discard Descartes' dualism but fail to discard the imagery of a central (but material) theatre in the mind where 'it all comes together' (Dennett 2002:83). He identified the problem at the heart of Hume's theory, which is that 'there is no literal place inside the brain that constitutes this theatre' (Blackmore 2003:71) and therefore no possible location.[3]

These theories comprise what has been called the 'orthodox' stance of cognitive science, which is challenged by the aforementioned 'pragmatic turn' of alternative enactive and situated approaches and is summarized thus:

- Cognition is understood as computation over mental (or neural) representations.
- The subject of cognition is not engaged in the world, but conceived as a *detached* 'neutral' observer.
- The processing architecture of cognitive systems is conceived as being largely modular and *context-invariant*.
- Explanatory strategies typically reference to *inner states* of individual cognitive systems. (Engel 2010:220, italics mine)

The connection between these 'representational' theories of mind and assumptions that have dominated certain areas of psychological-realist approaches to acting and actor training can be illustrated both by the reflections of Exeter students during the Body Map exercise described above, and in the words of the theatre student Sherry Dietchman:

> Until I began [psychophysical] training I thought that my focus problems were just mental. The fact that they may be physical as well simply never occurred to me...Most of my classes emphasized things such as emotional reality, script analysis, substitution, and memory recall. Body

training is either kept separate or ignored altogether ... I wonder what it is in our culture that perpetuates that split. (Dietchman in Zarrilli 2009:17)

In some approaches to acting (that is, some practices derived from Strasberg's translation of Stanislavsky's ideas, as discussed in Chapter 4) the 'interior' process is emphasized over an explicit rooting of the bodymind in space. As I argue through the chapter, a 'situated', 'enactive' approach to understanding the bodymind supports processes of acting and actor training that develop awareness and perception *through* space and action in space.

Part of the 'pragmatic turn' within cognitive science, discussed above, has involved not only 'new' research at the cutting edge of technology and understanding, but a re-examination of earlier pioneers of both scientific and philosophical thought. The following definition of 'situation' is written by the seminal philosopher and educationalist John Dewey and provides a key frame through which to examine the work of the contemporary psychophysical actor:

> In actual experience, there is never any such isolated singular object or event; an object or event is always a special part, phase, or aspect, of an environing, experienced world – a situation. (Dewey 1938:67)

The contemporary pragmatist philosopher Mark Johnson elucidates this understanding of 'situation' in his book *The Meaning of the Body* stating that Dewey did not just mean 'our physical setting, but the whole complex of physical, biological, social, and cultural conditions that constitute any given experience – experience taken in its fullest, deepest, richest, broadest sense' (Johnson 2007:72). Johnson gives the example that out of his office window he can see a huge oak tree so big that it makes up almost his entire field of vision, and through which he can occasionally glimpse other activity beyond the tree:

> In this moment there is only the situation, not as a mere visual scene, but as an experience with a pervasive unifying quality that is at once visual, auditory, tactile, social, and cultural. The pervasive quality changes as the day passes, and it changes also from day to day and season to season. (Johnson 2007:72)

It is this understanding of 'situation' that guides the work of this chapter, both as a central paradigm of the bodymind and as a metaphor for understanding the process of the actor. Before we now look at perception, emotion, and 'extension' for the performer from this perspective it is useful, momentarily, to turn back to the example of performing Beckett provided by Zarrilli in Chapter 1. We can see similarity with the process he describes to this notion of 'situation'. It is not only the external performance environment (the set, the auditorium, et cetera) that is the 'situation'. It is the 'experience with the pervasive unifying quality' including the actor's score of actions.

'Situated' perception and acting

'Situated' perspectives on perception posit that it is fruitless to search for any understanding of conscious experience by looking only at the brain, or as Alva Noë writes, 'Consciousness of the world around us is something that we do: we enact it, with the world's help, in our dynamic living activities. It is not something that happens in us' (Noë 2009:64).[4]

While most would agree that 'the character of conscious experiences is affected by the environment' (Prinz 2009:422), there are divergences of opinion on the extent to which consciousness actually resides in the world. What is most useful to glean from current research on consciousness for performance is that consciousness, in this context is seen as 'active' as I will elaborate further momentarily. As noted in Chapter 1, Varela, Thompson, and Rosch introduced their 'enactive approach' to cognition in their book *The Embodied Mind* (Varela, Thompson, and Rosch 1993) which aimed to free cognitive science from its 'Cartesian Anxiety'. This approach was developed further by Evan Thompson in 2007:

> Cognition is the exercise of skillful know-how in situated and embodied action. Cognitive structures and processes emerge from recurrent senso-rimotor patterns of perception and action. Sensorimotor coupling between organism and environment modulates ... the formation of endogenous, dynamic patterns of neural activity, which in turn inform sensorimotor coupling. (Thompson 2007:13)

In the 'enactive' view, therefore, cognition is dependent both on neural functioning in the brain, and also on the way our organism is 'coupled' to the environment through our senses.[5] Thinking emerges from sensing, modulated through the environment, which in turn forms neural activity in the brain. The notion of 'coupling' between organism and environment is a common one in 'situated' perspectives on consciousness and perception. David Lee refers to 'body-environment coupling':

> Like all animals, we exist by virtue of coupling our bodies to the environment through action ... Perception is necessary for controlling movement just as movement is necessary for obtaining perceptual information. Perception and movement compose a cycle that is action. (Lee 1993:43)

Among many examples cited to illustrate this relationship between perception and movement, Lee cites an experiment conducted by the seminal ecological psychologist James J. Gibson in which blindfolded participants were given a range of different shaped 'cookie cutters'. In one round of the experiment the cutters were pressed into the 'passive' palms of the participants. They were then asked to identify the shapes. Gibson discovered that during the next round, when the participants were able to actively handle the shapes with their fingers, they were far more likely to correctly identify which was which (Gibson 1962:486–487). The important point here is that the space is 'affording' the possibility of perception. If one is actively engaged in perception through movement, the perception is potentially more effective.

This experiment was a precursor to contemporary research in situated cognition on the notion of 'epistemic action' examining the computer game Tetris:

> Epistemic actions – physical actions that make mental computation easier, faster, or more reliable – are external actions that an agent performs to change his or her own computational state. (Kirsh and Maglio 1994:513–514)

Or, put another way, 'an epistemic action involves directly manipulating the environment to bring about a better state in a problem-solving/planning task, rather than constructing an internal representation and manipulating that' (Menary 2010:237).[6]

John Dewey's understanding of 'situation' is also pertinent here. I introduced above how Dewey's 'situation' is dominated by a 'pervasive unifying quality'. It is from this holistic sense that further discrete qualities within the situation can be discriminated. Johnson remarks how this understanding of the pervasive quality of a situation is in contrast to much prevailing assumptions about experience, where 'we learn to understand and to experience our world as consisting of pre-given, mind-independent objects' (Johnson 2007:73). Rather, in this view:

if you pay attention to how your world shows itself, you will indeed see that the flow of experience comes to us as unified wholes (*gestalts*) that are pervaded by an all-encompassing quality that makes the present situation what and how it is. (Johnson 2007:73)

What is most important to emphasize is 'active' engagement with the environment. One first perceives the whole and then discriminates within this situation.

We have seen in Chapter 5 how the relationship between the bodymind and space has been central to the creative practices of such seminal practitioners as Mary Wigman, Pina Bausch, Jerzy Grotowski, and Jacques Lecoq, and one could argue that this understanding of the bodymind is exactly what some practitioners have known, way before the term 'situated cognition' was coined. As Bausch says, in relation to the creation of her work:

I can't think without the time or without space. Everything belongs together. If it's together once, you can't take it apart. The feeling, the energy, all that you can hear, the music or the not-music, the space, all what is there, for me it's impossible [to separate them]. I can't think movement, only movement. (Bausch in Williams 2012:107)

Crucially, this research reminds us that perception is not a given and it is not static. In order to be able to translate these theories into performance, an actor needs to *train* the ability to perceive and be aware of the space around us. Several approaches to training this awareness have been addressed throughout the book. (Chapters 2, 3, 4, and 5)

Current research in developmental psychology uses the notion of a 'cross-modal' system to describe the individual's relationship to the world:

[We] have seen that from birth, actions of the infant and the perceived actions of others are coded in the same 'language', in a 'cross-modal' system that is directly attuned to the actions and gestures of other humans. In the case of imitated facial gestures, one does not require an intermediate theory or simulation to translate between one's proprioceptive experience of one's face and the visual perception of the other's face. This translation is already accomplished at the level of an innate body schema that integrates sensory and motor systems. (Gallagher 2005:225)

What Gallagher describes as 'cross-modal' in the context of relating to others is referred to as 'intermodal' by Mark Johnson to describe how babies learn to perceive and understand their world.

The notion of 'cross' or intermodality is a useful way to summarize the findings of this section and lead us into application in performance and training. We have learned, thus far, that the 'situated' body is actively engaged with its environment as it perceives, feels, and relates to others. Johnson defines 'intermodal' to mean 'patterns that do not exist outside or above our perceptual capacities' but that are not tied to only one modality such as touch, vision, or hearing (Johnson 2007:42) and continues:

> Infants have an ability to correlate structures experienced in one perceptual domain with those in a different perceptual modality and in various motor programs. Such correlations are what make it possible for a child to see a rolling ball, track its motion, move his or her body in pursuit, and eventually reach out to grab the ball.

I only need to look at my own eleven-month-old baby exploring his environment to appreciate the notion of an intermodal body. He looks at the toy, reaches for it, puts it in his mouth to feel and taste, shakes it, knocks it against the wall to hear the sound it makes before moving on. He is drawing on touch, taste, sight, sound, and smell. Johnson builds upon this work in infant cognitive psychology to argue that this intermodal or 'embodied' method of exploring the world continues as we become adults:

> When we grow up, we do not shed these embodied meanings or our bodily ways of meaning-making. Instead, we appropriate and recruit them in what we might think of as our more refined, abstractive modes of understanding and thinking. (51)

Many traditions of somatic awareness training practices that have been used in performance have argued, however, that in order to maintain a 'real' awareness of our environment, that we see in babies, and that has been recently named intermodal or cross-modal, we need to *train* our perception. The work of the German body-awareness pioneer Elsa Gindler (1885–1961), mentioned in Chapter 5, focuses on bringing attention to daily activities such as walking, eating, or speaking with an attitude of 'concentration':

> We ... come into a state that is more human because, when we are contented with ourselves in the doing, we experience *consciousness*. By

that I mean consciousness that is centered, reacts to the environment and can think and feel. (Gindler 1995:5–6, italics mine)

In Gindler's view, by focusing awareness on the present activity, the sensation of doing the action itself, one can become 'conscious'. And rather than disconnecting from the environment, this heightened awareness amplifies the reciprocal relationship between bodymind and space. In order to illustrate this point further, I draw on the writing of the dancer Gertrud Falke-Heller who taught Elsa Gindler's work at the Jooss-Leeder School of Dance at Dartington Hall in the 1930s. She began with work on 'various functions of the organism' through the activities of lying, sitting, standing, or walking. These activities, however, only had any meaning for Falke-Heller insofar as they enabled the students to become, 'sensitive to the whole environment with its actions and reactions' (Loukes 2010:109). She describes how her work attempted to cultivate an 'attitude of calm, absolute openness – an attitude that is prepared for all, but expecting nothing.' She asks the students to consider how a photograph is taken:

I reminded them that one needs a new unused plate for every snap-shot…they must try to rule out any memory or wish for repetition of a previous experience…and have the courage to surrender themselves completely to the unknown as the photographic plate surrenders its receptive quality to the influence of light'. (Falke-Heller in Loukes 2010:110)

When working with this attitude, she noted, '[t]hey became open and receptive to the forces of space and environment…As the awareness of their own body grew they began to sense the effect of the space as a dynamic quality; at the same time the awareness of each other developed and true contact began to be established' (Falke-Heller in Loukes 2010:110). I think that this understanding of space returns us again to Dewey's understanding of 'situation', which is, in fact, re-iterated in Falke-Heller's own words:

[O]nly if the environment can speak to us directly, immediately, only if we do not dim our capacity for 'awareness through habitual, mechanical' adaptation to circumstances (routine), but give ourselves up to the influ-ence and impressions of the *situation*, can we really partake of and be included in life. (Falke-Heller in Loukes 2010:111, italics mine)

What Falke-Heller understands is that in order to fully 'sense' our environment and therefore 'really partake of…life' we must first recognize the way we habitually 'adapt' to routine and then allow this growing awareness to cultivate the attitude that 'is prepared for all, but expecting nothing'. These practices were considered 'radically simple' at the turn of the twentieth century and also seem to align with the 'pragmatic' turn within contemporary cognitive studies; giving practical meaning in the actor training studio to some of the theoretical concepts explored here.

'Situated' emotion

> I cringe if I hear an actor say, 'If I feel it, they will feel it'. The notion that the actor and the audience feel the same sensations at the same moment leads to a solipsistic approach to acting and easy dismissal on the part of the audience. (Bogart 2010:x)

The question of whether an actor feels the emotion of the character she is playing has been debated since the Roman theorist Quintilian stated that 'the prime essential for stirring the emotions of others is, in my opinion, first to feel those emotions oneself' (Quinitilian in Roach 1993:24)[7]. Recent interdisciplinary scholarship within studies of acting has explored this question (Konijn 1997; Bloch 1993) and this reconsideration of the place of emotion in acting has grown out of the recent rise of 'situated' and 'enactive' approaches to research in cognition. Colombetti and Thompson argue that 'for many years emotion theory has been characterized by a dichotomy between the head and the body' (Colombetti and Thompson 2008:45). This has been rooted in the conceptualization from the 1960s until the latter part of the twentieth century, of cognition as 'an abstract, intellectual, heady process separate from bodily events' (2008:45).

Interestingly, and as we have seen in Chapter 5, the body played a crucial role in early emotion theory, and key authors have conceived of emotions as 'psychosomatic states'. Perhaps the most well-known of the early emotion theorists was William James, whose work has also been discussed in Chapter 4 in relation to Stanislavsky and avant-garde performance in 1960s America. James understood emotion as a physical event and stated that 'the bodily changes follow directly the *perception* of the exciting fact, and ... our feeling of the same changes as they occur *is* the emotion' (James 1884:189–199).[8] Going even further back in emotion theory Aristotle, Descartes, Spinoza, and Hume among others also believed that the body played an important role in emotion. But during the 1960s and 1970s, emotion theory became 'disembodied', according to Colombetti and Thompson, for two main reasons. Partly as a reaction to the radical activation and behavioral theories of the 1940s which 'neglected the cognitive and/or evaluative aspects of emotion' and also because of research that claimed that 'the role of the body in emotion started to be that of a mere enhancer – an affectively neutral support whose activation would, at best, influence the intensity of emotional feelings' (Colombetti and Thompson 2008:51).

Current research on emotion from a 'situated' perspective acknowledges the role that evolution has played in the organism/environment relationship. As Joseph LeDoux states, 'emotional systems evolved as ways of matching bodily responses with the demands being made by the environment' (LeDoux 1998:295). Antonio Damasio, one of the most well-known contemporary cognitive neuroscientists argues: 'Emotions are complex, largely automated programs of actions concocted by evolution.' In other words, emotions have developed to fulfill evolutionary needs. Current thinking also acknowledges the role culture plays in both the understanding and production of emotions (Griffiths and Scarantino 2009). Or, as Damasio writes, '[t]he situation you are in makes a difference for the emotional apparatus' (Damasio 2010:112):

> Feelings of emotion are composite perceptions of (1) a particular state of the body, during actual or simulated emotion; and (2) a state of altered cognitive resources and a deployment of certain mental scripts. In our minds, these perceptions are connected to the object that caused them. (Damasio 2010:116)

Damasio does not discriminate here between the perception of the bodymind state during 'actual or simulated' emotion. Damasio uses what he calls the 'as-if body loop' to propose how, in certain circumstances, 'brain mechanisms ... trick the brain into believing that the body is undergoing a change, when in fact it is not' (Colombetti and Thompson 2008:59), or, in other words:

> The brain can simulate, within somatosensing regions, certain body states, as if they were occurring; and because our perception of any body state is rooted in the body maps of the somatosensing regions, we perceive the body state as actually occurring even if it is not. (Damasio 2010:101–102)

Damasio explains that this simulation has emerged in the brain as a way to conserve time and energy. Some contemporary proponents of embodied and situated emotion theory have criticized Damasio's 'as-if body loop' idea as actually supporting a disembodied view of emotion because he is suggesting that it is just the brain supporting emotion *not* the whole organism. However, if Damasio's as-if body loop is understood as being dependent on 'bodily representations in the brain and in activity in the body proper' it is impossible to separate from its context:

> A bodily representation would eventually cease to represent in its normal way were it not embedded in a web of processes linking it to the world and to the possibility of action in the world. (Colombetti and Thompson 2008:61)

Evan Thompson and Giovanna Colombetti are currently developing an 'enactive' theory of cognition which incorporates an 'enactive emotion' approach. Thompson notes that the word 'emotion' (from the Latin verb *'emovere'*) can be translated literally as 'outward movement. Emotion is the welling up of an impulse within that tends towards outward expression and action' (Thompson 2007:363–364):

> According to the enactive approach, the human mind is embodied in our entire organism and embedded in the world, and hence is not reducible to structures inside the head. Meaning and experience are created by, or enacted through, the continuous reciprocal interaction of the brain, the body and the world. (Colombetti and Thompson 2008:56)[9]

The psychologist Elly Konijn's 'task-based acting theory' (Konijn 1997, 2002) has drawn on contemporary understanding within cognitive emotion theory, stating that 'emotions arise from an individual's interaction with the environment and that they are functional reactions regarding an individual's concerns in coping with environmental demands' (Konijn 2002:65). In relation to the perspective of this chapter on the notion of 'situation' Konijn says:

> Surroundings or situations offer opportunities or threats ... Simultaneously, the situation reveals possibilities or impediments that the individual has within this context. When the elements contributed by the situation combine with their potential meaning for the individual, this combination may create an emotional reaction. (Konijn 1997:16)

Later on in the chapter, I provide a short account of my own experience in performance which draws together these ideas in relation to a specific example.

The 'extended' bodymind?

'Wanderer the road is your footsteps, nothing else; you lay down a path in walking'. (Varela 1987 adapting the words of poet Antonio Machado)

These words used by Francisco Varela to describe his enactive approach to cognition, eloquently describe how the act (of walking) constructs the world one is able to perceive. We make our world through our actions. I have already argued that the 'situated' bodymind of the performer can develop its perceptual/sensual abilities to heighten its engagement with its environment. We have also seen how the body in daily life is 'non-situated'. As discussed in Chapter 1, one of the tasks of the contemporary performer is to find a way to be able to develop an awareness of both the bodymind and the action undertaken in order to be able to fully inhabit each moment of performance. It is this definition, which, seeming to be a good description of an optimal state of readiness for the performer, takes us forward to the most contro-versial aspect of 'situated' cognition – the 'extension thesis' or the notion that 'the boundaries of cognition extend beyond the boundaries of individual organisms' (Robbins and Aydede 2009:3). In the way that David Chalmers was thinking about his iPhone at the start of the chapter, can the body of the actor be described as 'extended' in this context? Alva Noë believes so:

[T]here's no principled reason even to think that our bodies stop where we think they do. Parts of me – tools – can be spatially discontinuous with me: What makes them me, what makes them part of my body, is the way my actions take them up. And insofar as I act in and feel with my extended body, my mind is extended too. (Noë 2009:80)

I have already mentioned how the bodymind can be 'extended' through the notion of the 'epistemic action' using the example of the Tetris computer game. Likewise, Alva Noë describes how air traffic controllers use paper strips to stand in for planes:

As a plane enters a controller's air-space, the clatter from the printing of the paper strip alerts the responsible controller. He manually annotates the strip and places it in a tray … When an airplane passes out of one con-troller's airspace and enters the space of one of his colleagues, he hands (or throws) the strip to him … Their active engagement with the paper strips was a kind of cognitive engagement with the planes. They thought about the planes with the strips. (Noë 2009:85–86)

Like the Tetris player, the air traffic controllers 'offload' the work that could be done mentally, internally onto and into their environment, and in doing so 'boost efficiency and extend [their] epistemic reach' (Robbins and Aydede 2009:6).

There are a number of ways we could consider the use of epistemic action for performers. Firstly, as Andy Clark notes, '[d]eeply integrated, progressively automated, epistemic actions figure prominently in the construction of complex skill hierarchies' (Clark 2011:75). Many forms of performer training involve the learning and assimilation of such 'complex skill hierarchies'. So, for example, we could view the learning of a sequence of movements in yoga, or the creation and assimilation of a physical 'score' of actions as a 'meta-system' of epistemic actions:

Humans build skill upon skill, creating very complex contingent hierarchies, as in driving or piano playing ... The result is an amazingly complex chain of habit systems ... each with its own executive demands, which must eventually be integrated into a massive meta-system that co-ordinates all of them. (Donald in Clark 2011:75)

Or, as Zarrilli writes, 'at optimal virtuosic levels of performance, one does the action/task while simultaneously being done by the action/task' (Zarrilli 2009:83).

Could we also consider something like Stanislavsky's work on physical actions as a method of extending our 'epistemic reach'? In using physical actions to construct a role, are we in fact 'offloading' the 'mental' work into our environment like the air traffic controllers and Tetris players? Chapter 4 discusses the Method of Physical Actions in detail, but it is worth remembering Stanislavsky's words:

People on stage act and these *actions* – better than anything else – uncover their inner sorrows, joys, relationships, and everything about the life of the human spirit on stage. (Stanislavsky in Carnicke 2009:165, italics mine)

To performers, perhaps this notion of the 'extended' body does not seem very radical. We know about Michael Chekhov's Psychological Gesture and Stanislavsky's Active Analysis. We have probably all participated in a workshop or a rehearsal where we are asked to create a 'character' by beginning with attention on a particular part of the body and leading the movement from that body part. But I think that if we let aspects of current science inform concrete working practices that allow us to develop awareness, perhaps we can start to move beyond the binaries of body/ mind that, we have seen, still underpin our fundamental ideas about acting.

I draw this out further with an example by turning, finally, to the use of 'tools' to 'extend' the body. The example of a blind person skillfully using a cane to physically 'extend' their perception of the world has been used by many phenomenologists (Polanyi, Merleau-Ponty). Noë's version explains:

> He feels the texture of the ground at the end of the cane. He feels in the cane even though there are no nerve endings in the cane, even though the cane is a bit of metal or wood…. Our experience and capacities depend on the full character of that skillful interaction. Where we are depends, in sig-nificant part, on what we're doing. And what we are – Is the cane part of me or not? What are the limits of my body? Of myself? – depends on more than the brain alone. Skillful experience with a cane can actually extend the body beyond its strictly biological limits. (Noë 2009:78–79)

This could relate to the experience of working with sticks in the theatre studio. To draw on a personal experience for a moment: I place the end of a bamboo cane in the centre of my open palm. A partner does the same with the other end. We look into each other's eyes while keeping our awareness 'open' to the space around us. We sense our feet on the floor and through the palms to the cane, and through the cane to the partner. We begin to move, but allow the movement to emerge through the sensing feet, through the body to the cane, through the cane to the partner and beyond into the space. The philosopher Michael Polanyi writes:

> We may say that when we learn to use language or a probe, or a tool, and thus make ourselves aware of these things as we are of our body, we interiorize these things and make ourselves dwell in them. (Polanyi 1969:148)

It is the task of making ourselves 'dwell' in these objects, as actors, that needs training. In their 2009 article, 'Making Sense of Sense-Making: Reflections on Enactive and Extended Mind Theories', Evan Thompson and Mog Stapleton distinguish between tools that only 'extend' the body and ones that the body 'incorporates':

> Resources that extend the body are familiar features of our environ-ment – pens, scissors, cars, computers, and so forth. These entities are

artifacts that we use and control in order to extend our abilities. Tools that the body incorporates also extend our abilities but they have a phenomenologically different status. (Thompson and Stapleton 2009: 28–29)

This 'different status' is articulated as the 'body-as-subject' (also referred to as the lived body or the body as *Leib*, referred to in Chapter 1) or 'the body-as-subject is a structure of experience; it is that through which the world is experienced. As such, the body-as-subject is transparent' (29). It is this notion of transparency, that distinguishes extension and incorporation:

For anything external to the body's boundary to count as part of the cognitive system it must function transparently in the body's sense-making interactions with the environment. (29)

So through the lens of this current research, David Chalmers' iPhone would not be included as part of the cognitive system but the use of the stick in the studio cited above could be, given an optimal engagement in the exercise. The stick can only become 'transparent' for me as an actor through training (as articulated throughout this book). It is not a given; it is something that is 'cultivated'.[10] This can be illustrated by recalling momentarily the example of Grotowski's actor and collaborator Cieslak cited in the previous chapter:

At first the exercises seemed to be merely strict physical forms, movement isolations invested with a sort of 'isometric' energy, as if the body part that moved was being pulled in two directions at once. But as Cieslak performed them, the *plastiques* also drew his attention into the space around him, as if they were simultaneously exciting his imagination to see things in the empty air. (Wangh 2000:75)

Acting from a 'Situated' perspective: an experience from performance

The final section of this chapter makes use of two examples from a piece of theatre I co-created and performed with RedCape Theatre in 2008 and 2009 in order to further tease out some of the ideas already discussed in this chapter.[11] In examining a particular set of moments from inside the actor's process in performance I provide one practical entry point into the theories introduced here.

The Idiot Colony Context and Process

The Idiot Colony, RedCape Theatre's first piece, was co-created by Coaché, Friend, and Loukes, Andrew Dawson (director) and Lisle Turner (writer). It opened at the Edinburgh Fringe Festival in August 2008 where it won both a Fringe First and Total Theatre Award for Visual Theatre. It toured the UK for the next two years.[12]

The piece told the fictional stories of three women (Joy played by Friend, Mary played by Coaché, and Victoria played by myself) admitted to an asylum in the 1940s after being classified as 'morally defective' as described in the 1913 Mental Deficiency Act. It was inspired by a story uncovered by Coaché's father, who used to fix hairdryers in salons in the West Midlands. One of the hairdressers he met used to work in the salon of St Margaret's Hospital (also known locally as the Great Barr Idiot Colony). The hairdresser said how she had cut the hair of women in the salon inside the hospital. These women had told her stories of people who had been 'locked away' in the hospital for having illegitimate children. Turner led an intensive pre-rehearsal, research process involving interviews with former staff at St Margaret's as well as mental health service users, local and national archival research and work on history of mental health in the UK.

In the performance, the three actors are all dressed identically throughout in white long-sleeved dresses, that could seem to be both patient's gowns and nurses uniforms. All wear white shoes. The actors play doctors and nurses as well as the main characters of Joy, Mary, and Victoria (see Figure 6.1).

Figure 6.1 Rebecca Loukes, Claire Coaché, and Cassie Friend in *The Idiot Colony* (photo by Nik Mackey with permission from Turtle Key Arts)

As the audience enters the auditorium they see a square box taped on the floor, lit by three hanging fluorescent strip-lights. The box marks the playing area and represents the walls of the asylum. Once the action begins no one leaves the area. Three chairs are placed at the back of this square alongside a hood hairdryer, a small white trolley with four drawers, a pile of folded towels and two white buckets. These are the only props used throughout the piece.

The Idiot Colony uses this minimal selection of props to move between the worlds of hospital, the hairdressing salon and scenes of reminiscence for each of the three 'characters', gradually revealing their 'stories' in fragments, as pieces of memory are uncovered. During the performance there are numerous 'shifts' between these worlds, marked in a range of ways; lighting and music changes, the repeated use of an institutional-sounding alarm bell to break the action. We made a conscious decision not to use blackouts and the transitions between the scenes gradually became important counterpoints for the main action of the 'scenes' themselves becoming opportunities to develop the notion of the mundane repetition, ritual, and routine of the institution.

After the initial research period and several short workshops, the actor-devisers worked with the director and writer to create and experiment with material which was gradually shaped into what became the final structure of the piece. At the start of this process Turner had created the outline of three 'characters', inspired by the real stories we had encountered during the research process. Turner then wrote three short pieces of prose describing a moment in the story of each of these characters. In an early rehearsal we each produced solo pieces of improvisation in response to the text. The piece of text for my character (Victoria) became a crucial step in the development of both her 'story' which was developed through the devising process, and the movement vocabulary that was used to tell that story. It describes a woman walking into a lake to drown herself and this ended up being the culmination of Victoria's story in the piece when she drowns herself in the lake in the hospital's grounds:

I look down at my feet, severed by the hem of my nightgown, and realise that they are already those of a ghost...

I take a step toward the lake...

I step into the water...

There is comfort in this embrace...

I yield...

I open my arms and walk forward to be held...

I am water returning to water…
(Extracts from unpublished rehearsal text for *The Idiot Colony*)

The piece of material I devised in response to the section of prose described above consisted of a slow series of movements executed as I embodied each of the images psychophysically, imagining that as I 'yielded' to the water, I was both disappearing *into* water and *becoming* water. As I engaged in this performance exercise I was using the imagery in the text to activate me to create movement. The style of this movement reflected the training I had undergone. Chapter 5 cites the dictionary definition of 'gesture' as 'to bear or to wield' and I think this is interesting. It implies that one can 'carry' or 'hold' gesture. Here, however, the gesture was not in any way separate from the rest of my body. In fact, it existed crucially also *beyond* the limits of my body in terms of my imagination. I am reminded of Mary Wigman's notion of the *Raumkoerper* or 'space body', which is reflected in her words:

> It is not the tangible, limited, and limiting space of concrete reality, but the imaginary, irrational space of the danced dimension, that space which can erase the boundaries of all corporeality…Height and depth, width and breadth, forward, sideward, and backward, the horizontal and the diagonal – these are not only technical terms or theoretical notions for the dancer. After all he experiences them in his own body. (Wigman 1966:12)

Through the 'danced dimension', Wigman argues, 'the boundaries of all corporeality' can be erased. It is this psychophysical 'situatedness' that becomes potentially available in performance.

This exercise based on Turner's text developed through the weeks of devising to become the following actions:

> *With her arms outstretched for balance she raises one foot as if stepping off something high in the air… She stops mid-step and struggles to maintain her balance. She then relaxes and steps onto the towel, sinking down into it, as if it were a lake.* (Stage directions, Scene 12, Turner 2009)

Victoria lays out a towel on the floor, steps onto it and slowly descends to the ground as a twisted, soaking towel is held above her by the other two and wrung out to allow water to fall over her body like rain, as described in the above extract from the text (Figure 6.2).

Turner's text became the basis of a movement 'score' that culminated in the scene where Victoria drowns, but also provided imagery that infused and drove the development of the rest of Victoria's performance

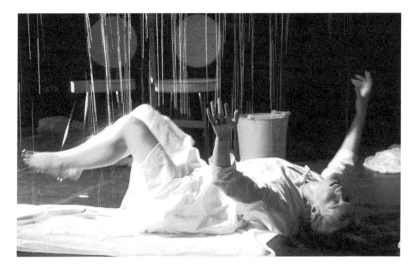

Figure 6.2 Rebecca Loukes as 'Victoria' in *The Idiot Colony* (photo by Lisle Turner)

material, as I explain further below. In understanding the actor's score, I find Lutterbie's definition, also cited in Chapter 1, helpful:

> An actor's score is a series of intentional acts that interweaves creative associations discovered through analysis and improvisation with the dynamics of technique. These acts are performed through movement, language, and gesture. They combine memories – those retrieved from the past as well as those derived from working on the current production – with data from external perceptions and internal proprioceptions … When all works, the result is a thoughtful, precise, intelligent, and effective series of actions that sustains the performer throughout the performance. (Lutterbie 2011:194)

I might also say that in this score, in which I step into 'the lake' to drown, I am making use of 'epistemic actions' as defined by computational researchers Kirsh and Maglio, which, as discussed earlier, 'involves directly manipulating the environment to bring about a better state in a problem solving/planning task, rather than constructing an internal representation and manipulating that' (Menary 2010:237). Here, I am working *with* the performance environment, feeling and being driven by the sensation of the water falling on my skin in order to facilitate and drive my acting 'state'.

Towards the end of the devising process we had generated a number of 'scenes'. We then spent some time deciding on the order of these scenes which were to become the overall final piece. The 'reveal' of all three 'stories' needed to serve the overall rhythm of the piece as a whole, but when we started performing *The Idiot Colony* after only a short rehearsal process, the 'logic' of this placement of the material had not become fully embodied. I was not yet clear *why* Victoria drowned herself in the lake at the particular chosen moment. It is important to say that the 'answer' that I eventually found, through repeated cycles of the piece, was not 'psychologically' or 'plot' driven. It did not depend on a finding a 'motivation' for the action but was rather an attempt to fully and meaningfully 'inhabit' the score I had developed in relation to the other actors and the performance environment. In this sense, it was very much what Barba describes as a 'subscore', as cited in Chapter 1; 'an inner support, a hidden scaffold which actors sketch for themselves' (Barba 2010:29). It emerged as a direct result of psychophysical listening and sensing the other actors. From my chair, 'observing' Coaché performing the monologue which directly precedes Victoria's drowning, I undertook the following actions:

1. Listen to the words Coaché is speaking;
2. Stare at a fixed point just above ground level;
3. Do not blink and allow water to form in eyes;
4. Allow body shape in sitting to collapse' very slightly;
5. Simultaneously I allow the words I am hearing to build up an internal desire for me to move, to stand up.

When Coaché finished her speech and I did then stand, the audience's attention shifted to me and they could see tears rolling down my face.

The planned score of actions which saw me then take a towel from Coaché, spread it on the ground and collect and assemble the other objects needed to 'create' the lake became charged (for me as a performer) with the preceding actions of my 'subscore':

> At each successive instant of a movement, the preceding instant is not lost sight of. It is, as it were, dovetailed into the present... [Movement draws] together, on the basis of one's present position, the succession of previous positions, which envelop each other. (Merleau-Ponty 1962:140)

Or in Gendlin's words 'a situation does not consist just of static truths; it involves the implying of further situations, events and actions'

(Gendlin 1991). A particular use of the space or 'situation' of the body in space affords possibilities for the actor. The use of Eugene Gendlin's 'felt-sense' and 'situation' perhaps can further clarify this. He says:

> Your felt sense is your body's interaction with your situations. Human bodies have situations and language implicit in them. Our bodies imply every next bit of our further living. An action can explicate this implicit further living, and can carry it forward. (Gendlin 1991)

So, translated into the studio, we might say that the aware, sensitive actor has a particular active relationship with the space around her as she is immersed in a particular form of psychophysical training or in performance. The actions she undertakes are implied within both her body and the 'situation'. Or as Gendlin puts it:

> We see that a situation consists of implicit actions, since actions reveal or explicate what it was. Actions explicate situations. The word 'explicate' travels here to say that a situation is implicitly its action-possibilities. (Gendlin 1991)

Viewing a 'situation' inherently consisting of 'action-possibilities' could be aligned with the notion of 'epistemic action' and that this understanding of the space 'implying' or 'carrying forward' action is an interesting one for the performer.

My full embodiment of the score at each moment depended on the deployment of my body 'intermodally', which is the result of long-term psychophysical training.[13] As I sit on the chair and stare out, I listen to the words Coaché is saying, feel the incremental tiny collapse of the outer shape of my body, my feet on the floor and I am fully sensing my own body, in relation to my partners on stage, the stage space itself, and the audience – the embodied, experienced situation.

But what was happening in terms of emotion? I was thinking about this in terms of Damasio's 'as-if body loop':

> The result of direct simulation of body states in body-sensing regions is no different from that of filtering of signals hailing from the body. In both cases the brain momentarily creates a set of body maps that does not correspond exactly to the current reality of the body. The brain uses the incoming body signals like clay to sculpt a particular body state in the regions where such a pattern can be constructed, i.e., the body-sensing regions. What one feels then is based on that 'false' construction, not on the 'real' body state. (Damasio 2004:116)

Could one say that by performing the score in the way I was, crying, with collapsed torso, I was 'simulating' the feeling body state of sadness the way Damasio suggests? The score certainly affected me psychophysically. By the time I stood by the edge of the towel/lake ready to lift my foot to step in and 'drown' I often felt the sensation of sadness. The 'felt sense' (as described by Eugene Gendlin) of the actions provoked an emotional reaction in me but the tasks I engaged in were physical; 'in my cells rather than in my thoughts'. I think Mark Johnson's reading of John Dewey's 'situation' is also pertinent here. He writes:

> Emotions are processes of organism-environment interactions. They involve perceptions and assessments of situations in the continual process of transforming those situations. The body states connected with feelings are states of both response to and remaking of experience. I say, 'I am fearful,' but this really means 'The *situation* is fearful'; fearfulness might appropriately be described as an objective aspect of the situation *for me at this moment*. However much the feeling of fear is 'in *me*', it is just as much 'in the *situation*' as I encounter it. (Johnson 2007:67)

The 'pervasive quality' of the scene, the 'situation', including the space, the lighting, the words spoken by one of the other performers was one of sadness. I remember one specific performance when after many, many times of repeating exactly the same actions I was struck by an almost overwhelming sense of this sadness that is difficult to describe. It seemed to me to emerge from my psychophysical engagement with the experience of the 'situation' – which I was both responding to and remaking, to paraphrase Johnson above. This also mirrors the understanding of Elly Konijn in her research on 'task-emotion theory'. She draws on the work of the Dutch psychologist Nico Frijda which 'views emotions as expressions of the individual which fulfill a central function in reacting to the environment':

> Surroundings or situations offer opportunities or threats; they pose certain demands for satisfying individual needs, desires or concerns and provoke engagement in relationships. Simultaneously, the situation reveals possibilities or impediments that the individual has within this context. When the elements contributed by the situation combine with their potential meaning for the individual, this combination may create an emotional reaction. (Konijn 1997:16)

In the context of acting this seems to align very clearly with my experience. Like Bausch's dancers described in Chapter 5, I was not trying to 'create' or 'show' emotion. But, importantly, this does not mean that the actor does not 'feel'. Current research in situated cognition is re-enforced by my experience as a contemporary actor, making and performing movement. This process was dependent on our sensing and sensitive engagement with our own actions in relation to each other, or in the words of Alva Noë:

> When we as dancers enter the 'image space' when we perform actions, when we issue calls and respond to calls, when we listen, and watch we make the environment. We enact our environments thanks to our skillful engagement with them. We enact our perceptual world by attuning ourselves to it. (Noë 2007:126–127)

Conclusion

Expanding on the 'enactive' approach discussed in Chapter 1, this chapter has examined additional dimensions of contemporary cognitive studies to consider whether current scholarship in 'situated cognition' can help, reflect, inform, and/or challenge how we understand the bodymind of the twenty-first-century psychophysical performer. Certainly the developments examined in this chapter might enable us to better articulate and therefore de-mystify aspects of the actor's process both in training and performance. By continuing to re-look at what we already think we know, in the light of new scientific research, we can keep questioning our practices and the way we attempt to describe them. Part of the premise of current science, as we have discovered, is an attempt to go beyond the old Cartesian binaries of mind/body, internal/ external, subject/object. The use of 'psychophysical', as Stanislavsky has proposed it, implies a holistic conception of the bodymind that does not privilege either one of these binaries. Maxine Sheets-Johnstone writes that the tautology of using the word 'embodied' actually re-enforces these old boundaries:

> In this sense, the term embodied is a lexical band-aid covering a three- hundred-fifty-year-old wound generated and kept suppurating by schizoid metaphysics. (Sheets-Johnstone 2009:215)

In the context of current science, the word 'psycho-physical' could also potentially be queried as a 'tautology.' But what is important to remember is what is implicit in the language we choose, and how we use it. Mark Johnson explains that from his perspective:

> What we call a 'person' is a certain kind of bodily organism that has a brain operating within its body, a body that is continually interacting with aspects of its environments (material and social) in an ever changing process of experience.

He goes on to say that we assign 'certain dimensions of these ongoing experiential processes' to mind and body, but that '"mind" and "body" are merely abstracted aspects of the flow of organism-environment interactions that constitutes what we call experience' (Johnson 2007:11–12). Thompson's enactive approach to cognition also supports this, stating that 'the spatial containment language of internal/external or inside/outside ... is inappropriate and misleading for understanding the ... lived body, or being-in-the-world.' Or, as Heidegger puts it; 'a living being is 'in' its world in a completely different sense from that of water being in a glass' (Heidegger 1995:165–166).

The actor has always been 'situated' and 'extended' in space. Performers have been attempting to understand and better articulate their own processes since Aristotle, Zeami and the *Natyasastra*, as we have seen throughout this book, but these current perspectives enable us to attempt to make what is 'implicit' in what we do 'explicit'. Griffiths and Scarantino discuss 'situated' research on emotions which is relevant here:

> The real theoretical payoff of the situated perspective on emotions is methodological. By shifting theoretical focus from the intrapsychic to the interpersonal, from the unbidden to the strategic, from the short lived to the long lived, from the context independent to the context dependent, from the static to the dynamic, the situated perspective points the attention of the research community to aspects of emotions that have been unduly neglected and that may hold the key to understanding the nature and function of a large class of emotions. (Griffiths and Scarantino 2009:449)

Current 'situated' research draws on work at the cutting edge of science to question and challenge our understanding of how human beings function in the world, but also re-examines and re-frames seminal work in the light of this new research. Shaun Gallagher, for example, encourages us to revisit the work of, for example, Dewey, Heidegger, Merleau-Ponty, and Wittgenstein not only in the light of recent developments in 'situated cognition' but also as 'untapped resources ... that may serve to enrich current accounts of situated cognition' (Gallagher 2009:35). Proponents of this work encourage us to return to 'the things themselves', after Husserl, rather than to rely on concepts or verbalized or written accounts of functioning; and to go beyond the purely material or neural to examine the bodymind in its range of contexts – social, cultural, and evolutional.

This does not mean, of course, that contemporary science has found all the answers. On the contrary, or as the neuroscientist Paul Broks puts it, 'phenomenal consciousness – the raw feel of experience – is invisible to conventional scientific scrutiny and will remain forever so' (Broks 2003:140). The last lines of the epilogue of *The Player's Passion* suggest that developments in scientific conceptions of the bodymind will keep returning to Denis Diderot's paradox of acting. In other words, as we continue to probe the edges of our understanding of what it is to be a human being we return again and again to what we thought we knew, and see it differently.

Notes

1. The philosophical and scientific antecedents to 'situated' cognition have already been used extensively by theatre practitioners and scholars. Research in theatre includes Herbert Blau (1984), Garner (1994), Fraleigh (1996), Sheets-Johnstone (2009), Zarrilli (2009), Welton (2011), Lutterbie (2011).
2. Shaun Gallagher's notion of 'body schema' furthers this view that we are not aware of much of our own perception. He distinguishes between a 'body image' which consists of 'a system of perceptions, attitudes, and beliefs pertaining to one's own body', and a 'body schema' as 'a system of sensory-motor capacities that function without awareness or the necessity of perceptual monitoring'. (Gallagher 2005:24). He goes on to say: 'The body schema... involves certain motor capacities, abilities, and habits that both enable and constrain movement and the maintenance of posture. It continues to operate, and in many cases operates best, when the intentional object of perception is something other than one's own body' (24). Gallagher emphasizes that perception happens away from the bodymind, which can leave the sensing bodymind dislocated.
3. The image of the mental theatre has persisted and been adapted by scientists such as the psychologist Bernard Baars who proposed the Global Workspace Theory (2001).
4. Philosopher David Chalmers coined the phrase 'the hard problem' to describe the question of 'how physical processes in the brain give rise to subjective experience' (Chalmers 1995:63), or, how is consciousness possible in the physical world? The search for the answer to this has been approached in a range of ways since William James stated in 1910 that 'the first and foremost concrete fact which everyone will affirm to belong to his inner experience is the fact that consciousness of some sort goes on' (James 2002).

5. See also Colombetti and Thompson (2008) for a useful summary of the enactive approach.

6. Players of Tetris must orient falling blocks, called 'Zoids' in layers at the bottom of the screen. When a layer is complete it disappears from the screen. The less skillful the player, the more unfilled layers build up, clog the screen and prevent more zoids from falling. As the game progresses the 'zoids' fall faster and the player has less time to decide where to place them. What Kirsh and Maglio discovered was that skilled players used the keyboard strokes to rotate the zoid on the screen to better see what shape it was and therefore where it might fit in the layer at the bottom. They chose to physically manipulate the zoid rather than mentally rotate it, despite the action seeming to be less efficient; ie. the zoid was initially moved further away from the target in order to rotate it, or to 'modify the external environment to provide crucial bits of information just when they are needed most' (Kirsh and Maglio 1994:542).

7. This research has been widely cited in recent work on theatre and cognitive science. See Blair (2008), Hurley (2010), McConachie (2008, 2013), Lutterbie (2011) for examples.

8. For further information on the enactive approach to emotion, see Colombetti (2013).

9. For a summary of the history of emotion theory in acting see Roach (1993) and Hetzler (2007).

10. Eastern mind-body theory uses the notion of cultivation as a way of integrating mind and body (Yuasa 1987), as discussed in Chapter 3.

11. RedCape Theatre makes devised work that draws inspiration from true stories, or from 'ordinary people in extraordinary situations' (RedCape website). The company was founded in 2007 by Claire Coaché, Cassie Friend and Rebecca Loukes. The core trainings of the three co-founders of RedCape reflect the diversity of the lineages of 'embodied' theatre practice discussed in Chapter 5 – drawing from early-twentieth-century European *Gymnastik* (through the body awareness work of Elsa Gindler via Eva Schmale in Germany and Charlotte Selver in the US), and the work of Jacques Lecoq as well as Asian martial-meditation arts with Phillip B. Zarrilli.

12. Venues included ICA as part of the London International Mime Festival, Warwick Arts Centre, Birmingham Rep, Plymouth Theatre Royal and Tron Glasgow. For images, reviews and other information, see http://www.redcapetheatre.co.uk/idiotcolony.html, and for short trailer, see http://www.youtube.com/watch?v=puhE0DGgoQI.

13. I have written about the influence of psychophysical awareness training on the devising and performance of the piece in Loukes (2013).

Afterword: Dialogue and Paradox

Jerri Daboo

The ideas presented within this book about psychophysical acting based in our questions and assumptions set out in the Preface, show a range of diverse, complex, and culture-specific approaches from different practices, philosophies, times, and places. One of our intentions in this book has been to demonstrate that these ideas have been debated and explored in different contexts and cultures for centuries, and are still developing today. In addition, paradigms of acting offer potential for thinking about issues from other fields such as consciousness studies, psychology, and philosophy, and likewise that theories of acting have drawn on these other fields in attempting to understand the practice and process of the experience of the performer.

The Preface to the book signposted that approaches to acting

- are highly diverse,
- have often been influenced by intercultural concepts and/or techniques,
- may be contradictory, and
- are often idiosyncratic.

This has certainly been indicated within the previous six chapters. In this way, it is difficult, if not perhaps even inappropriate, to suggest that there can be an over-arching 'conclusion' which squares all the circles. Instead, as a methodology we are attempting to create a dialogue. Through this dialogue and the connection between ideas, new ways of understanding and articulating practices may be found. This methodological approach can be situated within a selection of contemporary re-evaluations of the structure and assumptions of systems of analysis and discourse. As discussed in Chapters 1 and 6, the re-evaluations are occurring within interdisciplinary investigations, found particularly within the theoretical frameworks of such fields as cognitive science, phenomenology, the 'new sciences' including 'situated' cognition, quantum physics, ecology, and performance practice itself. In their study *The Embodied Mind*, an interdisciplinary exploration of cognitive science and Buddhism, Varela et al. explain that their proposition is to

> build a bridge between mind in science and mind in experience by articulating a dialogue between these two traditions of Western cognitive science and Buddhist meditative psychology. ...We do not intend to build some grand, unified theory ... [n]or do we intend to write a treatise of comparative scholarship. Our concern is to open a space of possibilities in which the circulation between cognitive science and human experience can be fully appreciated and to foster the transformative possibilities of human experience in a scientific culture. (Varela et al.:xviii–xix)

This proposition can also be applied to this book. Rather than intending to offer an absolute, unequivocal outcome, or a 'grand, unified theory', we hope to both 'articulate a dialogue' and 'open a space of possibilities' between selected theories and practices of a psychophysical approach to acting. In addition, Michael Kirby, author of *A Formalist Theatre*, has suggested that there is a need for analytical systems within the field of performance which can similarly offer an open or deductive investigation rather than one that is inductive, and that a way to approach this may be found through principles from other disciplines:

> The problem is that many analytical systems are inductive. They reason, as Aristotle did, from particular theatrical facts or known cases to general conclusions. [...] They reinforce the status quo. They codify tradition and rigidify convention. If turned into theatrical theory and used as a base for creation, these inductive analytical systems only justify more theatre like that which already exists.
>
> A deductive system – one that reasons from a known principle to an unknown one, from the general to the specific, from a premise to a logical conclusion – is one alternative. Another is to use or modify analytical systems set up for other disciplines and other phenomena. In both cases, the result is the same. There is the possibility that the unknown and the uncommon as well as the ordinary will have a place within the system.
>
> That is what is attempted here. An open deductive system is offered both as an analytical tool and as theory. As theory, it is not based upon an idea of what theatre should and should not be. It does not prescribe the kind of theatre it will produce. (Kirby:xix, 21)

To use Kirby's vocabulary, we could say that this book has aimed to be 'provocative and stimulating rather than prescriptive'. Rather than attempting to 'solve' the paradox, which can so often be the case within Western philosophy, instead the paradox is the way that things are. Understanding that it can be both this and not-this offers a place for dialogue where ideas are not resolved in a singular argument, but rather that the act of the dialogue itself articulates the process and intention of the methodology.

With this in mind, this concluding discussion highlights a number of themes which have run throughout the book in the different practices and theories to place them in dialogue, rather than to create a singular, unified conclusion, or solve the paradox. One recurring feature has been an approach to the bodymind of the performer, and the act of performance, as being that of process and embodiment rather than a fixed object. Chapters 2 and 3 demonstrated that long-term practice gradually trans-forms the bodymind of the actor through intense training systems, and that there is a continual 'becoming' in the performance context. In the work of Stanislavsky, the character is generated through the transfor-mation and generation process that the actor undergoes in relation to the actions, objectives, and score of the character in a particular moment of the play. In Chapter 5, we have seen how dance practices such as those by Pina Bausch are working on the psychophysical shifts in the performer, with a move from body-as-object to embodiment as a lived, changing process.

This idea may also be applied to the notion of performance. In its ever-present and non-fixable nature, performance can be seen as event and process, rather than object, as Nathalie Crohn Schmitt states, 'performance makes clear its nature as event rather than object' (Crohn Schmitt 1990:231–234). Peggy Phelan points to the 'eternal presence' of performance, in that it is '[p]oised forever at the threshold of the present' (Phelan 1993:27). It can only exist in its moment of performance, due to its nature of 'liveness', therefore performance 'continually marks the perceptual disappearance of its own enactment. [...] Performance's only life is in the present' (ibid.:115, 146). In its ever-present and non-fixable nature, performance can be seen as event and process, rather than object.

The idea of performance as being process may be applied further to the notion of performance 'tradition' as well. Many of the practices discussed in the book can be situated within the notion of 'tradition', whether *kutiy-attam* or *kathakali* in India, *nō* in Japan, Stanislavsky in Europe and America, or German Expressionism. However, what has also been observed is that these traditions themselves are not fixed, but rather always in process, adaptation and transformation. Chapter 1 pointed to the example of Japan, where the practices of Japanese theatre have demonstrated a process of interaction, exchange, influence, and adaptation with changes in political and social circumstances. Chapter 4, with the work of Stanislavsky, and Chapter 5 with that of Delsarte, showed what can happen when a student takes and adapts the work of a 'master' and develops it in their own way in another cultural context. This indicates a need to consider the notion of 'tradition' as being constantly in change, fluid, in process and multiple, as opposed to fixed and singular. The dance scholar Felicia Hughes-Freeland points out that

> tradition is a process, not a thing. [...] Indeed, tradition should not necessarily be understood as referring to customs that are authentic, indigenous, and long established, although there may be particular instances of this, but rather as an ideology that attributes precedents to practices that may have recently been revived, recast, or reinvented, even if the label or contexts refer back to a previous practice. (Hughes-Freeland 2006:55)

Many of the practices within this book have been commoditized, or labelled as 'authentic', which can mask the reality of the process of change and transformation which is ongoing within their development. This can also lead to some of the problems with theories of intercultural performance, as has been highlighted throughout the book, as there can be an over-simplification of the notion of 'one' culture interacting with 'another', and that the shifting boundaries of culture and forms are much more complex than this singularity implies. The notion of the 'transcultural' has been challenging that of the 'intercultural' and is becoming a more useful way to see and understand the global flow of cultures that leads to the development and change in forms of performance.

There have been different understandings of the notion of 'character' within this book, as well as various ways of approaching the process of acting and embodying a character. We could also use the term 'figure' rather 'character', as discussed in Chapter 3, and the use of the word 'character' in this section encompasses this notion of 'figure' as well. Some of these are culturally determined, if considering the difference in the construction of a character within *kathakali*, or that emerging from Naturalism as it influenced Stanislavsky. What connects them is the centrality of action, sensory awareness, and 'becoming'. It is the embodiment and relationship to the action, as well as the sensory field offered by the performance score, that creates the psychophysicalization of the character in the performance moment. These actions and awareness may be outlined specifically through a score or sub-score, as has been suggested throughout this book, which the actor can use as a guide and map to shape the creation of the character. Examples of this map may be found in forms of embodiment, vocalization, and bodymind consciousness through which specific types of characters discussed in Zeami's treatises in Chapter 3 are created, or through Lecoq's 'mimages' as internal states of the character, found in Chapter 5. What may be seen is that this creation of a character is in itself also a process of becoming, rather than fixed object, as is the bodymind of the performer and the nature of performance itself, discussed earlier in this section. The character emerges through the bodymind of the actor engaging in the embodiment of the score of actions, and so is in a state of being/becoming. It is the psychophysical process of becoming, or transforming, through precise scores of action, breath, gesture, and image that creates the embodied presence of a 'character' in a given moment of the performance.

Another key theme has been that of the relationship between 'inner' and 'outer'. This points to the problematic use of language to describe this process, as was indicated in Chapter 4 when discussing the difficulty with the term 'psychophysical' as a compound word which could imply a duality rather than a singular experience of body and mind as a continuum. Again, rather than attempting to 'solve' the problem by, for example, inventing a new term as discussed in Chapter 1, and seen in Chapters 2 and 3, it may be more suitable to acknowledge the problem as springing from aspects of Western philosophy which have historically separated body and mind. This has been challenged more recently as was seen in Chapter 6, with Mark Johnson's definition of a 'person' as 'a certain kind of bodily organism that has a brain operating within its body, a body that is continually interacting with aspects of its environments (material and social) in an ever changing process of experience' (Johnson 2007:11–12). Within other systems of philosophy where this separation has not occurred, such a reconsideration of terms may not be necessary. There can be problems with any term, as Derrida pointed out in his rethinking of Heidegger's idea of '*sous rature*', in that a word or terminology can be considered as 'inadequate but necessary'. The word 'psychophysical' is a signifier to be understood as implying a unity of body and mind, even if the limitations of language actually present it as a potential duality.[1] The psychophysical practices discussed throughout the book have shown that the actor explores the connection between 'inner' and 'outer' in a way that attempts to dissolve such distinctions in practice, whether through action and imagination, breath and subtle energy, or impulse and movement.

This again points to the need for dialogue, and understanding the connections between, rather than a fixed and singular interpretation. This is the potential for interdisciplinary and intercultural, or transcultural, studies, and also for examining different acting approaches both in their original context, and how they have developed when they moved beyond these into other contexts. It is in the debate that the paradox can fulfil itself. Where there is a commonality of underlying principles, as there has been throughout the chapters of this book, then perhaps it is possible, to repeat Varela et al. to build a bridge between 'mind in science and mind in experience', or even bodymind in science and in experience. The psychophysical actor may well be able to 'know' this at the level of embodiment, but 'knowing about', or talking about it, still requires further development to understand the nature of the paradox in language and thinking that encompasses the experience of the bodymind in all its complex aspects.

Note

1. With thanks to Franc Chamberlain for suggesting this connection to the work of Derrida and 'sous rature'.

Appendix I: An Historical/Contextual Introduction to Intercultural Theatre

Phillip B. Zarrilli

For readers not familiar with the history, context, or analysis of issues of intercultural theatre, I provide a brief introduction below. This introduction is not meant to be comprehensive, but to touch on important historical and analytical issues through discussion of selected examples of interculturalism.

The historical example of Japan

I begin this overview of historical interculturalism with a few examples from the history of Japanese theatre.[1] James Brandon, has described how at various periods during its history Japan has at times been open and turned outward to the influence and models of performance from others cultures, and then in other periods turned inward to develop its own indigenous arts. During the Nara period (646–794) the arts of Japan were shaped by a 'love of Chinese and Korean arts', that is,

> [p]erformers from these two countries (especially the latter) were invited to the imperial courts to learn at the feet of Korean and Chinese masters. In this way, elegant *bugaku* court dance and the didactic Buddhism processional dance play, *gigaku,* were introduced into Japan. (1990:89)

As discussed in detail in Chapter 3, in contrast during the Muromachi period (1392–1568) Kan'ami and his son Zeami 'developed *nō* theatre from various local, popular performing arts' (ibid.). Then, 1200 years after the Nara period, Japan again opened to the outside world from the end of the nineteenth century.

> Starting at the turn of this century, young actors, playwrights, musicians, and dancers journeyed to Europe to learn the new Western performing arts. These early pilgrims were particularly impressed by, and directly borrowed, Ibsen dramaturgy and Stanislavski performance theories. When Osanai Kaoru founded the Free Theatre (*jiyu gekijo*) in Tokyo in 1909 to serve the 'new drama' (*shingeki*), his purpose was to transplant into Japan the plays and performance style of Western realism. (1990:90)

In both instances these historically distinct ways of opening to other cultures for techniques, forms, and inspiration were impelled by an admiration for cultures other than Japan (Brandon 1990:90). Individual artists/performers travelled elsewhere to immerse themselves in learning something new, returned to Japan, and introduced what they had learned within either the Japanese courts or in the case of *shingeki* to the modern, cosmopolitan public. The introduction of *bugaku*, *gigaku*, and *shingeki* all required actor/performers to learn new approaches to performance appropriate to each of these new genres.

According to Brandon, today no one in Japan thinks of *bugaku* 'as foreign; it was naturalized and absorbed into Japanese culture'; however, this is *not* the case with *shingeki* which since its invention in Japan 'has remained foreign. It does not seem familiar' (1990:90).[2] These examples from Japanese history exemplify how new performances *can* develop from intercultural exchange that is actively sought out by specific segments of a society at specific points in history. But it is quite a different historical and political situation when there is a dominant, conquering, colonial/imperialist power that imposes itself and its norms, institutions, and culture on others, as did the Japanese in Taiwan from 1895 through the end of World War II in 1945.

Located just off the coast of mainland China, to the south of Japan, and north of the Philippines, like other islands in geographically strategic locations 'between', from the perspective of its earliest aboriginal inhabitants and each subsequent set of immigrants, the history of the island of Taiwan has been constantly re-shaped by a series of further migrations and/or occupations from near and far.

> Colonized by the Dutch (1624–1662) and ruled by the Chinese Ming loyalist Zheng Chenggong from 1662–1683, Taiwan was subsequently governed by the Chinese Qing imperial court (1683–1895). After China's defeat in the first Sino-Japanese War in 1895, Taiwan was ceded to Japan for fifty

years. China's Nationalist Party took over Taiwan at the end of Japanese colonial period in 1945 after Mao Zedong's army defeated them and drove them out of mainland China (the PRC was founded in 1949). The KMT [Kuomintang] moved the central government of the Republic of China (ROC) to Taiwan, and claimed sovereignty over mainland China until the late1980s. (Huang 2009:303; see also Chen Hui-Yun 2012:28ff)

The defeat of the Japanese at the end of the Second World War and the establishment of the Republic of China in Taiwan brought yet a further wave of immigration to Taiwan – a huge influx of 'Mainlander' Chinese. Although the Taiwanese welcomed the end of Japanese Imperial rule, the arrival of 'Mainlanders' added yet another complex layer to the ongoing processes of cultural (re)negotiation in Taiwan. Taiwanese history and the identities and subject positions of its various peoples and their languages (Taiwanese, Hakka, Mandarin) are a complex hybrid. The history of performance cultures in Taiwan is a result of the multiple colonizations (external and internal) listed above. Contemporary Taiwanese performance is in the process of constant (re)negotiation of its hybrid history.

One part of this complex history is the legacy of the introduction by the Japanese of *xing-ju* 'new theatre' in Taiwan. Chen Hui-Yun's recent research makes use of 'critical syncretism' to reconsider how *xing-ju* was transformed and refashioned after the Japanese departed in 1945 through a complex series of processes into a contemporary genre of performance that now includes 'a taste of Taiwan' (2012:250–252). These processes of transformation and re-negotiation of contemporary Taiwanese 'new theatre' include reformation of its content, performance style, and methods/approach to acting as various processes have been interwoven between and among a range of 'traditional' Taiwanese and Chinese performance techniques as well as the most recent, contemporary Western approaches to acting (see Chen Hi-Yun 2012:201ff; Huang 2009: 195ff). The complexities of Taiwanese theatre's 'inter-culturalism' today are born out of its geographical and historical position as a '"contact zone" and an immigrant society' with its 'hybrid cultural landscape' (Huang 2009:202).

Western colonialism, the rise of 'Orientalism', and unexpected re-negotiations

Western colonial expansion into Asia, Africa, and the Americas from the fifteenth century was prompted by the economic expansion of trade and brought the opening of new marketplaces, the establishment of outposts/

colonies, and direct imposition of colonial rule by force. Indigenous peoples were often conquered and/or displaced, and direct rule often led to highly problematic forms of cultural domination, misrepresentation, and/or misinterpretation of what was considered 'other'.

To take one Western example of many of the results of colonial encounter, during the nineteenth century the German philosopher Friedrich Hegel (1771–1831) represented Europe as open to change and development, but Asia as more or less static and unchangeable. The view of India in particular as unchangeable and absolutely different allowed the British to justify their colonization of India: they could provide the rules of reason and bureaucracy that Indians (ostensibly) could not provide for themselves. The legacy of India as the 'absolute other' is discernible even today in the West's continuing romance with India as the 'mystical' or 'spiritual Other'. In 1976 Edward Said identified this kind of ahistorical process of projecting onto cultures of the Middle East and Asia what the West desires them to be as 'orientalizing' the 'Other' (1976).

The roots of the 'universalist' form of Western interculturalism in theatre as 'a conscious program' appeared in Germany in the work of Johan Wolfgang von Goethe (Fischer-Lichte 1996:28) at the same time that Hegel was formulating his ideas about Asia. When Goethe was working with the Weimar Theatre between 1791 and 1817 and authored his version of *Faust*, he was inspired by his understanding of Indian Sanskrit drama, thus initiating 'a long tradition in the west of using intercultural links to access "truths" that were supposed to be universal' (Knowles 2010:11).

Whether it was the the Japanese in Taiwan, the Dutch in Indonesia, or the British in India, colonial rulers brought with them not only their political, social, institutional, intellectual, and ethical sensibilities, but also their own forms of theatre and drama. The importation of Western forms of drama performed by touring companies from 'home' countries created a complex set of responses and developments – some obvious and expected, and others unexpected.[3] First, colonial rulers and/or those among their subjects educated to assist them often looked down on indigenous, traditional performing arts when compared to those of the colonizing country. For example, *kathakali* dance-drama in Kerala, India, came to be pejoratively labelled a 'dumb show' as it was disdained by some of its educated elites in the late nineteenth century.

Second, the introduction of foreign/colonial forms of theatre and drama unexpectedly inspired the development of new forms of local theatre. For example, Parsi theatre was born in the mid-nineteenth century in Mumbai, India, and grew directly out of the marriage of

English-staging practices with the addition of indigenous Indian dance, content, music, etc.

As the work of late-nineteenth-century playwrights such as Henrik Ibsen (1828–1906) became known in Asia – as in Japan with *shingeki* – intellectuals, artists, and/or social-reformers were immediately drawn to the idea that theatre could stage plays addressing social issues of *immediate* concern. Ibsen in particular inspired the production of radical dramas calling for social reform, and in some instances helped spawn resistance to colonial rule as part of national movements.[4]

Another legacy of colonial rule has been the inventive renegotiation and assimilation of newly transformed modes of cultural practice and/or content. In India where the British introduced cricket as well as the plays of Shakespeare, both have been woven into the fabric of contemporary Indian cultural life in innovative ways.[5]

Notes

1. Two other quite different historical examples from the history of world theatre include the influence of Italian *commedia dell'arte* on the French playwright Jean-Baptiste Poquelin Moliere's plays (1622–1673) (Williams 2006:192ff), and the effect that the Spanish conquest had on the indigenous culture of the Mayans and performances of *Rabinal Achi* (Zarrilli 2006:68–71). For a comprehensive account of continuous East-West intercultural encounters see Nichola Savarese's comprehensive historical discussion *Eurasian Theatre* (2010).
2. I address this subject in Chapter 3 while focusing on Japan and examine three approaches to contemporary Japanese performance each of which exemplifies a different form of intercultural exchange both West to East and East to West – *butoh* dance/performance, Ōta Shōgo's work with quietude, and the theatre and training of the director Tadashi Suzuki.
3. These complex historical interactions are the subject of many new in-depth scholarly studies. For examples, see *Theatre Journal's* 1994 special issue on 'Colonial/Postcolonial Histories'; Evan Darwin Winet's *Indonesian Postcolonial Theatre* (2010); Cohen, Matthew's *Performing Otherness: Java and Bali on International Stages, 1905–1952* (2010); Aparna Dharwadker's *Theatres of Independence: Drama, Theatre, and Urban Performance in India since 1947* (2005); Rakesh Solomon's *Globalization, History, Historiography: The Making of a Modern Indian Theatre* (2014); and Min Tian's *The Poetics of Difference and Displacement: Twentieth-Century Chinese-Western Intercultural Theatre* (2008).
4. For example, the southwestern coastal region of India today known as Kerala State and home of *kathakali* dance-drama, had effectively been under British

colonial rule since 1790. From the late nineteenth century social reformers were so inspired by new forms of education and ideas introduced by the British that they began to conceive of the possibility of alternatives to Kerala's highly stratified, hierarchical socio-economic order. Social reformers wrote novels and short stories to highlight social issues. Social reformers also staged highly popular 'social dramas' which confronted contentious socio-political issues directly for the first time in the local, vernacular language. When the playwright/activist Thoopil Bhaasi wrote *You Made Me a Communist* in 1952, it focused on how a conservative peasant farmer Paramu Pillai is radicalized and makes a decision to become a communist. When Kerala People's Arts Club (sponsored by the Communist Party) gave performances across the length and breadth of Kerala, it helped communicate a clear message of socio-economic reform that no doubt contributed to the election of the first democratic communist government in Kerala State in 1957 (see Zarrilli 2006:391–399; Bhaasi 1996).The strength of the socio-political left in Kerala has been so strong that occasionally traditionally performing arts including *kathakali* have produced dance-dramas such as the 1987 performances of *People's Victory* where Marx met Imperialism on the *kathakali* stage (see Zarrilli 2000:196–205).

5. On the global spread of cricket, see Appadurai (1996) and Kaufman and Patterson (2005). On Shakespeare in India, see Sudipto Chatterjee's 'Moor or Less? *Othello* Under Surveillance, Calcutta, 1848,' and the other articles posted on the 'Shakespeare in Asia' web side at Stanford University (http://sia.stanford.edu/india/). Each February in India there is an annual Hamara Shakespeare ('Our Shakespeare') which stages plays and poems in any of the twenty-two major Indian languages (and some minor ones). Poonam Trivedi explains that 'although colonialism brought him to the subcontinent, Shakespeare has been utterly absorbed into the Indian imagination. He is a wise man – "Shekhu-pir" or "Shakespeare Sheikh" – whose stories and sayings have enduring wisdom. He crops up in surprising places in Bollywood, as when the super-gangster Amitabh Bachchan is told by his mother in the 1990 film *Agneepath* that "all the water of Mumbai will not wash his hands clean" of the taint of bloodshed' (Trivedi 2012).

References

Abram, D. (1997) *The Spell of the Sensuous: Perception and Language in a More-Than-Human World*, New York: Vintage Books.

Adler, Stella (2000) *The Arts of Acting*, comp. & ed. Howard Kissel, New York: Applause Books.

Aginski, Alice (1981) 'Elsa Gindler in the Nineteen Twenties and Thirties', in Mary Alice Roche (ed.), *Elsa Gindler*, Volume 2, Caldwell, NJ: Charlotte Selver Foundation.

Allain, Paul (1998) 'Suzuki Training', *TDR*, 42, 1:66–89.

Allain, Paul (2002) *The Art of Stillness: The Theatre Practice of Tadashi Suzuki*, London: Methuen.

Allain, Paul (2009) *The Theatre Practice of Tadashi Suzuki: A Critical Study with DVD*, London: Bloomsbury.

Amano, Yuka (2011) '"Flower" as Performing Body in *Nō* Theatre', *Asian Theatre Journal*, 28, 2:529–548.

Ames, Roger T., Thomas P. Kasulis and Wimal Dissayanake (eds) (1998) *Self as Image in Asian Theory and Practice*, Albany: State University of New York Press.

Appadurai, Arjun and Carol A. Breckenridge (1988) 'Why Public Culture?' *Public Culture*, 1, 1:5–9.

Appadurai, Arjun and Carol A. Breckenridge (1996) *Modernity at Large: Cultural Dimensions of Globalization*, Minneapolis: University of Minnesota Press.

Artaud, Antonin (1970) 'Athlete of the Heart', in Toby Cole and Helen Crich Chinoy (eds), *Actors on Acting*, New York: Crown Publishing, 235–240.

Aubel, Hermann and Marianne Aubel (2002) *Der Künstlerische Tanz unser Zeit*, Die Blauen Bücher, Königstein: Karl Robert Langewiesche Nachfolger Hans Köster Verlags KG.

Austin, James (1998) *Zen and the Brain*, Cambridge, MA: MIT Press.

Austin, James (2006) *Zen-Brain Reflections*, Cambridge, MA: MIT Press.

Baars, Bernard (2001) *In the Theater of Consciousness: The Workspace of the Mind*, Oxford: Oxford University Press.

Balme, Christopher B. (1999) *Decolonizing the Stage: Theatrical Syncretism and Post-Colonial Drama*, Oxford: Oxford University Press.

Barba, Eugenio (2010) *On Directing and Dramaturgy*, London: Routledge.

Barker, Clive (2002) 'Foreword', in T. Bicat and C. Baldwin (eds), *Devised and Collaborative Theatre: A Practical Guide*, Marlborough: Crowood Press, 6.

Beckett, Samuel (1984) *The Collected Shorter Plays*, New York: Grove Press.

Benedetti, J. (1990) *Stanislavski: A Biography*, London: Methuen.

Benedetti, J. (1998) *Stanislavski and the Actor*, London: Methuen.

Benedetti, J. (2005) *The Art of the Actor*, London: Methuen.

Berberich, Junko Sakaba (1984) 'Some Observations on Movement in *Nō*', *Asian Theatre Journal*, 1, 2:207–216.

Berberich, Junko Sakaba (1989) 'The Idea of Rapture as an Approach to Kyōgen', *Asian Theatre Journal*, 6, 1:31–46.

Betsuyaku Minoru (2004) '*Sick*', in Japan Playwrights Association (ed.), *Half a Century of Japanese Theater*, Volume 6: *1960s Part 1*, Tokyo: Kinokuniya, 245–286.

Bhaasi, T. (1996) *Memories in Hiding*, trans. J. George and P. B. Zarrilli, Calcutta: Seagull Books.

Bhabha, Homi K. (1994) *The Location of Culture*, London: Routledge.

Bharucha, Rustom (1993) *Theatre and the World: Performance and the Politics of Culture*, London: Routledge.

Bharucha, Rustom (1995) *Chandralekha: Woman Dance Resistance*, New Delhi: Indus.

Blacker, Carmen (1975) *The Catalpa Bow: A Study of Shamanistic Practices in Japan*, London: Allen & Unwin.

Blackmore, S. (2003) *Consciousness: An Introduction*, Abingdon: Hodder & Stoughton.

Blair, R. (2008) *The Actor, Image, and Action: Acting and Cognitive Neuroscience*, London: Routledge.

Blair, R. (2010) 'Cognitive Neuroscience and Acting: Imagination, Conceptual Blending, and Empathy', *TDR*, 53, 4:93–103.

Blau, H. (1984) *Take Up the Bodies*, Urbana: Illinois University Press.

Bloch, Susana (1993) 'Alba Emoting: A Psychophysiological Technique to Help Actors Create and Control Real Emotions', *Theatre Topics*, 3, 2:121–138.

Block, Ned (1995) 'On a Confusion about a Function of Consciousness', *Behavioral and Brain Sciences*, 18, 2:227–247.

Block, Ned, Owen Flanagan, and Güven Güzeldere (eds) (1997) *The Nature of Consciousness: Philosophical Debates*, Cambridge, MA: MIT Press.

Bode, Rudolph (1931) *Expression-Gymnastics*, New York: A.S. Barnes.

Bogart, Anne (2010) 'Foreword', in Erin Hurley, *Theatre & Feeling*, Basingstoke: Palgrave Macmillan, ix–xv.

Bottoms, Stephen and Matthew Goulish (eds) (2007) *Small Acts of Repair: Performance, Ecology and Goat Island*, London: Routledge.

Boyd, Mari (1990) 'Translator's Introduction: *The Water Station (Mizu no Eki)*', *Asian Theatre Journal*, 7, 2:151–153.

Boyd, Mari (2006) *The Aesthetics of Quietude: Ōta Shōgo and the Theatre of Divestiture*, Tokyo: Sophia University Press.

Boyd, Mari (2012) 'Quietude in Intercultural Performance: Phillip B. Zarrilli's *Told by the Wind* and Yojiro Okamura's *Aminadab*', *Comparative Theatre Review* (English issue), 11, 1:43–51.

Bradley, K. (2009) *Rudolph Laban*, London: Routledge.

Braidotti, Rosi (1991) *Patterns of Dissonance*, trans. Elizabeth Guild, New York: Routledge.

Brandon, James (1978) 'Training at the Waseda Little Theatre: The Suzuki Method', *TDR*, 22, 4:29–42.

Brandon, James (1989) 'A New World: Asian Theatre in the West Today', *TDR*, 33, 2:25–50.

Brandon, James (1990) 'Contemporary Japanese Theatre: Interculturalism and Intraculturalism', in Erika Fischer-Lichte, Josephine Riley and Michael Gissenwehrer (eds), *The Dramatic Touch of Difference*, Tubingen: Gunter Narr Verlag, 89–98.

Brandon, James (ed.) (1997) *Nō and Kyōgen in the Contemporary World*, Honolulu: University of Hawai'i Press.

Braun, Edward (1965) *Meyerhold: A Revolution in Theatre*, Iowa City: University of Iowa Press.

Braun, Edward (1969) *Meyerhold on Theatre*, New York: Hill and Wang.

Broks, Paul (2003) *Into the Silent Land: Travels in Neurophysiology*, London: Atlantic Books.

Brown, Margaret and Betty Sommer (1969) *Movement Education: Its Evolution and a Modern Approach*, Reading, MA: Addison Wesley.

Brownell, Susan (2009) 'The Global Body Cannot Ignore Asia', in Bryan S. Turner and Zheng Yangwen (eds), *The Body in Asia*, New York: Berghan, 23–42.

Bruder, Melissa (1986) *A Practical Handbook for the Actor*, New York: Random House.

Brunet-Lecomte, H. (1950) *Jacques Dalcroze: Sa Vie – Son Oeuvre*, Geneva: Edition Jeheber, The Dalcroze Institute.

Carnicke, S. (1998) *Stanislavsky in Focus*, Amsterdam: Harwood Academic Publishers.

Carnicke, S. (2000) *Stanislavsky in Focus* (2nd edition), London: Routledge.

Carnicke, S. (2010) 'Stanislavsky's System: Pathways for the Actor', in Alison Hodge (ed.), *Actor Training* (2nd edition), London: Routledge, 1–25.

Carreri, R. (1991) 'The Actor's Journey: "Judith" from Training to Performance', *New Theatre Quarterly*, 7, 26:137–146.

Carruthers, Ian and Takahashi Yasunari (2007) *The Theatre of Suzuki Tadashi*, Cambridge: Cambridge University Press.

Carter, Alexandra and Rachel Fensham (eds) (2011) *Dancing Naturally: Nature, Neo-Classicism and Modernity in Early Twentieth-Century Dance*, Basingstoke: Palgrave Macmillan.

Chakravarty, H. N. (1988) '*Prana*', in Bettina Baumer (ed.), *Kalatattvakosa: A Lexicon of Fundamental Concepts of Indian Arts*, Volume 1, New Delhi: Indira Gandhi.

Chalmers, David (1995) 'The Puzzle of Conscious Experience', *Scientific American*, 62–68.

Chalmers, David (2011) 'Foreword', in Andy Clark, *Supersizing the Mind: Embodiment, Action and Cognitive Extension*, Oxford: Oxford University Press, ix–xvi.

Chamberlain, Franc (2007) 'Gesturing towards Post-Physical Performance', in J. Keefe and S. Murray (eds), *Physical Theatres: A Critical Reader*, London: Routledge, 117–122.

Chamberlain, Franc and Ralph Yarrow (eds) (2002) *Jacque Lecoq and the British Theatre*, London: Routledge.

Chandradasan (2010) 'The Politics of Western Pedagogy in the Theatre of India', in Ellen Margolis and Lissa Tyler Renaud (eds), *The Politics of American Actor Training*, New York: Routledge, 46–61.

Chatterjee, Sudipto (2007) *The Colonial Staged: Theatre in Colonial Calcutta*, Calcutta: Seagull Books.

Chatterjee, Sudipto (2012) 'Moor or Less? *Othello* under Surveillance, Calcutta, 1848', http://sia.stanford.edu/india/

Chaudhuri, Harisas (1977) 'Yoga Psychology', in Charles T. Tart (ed.), *Transpersonal Psychologies*, New York, Harper and Row, 231–280.

Chaudhuri, Una (1991) *Interculturalism and Performance*, New York: PAJ Publications, 192–207.

Chekhov, M. (1983) 'Chekhov's Academy of Arts Questionnaire, 1923', *TDR*, 27, 2(Fall):22–33.

Chekhov, M. (1985) *Lessons for the Professional Actor*, New York: PAJ Publications.

Chekhov, M. (1991) *On the Technique of Acting*, New York: Harper Perennial.

Chekhov, M. (1996) *Michael Chekhov on Theatre and the Art of Acting: The Five-Hour Master Class* (audiocassettes), ed. Mala Powers, New York: Magi.

Chen, Hui-Yun (2012) 'In Search of "Taiwaneseness" – Reconsidering Taiwanese *Xing-ju* from a Post-colonial Perspective', unpublished PhD thesis, Drama Department, University of Exeter.

Chen, Kuan-Hsing (2010) *Asia as Method: Toward Deimperialization*, Durham, NC: Duke University Press.

Chin, Daryl (1991) 'Interculturalism, Postmodernism, Pluralism', in Bonnie Marranca and Gautam Dasgupta (eds), *Interculturalism and Performance*, New York: PAJ Publications.

Clancey, W. J. (2009) 'Scientific Antecedents of Situated Cognition', in P. Robbins and M. Aydede (eds), *The Cambridge Handbook of Situated Cognition*, Cambridge: Cambridge University Press, 11–34.

Clark, Andy (2011) *Supersizing the Mind: Embodiment, Action and Cognitive Extension*, Oxford: Oxford University Press.

Clark, E. R. (1914) 'The Difference between the Dalcroze Rhythmic Gymnastics and Ling's Swedish System', *Journal of Scientific Physical Training*, 7:3–5.

Claxton, Guy (1997) *Hare Brain, Tortoise Mind*, London: Fourth Estate.

Clifford, James (1988) *The Predicament of Culture*, Cambridge, MA: Harvard University Press.

Climenhaga, R. (2009) *Pina Bausch*, London: Routledge.

Climenhaga, R. (2012) *The Pina Bausch Sourcebook*, London: Routledge.

Cohen, Matthew (2010) *Performing Otherness: Java and Bali on International Stages, 1905–1952*, Basingstoke: Palgrave Macmillan.

Cohen, Robert (1978) *Acting Power*, Mountain View, CA: Mayfield.

Cole, David (1992) *Acting as Reading: The Place of the Reading Process in the Actor's Work*, Ann Arbor: University of Michigan Press.

Cole, T. and H. Chinoy (1963) *Directors on Directing*, London: Macmillan.

Cole, T. and H. Chinoy (eds) (1970 [1949]) *Actors on Acting*, New York: Crown Publishers.

Colombetti, Giovanna (2013) *The Feeling Body: Affective Science Meets the Enactive Mind*, Cambridge, MA: MIT Press.

Colombetti, Giovanna and Evan Thompson (2008) 'The Feeling Body: Towards an Enactive Approach to Emotion', in W. F. Overton, U. Muller and J. L. Newman (eds), *Developmental Perspectives on Embodiment and Consciousness*, New York: Lawrence Erlbaum Associates, 45–68.

Conroy, Colette (2010) *Theatre & the Body*, Basingstoke: Palgrave Macmillan.

Cox, Rupert A. (2003) *The Zen Arts: An Anthropological Study of the Culture of Aesthetic Form in Japan*, Milton Park, Abingdon: Routledge.

Crimp, Martin (1997) *Attempts on Her Life*, London: Faber & Faber.

Crimp, Martin (2005) *Fewer Emergencies*, London: Faber & Faber.

Crohn Schmitt, Natalie (1990) 'Theorizing about Performance: "Why Now?"', *NTQ*, 4:23.

Daboo, J. (2007) 'Michael Chekhov and the Embodied Imagination: Higher Self and Non-self', *Studies in Theatre and Performance*, 27, 3:261–273.

Daboo, J. (2012) 'Michael Chekhov and the Studio in Dartington: The Re-membering of a Tradition', in J. Pitches (ed.), *The Russians in Britain: British Theatre and the Russian Tradition of Acting*, London: Routledge, 62–85.

Dafoe, Willem (2001) 'Willem Dafoe', in Mary Luckhurst and Chloe Veltman (eds), *On Acting: Interviews with Actors*, London: Faber & Faber, 22–33.

Dalcroze, E. Jaques (1930) *Eurythmics, Art and Education*, London: Chatto & Windus.

Dalcroze, E. Jaques (1972) *Rhythm, Music and Education*, North Stratford, NH: Ayer Company Publishers.

Damasio, A. (2004) *Looking for Spinoza: Joy, Sorrow and the Feeling Brain*, London: Vintage Books.

Damasio, A. (2010) *Self Comes to Mind: Constructing the Conscious Brain*, London: William Heinemann.

Dartington Archives: The Michael Chekhov Studio archives owned by the Dartington Trust, held at the Devon Records Office, Exeter – from class notes, 16 January 1938 (DWE A 19 A).

de Gaynesford, Maximillian (2003) 'Corporeal Objects and the Interdependence of Perception and Action', in Mike Proudfoot (ed.), *The Philosophy of the Body*, Malden, MA: Blackwell, 21–39.

de Michelis, Elizabeth (2005) *A History of Modern Yoga: Patanjali and Western Esotericism*, London: Continuum.

Dennett, D. C. (2002) 'The Cartesian Theater and "Filling In" the Stream of Consciousness', in N. Block, O. Flanagan and G. Guzeldere (eds), *The Nature of Consciousness: Philosophical Debates*, Cambridge, MA: MIT Press, 83–89.

Depraz, Natalie, Francisco Cavela and Pierre Vermersch (2003) *On Becoming Aware: A Pragmatics of Experiencing*, Amsterdam: John Benjamins Publishing Company.

Descartes, R. (1984 [1641]) *Meditations on First Philosophy (with Objections and Replies)*. *The Philosophical Writings of Descartes*, Volume 2, Cambridge: Cambridge University Press.

Dewey, J. (1938) *Logic: The Theory of Inquiry*, New York: Holt, Rinehart and Winston.

Dharwadker, Aparna Bhargava (1995) *Theatres of Independence: Drama, Theory, and Urban Performance in India since 1947*, Iowa City: University of Iowa Press.

Di Benedetto, S. (2010) *The Provocation of the Senses in Contemporary Theatre*, New York and London: Routledge.

Donald, M. (2001) *A Mind So Rare*, New York: Norton.

Donnellan, Declan (2002) *The Actor and the Target*, London: Nick Hern Books.

Elberfeld, Rolf (2003) 'Sensory Dimensions in Intercultural Perspective and the Problem of Modern Media and Technology', in Peter D. Hershock, Marietta Stepaniants and Roger T. Ames (eds), *Technology and Cultural Values*, Honolulu: University of Hawai'i Press, 478–489.

Emmert, Richard (1997) 'Expanding *Nō*'s Horizons: Considerations for a New *Nō* Perspective', in James R. Brandon (ed.), *Nō and Kyōgen in the Contemporary World*, Honolulu: University of Hawai'i Press, 19–35.

Engel, Andreas K. (2010) 'Directive Minds: How Dynamics Shapes Cognition', in J. Stewart, O. Gapenne and E. A. Di Paulo (eds), *Enaction: Toward a New Paradigm for Cognitive Science*, Cambridge, MA: MIT Press, 219–244.

Evans, Mark (2012) 'The Influence of Sports on Jacques Lecoq's Actor Training', *Theatre, Dance and Performer Training*, 3, 2:163–177.

Fernandes, C. (2002) *Pina Bausch and the Wuppertal Dance Theater: The Aesthetics of Repetition and Transformation*, New York: Peter Lang.

Feuerstein, Georg (1980) *The Philosophy of Classical Yoga*, Manchester: Manchester University Press.

Filliozat, Jean (1964) *The Classical Doctrine of Indian Medicine*, Delhi: Munshiram Manoharlal.

Filliozat, Jean (1991) *Religion, Philosophy and Yoga*, New Delhi: Motilal.

Fischer-Lichte, Erika (1996) 'Interculturalism in Contemporary Theatre', in P. Pavis (ed.), *The Intercultural Performance Reader*, London: Routledge, 27–40.

Fischer-Lichte, Erika (2008) *The Transformative Power of Performance: A New Aesthetics*, London: Routledge (original German publication 2004).

Fischer-Lichte, Erika (2010) Personal interview/discussion, Berlin, 27 April, trans. Saskya Iris Jain.

Flood, Gavin (1996) *An Introduction to Hinduism*, Cambridge: Cambridge University Press.

Foard, James H. (1980) 'The Buddhist Orientation of a *Noh* Play', *Monumenta Nipponica*, 35, 4:437–456.

Foley, Kathy (2002) 'My Bodies: The Performer in West Java', in Phillip B. Zarrilli (ed.), *Acting Reconsidered*, London: Routledge, 168–180.

Fraleigh, Sondra (1996) *Dance and the Lived Body*, Pittsburgh: University of Pittsburgh Press.

Fraleigh, Sondra (1999) *Dancing into Darkness: Butoh, Zen, and Japan*, Pittsburgh: University of Pittsburgh Press.

Fraleigh, Sondra (2010) *Butoh: Metamorphic Dance and Global Alchemy*, Urbana: University of Illinois Press.

Fraleigh, Sondra and Tamah Nakamura (2006) *Hijikata Tatsumi and Ohno Kazuo*, London: Routledge.

Franco, S. (2007) 'Ausruckstanz: Traditions, Translations, Transmissions', in S. Franco and M. Nordera (eds), *Dance Discourses*, London: Routledge, 80–98.

Gainty, Denis (2009) '*Seki Juroji* and the Japanese Body: Martial Arts, *Kokutai*, and Citizen–State Relations in Meiji Japan', in Bryan S. Turner and Zheng Yangwen (eds), *The Body in Asia*, New York: Berghahn Books, 129–146.

Gallagher, Shaun (2005) *How the Body Shapes the Mind*, Oxford: Oxford University Press.

Gallagher, S. (2009) 'Philosophical Antecedents of Situated Cognition', in P. Robbins and M. Aydede (eds), *The Cambridge Handbook of Situated Cognition*, Cambridge: Cambridge University Press, 35–51.

Garner, S. (1994) *Bodied Spaces: Phenomenology and Performance in Contemporary Drama*, Ithaca, NY: Cornell University Press.

Gendlin, E. (1991) 'Thinking Beyond Patterns: Body, Language and Situations', http://www.focusing.org/tbp.html

Gerber, Ellen W. (1971) *Innovators and Institutions in Physical Education*, Philadelphia, PA: Lea and Febiger.

Gerber, Richard (2001) *Vibrational Medicine*, Rochester, NY: Bear & Company.

Gerow, E. (1981) '*Rasa* as a Category of Literary Criticism', in R. M. van Baumer and J. R. Brandon (eds), *Sanskrit Drama in Performance*, Honolulu: University of Hawai'i Press.

Ghosh, Manomohan (ed. & trans.) (1967 [1951]) *The Natyasastra*, Volumes 1 and 2, Calcutta: Graanthalaya.

Gibson, J. J. (1962) 'Observations on Active Touch', *Psychological Review*, 69:477–491.

Gibson, J. J. (1979) *The Ecological Approach to Visual Perception*, Hillsdale, NJ: Lawrence Erlbaum Associates.

Gindler, E. (1995) '*Gymnastik* for People Whose Lives Are Full of Activity', in D. H. Johnson (ed.), *Bone, Breath and Gesture: Practices of Embodiment*, Berkeley, CA: North Atlantic Press, 5–14.

Goff, Janet (1991) *Noh Drama and the Tale of Genji*, Princeton, NJ: Princeton University Press.

Gordon, Mel (1987) *The Stanislavski Technique: Russia: A Workbook for Actors*, New York and Tonbridge: Applause Theatre Books.

Gordon, Mel (2000) *Voluptuous Panic: The Erotic World of Weimar Berlin*, Los Angeles, CA: Feral House.

Gordon, Robert (2006) *The Purpose of Playing: Modern Acting Theories in Perspective*, Ann Arbor: University of Michigan Press.

Goulish, Matthew (2000) *39 Microlectures in Proximity of Performance*, London: Routledge.

Govan, E., H. Nicholson *et al.* (2007) *Making a Performance: Devising Histories and Contemporary Practices*, Basingstoke: Palgrave Macmillan.

Graesner, Wolfgang (1927) *Körpersinn*, Munich: Beck.

Graham, S. and S. Hoggett (2009) *The Frantic Assembly Book of Devising Theatre*, London: Routledge.

Griffiths, P. and A. Scarantino (2009) 'Emotions in the Wild: The Situated Perspective on Emotion', in P. Robbins and M. Aydede (eds), *The Cambridge Handbook of Situated Cognition*, Cambridge: Cambridge University Press, 437–453.

Grotowski, J. (1975) *Towards a Poor Theatre*, ed. Eugenio Barba, Holstebro, Denmark: Odin Theatre.

Grotowski, J. (1991) *Towards a Poor Theatre*, London: Methuen.

Guerts, Kathryn Linn (2002) *Culture and the Senses: Bodily Ways of Knowing in an African Community*, Berkeley: University of California Press.

Hagen, Uta (2008) *Respect for Acting*, Hoboken, NJ: John Wiley & Sons.

Hahn, Tomie P. (2007) *Sensational Knowledge: Embodying Culture through Japanese Dance*, Middletown, CT: Wesleyan University Press.

Hare, Tom (trans. & notes) (2008) *Zeami: Performance Notes*, New York: Columbia University Press.

Harrop, John (1992) *Acting*, London: Routledge.

Harvie, Jen and Andy Lavender (eds) (2010) *Making Contemporary Theatre: International Rehearsal Processes*, London: Routledge.

Heddon, D. and J. Milling (2006) *Devising Performance: A Critical History*, Basingstoke: Palgrave Macmillan.

Heidegger, M. (1995) *The Fundamental Concepts of Metaphysics: World, Finitude, Solitude*, trans. W. McNeill and N. Walker, Bloomington: Indiana University Press.

Henschke Durham, Else (1981) 'Elsa Gindler in the Nineteen Twenties and Thirties', in Mary Alice Roche (ed.) *Elsa Gindler*, Volume 2, Caldwell, NJ: Charlotte Selver Foundation.

Hetzler, Eric (2007) 'Actors and Emotion in Performance', *Studies in Theatre and Performance*, 28, 1:59–78.

Hijikata Tatsumi (2000a [1960]) *Inner Material/Material*, trans. Nanako Kurihara, *TDR*, 44, 2:34–42.

Hijikata Tatsumi (2000b [1962]) *To Prison*, trans. Nanako Kurihara, *TDR*, 44, 2:43–48.

Hijikata Tatsumi (2000c [1968]) 'Hijikata Tatsumi: Plucking Off the Darkness of the Flesh', an interview by Shibusawa Tatsukiko, trans. Nanako Kurihara, *TDR*, 44, 2:49–55.

Hijikata Tatsumi (2000d [1969]) *From Being a Jealous Dog*, trans. Nanako Kurihara, *TDR*, 44, 2:56–59.

Hijikata Tatsumi (2000e) *On Material II Fautrier*, trans. Nanako Kurihara, *TDR*, 44:60–61.

Hijikata Tatsumi (2000f [1977]) 'Fragments of Glass: A Conversation between Hijikata Tatsumi and Suzuki Tadashi', moderated by Senda Akihiko, trans. Nanako Kurihara, *TDR*, 44, 2:62–70.

Hijikata Tatsumi (2000g [1985]) *Wind Daruma*, trans. Nanako Kurihara, *TDR*, 44, 2:71–79.

Hilker, Franz (1926) 'Vom Sinn unserer Arbeit', *Gymnastik*, 1, 1:2.

Hill, Jackson (1982) 'Ritual Music in Japanese Esoteric Buddhism: Shingon Shōmyō', *Ethnomusicology*, 26, 1:27–39.

Hodge, A. (ed.) (2010 [2000]) *Twentieth Century Actor Training* (2nd edition), London: Routledge.

Holledge, Julie and Joanne Tompkins (2000) *Women's Intercultural Performance*, London: Routledge.

Hornby, Richard (1992) *The End of Acting: A Radical View*, New York: Applause Books.

Howe, Diane (1996) *Individuality and Expression: The Aesthetics of the New German Dance, 1908–1936*, New York: Peter Lang.

Howes, David (ed.) (2004) *The Empire of the Senses*, Oxford: Berg Publishers.

Huang, Alexander C. Y. (2009) *Chinese Shakespeares: Two Centuries of Cultural Exchange*, New York: Columbia University Press.

Hughes-Freeland, Felicia (2006) 'Constructing a Classical Tradition: Javanese Court Dance in Indonesia', in T. Buckland (ed.), *Dancing from Past to Present*, Madison: University of Wisconsin Press, 52–74.

Hulton, D. (1988) 'Creative Actor (Empowering Performers and Spectators)', in C. McCullough (ed.), *Theatre Praxis: Teaching Drama through Practice*, Basingstoke: Macmillan, 15–37.

Hulton, D. (2000) 'Joseph Chaikin and Aspects of Actor Training: Possibilities Rendered Present', in A. Hodge (ed.), *Twentieth-Century Actor Training*, London: Routledge, 151–173.

Hurley, Erin (2010) *Theatre & Feeling*, Basingstoke: Palgrave Macmillan.

Huston, Hollis (1992) *The Actor's Instrument: Body, Theory, Stage*, Ann Arbor: University of Michigan Press.

Ingold, Tim (2000) *The Perception of the Environment*, London: Routledge.

Ingold, Tim (2011) *Being Alive: Essays on Movement, Knowledge and Description*, London: Routledge.

James, W. (1884) 'What Is an Emotion?' *Mind*, 9, 34:188–205.

James, W. (2002) 'The Stream of Consciousness', in N. Block, O. Flanagan and G. Guzeldere (eds), *The Nature of Consciousness*, Cambridge, MA: MIT Press, 71–82.

Johnson, M. (1987) *The Body in the Mind: The Bodily Basis of Meaning, Imagination, and Reason*, Chicago, IL: University of Chicago Press.

Johnson, M. (2007) *The Meaning of the Body: Aesthetics of Human Understanding*, Chicago, IL: University of Chicago Press.

Jungr, Barb (2001) 'Barb Jungr', in Mary Luckhurst and Chloe Veltman (eds), *On Acting: Interviews with Actors*, London: Faber & Faber, 49–53.

Kalb, Jonathan (1989) *Beckett in Performance*, Cambridge: Cambridge University Press.

Kanze Hideo (1971) 'Noh: Business and Art, An Interview with Kanze Hideo', *TDR*, 15, 2:185–192.

Kapsali, Maria (2010) 'I Don't Attack It, but It's Not for Actors: The Use of Yoga by Jerzy Grotowski', *Theatre Dance and Performer Training*, 1, 2:185–198.

Karina, Lilian and Marion Kant (2005) *Hitler's Dancers: German Modern Dance and the Third Reich*, New York and Oxford: Berghahn Books.

Kasulis, Thomas P. (1993) 'The Body – Japanese Style', in Thomas P. Kasulis, Roger T. Ames and Wimal Dissanayake (eds), *Self as Body in Asian Theory and Practice*, Albany: State University of New York Press, 299–319.

Kasulis, Thomas P. (1998) 'Zen and Artistry', in Roger T. Ames with Thomas P. Kasulis and Wimal Dissanayake (eds), *Self as Image in Asian Theory and Practice*, Albany: State University of New York Press, 357–371.

Kasulis, Thomas P. with Roger T. Ames and Wimal Dissanayake (eds) (1993) *Self as Body in Asian Theory and Practice*, Albany: State University of New York Press.

Kaufman, Jason and Orlando Patterson (2005) 'Cross-national Cultural Diffusion: The Global Spread of Cricket', *American Sociological Review*, 70:82–110.

Kazan, E. (1988) *A Life*, London: Deutsch.

Kemp, Rick (2012) *Embodied Acting: What Neuroscience Tells Us about Performance*, London: Routledge.

Kigaya Shinko (2001) 'Western Audiences and the Emergent Reorientation of Meiji Nō', in Stanca Scholz-Cionca and Samuel L. Leiter (eds), *Japanese Theatre and the International Stage*, Leiden: Brill.

Kirby, E. T. (ed.) (1969) *Total Theatre: A Critical Anthology*, New York: E.P. Dutton.

Kirby, Michael (1987) *A Formalist Theatre*, Philadelphia: University of Pennsylvania Press.

Kirsh, D. and P. Maglio (1994) 'On Distinguishing Epistemic from Pragmatic Action', *Cognitive Science*, 18:513–549.

Kitizawa Masakuni (1995) 'The Twilight of a Tradition', *TDR*, 39, 2:106–114.

Knowles, Ric (2010) *Theatre & Interculturalism*, Basingstoke: Palgrave Macmillan.

Konijn, E. A. (1997) *Acting Emotions: Shaping Emotions on Stage*, Amsterdam: Amsterdam University Press.

Konijn, E. A. (2002) 'The Actor's Emotions Reconsidered: A Psychological Task-Based Perspective', in P. Zarrilli (ed.), *Acting (Re)Considered*, London: Routledge, 62–81.

Krasner, David (ed.) (2000) *Method Acting Reconsidered*, New York: St. Martin's Press.

Kumiega, Jennifer (1997) 'Laboratory Theatre/Grotowski/The Mountain Project', in Richard Schechner and Lisa Wolford (eds), *The Grotowski Sourcebook*, London: Routledge, 231–247.

Kunjunni, Raja K. (1964) *Kutiyattam: An Introduction*, Delhi: Sangeet Natak Akademi.

Kurihara Nanako (2000a) 'Hijikata Tatsumi: The Words of Butoh', *TDR*, 44, 1:10–28.

Kurihara Nanako (2000b) 'Hijikata Tatsumi Chronology', *TDR*, 44, 1:29–33.

Lakoff, George and Mark Johnson (1980) *Metaphors We Live By*, Chicago, IL: University of Chicago Press.

Lakoff, George and Mark Johnson (1999) *Philosophy in the Flesh*, New York: Basic Books.

Landes, Donald A. (2012) 'Introduction', in Maurice Merleau-Ponty, *Phenomenology of Perception*, trans. Donald A. Landes, London: Routledge.

Larlham, D. (2010) 'Dancing Pina Bausch', *TDR*, 54, 1:150–160.

Lecoq, J. (2002) *The Moving Body*, London: Methuen.

Leder, Drew (1990) *The Absent Body*, Chicago, IL: University of Chicago Press.

LeDoux, J. (1998) *The Emotional Brain*, New York: Phoenix.

Lee, D. N. (1993) 'Body–Environment Coupling', in U. Neisser (ed.), *The Perceived Self: Ecological and Interpersonal Sources of Self-Knowledge*, Cambridge: Cambridge University Press, 43–67.

Lehmann, Hans-Thies (2006) *Postdramatic Theatre*, trans. Karen Jurs-Munby, London: Routledge.

Lendra, I. Wayan (2002) 'Bali and Grotowski: Some Parallels in the Training Process', in Phillip B. Zarrilli (ed.), *Acting Reconsidered*, London: Routledge, 148–162.

Levine, David Michael (1985) *The Body's Recollection of Being*, London: Routledge.

Levith, Murray J. (2004) *Shakespeare in China*, New York: Continuum.

Li, Kay (2007) 'Performing the Globalized City: Contemporary Hong Kong Theatre and Global Connectivity', *Asian Theatre Journal*, 24, 2:440–469.

Lindh, Ingemar (2010) *Stepping Stones*, Wroclaw, Poland: Icarus Publishing, The Grotowski Institute (original Italian publication 1998).

Liu, Siyuan (2011) 'A.C. Scott', *Asian Theatre Journal*, 28, 2:404–425.

Lo, Jacqueline and Helen Gilbert (2002) 'Toward a Topography of Cross-cultural Theatre Praxis', *TDR*, 46, 3:31–53.

Lo, Jacqueline and Helen Gilbert (2007) *Performance and Cosmopolitics*, Basingstoke: Palgrave Macmillan.

Loukes, R. (2003) 'Psychophysical Awareness in Training and Performance: Elsa Gindler and Her Legacy', unpublished PhD thesis, University of Exeter.

Loukes, R. (2006) 'Concentration and Awareness in Psychophysical Training: The Practice of Elsa Gindler', *New Theatre Quarterly*, 22, 4:387–400.

Loukes, R. (2010) 'Gertrud Falke-Heller: Experiences of the Work with the Gindler Method in the Jooss-Leeder School of Dance, Dartington Hall, May 1937–June 1940', *Theatre, Dance and Performance Training*, 1, 1:101–115.

Loukes, R. (2013) 'Towards a Syncretic Ensemble? RedCape Theatre's *The Idiot Colony*', in John Britton (ed.), *Encountering Ensemble*, London: Methuen.

Luckhurst, Mary and Chloe Veltman (eds) (2001) *On Acting: Interviews with Actors*, London: Faber & Faber.

Ludwig, Sophie (2002) *Elsa Gindler – von ihrem Leben und Wirken*, ed. Marianne Haag, Hamburg: Christians Verlag.

Lutterbie, John (2011) *Toward a General Theory of Acting: Cognitive Science and Performance*, New York: Palgrave Macmillan.

Mabbett, Ian W. (1993–1994) 'Buddhism and Music', *Asian Music*, 25, 1/2:9–28.

Machon, J. (2009) *(Syn)aesthetics: Redefining Visceral Performance*, Basingstoke: Palgrave Macmillan.

Mackay, W. (1999) 'Is Paper Safer? The Role of Paper Flight Strips in Air Traffic Control', *ACM Transactions on Computer–Human Interaction*, 6, 4:311–340.

Mahoney, Elisabeth (2010) 'Told by the Wind', *The Guardian*, 2 February.

Manning, Susan (1993) *Ecstasy and the Demon: Feminism and Nationalism in the Dances of Mary Wigman*, Berkeley: University of California Press.

Manning, Susan (2007) '*Ausdruckstanz* across the Atlantic', in Susanne Franco and Marina Nordera (eds), *Dance Discourses*, London: Routledge.

Manning, Susan and Melissa Benson (1986) 'Interrupted Communities: Modern Dance in Germany', *TDR*, 30, 2:30–45.

Marchand, Trevor H. J. (2010) 'Introduction: Making Knowledge: Explorations of the Indissoluble Relation between Mind, Body, and Environment', in Trevor H. J. Marchand (ed.), *Making Knowledge*, Oxford: Wiley-Blackwell, 1–20.

Mazo, Joseph H. (1977) *Prime Movers: The Makers of Modern Dance in America*, Princeton, NJ: Princeton Book Company.

McAllister-Viel, Tara (2007) 'Speaking with an International Voice?' *Contemporary Theatre Review*, 17, 1:97–106.

McAllister-Viel, Tara (2009a) '(Re)considering the Role of Breath in Training Actors' Voices: Insights from Dahnjeon Breathing and the Phenomena of Breath', *Theatre Topics*, 19, 2:165–180.

McAllister-Viel, Tara (2009b) 'Dahnjeon Breathing', in J. Boston and R. Cook (eds), *Breath in Action*, London: Jessica Kingsley, 115–130.

McAllister-Viel, Tara (2009c) 'Voicing Culture: Training Korean Actors' Voices through the Namdaemun Market Projects', *Modern Drama*, 52, 4:426–448.

McConachie, B. (2006) 'Preface', in B. McConachie and F. E. Hart, *Performance and Cognition: Theatre Studies and the Cognitive Turn*, London: Routledge, ix–xv.

McConachie, B. (2008) *Engaging Audiences: A Cognitive Approach to Spectating in the Theatre*, Basingstoke: Palgrave Macmillan.

McConachie, B. (2013) *Theatre & Mind*, Basingstoke: Palgrave Macmillan.

McDaniel, June (1995) 'Emotion in Bengali Religious Thought: Substance and Metaphor', in Joel Marks and Roger T. Ames (eds), *Emotions in Asian Thought*, Albany: State University of New York Press, 39–63.

McDermott, Phelim (2007) 'Physical Theatre and Text', in John Keefe and Simon Murray (eds), *Physical Theatres: A Critical Reader*, London: Routledge, 201–208.

McGaw, Charles *et al.* (2012) *Acting Is Believing* (11th edition), Boston, MA: Wadsworth.

Meckler, Eva (1987) *The New Generation of Acting Teachers*, New York: Penguin.

Mee, Erin B. (ed.) (2001) *Drama Contemporary: India*, Baltimore, MD: The Johns Hopkins University Press.

Mee, Erin B. (2008) *Theatre of Roots: Redirecting the Modern Indian Stage*, Calcutta: Seagull Press.

Meeks, Lori (2011) 'The Disappearing Medium: Reassessing the Place of Miko in the Religious Landscape of Premodern Japan', *History of Religions*, 50, 3:208–260.

Menary, R. (2010) 'Cognitive Integration and the Extended Mind', *The Extended Mind*, Cambridge, MA: MIT Press, 227–243.

Mensendieck, Bess (1908 [1906]) *Körperkultur des Weibes: Praktisch, hygienische und praktisch asthetische Winke* (3rd edition), Munich: F. Bruckmann.

Merleau-Ponty, Maurice (1962) *Phenomenology of Perception*, London: Routledge and Kegan Paul.

Merleau-Ponty, Maurice (1964) *The Primacy of Perception*, ed. James J. Edie, Evanston, IL: Northwestern University Press.

Merleau-Ponty, Maurice (1968) *The Visible and the Invisible*, trans. Alphonso Lingus, Evanston, IL: Northwestern University Press.

Merleau-Ponty, Maurice (2012) *Phenomenology of Perception*, trans. Donald A. Landes, London: Routledge.

Merlin, B. (2002) *Beyond Stanislavsky*, London: Nick Hern.

Merlin, B. (2003) *Konstantin Stanislavsky*, London: Routledge.

Merlin, B. (2007) *The Complete Stanislavsky Toolkit*, London: Nick Hern.

Minagawa, Tatsuo (1957) 'Japanese *Noh* Music', *Journal of the American Musicological Society*, 10, 3:181–200.

Mishra, Pankaj (2012) *From the Ruins of Empire*, London: Allen Lane.

Mitchell, Katie (2008) *The Director's Craft: A Practical Guide*, London: Routledge.

Mitchell, Katie (2010) 'The Best Performance I've Ever Seen: Café Müller', *The Guardian*, 5 June.

Mnouchine, Ariane (1996) 'The Theatre Is Oriental', in Patrice Pavis (ed.), *The Intercultural Performance Reader*, London: Routledge, 93–98.

Monier-Williams, M. (1963) *A Sanskrit–English Dictionary*, Oxford: Clarendon Press.

Montemayor, Karen (1998) 'Notes on Ōta Shōgo and *The Water Station*', program for *The Water Station*, Madison: University of Wisconsin, University Theatre, 1–8.

Moore, Sonia (1960) *The Stanislavsky Method*, New York: Viking.

Moore, Sonia (1965) *The Stanislavsky System*, New York: Viking.

Moore, Sonia (1979) *Training an Actor: The Stanislavsky System in Class*, New York: Penguin.

Moser, Heike (ed.) (2011) 'Kutiyattam: 10 Years after the UNESCO-Declaration', special issue of *Indian Folklife*, 38 (June).

Müller, H. (1984) *Hamletmachine and Other Texts for the Stage*, New York: PAJ Publications.

Müller, H. and N. Servos (1986) 'Expressionism? *Ausdruckstanz* and the New Dance Theatre in Germany', souvenir program for the Festival International de Nouvelle Danse, Montreal, 10–15.

Murray, S. (2003) *Jacques Lecoq*, London: Routledge.

Murray, Simon and John Keefe (2007) *Physical Theatres: A Critical Reader*, London: Routledge.

Nagatomo, Shigenori (1987) 'An Analysis of Dogen's "Casting Off Body and Mind"', *International Philosophical Quarterly*, 27, 3:227–242.

Nagatomo, Shigenori (1992a) 'An Eastern Concept of the Body: Yuasa's Body-Scheme', in Maxine Sheets-Johnstone (ed.), *Giving the Body Its Due*, Albany: State University of New York Press, 48–68.

Nagatomo, Shigenori (1992b) *Attunement through the Body*, Albany: State University of New York Press.

Nancy, Jean-Luc (2007) *Listening*, New York: Fordham University Press.

Nearman, Mark (1978) 'Zeami's *Kyūi*: A Pedagogical Guide for Teachers of Acting', *Monumenta Nipponica*, 33, 3:299–332.

Nearman, Mark (1980) '*Kyakuraika*: Zeami's Final Legacy for the Master Actor', *Monumenta Nipponica*, 35, 2:153–197.

Nearman, Mark (1982a) '*Kakyō*: A Mirror of the Flower [Part One]', *Monumenta Nipponica*, 37, 3:343–374.

Nearman, Mark (1982b) '*Kakyō*: Zeami's Fundamental Principles of Acting [Part Two]', *Monumenta Nipponica*, 37, 4:459–496.

Nearman, Mark (1983) '*Kakyō*: Zeami's Fundamental Principles of Acting [Part Three]', *Monumenta Nipponica*, 38, 1:49–71.

Nearman, Mark (1984) 'Feeling in Relation to Acting: An Outline of Zeami's Views', *Asian Theatre Journal*, 1, 1:40–51.

Nearman, Mark (1995a) 'The Visions of a Creative Artist: Zenchiku's *Rokurin Ichiro* Treatises', *Monumenta Nipponica*, 50, 2:235–261.

Nearman, Mark (1995b) 'The Visions of a Creative Artist: Zenchiku's *Rokurin Ichiro* Treatises, Part 2', *Monumenta Nipponica*, 50, 3:281–303.

Nearman, Mark (1995c) 'The Visions of a Creative Artist: Zenchiku's *Rokurin Ichiro* Treatises, Part 3' *Monumenta Nipponica*, 50, 4:485–521.

Nearman, Mark (1996) 'The Visions of a Creative Artist: Zenchiku's *Rokurin Ichiro* Treatises', *Monumenta Nipponica*, 51, 1:17–52.

Newhall, Mary Anne Santos (2009) *Mary Wigman*, London: Routledge.

Nishino Haruo (2001) 'The Multilayered Structure of *Nō*', in Stanca Scholz-Cionca and Samuel L. Leiter (eds), *Japanese Theatre and the International Stage*, Leiden: Brill, 149–160.

Noda Hideki and Colin Teevan (2006) *The Bee*, London: Oberon Books.

Noda Hideki and Colin Teevan (2008) *The Diver*, London: Oberon Books.

Noë, A. (2004) *Action in Perception*, Cambridge, MA: MIT Press.

Noë, A. (2007) 'Making Worlds Available', in S. Gehm, P. Huseman and K. von Wilcke (eds), *Knowledge in Motion: Perspectives on Artistic and Scientific Research in Dance*, London and New Brunswick, NJ: Transaction, 121–128.

Noë, A. (2009) *Out of Our Heads: Why You Are Not Your Brain, and Other Lessons from the Biology of Consciousness*, New York: Hill and Wang.

Noguchi Hiroyuki (2004) 'The Idea of the Body in Japanese Culture and Its Dismantlement', *International Journal of Sport and Health Science*, 2:8–24.

Nomura Mansaku (1997) 'Experiments in *Kyōgen*', in James R. Brandon (ed.), *Nō and Kyōgen in the Contemporary World*, Honolulu: University of Hawai'i Press, 173–182.

Nomura Shirō (1997) 'Teaching the Paradox of *Nō*', in James R. Brandon (ed.), *Nō and Kyōgen in the Contemporary World*, Honolulu: University of Hawai'i Press, 202–209.

Ohno Kazuo (1986a) 'Kazuo Ohno Doesn't Commute', an interview by Richard Schechner, *TDR*, 30, 2:163–169.

Ohno Kazuo (1986b) 'The Dead Sea Vienna Waltz and Ghost', *TDR*, 30, 2:170.

Ohno Kazuo and Ohno Yoshito (2004) *Kazuo Ohno's World from Without and Within*, trans. John Barrett, Middletown, CT: Wesleyan University Press.

Oida, Yoshi with Lorna Marshall (1992) *An Actor Adrift*, London: Methuen.

Oida, Yoshi with Lorna Marshall (1997) *The Invisible Actor*, London: Methuen.

Ortolani, Benito (1984) 'Shamanism in the Origins of *Nō* Theatre', *Asian Theatre Journal*, 1, 2:166–190.

Ortolani, Benito (2001) 'Zeami's Mysterious Flower: The Challenge of Interpreting It in Western Terms', in Stanca Scholz-Cionca and Samuel L. Leiter (eds), *Japanese Theatre and the International Stage*, Leiden: Brill, 113–132.

Ōta Shōgo (1985) 'From *Water Station*'s Program: "Silence as a Means of Expression"', in Robert K. Sarlos, 'Tenkei Gekijo (Tokyo): *Water Station*', *TDR*, 29, 1:137–138.

Ōta Shōgo (1990) *Mizo no Eki* [*The Water Station*], trans. Mari Boyd, *Asian Theatre Journal*, 7, 2:150–184.

Ōta Shōgo (2004) *The Tale of Komachi Told by the Wind*, in Japan Playwrights Association (ed.), *Half a Century of Japanese Theater*, Volume 6: *1960s Part 1*, Tokyo: Kinokuniya, 209–244.

Ozawa-De Silva, Chikako (2002) 'Beyond the Body/Mind? Japanese Contemporary Thinkers on Alternative Sociologies of the Body', *Body and Society*, 8, 2:21–38.

Partridge, Eric (1983) *Origins: A Short Etymological Dictionary of Modern English*, New York: Greenwich House.

Partsch-Bergsohn, Isa (1994) *Modern Dance in Germany and the United States: Crosscurrents and Influences*, Basel: Harwood Academic Publishers.

Paulose, K. G. (2006) *Kutiyattam Theatre*, Kottayam: D.C. Books.

Pavis, Patrice (1981) 'Problems of a Semiology of Theatrical Gesture', *Poetics Today*, 2, 3:65–93.

Pavis, Patrice (1990) 'Interculturalism in Contemporary Mise en Scene: The Image of India in "The Mahabharata"', in Erika Fischer-Lichte, Josephine Riley and Michael Gissenwehrer (eds), *The Dramatic Touch of Difference: Theatre, Own and Foreign*, Tubingen: Gunter Narr Verlag, 57–72.

Pavis, Patrice (1992) *Theatre at the Crossroads of Culture*, London: Routledge.

Pavis, Patrice (ed.) (1996) *The Intercultural Performance Reader*, London: Routledge.

Pavis, Patrice (2003) *Analyzing Performance*, Ann Arbor: University of Michigan Press.

Petit, Lenard (2010) *The Michael Chekhov Handbook for the Actor*, London: Routledge.

Phelan, Peggy (1993) *Unmarked: The Politics of Performance*, London and New York: Routledge.

Pilgrim, Richard B. (1969) 'Some Aspects of Kokoro in Zeami', *Monumenta Nipponica*, 24, 4:393–402.

Pilgrim, Richard B. (1986) 'Intervals (*Ma*) in Space and Time: Foundations for a Religio-Aesthetic Paradigm in Japan', *History of Religions*, 25, 3:255–277.

Pinnington, Noel J. (1997) 'Crossed Paths: Zeami's Transmission to Zenchiku', *Monumenta Nipponica*, 52, 2:201–234.

Pinnington, Noel J. (2006) 'Models of the Way in the Theory of *Noh*', *Japan Review*, 18:29–55.

Pitches, Jonathan (2003) *Vsevolod Meyerhold*, London: Routledge.

Pitches, Jonathan (2009 [2006]) *Science and the Stanislavski Tradition of Acting*, London: Routledge.

Pitches, Jonathan (2012) *Russians in Britain: British Theatre and the Russian Tradition of Actor Training*, London: Routledge.

Polanyi, M. (1969) *Knowing and Being*, Chicago, IL: University of Chicago Press.

Powers, Mala, (2002) 'The Past, Present and Future of Michael Chekhov', *To The Actor on the Technique of Acting*, London: Routledge, xxv–xlviii.

Premkumar (1948) *The Language of Kathakali: A Guide to Mudras*, Allahabad: Kitabistan.

Preston-Dunlop, Valerie and Susanne Lahusen (1990) *Schrifttanz: A View of German Dance in the Weimar Republic*, London: Dance Books.

Prinz, J. J. (2009) 'Is Consciousness Embodied?' in P. Robbins and M. Aydede (eds), *The Cambridge Handbook of Situated Cognition*, Cambridge: Cambridge University Press, 419–436.

Punpeng, Grisana (2012) 'From Meditation to Presence in Performance: A Psychophysical Approach to Actor Training for Thai Undergraduate Drama Programmes', unpublished PhD thesis, Drama Department, University of Exeter.

Quinn, Shelley Fenno (2005) *Developing Zeami: The Noh Actor's Attunement in Practice*, Honolulu: University of Hawai'i Press.

Rao, Maya Krishna (1999) '*Khol Do*', program note for a performance sponsored by the Centre for Performance Research, Aberystwyth, Wales, UK.

Rao, Maya Krishna (2010) Program note, Bharat Rang Mahotsav 2010, New Delhi: NSD, 156–157.

Rao, Maya Krishna (2012) Presentation on performance practice, Institute for Interweaving Performance Cultures, Freie Universität Berlin, 12 September.

Rath, Eric C. (2003) 'Remembering Zeami: The Kanze School and Its Patriarch', *Asian Theatre Journal*, 20, 2:191–208.

Rayner, Alice (1994) *To Act, to Do, to Perform*, Ann Arbor: University of Michigan Press.

Reinelt, Janelle and Brian Singleton (2010) 'Series Editors' Preface', in Evin Darwin Winet, *Indonesian Postcolonial Theatre*, Studies in International Performance, London: Routledge, xi.

Renaud, Lissa Tyler (2010) 'Training Artists or Consumers? Commentary on American Actor Training', in Ellen Margolis and Lissa Tyler Renaud (eds), *The Politics of American Actor Training*, New York: Routledge, 76–93.

Reynolds, D. (2007) *Rhythmic Subjects: Uses of Energy in the Dances of Mary Wigman, Martha Graham and Merce Cunningham*, London: Dance Books.

Richmond, Farley (1999) *Kutiyattam: Sanskrit Theater of Kerala*, Ann Arbor: University of Michigan Press (CD-ROM).

Richmond, Farley, Darius Swann and Phillip B. Zarrilli (1990) *Indian Theatre: Traditions of Performance*, Honolulu: University of Hawai'i Press.

Riley, Jo (1997) *Chinese Theatre and the Actor in Performance*, Cambridge: Cambridge University Press.

Rimer, J. Thomas and Yamazaki Masakazu (1984) *On the Art of the Nō Drama: The Major Treatises of Zeami*, Princeton, NJ: Princeton University Press.

Roach, J. (1993) *The Player's Passion: Studies in the Science of Acting*, Ann Arbor: University of Michigan Press.

Robbins, P. and M. Aydede (2009) 'A Short Primer on Situated Cognition', in P. Robbins and M. Aydede (eds), *The Cambridge Handbook of Situated Cognition*, Cambridge: Cambridge University Press, 3–10.

Romdenh-Romluc, Komarine (2011) *Merleau-Ponty and Phenomenology of Perception*, London: Routledge.

Rowell, Lewis (1992) *Music and Musical Thought in Early India*, Chicago, IL: University of Chicago Press.

Ruyter, N. L. C. (1996) 'The Delsarte Heritage', *Dance Research Journal*, 14, 1:62–74.

Ruyter, Nancy (1999) *The Cultivation of Body and Mind in Nineteenth Century Delsartism*, Westport, CT: Greenwood.

Said, Edward (1976) *Orientalism*, New York: Pantheon.

Sant, Toni (2003) 'Suzuki Tadashi and the Shizuoka Theatre Company in New York', an interview by Toni Sant', *TDR*, 47, 3:147–158.

Sarlos, Robert K. (1985) 'Tenkei Gekijo (Tokyo): *Water Station*', *TDR*, 29, 1:131–138.

Savarese, Nicola (2010) *Eurasian Theatre: Drama and Performance between East and West from Classical Antiquity to the Present*, Malta: Icarus Publishing.

Schechner, R. (2002) *Performance Studies: An Introduction*, London: Routledge.

Schechner, R. (2006) 'Towards Tomorrow: Restoring Disciplinary Limits and Rehearsals in Time? Richard Schechner Interviewed by Richard Gough', in Judie Christie, Richard Gough and Daniel Watt (eds), *A Performance Cosmology*, London: Routledge.

Schechner, R. and T. Hoffman (1997) 'Interview with Grotowski', in R. Schechner and Lisa Wolford (eds), *The Grotowski Sourcebook*, London: Routledge.

Schechner, R. and L. Wolford (eds) (1997) *The Grotowski Sourcebook*, London: Routledge.

Schmitt, Natalie Crohn (1990) *Actors and Onlookers: Theater and Twentieth-Century Scientific Views of Nature*, Evanston, IL: Northwestern University Press.

Schrag, Calvin O. (1969) *Experience and Being*, Evanston, IL: Northwestern University Press.

Scott, A. C. (1993) 'Underneath the Stewpot, There's the Flame … *T'ai chi ch'uan* and the Asian/Experimental Theatre Program', in Phillip B. Zarrilli (ed.), *Asian Martial Arts in Actor Training*, Madison: Center for South Asia, University of Wisconsin-Madison, 48–61.

Senda Akihito (1997) *The Voyage of Contemporary Japanese Theatre*, trans. J. Thomas Rimer, Honolulu: University of Hawai'i Press.

Serper, Zvika (2000) '*Kotoba* ("Sung" Speech) in Japanese *Nō* Theater: Gender Distinctions in Structure and Performance', *Asian Music*, 31, 2:129–166.

Shapiro, Lawrence (2011) *Embodied Cognition*, London: Routledge.

Sheen, Michael (2001) 'Michael Sheen', in Mary Luckhurst and Chloe Veltman (eds), *On Acting: Interviews with Actors*, London: Faber & Faber, 115–123.

Sheets-Johnstone, M. (2009) *The Corporeal Turn: An Interdisciplinary Reader*, Exeter: Imprint Academic.

Shigenori Nagatomo (1987) 'An Analysis of Dogen's "Casting Off Body and Mind"', *International Philosophical Quarterly*, 27, 3:227–242.

Shusterman, R. (2000) *Performing Live: Aesthetic Alternatives for the Ends of Art*, Ithaca, NY: Cornell University Press.

Shusterman, R. (2008) *Body Consciousness: A Philosophy of Mindfulness and Somaesthetics*, Cambridge: Cambridge University Press.

Singleton, Brian (1997) 'K.N. Panikkar's *Teyyateyyam*: Resisting Interculturalism through Ritual Practice', *Theatre Research International*, 22, 2:162–169.

Singleton, Mark (2010) *Yoga Body: The Origins of Modern Posture Practice*, Oxford: Oxford University Press.

Slowiak, J. and J. Cuesta (2007) *Jerzy Grotowski*, London: Routledge.

Smith, Michael (1969) *Theatre Trip*, Indianapolis and New York: Bobbs-Merrill.

Soelberg, Louise (1941) 'Modern Dance … What Is It?' *Physical Education and School Hygiene*, 33:157–163.

Solomon, Rakesh (1994) 'Culture, Imperialism and National Resistance: Performance in Colonial India', *Theatre Journal*, 46:323–347.

Solomon, Rakesh (2004) 'From Orientalist to Postcolonial Representations: A Critique of Indian Theatre Historiography from 1827 to the Present', *Theatre*, 2:117–127.

Solomon, Rakesh (2014) *Globalization, History, Historiography: The Making of a Modern Indian Theatre*, London: Anthem South Asian Studies.

Sorrell, W. (1986) *Mary Wigman: Ein Vermaechtnis*, Wilhelmshaven, Germany: Florian Noetzel Verlag.

Soto-Morettini, Donna (2010) *The Philosophical Actor: A Practical Meditation for Practicing Theatre Artists*, Bristol: Intellect.

Staniewski, Wlodzimierz with Alison Hodge (2004) *Hidden Territories: The Theatre of Gardzienice*, London: Routledge.

Stanislavsky, K. (1962) *Creating a Role*, trans. Elisabeth Reynolds Hapgood, New York: Theatre Arts Books.

Stanislavsky, K. (1980 [1936]) *An Actor Prepares*, trans. & ed. Elisabeth Reynolds Hapgood, London: Methuen.

Stanislavsky, K. (2008) *An Actor's Work*, trans. & ed. Jean Benedetti, London: Routledge.

Stanislavsky, C. and P. Rumyantsev (1975) *Stanislavski on Opera*, trans. & ed. Elisabeth Reynolds Hapgood, New York: Theatre Arts.

States, B. O. (1971) *Great Reckonings in Little Rooms: On Phenomenology of Theatre*, Ithaca, NY: Cornell University Press.

Stebbins, G. (1977 [1902]) *Delsarte System of Expression*, New York: Dance Horizons.

Stein, Bonnie Sue (1986) 'Butoh: "Twenty Years Ago We Were Crazy, Dirty, and Mad"', *TDR*, 30, 2:107–120.

Stein, Bonnie Sue (1987) '"If a Man Eats Vacuum" – Akaji Maro and Japanese Butoh', *Playbill, The National Theatre Magazine*, 87, 4:34, 39.

Stein, E. (1989) *On the Problem of Empathy*, Washington, DC: ICS Publications.

Stewart, John, Olivier Grapenne and Ezequiel A. Di Paolo (eds) (2010) *Enaction: Toward a New Paradigm for Cognitive Science*, Cambridge, MA: MIT Press.

Stoller, P. (1989) *The Taste of Ethnographic Things: The Senses in Anthropology*, Philadelphia: University of Pennsylvania Press.

Strasberg, L. (1966) *Strasberg at the Actors' Studio*, ed. R. Hethmon, New York: Theatre Communications Group.

Streicher, Margarete (1970) *Reshaping Physical Education*, ed. Betty E. Strutt, Manchester: Manchester University Press.

Suzuki Tadashi (1986) *The Way of Acting: The Theatre Writings of Tadashi Suzuki*, trans. J. Thomas Rimer, New York: Theatre Communications Group.

Takahashi Yasunari (2004) 'Introduction: Suzuki's Work in the Context of Japanese Theatre', in Ian Carruthers and Takahashi Yasunari, *The Theatre of Suzuki Tadashi*, Cambridge: Cambridge University Press, 1–5.

Tamba Akira (1981) *The Musical Structure of Nō*, Tokyo: Tokai University Press.

Tanabe, Willa Jane (1998) 'The Persistence of Self as Body and Personality in Japanese Buddhist Art', in Roger T. Ames with Thomas P. Kasulis and Wimal Dissanayake (eds), *Self as Image in Asian Theory and Practice*, Albany: State University of New York Press, 406–420.

Tanaka Min (1986a) 'Farmer/Dancer or Dancer/Farmer', an interview by Bonnie Sue Stein, *TDR*, 30, 2:142–151.

Tanaka Min (1986b) 'Stand by Me!' *TDR*, 30, 2:152.

Tanaka Min (1986c) '"From" I Am an Avant-Garde Who Crawls the Earth: Homage to Tatsumi Hijikata', *TDR*, 30, 2:153–155.

Tanaka Min (2006) 'Min Tanaka's Butoh', interview by Jiae Kim, trans. Kazue Kobata, *Theme*, 7(Fall), http://www.thememagazine.com/stories/min-tanaka/

Tatsuro Ishii (1985) 'Kazuko Yoshiyuki on Acting', *TDR*, 29, 4:31–38.

Thompson, E. (2007) *Mind in Life: Biology, Phenomenology, and the Sciences of Mind*, Cambridge, MA: Belknap Press of Harvard University Press.

Thompson, E. and M. Stapleton (2009) 'Making Sense of Sense-Making: Reflections on Enactive and Extended Mind Theories', *Topoi*, 28, 1:23–30.

Thornhill, Arthur H. (1993) *Six Circles, One Dewdrop: The Religio-Aesthetic World of Komparu Zenchiku*, Princeton, NJ: Princeton University Press.

Thornhill, Arthur H. (1997) 'Yūgen after Zeami', in James R. Brandon (ed.), *Nō and Kyōgen in the Contemporary World*, Honolulu: University of Hawai'i Press, 36–64.

Tian, Min (2008) *The Poetics of Difference and Displacement: Twentieth-Century Chinese-Western Intercultural Theatre*, Hong Kong: Hong Kong University Press.

Toepfer, K. (1997) *Empire of Ecstasy: Nudity and Movement in German Body Culture, 1910–1935*, Berkeley and Los Angeles: University of California Press.

Toporkov, V. (1979) *Stanislavski in Rehearsal: The Final Years*, New York and London: Routledge.

Trivedi, Poonam (2012) 'Why Shakespeare Is...Indian', *The Guardian*, 4 May, http://www.guardian.co.uk/stage/2012/may/04/why-shakespeare-is-indian.

Turner, Bryan S. and Zheng Yangwen (2009a) 'Introduction: Piety, Politics and Philosophy: Asia and the Global Body', in Bryan S. Turner and Zheng Yangwen (eds), *The Body in Asia*, New York: Berghahn Books, 1–21.

Turner, Bryan S. and Zheng Yangwen (eds) (2009b) *The Body in Asia*, New York: Berghahn.

Turner, Lisle (2008) *The Idiot Colony*, unpublished performance text (co-created by Claire Coaché, Cassie Friend, Rebecca Loukes and Andrew Dawson).

Tyler, Royall (1982) *Funa Benkei or Benkei Aboard Ship*, trans. Royall Tyler, unpublished manuscript for performance of the Kita nō school text, Madison: University of Wisconsin.

Tyler, Royall (1987) 'Buddhism in Noh', *Japanese Journal of Religious Studies*, 14, 1:19–52.

Tyler, Royall (1997) 'The *Waki-Shite* Relationship in *Nō*', in James R. Brandon (ed.), *Nō and Kyōgen in the Contemporary World*, Honolulu: University of Hawai'i Press, 65–190.

Unschuld, Paul U. (1985) *Medicine in China*, Berkeley: University of California Press.

Van Erven, Eugene (1992) *The Playful Revolution: Theatre and Liberation in Asia*, Bloomington: Indiana University Press.

Van Maanen, Hettie (1981) 'La Rythmique Jacques-Dalcroze: Stories Yesterday and Today', unpublished collection of essays from the archive of Gerda von Bülow, Copenhagen.

Varela, Francisco J. (1987) 'Laying Down a Path in Walking', in William Irwin Thompson (ed.), *Gaia: A Way of Knowing – Political Implications of the New Biology*, New York: Lindisfarne Press, 48–64.

Varela, Francisco J. and Natalie Depraz (2003) 'Imagining: Embodiment, Phenomenology and Transformation', in B. Alan Wallace (ed.), *Buddhism and Science*, New York: Columbia University Press, 195–230.

Varela, Francisco J., E. Thompson and E. Rosch (1993) *The Embodied Mind: Cognitive Science and Human Experience*, Cambridge, MA: MIT Press.

Varenne, Jean (1976) *Yoga and the Hindu Tradition*, Chicago, IL: University of Chicago Press.

Varley, Julia (2011) *Notes from an Odin Actress: Stones from Water*, London: Routledge.

Vatsyayan, Kapila (1983) *The Square and the Circle of the Indian Arts*, Atlantic Highlands, NJ: Humanities Press.

Venu, G. (1984) *Mudras in Kathakali: Notations of 373 Hand Gestures*, Irinjalakuda: Natan Kairali.

Venu, G. (1989) *Production of a Play in Kutiyattam*, Irinjalakuda: Natan Kairali.

Venu, G. (2002) *Into the World of Kutiyattam*, Irinjalakuda: Natan Kairali.

Vidal, J. (1988) 'Opening Moves: Interview with Jacques Lecoq', *The Guardian*, 22 March.

Waguri, Yukio (1998) *Butoh-Kaden*, Tokushima: Justsystem (CD-ROM and booklet).

Wallace, B. Alan (2007) *Contemplative Science: Where Buddhism and Neuroscience Converge*, New York: Columbia University Press.

Wangh, S. (2000) *An Acrobat of the Heart: A Physical Approach to Acting Inspired by the Work of Jerzy Grotowski*, New York: Vintage.

Watson, I. (2002). 'Interculturalism and the Individual Performer: An Interview with Roberta Carreri', in I. Watson (ed.), *Negotiating Cultures: Eugenio Barba and the Intercultural Debate*, Manchester: Manchester University Press.

Watson, I. (ed.) (2002) *Negotiating Cultures: Eugenio Barba and the Intercultural Debate*, Manchester: Manchester University Press.

Webster's Third New International Dictionary, Volume 1 (1976), Chicago, IL: Encyclopedia Britannica, Inc.

Welton, M. (2011) *Feeling Theatre*, Basingstoke: Palgrave Macmillan.

White, David Gordon (1996) *The Alchemical Body: Siddha Traditions in Medieval India*, Chicago, IL: University of Chicago Press.

White, David Gordon (2009) 'Yogic Rays: The Self-Externalization of the Yogi in Ritual, Narrative and Philosophy', *Paragrana: Internationale Zeitschrift für Historische Anthropologie*, 18, 1:64–77.

Whyman, R. (2008) *The Stanislavsky System of Acting: Legacy and Influence in Modern Performance*, Cambridge: Cambridge University Press.

Wichmann, Elizabeth (1991) *Listening to Theatre: Oral Dimension of Beijing Opera*, Honolulu: University of Hawai'i Press.

Wigman, M. (1966) *The Language of Dance*, Middleton, CT: Wesleyan University Press.

Wigman, M. (1973) *The Mary Wigman Book: Her Writings*, Middletown, CT: Wesleyan University Press.

Wigman, M. (1983) 'The Philosophy of the Modern Dance', in Marshall Cohen and Roger Copeland (eds), *What Is Dance? Readings in Theory and Criticism*, New York and Oxford: Oxford University Press.

Wigman, M. (1998) 'Stage Dance – Stage Dancer', in J. Morrison Brown, N. Mindlin and C. H. Woodford (eds), *The Vision of Modern Dance: In the Words of Its Creators*, London: Dance Books, 33–40.

Williams, David (ed.) (1991) *Peter Brook and the Mahabharata: Critical Perspectives*, London: Routledge.

Williams, Faynia (2012) 'Working with Pina Bausch: A Conversation with Tanztheater Wuppertal', in R. Climenhaga (ed.), *The Pina Bausch Sourcebook*, London: Routledge, 103–108.

Williams, Gary Jay (2006) 'Case Study: Moliere and Carnival Laughter', in Phillip B. Zarrilli *et al.*, *Theatre Histories: An Introduction*, London: Routledge, 192–200.

Wilson, R. A. and A. Clark (2009). 'How to Situate Cognition: Letting Nature Take Its Course', in P. Robbins and M. Aydede (eds), *The Cambridge Handbook of Situated Cognition*, Cambridge: Cambridge University Press, 55–77.

Winet, Evan (2010) *Indonesian Postcolonial Theatre: Spectral Genealogies and Absent Faces*, Basingstoke: Palgrave Macmillan.

Winter, Jessica (2012) 'Daniel Day-Lewis: How the Greatest Living Actor Became Lincoln', *Time*, 25 October, http://entertainment.time.com/2012/10/25/daniel-day-lewis-in-lincoln-hail-to-the-chief/

Wolford, L. (2010) 'Grotowski's Vision of the Actor: The Search for Contact', in A. Hodge (ed.), *Actor Training* (2nd edition), London: Routledge, 199–214.

Wylie-Marques, Kathry (2003) 'Opening the Actor's Spiritual Heart: The Zen Influence of *Nō* Training and Performance', *Journal of Dramatic Theory and Criticism*, 18, 1:131–160.

Yan, Haiping (1994) 'Theatre and Society: Reflections on Research Needs in Chinese Theatre Studies', *Asian Theatre Journal*, 11, 1:104–113.

Yasumi Akihito (2004) 'Introduction' to Ōta Shōgo, *The Tale of Komachi Told by the Wind*, trans. Mari Boyd, in Japan Playwrights Association (ed.), *Half a Century of Japanese Theater*, Volume 6: *1960s Part 1*, Tokyo: Kinokuniya, 216–239.

Yogi Ramacharaka (2004) *Series of Lessons in Raja Yoga*, Project Gutenberg (online).

Yogi Ramacharaka (2007) *Hatha Yoga: The Science of Breath and Posture*, Sydney: Axiom Publishing.

Yoo, Jeung-sook (2007) 'Moving *ki* in Inner and Outer Space – A Korean Perspective on Acting Process in *The Water Station*', *Contemporary Theatre Review*, 17, 1:81–96.

Yoo, Jeung-sook (2008a) 'Toward a Korean Language and Psychophysical Process of Approaching Acting and Actor Training', unpublished PhD thesis, Drama Department, University of Exeter.

Yoo, Jeung-sook (2008b) 'Exploring an Actor's Active-Passiveness through Training *ki*', *Forum of Theatre and Drama*, Seoul: Korean National University of the Arts.

Yuasa Yasuo (1987) *The Body: Toward an Eastern Mind–Body Theory*, Albany: State University of New York Press.

Yuasa Yasuo (1993) *The Body, Self-Cultivation, and Ki-Energy*, trans. Shigenori Nagatomo and Monte S. Hull, Albany: State University of New York Press.

Yuka Amano (2011) '"Flower" as Performing Body in *Nō* Theatre', *Asian Theatre Journal*, 28, 2:529–548.

Zachariah, Mathew and R. Sooryamoorthy (1994) *Science for Social Revolution? Achievements and Dilemmas of a Development Movement – The Kerala Sastra Sahitya Parishad*, New Delhi: Vistaar Publications.

Zarrilli, Phillip (1984) *The Kathakali Complex: Actor, Performance, Structure*, New Delhi: Abhinav Publishers.

Zarrilli, Phillip (1998) *'When the Body Becomes All Eyes': Paradigms and Practices of Power in Kalarippayattu*, New Delhi: Oxford University Press.

Zarrilli, Phillip (2000) *Kathakali Dance-Drama: Where Gods and Demons Come to Play*, London: Routledge.

Zarrilli, Phillip (2001) 'Negotiating Performance Epistemologies: Knowledges "about", "in" and "for"', *Studies in Theatre and Performance*, 21, 1:31–46.

Zarrilli, Phillip (2002) *Acting (Re)considered* (2nd edition), London: Routledge.

Zarrilli, Phillip (2006a) 'Case Study: Social Drama in Kerala, India: Staging the "Revolution"', in Phillip B. Zarrilli *et al.*, *Theatre Histories: An Introduction*, London: Routledge, 391–399.

Zarrilli, Phillip (2006b) 'Sung Dance-Drama: The Mayan Rabinal Achi', in Phillip B. Zarrilli *et al.*, *Theatre Histories: An Introduction*, London: Routledge, 68–71.

Zarrilli, Phillip (2009) *Psychophysical Acting: An Intercultural Approach after Stanislavski*, London: Routledge.

Zarrilli, Phillip (2012) '"... Presence..." as a Question and Emergent Possibility: A Case Study from the Performer's Perspective', in Gabriella Giannachi and Nick Kaye (eds), *Archeologies of Presence*, London: Routledge, 119–152.

Zimmermann, Francis (1983) *Jungle and the Aroma of Meats*, Chicago, IL: University of Chicago Press.

Zimmermann, Francis (1986) *Susruta Samhita, Cikitsasthana*, 24:38–49 (unpublished translation).

Index

291